Polit

MW01490808

American Revolution:
A Reader

Volume II:
Revolutionary Constitution-Making
and Social Reform

Also by C. Bradley Thompson

Political Thought of the American Revolution: A Reader
Volume I: The Imperial Crisis and Independence

What America Is

America's Revolutionary Mind: A Moral History of the American Revolution and the Declaration that Defined It

Freedom and School Choice in American Education
(editor, with Greg Forster)

Neoconservatism: An Obituary for an Idea
(with Yaron Brook)

Antislavery Political Writings, 1833-1860: A Reader

The Revolutionary Writings of John Adams

John Adams and the Spirit of Liberty
(Winner of the Best First Book in Political Theory Prize
from the American Political Science Association)

Political Thought
of the
American Revolution:
A Reader

Volume II:
Revolutionary Constitution-Making
and Social Reform

Edited with an Introduction and Commentary
by C. Bradley Thompson

LOCO-FOCO PRESS
Seneca, South Carolina

For my students—past, present, and future

TABLE OF CONTENTS

PREFACE

On July 4, 2026, Americans will celebrate the 250th anniversary of the Declaration of Independence. Few thought that the United States would last this long. Others worry that America has seen better days and is in a state of decline. An occasion such as the semiquincentennial of the United States of America grants us, however, a special opportunity—indeed, an obligation—to undertake a comprehensive reexamination of our revolutionary principles and institutions. The American Revolution is the most written about subject in American history. All that America is—its virtues and vices—can be traced in one way or another to that moment in 1776 when colonial Americans declared their independence from Great Britain.

For 200 years, the American people were proud of their revolutionary past and remarkably patriotic. The last five decades have not been so kind to the principles and institutions established by America's revolutionary founders. Our best universities rarely teach courses on the American Revolution or the American Founding. In many ways, the field seems to be dying. Even worse, two generations of academic writers have denigrated the accomplishments of the revolutionary generation. To the extent that academics do write and teach about the revolutionary and founding periods, they do so mostly as hostile critics. They typically claim that the founding of the United States of America was immoral, that its founding documents were grounded in self-evident lies, and that its founding fathers were racist, sexist, classist, homophobic, etc. Scholarly study of the American Founding is therefore in a state of rapid decline and with it the way in which ordinary Americans view their past—and hence their present and future.

The current situation should be viewed, however, as an opportunity and for one very important reason: most ordinary Americans still have a profound interest in and appreciation (if not a love) for America's founding fathers and the principles and institutions on which this nation was founded. This is why best-selling books on America's revolutionaries and founding fathers (typically written by amateur historians and journalists) are published every year. There is, in other words, a disconnect between what American academics say about the American Revolution and what the American public wants to know about the subject.

The time has come for a new volume (or two) of the best, deepest, and most influential primary source readings from the revolutionary era. In fact, the two volumes of *Political Thought of the American Revolution: A Reader* represent the most comprehensive collection of primary source readings ever collected and published on the American Revolution. These two volumes feature the ideas, strategies, and policies of the best minds amongst

American revolutionaries and loyalists, and it also includes the most important laws and policies advanced by British imperial legislators and officials during the years of the imperial crisis. On display in these two volumes are the best minds in eighteenth-century Great Britain and America as they discussed, deliberated, speculated, theorized, compromised, and decided which path forward to take. It is hoped these volumes will launch a renaissance in the teaching, study, and scholarship of the American Revolution.

This two-volume collection of the most illuminating and influential writings of this nation's revolutionary founders has been produced for academics, students, and the general public who have an interest in the underlying philosophy that led to and came out of the American Revolution. *Political Thought of the American Revolution: A Reader* is a primary source anthology, the purpose of which is to introduce teachers and students of the American Revolution to the thought of the best thinkers and statesmen of the period from 1761 to 1780. The first volume, subtitled "The Imperial Crisis and Independence," assembles some of the most important tracts of the conflict between Great Britain and her American colonies in the years between 1760 and 1776. The second volume, subtitled "Revolutionary Constitution-Making and Social Reform," presents dozens of documents concerned with the attempts by American revolutionaries to construct new constitutions and governments after 1776 and to reform the laws of their societies. The tracts of both volumes allow readers to study the colonists' grievances against Great Britain, their various rhetorical strategies, and the development of their moral and political thought that led to the Declaration of Independence and the revolutionary state constitutions and governments. Each document is preceded by a headnote, which provides readers with a relatively brief introduction to the author or authors of each document and the context in which it was written.

The documents included in these volumes represent a fraction of American and British thinking on the key issues debated during the years of the imperial crisis and the Americans' subsequent development of a revolutionary moral, constitutional, and political philosophy in the years after 1776. Between 1761 and 1780, hundreds of pamphlets, essays, and newspaper articles appeared in the colonies and then in the states. I have included in these two volumes what I consider to be the most important and influential documents of the revolutionary era. Hopefully, the selections included in both volumes will allow students of the American Revolution to see inside the minds of the leading revolutionaries and their opponents to better understand why they thought and acted as they did.

A final pedagogical note to both teachers and students of this volume: In the introductory essay that immediately follows this Preface, I have decided to eschew the conventional summaries of the various tracts in this volume. The truth of the matter is that there are far too many entries to write even the briefest of summaries. Besides, I have done some of that in the headnotes at the top of each document. What I have done instead is to write a somewhat impressionistic essay that provides a high-level view of the intellectual and political context of the time as well as an examination of the most important questions and themes of the imperial crisis and revolutionary period. I would recommend that teachers and students read the Introduction first before they dive into the primary source material.

Acknowledgements: I wish to thank several former teachers, colleagues, and friends who assisted me directly or indirectly in the development of this book. As a young man I was fortunate to have studied with some of the nation's greatest scholars of what I call America's revolutionary-founding period, including Gordon S. Wood, Bernard Bailyn, Ralph Lerner, and Harvey Mansfield. Their work on this period has always inspired my own. My colleague Samuel Postell helped to format the manuscript for publication. Finally, my wife, Sidney Thompson, designed the cover of this volume, and she has ably managed the legal, production, and marketing side of Loco-Foco Press. She has also demanded of me that I stop wasting time and finish this project.

C. Bradley Thompson
January 24, 2025

INTRODUCTION:
AMERICAN REVOLUTIONARY CONSTITUTIONALISM

The American Revolution is *the* great event of the modern world. Its character and ultimate meaning should not be seen in what it overthrew or destroyed, but rather in the permanent institutions that it created. The destruction of the old requires the building of the new, and it was through the creation of new constitutions and governments that American revolutionaries distinguished themselves as the most constructive statesmen in both ancient and modern history. During the years of the imperial crisis, American revolutionaries thought long and hard about their constitutional relationship with Great Britain and then, ultimately, about the nature of constitutions themselves. And when it became clear that the political conflict between Britain and America could not be resolved constitutionally, America's best legal and political minds set out to revolutionize the very idea of a constitution.

By 1776, American revolutionaries were ready to put their new ideas into practice. Over the course of the next four years, during a war for their very survival, they applied their minds and labors to transforming forever the way men and women around the world would understand the idea and practice of constitutions and the role of government in human affairs. Between 1776 and 1791, from the Declaration of Independence to the Bill of Rights, American revolutionaries initiated the most creative and fruitful period of political thinking and practice the world has ever seen. In fact, they revolutionized the very idea of government. More specifically, in the four years from 1776 to 1780, three American colonies (before July 4, 1776) and then nine states (after July 4, 1776) drafted or redrafted written constitutions and established new republican governments. It was a bold experiment the likes of which had never been seen before.

The newly drafted American constitutions were founded on an entirely new foundation—a foundation grounded in nature, reason, the laws and rights of nature, the sovereignty of the individual, consent, and contract. The philosophic process by which the Americans discovered their new principles and institutions has a history as important and as fascinating as any competing political or military event of the Revolution.

This introductory essay examines *how* American revolutionaries made that quantum leap in theory and practice, *how* they revolutionized the very idea of a constitution, and *how* they invented and put into practice the idea of a written constitution as fundamental law. Ultimately, our task is to consider not so much how the revolutionary generation came to draft written constitutions but rather how they transformed written constitutions into fundamental law. It is the idea of *fundamentality* that is most important and most revolutionary.

What is the difference between a written constitution that is fundamental law and a written constitution that is not? More to the point: what is it that makes a written constitution the fundamental or higher law of the land? And why did American revolutionaries come to reject their own former claim that the British constitution was a fundamental law?

To answer these questions, we must examine the actual method and processes by which American revolutionaries established new governments in America, and how they understood the very idea of their founding act. This was a transforming event in world history and the Americans knew it. They were consciously creating a *novus ordo seclorum*—a "new order of the ages." Theirs was to be an experiment to determine whether it was actually possible to establish free government on the moral foundation of individual rights.

America's revolutionary constitution-makers were confronted with the daunting task of beginning *de novo*, with converting abstract ideas into working and long-lasting institutions. Translating theory into practice was, however, no small task. It requires more than just brilliant thinkers and a good philosophy shared by most people; it also requires sobriety of judgment, great political capacity, a people capable of governing themselves, and favorable socio-economic circumstances. Ironically, the Americans were also aided by the fact that they were motivated to design and implement constitutions so that they could have the governments necessary to fight the war against the British. New state and national constitutions had to be designed and governments established. The moment was unprecedented in modern history.

Nothing strikes the student of the American Revolution more forcibly than the conscious awareness attached by the revolutionary generation to the novelty and importance of their founding act. The American constitutions were created at a particular moment in time; they were the result of a deliberate *"founding"* act. The very idea of a founding was critical to American revolutionaries' self-understanding, and it fired their ambition. It was an intoxicating moment, but America's revolutionary constitution-makers never lost sight of the enormous practical difficulties that stood in front of them. To create or found a new nation based on reflection and choice was unprecedented, and history and philosophy provided no examples of how to do it. The great challenge confronting America's revolutionary statesmen was to convert theory into practice. To create permanent institutions that could withstand the storms of time was a task of enormous complexity and responsibility, a task that would affect the lives of tens and then hundreds of millions of people over the course of many generations.

What is truly astounding about the American Revolution is that not only did America's great founding statesmen *think* philosophically and *act* prudently, but so did hundreds if not thousands of ordinary citizens. One of the great-untold stories of the American Revolution is the degree to which a broad cross-section of American society, including uneducated, hard-scrabble farmers living along the Appalachian frontier from New Hampshire to South Carolina, imbibed not only the moral and political philosophy of John Locke, but they put it into practice. These simple yeoman farmers grappled with fundamental principles such as the nature and extent of equality and liberty, consent, rights, sovereignty the purpose and forms of government, and the role of constitutions in a free society. In the pages that follow, we tell the story of *ordinary* people doing *extraordinary* things. In their own way, these men deserve to be counted among the heroes of the American Revolution.

It all seems so obvious and natural to us today, but the actual design and construction of new revolutionary governments was an extraordinarily difficult and complicated process. It did not just happen overnight or without great trials and tribulations. American revolutionaries around the United States did not get it exactly right the first, second, or third times they tried to build constitutional republics; in fact, they did not get it quite right until the eleventh try when the Massachusetts Constitution was ratified in 1780.

Why was it so difficult? What were the theoretical and practical challenges confronted by American constitution-makers in the years between 1776 and 1780? This introductory essay answers these questions. It tells the remarkable story of how American revolutionaries built a new system of government—nay, a system of governments—unlike anything ever before seen in the history of the world.

CONSTITUTIONS OLD AND NEW

To fully understand and appreciate the nature and meaning of what American revolutionaries accomplished over a thirty-year period between 1761 and 1791, we should step back and examine the broader historical context that defined the boundaries of their ideas and actions. The American Revolution began as a contest over competing interpretations of the British constitution, and it ended as a battle over the very idea of a "constitution." The controversy started in 1765 when American colonists challenged the constitutionality of the British Parliament's infamous Stamp Act. The colonists considered the new Stamp tax to be unjust and therefore unconstitutional, while English imperial officials believed that it was legal and therefore constitutional. Both sides of the controversy sought to preserve the British constitution as each understood it. No one on either side of the Atlantic doubted the authority of Parliament to pass such a tax for Englishmen within the realm, but the question at hand concerned Parliament's constitutional right to legislate a tax for colonies beyond the realm. The meaning of the word "constitution" was therefore central to the crisis in Anglo-American relations in the decade or so before 1776.

At the start of the revolutionary controversy in 1765, the colonists' understanding of what a constitution is was virtually indistinguishable from the British view. Both sides of the Anglo-Atlantic world defined a constitution as the manner in which the extant governmental institutions, laws, customs, and practices functioned and were held together by certain animating moral principles, legal rules, and cultural assumptions. Virtually all colonial Americans—future Whigs and Tories alike—viewed the British constitution as the repository of all their customary rights and liberties, such as the rights to habeas corpus, trial by jury, not to be taxed without representation, etc. It was a constitution of liberty for all Anglo-Americans. Within a few short years after Parliament's passage of the Stamp Act, the constitution that had held the greater Britannic world together for over a century and a half not only began to fray at the seams, but it started to rip apart. It became clear to both the British and their American cousins that each side interpreted the constitution they shared and admired so much in radically different ways. To understand how and why this happened is the penultimate causal factor in explaining the coming of the American Revolution.

To make sense of what happened to the British constitution in America during the years of the imperial crisis and to understand the colonists' newly emerging view of what a constitution should be, we must step away from the political crises of the imperial crisis and put these different understandings of what a constitution is in a broader historical context. The easiest way to understand this transformation is to contrast how Americans defined what a constitution is in the years leading up to 1765 with their definition in 1780 and beyond. To understand the constitutional revolution that occurred in America in the fifteen years before and 1780, we must consider both its origin and its *telos*.

How did mid-eighteenth-century Anglo-Americans understand the very idea of a constitution, and, more particularly, how did they understand the nature and meaning of the British constitution? One thing is certain: the colonists' conception of a constitution was very different than it is today. Most mid-eighteenth-century Britons living at home or abroad would have accepted Lord Viscount Bolingbroke's well-known definition of a constitution, which he enunciated in his "A Dissertation upon Parties," published in 1734:

> By Constitution we mean, whenever we speak with propriety and exactness, that assemblage of laws, institutions, and customs, derived from certain *fixed* principles of reason . . . that compose the general system, according to which the community hath agreed to be governed.

Bolingbroke's constitution was unwritten, although it consisted of certain written charters, declarations, legal decisions, and laws that had accumulated over the centuries, and which had taken on the status of fundamental law. The standard eighteenth-century definition of a constitution included the forms and formalities of the extant institutions, structures, laws, customs, rules and procedures, and principles of the British government as it was constituted at any point in time. A constitution was, according to Anglo-American constitutionalists, an inheritance, an accretion, an amalgam of cultural, political, and legal institutions, of written and unwritten laws, past and present. The British constitution was not the product of conscious design, creative wisdom, and choice. It knew neither Solon nor Lycurgus, and it had no founding father(s). Instead, it was the result of slow, organic growth and adaptation taking place over the course of many centuries.

This is precisely how British Americans throughout the eighteenth century understood and defined the term, *constitution*. American colonials before 1765 thought of the British constitution and the pseudo-constitutions that governed their separate colonies (i.e., the colonial charters) as the way in which political bodies were constituted—that is, the different ways in which the animating principles, institutions, laws, and customs of government were combined and brought to life. Their colonial charters and governments were a part of the British constitution's complicated labyrinth of connected institutions and customs.

When an eighteenth-century jurist, statesman, politician, or writer described a particular course of action by a government as constitutional (e.g., an act of Parliament or an act of a colonial assembly), what he meant to say was that the action had proceeded in conformity with common usages and rules established by law, custom, and the extant political forms and formalities. By this standard, the Stamp Act was, according to British imperial officials, legal and therefore constitutional. During the imperial crisis, however, colonial Americans began a rapid retreat from this traditional definition of a constitution. By 1773, America's Revolutionary statesmen openly challenged the conflation of the "legal" with the "constitutional." This seemingly technical distinction cut to the core of what the American Revolution was all about.

The traditional eighteenth-century definition of a constitution can best be understood when contrasted with the radically new definition that developed out of the American Revolution. By seeing our beginning and end points at the outset, we can better understand the complicated historical *process* that led from one to the other. Consider, for instance, Thomas Paine's definition of a constitution in his 1790 work, *Rights of Man*:

> A constitution is not a thing in name only, but in fact. It has not an ideal, but a real existence; and wherever it cannot be produced in a visible form, there is none. A constitution is a thing *antecedent* to a government, and a government is only the creature of a constitution. The constitution of a

> country is not the act of its government, but of the people
> constituting a government. . . . A constitution, therefore, is
> to a government, what the laws made afterwards by that
> government are to a court of judicature. The court of judi-
> cature does not make the laws, neither can it alter them; it
> only acts in conformity to the laws made; and the govern-
> ment is in like manner governed by the constitution.

Paine's definition of a constitution was entirely different from the common mid-eighteenth century understanding. For Paine, the constitution de-scribed by Bolingbroke was not a constitution at all. It was merely a form of government that gave itself whatever powers it pleased. The problem with the British constitution from Paine's perspective is that it would not stand still; it was constantly changing, growing, and evolving. There was nothing permanently "fixed" about it; nothing to appeal to as a final standard. It was precisely the Americans' search for greater fixity that would come to distin-guish their revolutionary constitutions from all others throughout history. A "fixed" constitution for the Americans was a written document grounded in the moral laws of nature that are absolute, certain, universal, and permanent.

For Paine and his post-revolutionary fellow Americans, a constitution was something permanently fixed—an unmoved mover. A proper constitu-tion is, the Americans' argued, a cause and not an effect; it is a written docu-ment that establishes, defines, and limits the powers of government. After 1776, the very idea of a constitution took on a meaning and an importance quite different from that of any other place in the world. Over the course of one generation, the American mind changed from a revolutionary to a con-stitutional mindset.

This uniquely American idea of a constitution was not, however, born phoenix-like, at one singular moment in time or in the head of one man. It has a fascinating and complicated history that can be seen in the polemical debates of the 1760s and 1770s.

From the very outset of the imperial crisis, American Patriots embraced a much more philosophical form of argument than their British or Loyalist opponents. They stood toe-to-toe with the British in their use of historical and constitutional arguments, but they also appealed to a moral tradition that the British accepted only partially in theory and rejected almost entirely in practice. American Whigs typically assumed that the so-called "rights of Englishmen" were ultimately grounded not just in the history of the English way of life but in something not uniquely English in any way—i.e., the moral laws of nature, which are discoverable and revealed to man through unaided reason. In other words, they were grounded in something more permanent than the vagaries of time, place, usage, and convention. Such rights were not historically relative or politically contextual, nor were they made real or jus-tified through legislation or codification. They were understood by revolutionary Americans to be certain, permanent, universal and absolute, and they were discovered and declared through right reason but not created by men. The book of nature was open to all men with eyes to see and to be read using their rational faculty.

But how, one might ask, are the "Rights of Nature" interwoven in the British constitution? The common law, for instance, embodied and protected natural rights such as the rights to life, liberty, and property by discovering, declaring, incorporating, and enshrining certain civil rights that had developed historically from time immemorial such as the right not to be taxed without one's consent, right to jury trial, and habeas corpus. From beginning to end, this was the moral foundation on which American Whigs interpreted the English constitution, and it was a foundation from which they would never budge.

As a result, the American mind was becoming what we might call *constitutionalized*. During the imperial crisis, American colonists were constantly searching for some kind of constitutional Holy Grail, a standard by which to measure and judge the actions of Parliament. Over the course of the next six years, a consensus in American thinking began to develop around a new conception of what a constitution is. A proper constitution is a fundamental law that creates and defines the powers of government, and which cannot be altered by that same government. Fundamental constitutions cannot be altered by any part of the government, by King or Parliament, without resorting to the will of the people and securing their consent to any changes. The constitution is the cause, and the government and its laws are the effects.

The Americans' final break with British constitutionalism came in 1776. After ten years of debating the nature of the British constitution, the most advanced revolutionary thinkers were now prepared to offer a radically new definition of a constitution that broke decisively with the entire tradition of Western constitutional thought and practice. Legitimate constitutions, they argued, must be grounded in moral "first principles"—moral principles considered to be fundamental, absolute, and permanent. For the fundamental law to be truly fundamental, it must exist beyond the temporal order or the ebb and flow of history. It must be "natural" in the sense of "eternal" or timelessly accessible to human reason and unvarying from one place to another. The Americans were now on the verge of reinventing the idea of a constitution.

By the early 1770s, America's leading Whig thinkers began to identify, isolate, and define the principles that would distinguish their constitutional jurisprudence from that of their British cousins, and they developed a radically forward-looking theory of constitutional government. American revolutionaries constructed their new constitutional theory based on six fundamental principles: first, constitutions should be grounded on immutable, antecedent rights; second, constitutions should be defined by fixed principles

and rules that control the operations of government; third, constitutions create governments and are paramount to them; fourth, constitutions define
and limit the powers and actions of government, particularly the lawmaking
power; fifth, constitutions should be written; and sixth, constitutions must
be distinguished from ordinary law and they must be instituted as the permanent and fundamental law of the land.

This new conception of a constitution revolutionized American political
and jurisprudential thought and practice. It was a daring leap into the future,
but no one on either side of the Atlantic in the mid-1770s knew quite how
this new understanding of a constitution would work in the realm of practice. In the end, the central question for the Americans was this: how can the
moral laws and rights of nature be *constitutionalized*? With independence,
the colonists could put into practice the ideas they had been developing over
the course of the previous decade.

THE FALL OF ROYAL GOVERNMENT AND THE STATE OF NATURE

Let us turn now and zero in on the immediate historical context that led
to the creation of revolutionary constitutions and governments in America.
Our focus will be mostly limited to Massachusetts, where the most consistently radical and important constitutional developments occurred in both
theory and practice.

The overriding historical and sociological fact explaining the political
culture of eighteenth-century Massachusetts was the devotion of its residents
to their self-governing political institutions and customs, a devotion they
proudly identified with their royal charter dating back to the end of the seventeenth century. The Massachusetts charter of 1691 represented to the residents of the Bay Colony the shining palladium of all their liberties. It was
their constitution and its protection of their rights and liberties made them
the freest people in the world—and they knew it.

The tipping point in the imperial crisis came in 1774 when Parliament
passed and George III assented to the Coercive Acts (May 20, 1774), which
were the most arbitrary and oppressive ever passed by Parliament against the
colonies. The legislation was both arbitrary and punitive, particularly in its
punishment of Massachusetts. For our purposes, the most important of the
four Coercive Acts was the Massachusetts Government Act, which radically
altered the Massachusetts charter of 1691. It was one thing for the British
Parliament to tax the colonies without representation, but it was of an entirely different magnitude to openly overturn the colonists' "constitution."
Without the charter, there could be no rights and liberties for the people of
Massachusetts. All would be lost.

Under the terms of the Massachusetts Government Act, the Crown rather than the Massachusetts Assembly now had the authority to appoint
members to the Governor's Council (i.e., the legislative "upper" house) as
well as almost all judges and sheriffs in Massachusetts; and, most alarmingly,

the famed Massachusetts town meeting, the heart and soul of New England politics and self-government, was forbidden to meet except for the election of town officials. The Massachusetts Government Act represented the death-knell of the colonists' traditional charter constitution.

More fundamentally, the legislation told the colonists that their under-standing of a constitution was entirely different from that of their imperial overlords. The Massachusetts Government Act brought to the surface the colonists' deeply held belief that their charter was a de facto constitution founded on a compact between the King and his colonial subjects and sub-ject to alteration only with the consent of both parties. The seventeenth-cen-tury charter was the colonists' Magna Carta. By contrast, British imperial of-ficials made it clear that they viewed the Massachusetts constitution as sub-ject to change at their will in the same way that William Blackstone, the great eighteenth-century English jurist, had written in his *Commentaries on the Laws of England* that the British constitution was changeable at the hands of Parliament. The chasm between colonies and mother country was now un-bridgeable. One-hundred and fifty years of self-government in Massachu-setts was now at an end.

In response to the Massachusetts Government Act and the suspension of the assembly, Massachusetts revolutionaries essentially shut down all gov-erning institutions in the colony. Royal government in America, particularly in the Bay Colony, effectively came to an end. In fact, some crown-appointed governors were forced to relocate their residences to either armed forts on local islands or to British warships anchored in a local harbor. Back in Mas-sachusetts, American patriots led by the Sons of Liberty denounced the new royal government as illegitimate, and they pressured sheriffs, judges, and ju-ries to either resign their positions or to not enforce the law. As a result, courts were unable to conduct business, and it was impossible to form juries for trials. Massachusetts was in a state of open rebellion.

Remarkably there would be no legally functioning government in Mas-sachusetts for six years between 1774 and 1780. As Patrick Henry announced in the Continental Congress in 1774: "Government is dissolved, . . . We are in a State of Nature." Notice Henry's use of John Locke's state of nature met-aphor. Henry's identification is important, and he was not alone in using it. In Massachusetts, outlawed town meetings typically declared themselves to be in a state of nature. The colonists' use of the state of nature metaphor served a twofold purpose: first, it was the best way to describe their actual condition and, second, it gave them the opportunity to think about recon-structing government in purely Lockean terms.

It was an ominous moment. Threatened at first by tyranny, the colony now seemed on the verge of anarchy. The only government that the colonists had ever known—indeed, the only form of government known to most Eu-ropeans for close to a thousand years—was now at an end. The Americans were in a state of nature and the obvious question now was: how would they escape it? It is both true and remarkable that the residents of Massachusetts lived without formal and legal government during wartime for six years. How did they manage?

First and most importantly, though in a state of nature, the residents of Massachusetts were not without *civil* society. As the toothless power of the old colonial governments collapsed, new forms of civil and political association developed spontaneously or were reborn at the local, county, provincial, and eventually at the continental level. These independent, eighteenth-century colonial Americans easily reverted to, and were able to live off, the reserves of the social, political and moral capital that they had built up over the course of the previous 150 years. Yes, it is true that there was no legal government functioning in Massachusetts but there certainly was civil society, and a civil society of a very peculiar kind. Once legal government came to an end in Massachusetts, the day-to-day functions of government were mostly assumed at the local town level where they had largely been anyway. The implosion of power down to the local town or county level in seventeenth- and eighteenth-century New England gave these hardy Yankees that fiercely independent spirit and tradition of local self-government, which they reassumed with great vigor after 1774.

Almost immediately, the residents of Massachusetts and many of the other colonies began to set up what were, technically speaking, *illegal* or *extra-legal* governments. Political authority and power during this period became radically decentralized. Provincial political authority imploded downward first to counties and then to cities, towns, and townships. On their own, despite the Massachusetts Government Act, the freemen of Massachusetts resurrected their local town meetings to assume some of the functions of government and they reestablished their criminal and civil courts. This period also saw the rise of various other voluntary associations, committees, and conventions that would typically assume authority over projects (e.g., intra- and interstate correspondence, writing and publishing newspaper articles, organizing boycotts, distributing broadsides and handbills, and administering defense and loyalty oaths)—projects formerly managed by the provincial government. In some counties, local conventions even acquired police powers, and several provincial congresses established "committees of safety" to keep civil order. During a two-year period between 1774 and 1776, the colonies were mostly governed from the bottom up by informal and sometimes illegal town meetings, voluntary associations and committees, county conventions, and provincial congresses at the local, county, and provincial levels.

The Bay Colony's first provincial congress met in Salem for most of October 1774. In a direct challenge to the authority and power of the crown-appointed military governor, Thomas Gage, the provincial congress appointed an executive committee (referred to as the council of safety), which was authorized to call out the militia if necessary. All in all, these *shadow* or *para*-governments were, in a sense, competing with, if not supplanting, the royal government until General Thomas Gage was recalled as governor of Massachusetts by George III on September 26, 1775. From this point forward, all functions of government thereafter were assumed by the revolutionary provincial congress.

Over the course of the next several years, the regular functions of government in Massachusetts and in the other colonies were assumed by these extra-legal, voluntarily associated political bodies, and they did so with remarkable success. One cannot help but be impressed with the ability of the American people to govern themselves in the absence of legal government. Still, what can't go on forever, won't. Most colonists knew that the informal state of natural society could only represent a transition period to the formal state of civil society. No one thought it was either possible or desirable to live in a civil society governed simply by inherited cultural mores and informal associations, committees, conventions, and congresses.

Virtually all Americans understood that this virtual state of nature would ultimately become a Hobbesian state of war. This precarious situation could not last indefinitely and the colonists knew it. By early 1776, it was clear to most American patriots that new structures of political association and authority had to be developed at the local, county, provincial, and continental levels. The failure to construct sufficiently energetic governments at home would almost certainly result in the collapse of the Continental Army and with it the failure of the Revolution itself. The time was fast approaching when the informal political order of associations, committees, conventions, and congresses would have to give way to regular government. Voluntary self-government was a temporary fix during a period of extreme necessity when external exigencies and internal virtue were at a fever pitch.

As royal governments imploded around them and as their own shadow governments began to show their limitations, American revolutionaries were confronted with a host of difficult questions: who, how, by what process, on what authority should they institute new governments? Should they follow the simplest and quickest course and reconstitute their colonial governments to meet the exigencies of an emergency, should they revise and liberalize the old charters along lines more suited to the local conditions of the 1770s, or should they take their time to design and construct their governments with the care necessary to do the job well? These were the first and most important questions they had to address even before they tackled the extraordinarily difficult problems of choosing and putting into practice any one form of government.

THE BIRTH OF CIVIL SOCIETY AND SELF-GOVERNMENT

By the beginning of 1775, circumstances on the ground and necessity dictated a much less random and catch-as-catch-can process of political reconstruction. Informal self-government by association, committee, convention, and congress could not be sustained much longer. The reign of shadow governments would have to end. In the eighteen months leading to July 4, 1776, the need for some kind of formal government in Massachusetts became acute, particularly after the passage of the "Intolerable Acts" and then certainly after blood had been shed at the battles at Lexington and Concord. Massachusetts was fast moving toward a revolutionary point of no return.

On June 17, 1775, shortly after the Battles of Lexington and Concord, the extra-legal provisional government of Massachusetts petitioned the extra-legal Continental Congress for advice on how to restore government to the Bay Colony. The Congress replied to Massachusetts by encouraging the residents of the Bay Colony to institute a modified charter government to serve their interests temporarily until the crisis with Great Britain had been resolved. And this is precisely what Massachusetts did. A General Court (the primary legislative body) was elected, which in turn elected a Council or upper house. The new interim government then appointed judges and other officials for the province's fourteen counties, thereby allowing for various county courts to reopen. Government for the moment—even if informal— was restored. It is important to keep in mind, though, that this was still, strictly speaking, *royal* government—that is, the officers of this interim government were still required to take oaths of allegiance to George III.

And now we come to the most fascinating part of our story. It turns out that not everyone in Massachusetts was pleased with this new arrangement. An outspoken minority in Berkshire County, at the western end of the colony, objected to the Continental Congress's recommendation. Known sometimes as the "Constitutionalists," and centered in the town of Pittsfield, they called a county convention for December 1775. Meeting in the nearby town of Stockbridge, the convention's delegates protested the authority of the Council to name local officials. Instead, they recommended that county judges be nominated by the people at the local level and commissioned by the Council. The Berkshire Constitutionalists defended their position by keeping their county courts closed for several years. In fact, more fundamentally, they viewed both the old charter government and the newly modified provincial government—to be without proper moral or legal standing. They resolved therefore to withdraw their sanction from the new provisional government.

What is most fascinating about the Berkshire Constitutionalists is how radicalized they had become in a very short period of time. Just a few years before, as we have seen already, most American revolutionaries were defending their colonial charters as their only legitimate and ruling constitutions. By 1775, however, the Berkshire Constitutionalists had rejected the old charter completely as the basis of government. When did the people expressly consent to it, they asked repeatedly?

What is genuinely revolutionary about the Berkshire Constitutionalists is that they were completely re-centering the foundation of government in America from the Crown to the people themselves. Any new government, they argued repeatedly, should be formed "*De novo*"—that is, anew. They were attempting, in other words, to elevate their constitutions above the exigencies of time. Remarkably, it was these frontier pioneers who led their better-educated fellow revolutionaries in the search for that permanent constitutional foundation that would ultimately define the Revolution's most important and unique accomplishment. And that permanent foundation, the only proper basis of government, they declared, was the consent of the people, which in turn was grounded in the inalienable rights of individuals. As we shall see momentarily, it was a truly radical position that would serve as the foundation for the future development of American constitutional thought and practice.

By July 4, 1776, it became increasingly difficult to support piecemeal reform of the modified Charter of 1691. Now that reconciliation with Great Britain was no longer possible, all arguments to retain and reform the old charter were irrelevant. Most Massachusetts residents now saw the logic and necessity of the Berkshire Constitutionalists' argument that the old charter and the provisional government had no proper standing and that a new beginning grounded on new assumptions was required. Still, the fact remained that they needed a government, and they needed one as soon as possible.

And thus, we return to our guiding questions: *how* should the colonists establish this new government? More to the point, *who* should design and construct this new constitution?

In the fall of 1776, the Massachusetts General Court sent a resolution to 260 towns offering to draft a new constitution for Massachusetts. This seemed like the simplest and most obvious way to proceed. Nearly three-fourths of the towns that responded sanctioned the General Court to begin at once. In proceeding this way, Massachusetts was following the example set by most of the other states. Virtually all the state constitutions drafted in 1776 and 1777 were the product of sitting legislatures. Typically, these provincial assemblies would draft and ratify the new constitution, declare it to be the law of the land, and then immediately vote themselves as the first sitting legislature under the new constitution. The provincial congresses justified this procedure on the grounds that they fully represented the people in their respective states.

With no real models either philosophical or historical to guide them and in the face of war, it seemed both natural and expedient for the various provisional governments to draft and ratify the new constitutions. Many leading revolutionaries quite reasonably sought the quickest and easiest way to form their new governments. Besides, who else would do it? No one really knew. The provincial congresses therefore wrote and ratified constitutions in the very same way that they drafted and passed ordinary bills. It was all part and parcel of the regular legislative process.

Not everyone in Massachusetts was happy with this procedure, however. The Berkshire Constitutionalists and their allies around the state denied the right and the propriety of having the existing legislature draft the constitution. Over the course of the next four years, they held firm to the view that a legitimate constitution could only be created and sanctioned by the people. For the moment, however, this was a decidedly minority view. Still, the question at hand was this: *who* should draft the constitution?

Having received the go-ahead from a large majority of the towns, the Massachusetts General Court declared itself in 1777 to be in session as a constitutional convention and then it proceeded to draft a constitution for the state. The constitution took four months to write and was then submitted to the people for ratification. Town meetings around the state then examined, discussed, and debated the proposed constitution in the spring of 1778. The overwhelming response of the towns, however, was negative. The Constitution of 1778 was rejected by a margin of almost 5 to 1. It was rejected on both substantive and procedural grounds. Substantively, the constitution was rejected for several reasons: first, it lacked a bill of rights; second, it had no proper method of amendment other than by the legislature itself; and third, its plan of representation was unequal. Procedurally, some of the towns rejected the constitution because the procedure that was used to create it was illegitimate. There was no special convention above the legislature to create it.

The rejection of the 1778 Constitution only emboldened the Berkshire County Constitutionalists to resist attempts to force on them either an illegitimate provisional government or constitution. Despite pressure from surrounding counties and the General Court, they remained steadfastly opposed to the re-opening of their Quarter Session Courts recently ordered by the General Court. To their credit, the Constitutionalists stood on principle, insisting that legitimate government had to be created and sanctioned directly by the people. By holding firm and refusing to re-open their County Courts, the Berkshire Constitutionalists were forcing not only the General Court but all residents of Massachusetts to think seriously about the proper methods by which to establish their constitution. They were not anarchists, nor were they debtor criminals trying to avoid law and justice as some of their contemporaries suggested. Rather, they were men of principal who insisted that for government to be *legitimate*, it must be established on a proper moral foundation. And on this point, they would not compromise.

THE CONSTITUTIONALISTS' CONSTITUTION

What stands out most prominently in the Constitutionalists' thought (and this was true of virtually all American revolutionaries) was their repeated demand for the creation of what they referred to as a *"fundamental* constitution"—a fundamental constitution that is *permanent* and *fixed*. But what exactly did they mean by a "fundamental" constitution, and what makes it different from just a constitution?

To answer these two important questions, we need to ask three more specific questions. First, why did the Berkshire Constitutionalists want a "fundamental" constitution? Second, what are the defining characteristics of a "fundamental" constitution? And third, by what process did the Constitutionalists propose to convert their written constitutions into the fundamental law of the land?

Let us examine each of these questions in turn.

1. Why did the Berkshire Constitutionalists and many other American revolutionaries want a "fundamental" constitution?

The answer to this question should be obvious by now. At the deepest level, the imperial crisis was largely inspired by the Anglo-American debate over the nature of the British constitution. American colonials interpreted the British constitution through the lens of an older seventeenth-century English constitution (i.e., the so-called "ancient" or "Saxon" constitution), the principles of which were thought to be "fundamental," "permanent," "and "fixed." By contrast, eighteenth-century British Parliamentarians had largely abandoned, indeed, most had rejected the idea that there was some kind of fundamental or higher law grounding and guiding the actions of Parliament. And to the extent that any British jurists interpreted law or members of Parliament drafted legislation in the light of the law of nature principles, it was only a theoretical disposition on the part of a small minority of individuals and without legal standing. In the end, the problem of course was that most British jurists and statesmen simply rejected the American interpretation of the ancient English constitution. Instead, they had come to equate the eighteenth-century British constitution as synonymous with the commands of Parliament, which is to say that it was neither "fundamental," "permanent," nor "fixed."

More importantly, even the Anglo-American defenders of the so-called ancient or Saxon constitution had difficulty in locating and defining the principles and institutions that made the traditional English constitution fundamental, permanent, and fixed. But how could they? There was no written constitution to turn to for explicit guidance. Consider, for instance, the idea typically associated with the ancient constitution that common-law rights and liberties were emanations of natural rights. Now it is true that the English constitution did protect common-law rights that mirrored the so-called natural rights, but the actual origin of these common-law rights and their incorporation in the ancient constitution was buried in history and steeped in mystery. And it was steeped in mystery because ultimately these natural rights were thought to be in some way intrinsic *in* nature. Their ultimate source was said to be in God and their incorporation in the English constitution was said to be found in the mystic cords of the past. In other words, the explicit philosophical and historical identification and validation of these of these rights was asserted rather than proved.

By 1776, American revolutionaries in general, and the Berkshire Constitutionalists in particular, came to see serious deficiencies in their vaunted English constitution and the rights it was said to protect. They sought therefore to retain and restore the best features of the lapsed seventeenth-century English constitution, but they also sought to improve upon it, to *rebuild* it on a new and improved philosophic foundation—i.e., the laws and rights of nature as enumerated in the philosophy of John Locke.

2. What are the defining characteristics of a fundamental constitution?

American revolutionaries typically defined a fundamental constitution by two principal characteristics: *permanence* and *fixity*. This new American idea of a fundamental constitution was diametrically opposed to the British view: a constitution is not a living organism subject to growth; it is not the sum of its past and a product of history. In fact, the Americans hoped to design and build constitutions that could withstand the vagaries of time. A constitution's fundamentality, they argued, should be ultimately anchored by permanent, unchanging principles, thereby making the constitution itself permanent and unchanging.

During the debates of the 1760s and 1770s the colonists searched high and low in the British constitution for immutable principles of right and justice. But when their search yielded inconclusive results, they eventually abandoned history and English jurisprudence as the source of their constitutional rights. By 1776, American revolutionaries no longer spoke of the "rights of Englishmen." Instead, they sought a new constitutional foundation rooted unalterably in nature or the rights and laws of nature. A fundamental constitution, according to the Berkshire Constitutionalists, is one grounded in man's fundamental, inalienable rights. *That* is the unalterable foundation, the cornerstone, as they often called it, of a fundamental constitution. Protecting these rights defined for the Americans the ultimate nature and purpose of government. It was the ultimate standard of legitimacy.

The first characteristic of a fundamental constitution is its "permanence," which means that the constitution must be grounded in unchanging principles. To that end, the first task of the Berkshire Constitutionalists and their allies was, accordingly, to identify, isolate, and define rights that were in some way grounded permanently in reality or nature. This was clearly the hardest undertaking, because it was the most philosophically challenging. Readers of American revolutionary literature cannot help but be impressed with the quantity and sometimes even the quality of philosophic thinking undertaken by these ordinary Americans, even if they were ultimately unsuccessful in validating their rights in nature. The second task for American revolutionaries was more practical, but hardly less difficult, particularly given that they had no experience in the matter: i.e., they had to find some method by which to institutionalize man's natural rights in their new constitutions and they had to do it in a way that would permanently separate those rights from, and elevate them above, the grasping power of government. To get even to this point represented a profound and important shift in Western constitutional thinking.

The second characteristic of a fundamental constitution is its "fixity," which means that the forms and formalities, the powers and procedures of government must be permanently "fixed" or cast in stone. The idea that constitutions should be "fixed" was central to American revolutionary constitutionalism. The permanence and fixity of a fundamental constitution are, however, ultimately embodied in its *written-ness*. From John Locke, American revolutionaries and the Berkshire Constitutionalists learned that legitimate governments must create and dispense justice according to known and settled rules, which meant that the constitutions and laws must be written.

Two important and related corollary characteristics of a fundamental constitution derived from its fixity and writtenness are *certainty* and *predictability*. It was a basic tenet of the founding generation that government officials and private citizens know clearly and hold with absolute confidence, and in advance of taking any action, what the constitution allows and forbids them to do. Written and fixed constitutions therefore provide an objective standard of what is and is not permitted by the constitution. By explicitly and exactly defining the power that may be exercised by government and by explicitly and exactly defining the rights of individuals, written constitutions (and bills of rights) create spheres of human action that are knowable, predictable, and therefore non-arbitrary. If a constitution is not clearly known and understood by those whose behavior it is meant to control, it will cease to have any meaningful authority and will become a mere parchment barrier. Without certainty and predictability, power and liberty become synonymous.

The way in which the permanence and fixity of a written constitution best guaranteed its fundamentality is most clearly seen in the important role American revolutionaries attributed to a bill of rights in their new constitutional order. An essential element of the rule of law is that it must clearly define the boundaries of government power in the light of the rights held inalienably by its citizenry. A bill of rights is just that: it is a written list or catalogue of the rights retained by individuals against their government. The writ of habeas corpus, for instance, prohibits the government from physically seizing and holding (i.e., jailing) an individual for an indefinite duration without bringing charges against him in a court of law. American revolutionaries in general, and the Berkshire Constitutionalists in particular, insisted that their constitutions be preceded by a written bill of rights, which would serve as the foundation and standard by which the actions of government could be measured and evaluated. In other words, the natural rights of men should serve as the immoveable foundation and standard of government.

American Constitutionalists thought it was critical that man's natural rights be enumerated in a constitution for three reasons. First, a bill of rights can serve an educative function: it teaches all men about their rights. Second, a bill of rights necessarily limits the powers of government by serving as a benchmark beyond which it shall not go. And third, it can also serve to remind legislators that the purpose of legislation is to make laws that further protect the rights of individuals. In other words, the purposes and powers of government should always be guided by the protection of individual rights.

3. *How, and by what process, did the Constitutionalists propose to make their constitutions the fundamental law of the land?*

Ultimately, the fundamentality of a constitution is established less by simply declaring it so, or giving it certain forms and formalities, than it is by making it *operationally effective* as the fundamental law. A constitution's status as the fundamental law of the land is determined by the way in which it is created or brought into being. For a constitution to be the fundamental law of the land it must be created in a certain way, by a certain process. The critical discovery made by the Berkshire Constitutionalists—a discovery that signaled their final break with British constitutionalism—was this: there must be distinction between the constitution and legislation.

A constitution's fundamentality is not determined primarily by its age; it is not something that develops spontaneously over the course of many centuries as with the ancient English constitution, nor should it be created or changed by a regular legislative body as with the eighteenth-century British constitution. A constitution subject to the whims of legislative fancy could not by definition be the fundamental law. In that case, the legislature would be the fundamental law. For a constitution to be the fundamental law of the land it must be somehow separated from, elevated above, and superior to, the legislature. The fundamental principles of the constitution must be permanently distinguished from ordinary statutory law. Constitutions create governments, not the other way around.

But if constitutions create governments, who then creates constitutions and by what process? How and by whom did the Massachusetts Constitutionalists think that written constitutions could be created as the fundamental law? How could such a constitution's legitimacy be established?

To put it simply, the Massachusetts Constitutionalists began, theoretically speaking, with John Locke's political philosophy. They were pure, thoroughgoing Lockeans—the "great Mr. Locke" they often called him. These simple yeoman farmers and small-town lawyers and ministers living in the Connecticut River Valley obviously read Locke with great seriousness, they rehearsed his theory of government almost verbatim and, most importantly, they worked out, improved upon and completed the Englishman's theory by putting it into practice. Locke was useful to them, initially at least, because his account of a state of nature described their situation. With the collapse of royal government in Massachusetts, they thought of themselves as being in a state of nature. The Constitutionalists therefore insisted that they begin *de novo*, that they follow Locke's account of the formation of government from the *Second Treatise*.

Virtually all the American Constitutionalists begin from this point. They all argued that the people—by which they meant a voluntary association of autonomous individuals—must consent through a social compact to create a constitution, which in turn creates a government. But what exactly does that mean? How does it happen? How is the will of the people to be captured and represented institutionally?

In their attempt to answer these questions, the Berkshire Constitutionalists discovered the missing link in Locke's theory of government. John Locke, who was the Constitutionalists' philosophic doyen, provides no guidance to this critical question. There is a gaping chasm in Locke's *Second Treatise* between the moment a people come together to form a social compact and the emergence of a constitution, which appears in the *Second Treatise* as fully formed. Utterly absent from the *Second Treatise* is any discussion of how and by whom constitutions are formed.

Locke never really tells his readers except to say that the authority to establish government is put in the hands of the majority. But several difficult questions arise immediately. For instance: By what process will a majority of ordinary people, numbering in the tens or hundreds of thousands or possibly even millions, make this decision? How are such people supposed to design, build and agree upon such an extraordinarily complicated structure as a constitution or a form of government? And what about the actual forms and formalities of the government being created?

One could ask scores of important questions that Locke does not address in the *Second Treatise*. For instance: What is the best form of government? What or whom should be represented in the legislature? Should the legislature be uni- or bi-cameral? How many members should be seated in each legislature? On what basis shall representation be determined (e.g., by population, property, or corporate entity such as towns, counties or districts)? What should be the term of office for various legislative, executive and judicial offices? Will there be property and age qualifications to vote and to hold office? What powers should be given to the government and who should wield them? Should the legislative, executive, and judicial powers be separated, and if so, how? Should the constitution be subject to alteration? If yes, how and by whom? What kind of society should government foster? Locke is mostly silent or agnostic on these crucially important questions. The residents of Massachusetts therefore had to come up with their own Lockean solutions to these Lockean problems.

We come now to the most important invention in the creation of a written constitution as fundamental law. In several towns, but in Concord, Massachusetts, most importantly, a quantum leap in constitutional theory took place. The so-called "Concord Return" of 1776 laid out a revolutionary method for creating a constitution as fundamental law. The Berkshire and Concord Constitutionalists were calling for a constitution that would serve as the fundamental or higher law of the state, which meant that the constitution must therefore precede—indeed, it must create—the government, and not the other way around. And so, our question now becomes: How can that be done? How can a constitution exist before the existence of government to create it? Such a constitution had never existed in world history.

The Constitutionalists' stunning solution to the problem was the invention of a two-step process that would simultaneously capture the sovereignty of the people without indulging the vice of assembling all the people in one place at one time. This two-step process called, first, for the creation of a special constitutional convention or constituent assembly to create a constitution, and, second, for the constitution to be ratified by the people.

In February 1779, the General Court finally acquiesced to the demands of the Berkshire Constitutionalists and called for a special constitutional convention to meet in September 1780. The sole purpose of the convention was to draft a constitution that would in turn be sent back to the people for ratification. Once it had finished its task, the convention would be disbanded. Each town was permitted to send as many delegates to the constitutional convention as it was entitled to elect representatives to the General Court. On September 1, 1779, the residents of Massachusetts made history by sending representatives to Cambridge that would sit in the first true constitutional convention based on the Lockean principles of individual sovereignty, consent, and social-compact theory.

Once the convention met, a committee of thirty was chosen to draft the constitution, which in turn was delegated to a subcommittee of three—James Bowdoin, Samuel Adams, and John Adams. Ultimately, the constitution's principal architect was John Adams, the American Solon. Beginning on October 28, 1779, Adams's draft declaration of rights and constitution were presented to the entire convention, which then examined and debated their contents over the course of the next four months. Adams's finished product was accepted by the convention with only minor revisions on March 2, 1780. The proposed constitution was then printed and sent out to 290 towns for ratification. Over the course of the next several months the towns examined the draft constitution. A ratifying convention then examined the returns from the towns and counted the votes. Formal ratification required the approval of two-thirds of the voting population. On June 16, 1780, the ratifying convention declared the Constitution ratified, and on October 25, 1780, it went into effect.

CONCLUSION

In many ways, the struggle for a constitution in Massachusetts embodies and represents the defining principles of the American Revolution. The new political order was founded on the principle of the consent of the people, and it was defined by a written constitution. From beginning to end, the Berkshire Constitutionalists insisted that the consent of the people was the only proper foundation legitimizing a written constitution as fundamental law. By inventing the idea of special constituent and ratifying conventions chosen by manhood suffrage for the sole purpose of creating and institutionalizing a constitution, the residents of Massachusetts found a means by which to sanctify their constitution as a fundamental law superior to ordinary legislation. In other words, they found a Lockean solution to the Lockean problem of how to frame a constitution based on Lockean principles. That is, they discovered how to put theory into practice, to reconcile consent of the governed with the need for the wisdom of the wise few.

That these simple yeoman farmers, shopkeepers, merchants, sailors, blacksmiths, preachers and lawyers could design and construct their own constitution, that they could redefine the way that all peoples would hitherto think about and look at government, that they could do all this during wartime and in such a brief period of time is one of the truly great stories not only in American history but in the history of all civilized peoples. They demonstrated to the world that it is possible to peaceably alter or even abolish one's form of government without destroying civil society and to reconstruct new governments based on certain self-evident truths. It was a revolutionary invention to end a revolution.

All in all, it was a remarkable achievement.

PART ONE:

REVOLUTIONARY THEORIES OF GOVERNMENT

1. DANIEL SHUTE
"AN ELECTION SERMON"
1768

Daniel Shute was born in Malden, Massachusetts (1722) and died in Hingham, Massachusetts (1802). Shute graduated from Harvard College in 1743, and he was ordained a Congregational minister in 1746. Reverend Shute also served was a member of the Massachusetts convention that ratified the national Constitution. He supported ratification of the new Constitution and was a strong proponent of its provision forbidding the use of religious tests in choosing persons for public office. In 1768, Shute delivered the prestigious "Election Sermon" to Governor Hutchinson, the Council, and House of Representatives. Like many Election Day sermons of the revolutionary era, Shute demonstrates his Enlightenment bona fides by grounding America's constitutional arguments against Great Britain on the laws and rights of nature. His theological arguments serve as window dressing to his more philosophical arguments. Readers should pay close attention to Shute's repeated use of terms such as the "general constitution of things," the "moral fitness of things," and the "relation of things," and his view of men as "rational moral agents." Readers should also be concerned with Shute's philosophic "method."

He whose happiness can admit no accession, and whose perfect rectitude excludes every degree of malevolence, must design the happiness of those creatures he calls out of nothing into existence; to suppose the contrary is inconsistent with absolute perfection, and implies the worst of characters.

The communication of happiness being the end of creation, it will follow, from the perfections of the creator, that the whole plan of things is so adjusted as to promote the benevolent purpose; to which the immense diversity in his works; the gradation in the species of beings that we know of, and many more perhaps than we know of, and the somewhat similar gradation in the same species, arising from their make, their connections, and the circumstances they are placed in, are happily subservient. And every creature in the universe, according to its rank in the scale of being, is so constituted, as that acting agreeably to the laws of its nature, will promote its own happiness, and of consequence the grand design of the creator.

Agreeably hereto, all beings in the class of moral agents are so formed, that happiness will result to them from acting according to certain rules prescribed by the creator, and made known to them by reason or revelation. The rules of action, conformity to which will be productive of happiness to *such* beings, must be agreeable to moral fitness in the relation of things; in perfect conformity to which the rectitude, and happiness of the creator himself consists. And such is the connection and dependency of things, that happiness will result from conformity to these rules, not only to individuals, but likewise to the whole; for the beneficial effects of such conformity are reciprocal.—It naturally tends to promote the order and harmony of the moral system, and so the general good.

The plan of the creator being thus manifestly adapted to promote the happiness of his creation, his conduct herein becomes a pattern to his creatures that are rational moral agents, and the rule of their duty, according to their measure; for all moral obligation on such, indubitably, arises from the will of God, as there is so exact a coincidence between his will, and the relative fitness of things; so that the nearer they resemble him, the nearer they will come to the perfect standard of right action, and the nearer they come to *this* the more happiness will be produced.

It being so evidently the will of God, from the general constitution of things, that the happiness of his rational creatures should be promoted, all such are under moral obligation in conformity thereto, according to their ability, to promote their own, and the happiness of others.

The nature of the human species, therefore, being so adapted to society as that society will afford vastly more happiness to them, than solitary existence could do, indicates the will of their creator, and makes it morally fit that they should associate. From the make of man, the disadvantages of a solitary, and the advantages of a social state, evidently appear. A state of separation from the rest of the species will not admit the exercise of those *affections and virtues,* in which, from his natural constitution, his happiness very much consists; but in connection with others there will be opportunity for the exercise of them. As each individual living in a separate state would be preventive of the happiness for which men were evidently formed; and as this happiness can be obtained only in a social state, to form into society must be not only their interest, but their duty.

The instinct, or propensity, implanted in the human species leading them, as it were mechanically, to *that* to which they are morally obliged, is an instance of the creator's goodness as it facilitates the performance; and in the same proportion it does so, must make their neglect the more inexcusable.

Mankind being formed into society, the moral obligation they are under to civil government will appear from the same principle, as being necessary to secure to them those natural rights and privileges which are essential to their happiness. Life, liberty, and property, are the gifts of the creator, on the unmolested enjoyment of which their happiness chiefly depends: yet they are such an imperfect set of beings that they are liable to have these invaded by one another: But the preservation of them in every fit method is evidently their duty. The entering into society lays the foundation of a plan for securing them; but this plan will be incomplete without the exertion of the united power of the *whole* for their mutual safety. The exertion of this power for that purpose, correspondent to the everlasting rules of right, is what is, here, intended by civil government; and as this is a method the best adapted, in their power, to secure the rights and privileges necessary to their happiness, to go into it is morally fit, and evidently the will of their creator.

Whatever mankind are obliged to perform must be within the verge of their power: The impracticability of the human species continuing to be one society for the purpose before mentioned, makes it necessary and fit they should form into distinct and separate societies, and erect civil government in them for that end.

Upon the same principle, still, the natural rights of one society being invaded by the superior power of another, so long as the former are unable to assert their freedom, it is morally fit they should receive laws from the latter tending to their happiness, as being the best means in their power to promote it, rather than admit a state of anarchy, big with *confusion and every evil work:* But from these circumstances it is morally fit they should rescue themselves whenever it is in their power, only it may be as fit to use caution, that by such attempts they do not plunge themselves the deeper into distress.

The obligation mankind are under to civil government, in some form, as essential to their happiness in the present state, and perhaps not without its influence upon their happiness in a future, is not only deducible from the natural constitution of things, but also supported by written revelation; in which it is represented as greatly tending to their *good,* and therefore an ordinance of the great benefactor of the world, whose *tender mercies are over all his works.* In the epistle to the Romans, the civil power is expressly said to be *of God,* to be *ordained* of him, and the civil ruler to be *the minister of God for good.*

The line, indeed, between one society, and another, is not drawn by heaven; nor is the particular form of civil government; as whether it shall be conducted immediately by the whole society, or by a few of their number, or if by a few, who they shall be, expressly pointed out; but, as mankind are rational and free agents, these are left to their determination and choice; only herein they are restricted by those rules which arise from the moral fitness of things productive of the general good, which they are ever bound invariably to observe.

Nor does the sacred story of the *Hebrew* polity militate against the established order of things relative to civil government among men. The theocracy of the Jews, was an extraordinary vouchsafement of God to that particular nation, but not counter to, or designed to alter, the general constitution of mankind.

The right the supreme ruler of the world has to bestow favours upon *some* out of the common course of things, while *others* are left in the enjoyment of their natural privileges, can, in reason, no more be doubted, than his right to create one being superior to another; for, though unknown to us, *that,* as well as *this,* may be in the original plan for the communication of happiness. . . .

No set of beings can, in reason, suppose themselves wiser than their maker; but must think *that* to which he directs to be wisest and best; and, therefore, when they have certain notice of his pleasure respecting any transaction of theirs, both duty and interest urge them to a compliance. And what nation of men on earth, in the exercise of this natural right, unalienable to any mortal, would not be glad of immediate indubitable direction from heaven? But when these special directions are not obtainable, as according to the natural constitution of mankind they are not, the affair being so important to society, and the happiness of the whole so intimately connected with it, it is fit that they should first implore the influence of providence, which may be real, though not immediate and sensible; and then transact it in the exercise of that liberty wherewith the creator has made them free. . . .

And FIRST, The part of civil rulers, in general is to keep in view the end of civil government, and of their own particular advancement, and to act accordingly.

Though in the constitution of things it does not belong to man to live alone, or without government in society; yet he is invested with certain rights and privileges, by the bounty of the creator, so adapted to his nature that the enjoyment of them is the source of his happiness in this world, and without which existence here would not be desirable. And mankind have no right voluntarily to give up to others those natural privileges, essential to their happiness, with which they are invested by the Lord of all: for the improvement of *these* they are accountable to him. Nor is it fit, that any of the sons of men should take from others *that* which they have no right to give, nor by their misconduct have forfeited; though in this case there should be mutual consent, the compact would be illegal, and both parties indictable at the bar of heaven.

Civil government among mankind is not a resignation of their natural privileges, but that method of securing them, to which they are morally obliged as conducive to their happiness: In the constitution of things, they can naturally have no rights incompatible with this; and therefore none to resign. For each individual to live in a separate state, and of consequence without civil government, is so pregnant with evil, and greatly preventive of that happiness of which human nature is made capable, that it could never be designed as a privilege to man by the munificent creator: And, perhaps, is not a privilege to other orders of rational creatures, as much superior to man, in virtue, as in rank of being.

Mankind may naturally have a liberty to live without civil government in the same sense that they have a liberty, *i.e.* a power to neglect any moral duty: But they are evidently made dependent on one another for happiness; and that method of action, which in the constitution of things, will prevent misery, and procure happiness to the species, on supposition of their being acquainted with it, and in a capacity of going into it, is not only wrong in them to neglect, but even duty indispensible to pursue. From hence arises their obligation to civil government as mentioned before; and when the same reason urges the lodging this government in the hands of a few of the number associated, the same obligation lies on them to do so.

A Community having determined that to commit the power of government to some few of their number is best, the right the some few can have to it, must arise from the choice of the whole; for in this state the government belongs to the whole, and one has no more right to govern than another; the right therefore that individuals can have to this must be delegated. This delegation is not indeed the giving away of the right the whole have to govern, but providing for the exercise of their power in the most effectual manner.

It is by virtue of the previous consent of society as being best, that government may devolve on some by succession, and that others may be appointed to rule by those already in authority.

A compact for civil government in any community implies the stipulation of certain rules of government. These rules or laws more properly make the civil constitution. How various these rules are in different nations is not the present enquiry; but that they ought in every nation to coincide with the moral fitness of things, by which alone the natural rights of mankind can be secured, and their happiness promoted, is very certain. And such are the laws of the constitution of civil government that we, and all *British* subjects are so happy as to live under.

The rectitude of the laws of a civil constitution are of more importance to the well-being of society than the particular form of administration, but that form which is best adapted to secure the uninterrupted course of such laws is most eligible, and herein also we outvie other nations.

Those laws which prescribe the rights of prerogative, and the rights of the people, should be founded on such principles as tend to promote the great end of civil institution; and as they are to be held sacred by both, it may be supposed, ought to be as plain as the nature of the thing will admit: Mysteries in civil government relative to the rights of the people, like mysteries in the laws of religion, may be pretended, and to the like purpose of slavery, *this* of the souls, and *that* of the bodies of men.

The design of mankind in forming a civil constitution being to secure their natural rights and privileges, and to promote their happiness, it is necessary that the special end of the electors in chusing some to govern the whole, should be assented to by the elected to vest them with a right to govern, so far at least as to direct the administration, without which they are indeed vested with no authority; for the being chosen to a particular purpose by those in whom the right of choice is, can give no rightful power to act beside or counter to this purpose. And therefore to the proper investiture of any in the office of civil rulers to which they are chosen by the people, it is necessary they should consent to act the part for which they are chosen; and this sets them in the high office of government, and gives them authority to regulate the whole.

Their consent to take the office to which they are chosen by the community lays rulers under a moral obligation to discharge the duties of it with fidelity. And if for the greater security of society, they who are thus introduced into office are bound to the faithful discharge of it by the solemnity of an oath, their obligation hereto is the greater.

What is right in the relation of things, and which has the general consent of mankind, being the rule of civil government in a well constituted state, civil rulers are to be so far from invading, that they ought to be the guardians of the natural and constitutional rights of their subjects; which are here supposed to be so nearly the same that there is no interfering between them. To form a civil constitution otherwise would be to establish iniquity by law.

The various duties of their office then centre in one point, the end of their election, and that is to promote the public welfare.

Minutely to enumerate these duties is not indeed pretended, not only as it would take up too much time, but also as the wisdom of the politician can better apply general rules to particular cases as circumstances vary; I therefore shall take the liberty only in a more general way to observe: That whatever is injurious to the community, whether foreign or intestine, is theirs to endeavor to prevent. In this state of imperfection and sin, particular societies are liable to injuries from one another, hence vigilance becomes one part of the duty of civil rulers; to this they are more obliged than other men: In office they are as eyes to the political body, the proper use of which is necessary to its safety. It is no small part of their care to descry danger, to penetrate the designs formed abroad to the detriment of the community. And as they are set for the public defence, when such dangers are discovered by them, it is their part to provide against them at the public expense; which must be in their power at all times, or at some times it may not be in their power to act in the character of guardians to the public. Individuals of the same society are likewise liable to unequal treatment from one another, which also claims their attention. They are to rescue the weak and helpless, the widow and fatherless, from the cruel hands of oppression, and equally secure to all, high and low, their rights.

And whatever is for the advantage and emolument of society, is also their part to promote, not only barely to secure to their subjects the cardinal privileges of human nature, but also kindly endeavour to heighten their happiness in the enjoyment of them. Those methods which will be most conducive to the preservation and prosperity of the *whole* are to be studiously devised, and faithfully urged by them; hence agriculture and commerce, liberal and mechanical arts should be encouraged, as pointed out in providence for the benefit of mankind; in proportion to improvement in which will be the benefit resulting from them, by which a supply may be obtained not only for necessity, but also for delight; and hereby their political strength will be increased, and they become more able to support the common cause. The wealth of the people is the strength of the state; and therefore, as *the diligent hand maketh rich,* they should reduce the vagrant, and call the idle to labor, and all to industry in their respective callings, so essential to the public utility.

But *wisdom is a defence* as well as *money,* and necessary to the well being of a community. The education of the youth is therefore carefully to be provided for; that hereby such improvements may be made, as happily tend to abate the ferocity of uncultivated nature, to soften the temper, and give a high relish to the sweets of social life; and such geniuses may be formed as public offices require; that the *people,* in church or state, may not be *destroyed for lack of knowledge;* but *wisdom and knowledge* may *be the stability of the times.*

The civil power also should be exerted to suppress vice as pregnant with mischief to society; and to support virtue as the foundation of social happiness.

That public homage which the community owe to the great Lord of all; and which is equally their interest as their duty to pay, should be earnestly promoted by their rulers. The fitness of which, reason dictates and revelation confirms, as a proper expression of the dependence of mankind on him, and of their grateful sentiments towards him, *who giveth to all life and breath and all things;* and also as the way more deeply to impress on their minds a sense of their obligations to conform to his will; conformity to which will produce order and harmony, and, qualify for the blessings of his providence.

The great advantages acruing from the public social worship of the Deity may be a laudable motive to civil rulers to exert themselves to promote it; and will have an influence on them who have the public good at heart, as well as a proper sense of duty to him, who *is higher than the highest:* In this way, while the ministers of religion are under the patronage of the civil power, the people will be instructed in those principles, and urged to those practices, which will greatly subserve the interest of the community, and facilitate the end of government. . . .

It is therefore the part of civil rulers to make, and as occasion shall offer, to execute such laws as tend to promote the public welfare. *These* indeed are in some measure to be varied, according to the temper and circumstances of the subjects, by the wisdom of the legislators; but yet it is necessary there should be in them a conformity to the immutable laws of nature, to answer the true design of civil institution.

To these laws it is fit they should add such sanctions as will give them energy if they are suitably applied by those in civil office whose part it is to put the laws into execution.

Provided always, that no laws be made invasive of the natural rights of conscience, and no penalties inflicted by the civil power in things purely religious, and which do not affect the well being of the state: In *these,* every

man has an unalienable right, in the constitution of things, to judge for himself: No man, and no number of men therefore have a right to assume jurisdiction here.

On the free exercise of their natural religious rights the present as well
as future happiness of mankind greatly depends; the abridgement of which
by penal laws is evidently incongruous to the eternal rules of equity; but
these rules are never to be violated in the exercise of civil power. Civil laws,
of right, can relate only to those actions which have influence on the welfare
of the state; and to all *such* the subject may be urged by the civil authority
consistently with that freedom of mind, in judging of points of speculation,
and that liberty of conscience relative to modes of worship, which he has a
natural right unmolested to enjoy.

Obligation on civil rulers to secure the rights and promote the happiness
of the people, most certainly implies a power in them to that purpose,—to
make laws and execute them; without which, ruler is but an empty name: To
this purpose they are indeed cloathed with authority, and armed with the
united power of the community; only in the exercise of this power they are
under the same moral restrictions with those by whom it was delegated to
them.

As in a well constituted civil state there is a subordination among rulers,
and each has his respective part to act with a view to the public good; so to
carry the grand design into execution it is necessary that each should keep
the line of his own particular department; every excentric motion will introduce disorder and be productive of mischief: But each keeping a steady and
regular course in his own sphere, will dispense a benign influence upon the
community, and harmoniously conspire to promote the general good: As in
the solar system, every planet revolving in its own orbit round the sun pro-
duces that order and harmony which secures the conservation of the whole.

The part that civil rulers have to act supposes qualifications for that purpose, and accordingly we have begged leave in the SECOND place . . . to
suggest some of them.

Religion, learning, and firmness of mind in the discharge of the duties
of his office, were conspicuous parts of his character, and comprehend perhaps most of the qualifications requisite in civil rulers.

Religion includes piety and virtue, and is acting agreeably to the will of
God according to the capacity of the moral agent. To *this* all men are under
obligation as they would answer the end of their creation, and qualify themselves for the happiness for which they were formed: And to *this* they are
obliged in their social connections, that the happy effects of it may be felt not
only by themselves but also by others. Nor is there any station among mankind so elevated as to free from this obligation.

The public good is in proportion to right action in every individual.—
But as in the civil subordination among men *some* have it in their power to
do more *good* or *mischief* to the *whole* than others, so it is of more

importance to society that *such* should be more virtuous than others. There is an essential difference between virtue and vice, and their different consequences to society will be sensibly felt: nor is it in the power of earth, or hell, to alter the natural constitution of things.

Vice is detrimental to society in some degree in *any* of its members, but is more so in *those* who manage the public affairs of it. It disqualifies for public services at the same rate, as it debases the mind, weakens the generous movements of the soul, and centres it's views in the contracted circle of self-interest.

But virtue qualifies for public offices as it dilates the mind with liberal sentiments, inspires with principles of beneficent actions, and disposes to a ready compliance with the apostolic injunction, *look not every man on his own things, but every man also on the things of another.*

The religion of Jesus is designed to *destroy the works of the devil,* to bring men *from darkness to light,* from error to the truth, *and from the power of Satan unto God*—It inspires the mind with a sacred regard to God, and with benevolence to men,—it is an imitation of his example, *who came down from heaven* and *went about doing good,*—of *his, who is good to all,* and *whose mercy endures forever*—and it also more powerfully inforces all moral obligations, as it illucidates a future state of rewards and punishments.

That character therefore which is formed from those principles, which are abhorrent to sinister views, and indirect measures to promote a man's own private interest, and lead to generous godlike actions diffusive of goodness to mankind, and which afford the strongest motives to such actions, evidently corresponds to a public station, and is most likely *ceteris paribus,* to discharge with fidelity the duties of a civil post.

Nor is the influence, the example of rulers will, in high probability, have upon others, unimportant to society: Facts demonstrate examples to be very forcible on human nature. Inferiours especially are apt to copy the pattern set them by superiors, and too often even to servile imitation. In some proportion then as the example of those who are in exalted stations is virtuous or vicious it may naturally be expected the character of the *whole* will be: Nor is sacred history silent as to the influence public characters have had upon the morals of a people; in this view therefore it is the wisdom and interest of a community to prefer the virtuous to the vicious for their rulers.

But the goodness of the heart influential on the life, without discernment in the head, will yet leave civil rulers short of a qualification necessary to discharge the duties of their office. Men may be pious and virtuous and yet not capable of penetrating very far into the nature and connection of things, and therefore unequal to transactions which require more than common abilities. . . .

Capacity for posts of public trust without virtuous principles is indeed precarious, and not safely to be depended on; but when probity and wisdom unite in the same person they form a character that tends greatly to support the confidence, and secure the happiness of the people.

But to *these* we may yet add firmness of mind in the execution of their office as a very necessary qualification in civil rulers, without *which* an habitual disposition to do their duty, and the good sense to understand it, may not in all circumstances answer the end. . . .

The present state of things will afford frequent occasions of trying the virtue as well as the wisdom of rulers.—Like other men they are exposed to temptations, and perhaps to more and greater than others; and human nature at best is very imperfect. The temper of domination so strongly interwoven in the make of man may induce them to a wanton exercise of the power reposed in them. Flattery by its soothing addresses and artful insinuations may insensibly divert them from a right course, and lead them to dispense the blessings of government with a partial hand. Calumny and cruel censure may provoke in them too great resentment, or subject them to that *fear of man* which *bringeth a snare:* Firmness of mind is therefore necessary to repel *these* and a thousand other temptations—to supress every undue sally of the soul, and to urge the spring of action, that they may pursue with steadiness and vigor the great end of their office.

Those noble exertions of mind which a due administration requires clearly evinces the necessity of this temper in civil rulers: As in order hereto the art of self-denial must be learned and frequently practised by them;—a prevailing attachment to their own private interests and gratifications be given up to the public—angry resentments be tempered down to the standard of right action,—their ease superseded by incessant labors, and sacrificed to the benefit of others.

Softness and timidity of mind indulged into habit will weaken resolution, and relax the nerves of effort in the most trying seasons, and perhaps betray the cause their office calls, and their virtue inclines them to support. But firmness and fortitude of soul arising from principle, and cultivated with care, will not easily admit those sordid views that lead *supinely* to neglect, or *tamely* to surrender the interest of society, but enable them to comport with personal inconveniences, and stand firm amidst the severest trials, in executing the duties of their office.

Good may indeed be done by him, who is *distinguished* by one of these qualifications alone, and more especially in his connections with others employed in the same office; their different qualities may operate in subserviency to each other, and by their mutual aid lead into measures conducive to the general safety; and happy to mankind that in this imperfect state it is so! But without determining which of them being wanting in civil rulers would be of most dangerous consequence to society, it is very certain their meeting in the same person forms a character that will best answer the design of such promotion; and the more there are of this character among them, the more likely it is that the public welfare will be promoted.

But, if every good quality should meet in civil rulers yet THIRDLY, the united exertions of the people with them are necessary to answer the salutary purposes of civil government.

A community having delegated to some of their number the power of civil government as a method of exercising that power the best adapted to secure their natural rights and promote their happiness are not at liberty to counteract the method, but under obligation, in every fit way, to support it; and indeed without their exerting themselves to this purpose, their rulers, however well qualified, will be unable to answer the end of their advancement.

The cause in which rulers and ruled are engaged is the same, though the parts they have to act are different; *these* all tend to one grand point, the welfare of the community; and people are as much, obliged to fidelity and ardor in the discharge of their duty, as rulers to theirs, in supporting the common cause.

The discharge of the duties of civil office merits an adequate reward from them whose business is done thereby; and the community are unquestionably obliged to see that business performed. Rulers devoting their time and their talents to the service of the public entitles them to an easy and honourable support: For real service and great benefit done them, it is the duty of the *people to render to all their dues, tribute to whom tribute is due,* and *custom to whom custom.* If *this* should not be afforded *them* by the public, they could not attend *continually* upon the duties of their station; and of consequence civil government, on which so much depends, could not be upheld to advantage.

A respectful treatment of their rulers is also due from the people, and greatly conducive to the end of civil institution. *They* are raised to exalted station by the *people,* under the governance of his providence, who wills the happiness of *all men,* and in promoting which they are to be considered as his vicegerents executing his will, and therefore worthy of esteem and veneration. Their success in administration also very much depends upon this respectful deportment toward them: To pour contempt upon rulers is to weaken government itself, and to weaken government is to sow the seeds of libertinism, which in a soil so prolific as human nature, will soon spring up into a luxuriant growth; nor will it be in the power of rulers to stop the growing mischief, or, to keep things in a proper situation, without, the concurring aid of the people.

A sacred regard to civil authority, according to the true design of it, is to be cultivated in all; and as a means naturally tending to this, including the necessity of divine influence in their arduous and benevolent work, it is directed by the supreme law-giver, *that supplications; and prayers, intercessions, and giving of thanks be made—for kings, and for all that are in authority, that we may lead a quiet and peaceable life in all godliness and honesty.*

To keep up a veneration for rulers, is to keep up a regard to government itself in the community, and to open the way for its happier influence. Honor therefore should be rendered to them to whom it is due for the good services they have already done, and as being the way to give them opportunity of doing more, and to stimulate them to improve the opportunity by the vigorous exertions of their abilities to that purpose.

But still and more especially, the united efforts of the people with their rulers are necessary to the putting those laws into execution that are made for the good of the community.

It is here supposed, that the laws made by civil rulers coincide with moral fitness, and are calculated to answer the end for which only they are impowered to make laws; if otherwise, the subject can be under no obligation to observe them; but may be morally obliged to resist them, as it must ever be right *to obey God rather than men.* The doctrine of *passive obedience* and *non-resistance* in the unlimited sense it has been urged by some, came not down from above, as it can be supported neither by reason nor revelation; and therefore if any where, may be urged with a better grace by *the rulers of darkness,* in the regions below, upon those who by the righteous decree of heaven, are excluded the common benefits of creation, than by those *powers that are ordained of God* for the *good* of mankind. But though with the highest propriety this doctrine may be exploded, it does not at all lessen the moral obligation of obedience in the people to an equitable administration; and to use their endeavours that the laws made by their rulers to promote the good of the community should take place to that purpose: This is only the continued exertion of that power which is necessary to carry into effect the plan of civil government laid by themselves, and without which the best laws will fall short of it. There may be *good* laws, and *faithful* executors of them, and yet such a practical combination of the subjects as in some measure to frustrate the happy effects of them: The violation of *these* laws may be so connived at in one another, as to prevent the executors having the opportunity to suppress them. The laws of the supreme legislator of the world are unquestionably *just and good,* and yet are transgressed by daring mortals every day: And though under his all-discerning eye the impenitent shall not finally escape with impunity, yet the transgressors of human laws founded on the same principles as the divine, may illude the inspection of man and the force of his laws: And when this practice shall become general in civil society, the energy of government will of course be relaxed. Nor can it be in the power of rulers the best qualified and the most sedulously attentive to the duties of their office to prevent it, unless they were gods in a higher sense than the scripture intends by giving them that title, and were able not only to make *good* laws, but also to inspire their subjects with a principle of obedience to them.

It is therefore plain, that the united efforts of the people are necessary to support civil government, and make it efficacious to the great and happy end for which it was instituted: And as rulers are holden by the strongest ties to consult and endeavour the welfare of the people; the *people* are equally bound to aid and assist them in these endeavours.

What has been imperfectly suggested in this discourse may lead to some reflections on the goodness of the supreme ruler of the world, to mankind in general and to ourselves in particular, in the present state, more especially as expressed in the institution of civil government: And give occasion to urge the attention of rulers and people to the duties of their respective stations.

The goodness of the Creator appears through all his works, but more illustriously to man than to any other creature on this earth; him he hath set at the head of this part of his creation: The place of his present abode is accomodated to his necessity and pleasure; and his mind is endowed with reason and understanding to guide and regulate him in the enjoyment. With a view to secure him in the possession of the munificence of his creator, he is directed by instinct and reason to associate, and amicably unite the strength of individuals for the defence and safety of the whole.

And this method is peculiarly adapted to the present depraved state of mankind, in which by leaping the mounds of right man is the greatest enemy to man. If there was no such thing as civil government among them, what ravages! and what depredations would there be! This earth would be the habitation of cruelty, and a field of blood. The consequences of perfect anarchy among mankind would be more unhappy and mischievous to them, than if *the foundations of the earth* were *out of course, the sun* should *be darkened, and the moon not give her light, and the stars fall from heaven;* And the natural order of this system should be interrupted by a general and most ruinous confusion.

But the plan of civil government, as included in the constitution of things, and obvious to the common sense of mankind, well executed by them, gives such a check to *evil doers,* and support to *them that do well,* that the nearer mankind pursue it, in its true intention, the more this earth will become a habitation of peace, of security and happiness. This privilege is put into their hands by the Lord of all, as the great security and completion of their earthly felicity; to him therefore their united acknowledgements should like incense, with fervor ascend.

We ourselves have reason, not only to join in the universal tribute, as partaking of the blessings of the creator in common with mankind, but also in particular to express our warmest gratitude to him whose providence determines *the bounds of the habitations of all the nations of men that dwell on the face of the earth;* that we live under a constitution of civil government the best adapted to secure the rights and liberties of the subject: The fundamental laws of which are agreeable to the laws of nature resulting from the relation of things, worthy of men and christians; and the form of administration the best contrived to secure a steady adherence to those laws in the exercise of civil power. Our King sways the sceptre in righteousness, *and his throne is upholden by mercy:* The legislative and executive powers are guided by the same laws.

The beneficial effects of the happy constitution extend to the remotest parts of the *British* empire: *Britons* exult in the enjoyment of their natural rights under its auspicious influence, nor less the colonists in *North-America* while they participate with grateful and loyal hearts the like blessings from the same source.

The colonists indeed on account of local circumstances, have been indulged to form into little distinct states under the same head, and to make laws and execute them, restricted at the same time by the laws and dependent on the supreme power of the nation as far as it is consistent with the essential rights of *British* subjects and necessary to the well-being of the whole. And this is so far from being the ground of their complaint that it is in their opinion the very foundation of their happiness; from the antient stock they delight to draw nutrition as hereby they flourish, and in their turn bear to *that* proportionable fruit. Nor could any thing more sensibly affect them, or be thought of with more regret, than to be rescinded from the body of the empire, and their present connections with *Great-Britain.*

In their little dependent states they have long enjoyed her parental smiles, which has greatly increased their attachment to her: The relief she has kindly afforded them in times of danger and distress will always invigorate the addresses, and support the confidence of her children towards her, under the like circumstances, till they shall find themselves discarded by her. Which sad catastrophe may all-gracious Heaven prevent! But the same patronage is still to be hoped for by the colonists while they do nothing to forfeit it. Nor is it to be thought that *Great-Britain* would designedly enslave any of her free-born sons, and thereby break in upon that constitution so friendly to liberty, and on which her own safety depends.

This Province has not the least share in privileges derived from the civil constitution of her parent country, and which are amply secured to us by royal charter.

Our Governor is by deputation from our most gracious Sovereign as the representative of his sacred person in our provincial model of civil government. His Majesty's paternal care in this respect is most readily acknowledged by us, as the Gentleman who has this honor at present is well acquainted with the laws and formalities of our civil constitution, and has abilities equal to the important post. Whose presence forbids every thing that looks like adulation, but may admit of the warmest wishes for his happiness in this world and the next.

The other two branches of the legislature are chosen by the people, either immediately by themselves or mediately by their representatives, which coincides with the freedom of the *British* constitution, and we shall always esteem as a pledge of the Royal favor. . . .

The happiness of this people in the enjoyment of their natural rights and privileges under providence is provided for by their being a part of the *British* empire, by which they are intitled to all the privileges of that happy constitution; and also by the full and ample recognition of these privileges to them by character.

Their civil constitution as the basis of all their temporal felicity is their dearest stake. Every privation of their natural rights is subversive of their happiness, and every infringement of the form of their constitution has a tendency to such privation: The preservation of their constitutional rights, in every fit method, will therefore ever forceably claim their attention; and to this purpose, while they are awake to a sense of their interest, the vigilance and care of their rulers will, of right, be earnestly expected by them.

Their being dependent on the supreme power of the nation as a part of the *whole,* is so far from making it unfit to remonstrate under grievances of this nature, that it is a reason why they should do so; when by the constitution every subject has an equal claim to protection and security in the exercise of that very power.

Their being loyal subjects to the best of Kings, whom may God long preserve! and disposed to cultivate, and if possible to increase their loyalty, will always incline his gracious ear; and give weight to their petitions with his parliament.

With indifference to surrender constitutional rights, or with rashness to oppose constitutional measures, is equally to *rebel* against the state. Anarchy and slavery are both diametrically opposite to the genius of the *British* constitution, and indeed to the constitution of the God of nature; and equal care at least is to be taken to avoid the former as the latter. A ready compliance with constitutional measures will always justify a tenacious claim to constitutional privileges, and support the hope of their continuance.

The wellfare of the province, at all times, demands the attention of the guardians of our natural and civil rights; to this purpose the legislative and executive powers are to be exercised. But laws are useless in a state, unless they are obeyed; nor will putting the executive power into the best hands avail to the designed purpose, if there is not proper application made to it upon those occasions that require the exercise of it; for in proportion to the want of this application the most excellent *code* of laws will be a dead letter. It is necessary in the nature of the thing, and indispensably obligatory upon the people to unite their endeavours with their rulers to give life and energy to the laws in producing the designed happy effects.

We have good laws; and magistrates appointed to put *those* laws into execution, whose fidelity may not be impeached: What therefore seems to remain to complete our political happiness is the exerting ourselves to aid the civil power, in surpressing every thing that may be detrimental, and in promoting that which may be of advantage to the *whole.*

Though *some* are appointed and bound by oath to give information of breaches of the law which come within their knowledge, yet *all* are under certain obligation to assist in conveying such information through the proper channels to the executive power, as it is the *ordinance of God* for the good of the community. But from the want of a due regard to the public—or from a misguided fondness for ourselves, we are too apt to be criminally indulgent to one another, and of consequence to desert the magistrate, and in some degree frustrate the design of his office. We have laws *wisely* provided against the evils of *idleness* and *intemperance*—and whatever has appeared to the wisdom of the legislature to be hurtful to society; to whom then may the increase of such disorders be attributed? to *those* whose business it is to execute the law upon offenders, on due information, or *those* who rather than give, such information chuse to have *fellowship* with iniquity:—But not only they who are specially appointed for the purpose, but *all* should attend to the moral obligation they are under to exert themselves, in their respective stations, to prevent the interruption of the happiness of society, and instead of leaving the magistrates unaided, should voluntarily *rise up for* them *against the evil doers,* and lend their assistance to bring *the workers of iniquity* to condign punishment.

By this general exertion the most happy effects would be produced;—transgressors would soon be taught a greater reverence for the law, and all be more secure in the enjoyment of their rights: Hereby obstructions would be removed, and the executive power have free course; and *judgment* would *run down as waters and righteousness as a mighty stream.*

Instead therefore of speaking *evil of dignities,* and cruelly charging them with the blame of prevailing disorders, we should recriminate on ourselves, and do our part to aid the magistrates in putting the laws *already* made into execution, and confide in the wisdom and fidelity of the legislators to make such *new ones* as the circumstances of the community may require.

And while the guardians of this people are intent upon securing their rights and promoting their happiness, in every wise and laudable method, liberal support should be granted, great honors done, and cheerful obedience yielded to them.

Our safety and happiness must always arise from the united exertions of rulers and ruled to the same salutary purposes. The security of our liberty and property by the fundamental laws of our civil constitution is the strongest motive to maintain an inviolable attachment to it; and to exert ourselves to promote the interest of the nation to which we belong. Every well-directed effort to support the constitution on which the happiness of the *whole* depends, and to augment the wealth and strength of the *British* empire, as our duty and interest, should be readily made by us. To multiply settlements on the uncultivated lands, and reduce the *wilderness* to *a fruitful field,* by emigration from our older towns, and especially by the introduction of foreigners not unfriendly to our constitution—to make greater improvements in agriculture and in every useful art evidently tends to the general welfare.

Arbitrary and oppressive measures in the state would indeed dispirit the people and weaken the nerves of industry, and in their consequences lead to poverty and ruin; but a mild and equitable administration, will encourage their hearts and strengthen their hands to execute with vigor those measures which promote the strength and safety of the whole.

To lay a foundation of greater security to *ourselves* is indeed a laudable motive to such efforts; and may be justified by the principle of self-preservation: But the advantages of such improvements will not be confined to ourselves—the more populous and opulent we grow, the more able we shall be to defend this important part of the *British* dominions—the more our nation will be a terror to her enemies—and the better able shall we be to make remittance for what we shall necessarily want of her manufactures.

By a proper attention to the general interest, and vigorous pursuits of measures that tend to promote it, things may be put into such a situation as to be of mutual advantage. The growth and prosperity of her colonies must be of real advantage to *Great-Britain.*—The means for exportation being increased in them, will be so to the colonies, by which they may sink their present heavy debts, and more easily defray necessary public charges.

The same attention, with a little prudence, would lead us to retrench extravagant expences, and to promote frugality, good order, and industry, that we might give a seasonable check to increasing debility, enjoy what we possess to more advantage and widen the foundation of future felicity. Under greater advantages we may receive monitory and directive hints, by turning our eye to the provident ant, *which having no guide, overseer or ruler provides her meat in the summer and gathereth her food in the harvest.*

We are now reaping the happy fruits of our Fathers *hard* labor and *ineffable* sufferings; and shall not a concern for future generations warm our hearts—produce some acts of self denial, and closer application for their sakes? or shall we do nothing for our *posterity* when the first renowned settlers, here, did so much for *theirs?* Could *they* look down—or rather be permitted in flesh to visit their dear-bought country, with what astonishment would they behold the ungrateful neglect—with what severity reprove the prostitution of patrimonial privileges, and chide the criminal want of philanthropy, in their degenerate offspring: and with what ardor would they urge them to perfect the work they had nobly begun, and thereby make room for millions yet unborn quietly to enjoy their natural, their civil, and religious liberties.

In fine. To secure his own, and to promote the happiness of others, is the part of every one in this great assembly. *To this end* were we *born, and for this cause came* we *into the world.* We were placed in that rank of being, and under those circumstances, which the infinitely wise and good Creator saw proper. And as we are moral agents, and accountable; it is of great importance to us in every station, to keep in view the *end* of our being called into existence.

This is but the bud of being—we are candidates for a succeeding state; into which, we are assured by the *gospel* of the Son of God, the consequences of our actions in *this,* will follow us. Nor in the constitution of things have we long to continue here, but mortality will soon translate us to the state of retribution. With what care then should we avoid every action debasing to the mind, and with what assiduity pursue those that tend to raise it to nobler heights.

By inattention and vice we may forfeit the blessings of *creation* and *redemption,* and by a continued course of sordid and unworthy actions, dishonorary to God and unfriendly to mankind, we may finish the ruins of our nature; and put ourselves into such a state, that it would have been *good* for us if we *had never been born.* But by a diligent improvement of the talents committed to our trust in exercises of piety towards God, and charity to men, we may enoble the mind, and qualify it for the sublime happiness for which it was originally designed. Having therefore acted our part with fidelity in the service of God and our generation, we shall quit this imperfect state with dignity and honor, and rise superior to the highest grandeur and felicity in these regions of mortality; and by the immerited munificence of the Creator

---

SOURCE: Extracts from Daniel Shute, "A sermon preached before His Excellency Francis Bernard, Esq; governor, His Honor Thomas Hutchinson, . . . of the province of the Massachusetts-Bay in New-England, May 25th. 1768." In the digital collection *Evans Early American Imprint Collection.* https://name.umdl.umich.edu/n08656.0001.001. University of Michigan Library Digital Collections. Accessed December 21, 2024.

2. JOHN ADAMS
"THOUGHTS ON GOVERNMENT"
1776

John Adams was born in Braintree, Massachusetts (1735), and he died a few miles away from his birthplace in Quincy, Massachusetts (1826). Adams was a lawyer, politician, statesman, political philosopher, diplomat, first vice-president of the United States under George Washington, second President of the United States, and founding father. In late 1775 and early 1776, John Adams assumed a leading role in the Continental Congress to encourage the thirteen colonies to begin designing and constructing new governments. In the spring of 1776, when it was clear that the Americans were heading toward independence, many delegates turned to Adams to produce a model constitution that could be used by the prospective new states. Adams responded to their requests with his most influential writing of the Revolutionary period, Thoughts on Government. Adams also wrote the "Thoughts" as an antidote to the political prescriptions advanced in Thomas Paine's recently published "Common Sense." "Thoughts on Government" stands as a distillation of Adams's most advanced political thinking. The principles that he would later put forth in his great treatise, A Defence of the Constitutions of Government of the United States of America (1787-88), *are all found in "Thoughts": republican government, frequent elections, separation of powers, bicameralism, a unitary executive armed with a strong veto power, and an independent judiciary. The influence of "Thoughts on Government" on American constitution-makers was widespread. The historical evidence strongly suggests that Thoughts was used as a constitutional blueprint in North Carolina, Virginia, New Jersey, New York, and Massachusetts.*

If I was equal to the task of forming a plan for the government of a colony, I should be flattered with your request, and very happy to comply with it; because as the divine science of politicks is the science of social happiness, and the blessings of society depend entirely on the constitutions of government, which are generally institutions that last for many generations, there can be no employment more agreeable to a benevolent mind, than a research after the best.

Pope flattered tyrants too much when he said,

> "For forms of government let fools contest,
> That which is best administered is best."

Nothing can be more fallacious than this: But poets read history to collect flowers not fruits—they attend to fanciful images, not the effects of social institutions. Nothing is more certain from the history of nations, and the nature of man, than that some forms of government are better fitted for being well administered than others.

We ought to consider, what is the end of government, before we determine which is the best form. Upon this point all speculative politicians will agree, that the happiness of society is the end of government, as all Divines and moral Philosophers will agree that the happiness of the individual is the end of man. From this principle it will follow, that the form of government, which communicates ease, comfort, security, or in one word happiness to the greatest number of persons, and in the greatest degree, is the best.

All sober enquiries after truth, ancient and modern, Pagan and Christian, have declared that the happiness of man, as well as his dignity consists in virtue. Confucius, Zoroaster, Socrates, Mahomet, not to mention authorities really sacred, have agreed in this.

If there is a form of government then, whose principle and foundation is virtue, will not every sober man acknowledge it better calculated to promote the general happiness than any other form?

Fear is the foundation of most governments; but is so sordid and brutal a passion, and renders men, in whose breasts it predominates, so stupid, and miserable, that Americans will not be likely to approve of any political institution which is founded on it.

Honor is truly sacred, but holds a lower rank in the scale of moral excellence than virtue. Indeed the former is but a part of the latter, and consequently has not equal pretensions to support a frame of government productive of human happiness.

The foundation of every government is some principle or passion in the minds of the people. The noblest principles and most generous affections in our nature then, have the fairest chance to support the noblest and most generous models of government.

A man must be indifferent to the sneers of modern Englishmen to mention in their company the names of Sidney, Harrington, Locke, Milton, Nedham, Neville, Burnet, and Hoadley. No small fortitude is necessary to confess that one has read them. The wretched condition of this country, however, for ten or fifteen years past, has frequently reminded me of their principles and reasonings. They will convince any candid mind, that there is no good government but what is Republican. That the only valuable part of the British constitution is so; because the very definition of a Republic, is "an Empire of Laws, and not of men." That, as a Republic is the best of governments, so that particular arrangement of the powers of society, or in other words that form of government, which is best contrived to secure an impartial and exact execution of the laws, is the best of Republics.

Of Republics, there is an inexhaustable variety, because the possible combinations of the powers of society, are capable of innumerable variations.

As good government, is an empire of laws, how shall your laws be made? In a large society, inhabiting an extensive country, it is impossible that the whole should assemble, to make laws: The first necessary step then, is, to depute power from the many, to a few of the most wise and good. But by what rules shall you chuse your Representatives? Agree upon the number and qualifications of persons, who shall have the benefit of choosing, or annex this priviledge to the inhabitants of a certain extent of ground.

The principal difficulty lies, and the greatest care should be employed in constituting this Representative Assembly. It should be in miniature, an exact portrait of the people at large. It should think, feel, reason, and act like them. That it may be the interest of this Assembly to do strict justice at all times, it should be an equal representation, or in other words equal interest among the people should have equal interest in it. Great care should be taken to effect this, and to prevent unfair, partial, and corrupt elections. Such regulations, however, may be better made in times of greater tranquility than the present, and they will spring up of themselves naturally, when all the powers of government come to be in the hands of the people's friends. At present it will be safest to proceed in all established modes to which the people have been familiarised by habit.

A representation of the people in one assembly being obtained, a question arises whether all the powers of government, legislative, executive, and judicial, shall be left in this body? I think a people cannot be long free, nor ever happy, whose government is in one Assembly. My reasons for this opinion are as follow.

1. A single Assembly is liable to all the vices, follies and frailties of an individual. Subject to fits of humour, starts of passion, flights of enthusiasm, partialities of prejudice, and consequently productive of hasty results and absurd judgments: And all these errors ought to be corrected and defects supplied by some controuling power.

2. A single Assembly is apt to be avaricious, and in time will not scruple to exempt itself from burthens which it will lay, without compunction, on its constituents.

3. A single Assembly is apt to grow ambitious, and after a time will not hesitate to vote itself perpetual. This was one fault of the long parliament, but more remarkably of Holland, whose Assembly first voted themselves from annual to septennial, then for life, and after a course of years, that all vacancies happening by death, or otherwise, should be filled by themselves, without any application to constituents at all.

4. A Representative Assembly, altho' extremely well qualified, and absolutely necessary as a branch of the legislature, is unfit to exercise the executive power, for want of two essential properties, secrecy and dispatch.

5. A Representative Assembly is still less qualified for the judicial power; because it is too numerous, too slow, and too little skilled in the laws.

6. Because a single Assembly, possessed of all the powers of government, would make arbitrary laws for their own interest, execute all laws arbitrarily for their own interest, and adjudge all controversies in their own favour.

But shall the whole power of legislation rest in one Assembly? Most of the foregoing reasons apply equally to prove that the legislative power ought to be more complex—to which we may add, that if the legislative power is wholly in one Assembly, and the executive in another, or in a single person, these two powers will oppose and enervate upon each other, until the contest shall end in war, and the whole power, legislative and executive, be usurped by the strongest.

The judicial power, in such case, could not mediate, or hold the balance between the two contending powers, because the legislative would undermine it. And this shews the necessity too, of giving the executive power a negative upon the legislative, otherwise this will be continually encroaching upon that.

To avoid these dangers let a distant1 Assembly be constituted, as a mediator between the two extreme branches of the legislature, that which represents the people and that which is vested with the executive power.

Let the Representative Assembly then elect by ballot, from among themselves or their constituents, or both, a distinct Assembly, which for the sake of perspicuity we will call a Council. It may consist of any number you please, say twenty or thirty, and should have a free and independent exercise of its judgment, and consequently a negative voice in the legislature.

These two bodies thus constituted, and made integral parts of the legislature, let them unite, and by joint ballot choose a Governor, who, after being stripped of most of those badges of domination called prerogatives, should have a free and independent exercise of his judgment, and be made also an integral part of the legislature. This I know is liable to objections, and if you please you may make him only President of the Council, as in Connecticut: But as the Governor is to be invested with the executive power, with consent of Council, I think he ought to have a negative upon the legislative. If he is annually elective, as he ought to be, he will always have so much reverence and affection for the People, their Representatives and Councillors, that although you give him an independent exercise of his judgment, he will seldom use it in opposition to the two Houses, except in cases the public utility of which would be conspicuous, and some such cases would happen.

In the present exigency of American affairs, when by an act of Parliament we are put out of the royal protection, and consequently discharged from our allegiance; and it has become necessary to assume government for our immediate security, the Governor, Lieutenant-Governor, Secretary, Treasurer, Commissary, Attorney-General, should be chosen by joint Ballot, of both Houses. And these and all other elections, especially of

Representatives, and Councillors, should be annual, there not being in the whole circle of the sciences, a maxim more infallible than this, "Where annual elections end, there slavery begins."

These great men, in this respect, should be, once a year

"Like bubbles on the sea of matter borne,
They rise, they break, and to that sea return."

This will teach them the great political virtues of humility, patience, and moderation, without which every man in power becomes a ravenous beast of prey.

This mode of constituting the great offices of state will answer very well for the present, but if, by experiment, it should be found inconvenient, the legislature may at its leisure devise other methods of creating them, by elections of the people at large, as in Connecticut, or it may enlarge the term for which they shall be chosen to seven years, or three years, or for life, or make any other alterations which the society shall find productive of its ease, its safety, its freedom, or in one word, its happiness.

A rotation of all offices, as well as of Representatives and Councillors, has many advocates, and is contended for with many plausible arguments. It would be attended no doubt with many advantages, and if the society has a sufficient number of suitable characters to supply the great number of vacancies which would be made by such a rotation, I can see no objection to it. These persons may be allowed to serve for three years, and then excluded three years, or for any longer or shorter term.

Any seven or nine of the legislative Council may be made a Quorum, for doing business as a Privy Council, to advise the Governor in the exercise of the executive branch of power, and in all acts of state.

The Governor should have the command of the militia, and of all your armies. The power of pardons should be with the Governor and Council.

Judges, Justices and all other officers, civil and military, should be nominated and appointed by the Governor, with the advice and consent of Council, unless you choose to have a government more popular; if you do, all officers, civil and military, may be chosen by joint ballot of both Houses, or in order to preserve the independence and importance of each House, by ballot of one House, concurred by the other. Sheriffs should be chosen by the freeholders of counties—so should Registers of Deeds and Clerks of Counties.2

All officers should have commissions, under the hand of the Governor and seal of the Colony.

The dignity and stability of government in all its branches, the morals of the people and every blessing of society, depends so much upon an upright and skillful administration of justice, that the judicial power ought to be distinct from both the legislative and executive, and independent upon both, that so it may be a check upon both, as both should be checks upon that. The

Judges therefore should always be men of learning and experience in the laws, of exemplary morals, great patience, calmness, coolness and attention. Their minds should not be distracted with jarring interests; they should not be dependant upon any man or body of men. To these ends they should hold estates for life in their offices, or in other words their commissions should be during good behaviour, and their salaries ascertained and established by law. For misbehaviour the grand inquest of the Colony, the House of Representatives, should impeach them before the Governor and Council, where they should have time and opportunity to make their defence, but if convicted should be removed from their offices, and subjected to such other punishment as shall be thought proper.

A Militia Law requiring all men, or with very few exceptions, besides cases of conscience, to be provided with arms and ammunition, to be trained at certain seasons, and requiring counties, towns, or other small districts to be provided with public stocks of ammunition and entrenching utensils, and with some settled plans for transporting provisions after the militia, when marched to defend their country against sudden invasions, and requiring certain districts to be provided with field-pieces, companies of matrosses and perhaps some regiments of light horse, is always a wise institution, and in the present circumstances of our country indispensible.

Laws for the liberal education of youth, especially of the lower class of people, are so extremely wise and useful, that to a humane and generous mind, no expence for this purpose would be thought extravagant.3

The very mention of sumptuary laws will excite a smile. Whether our countrymen have wisdom and virtue enough to submit to them I know not. But the happiness of the people might be greatly promoted by them, and a revenue saved sufficient to carry on this war forever. Frugality is a great revenue, besides curing us of vanities, levities and fopperies which are real antidotes to all great, manly and warlike virtues.

But must not all commissions run in the name of a king? No. Why may they not as well run thus, "The Colony of to A. B. greeting," and be tested by the Governor?

Why may not writs, instead of running in the name of a King, run thus, "The Colony of to the Sheriff, &c." and be tested by the Chief Justice.

Why may not indictments conclude, "against the peace of the Colony of and the dignity of the same?"

A Constitution, founded on these principles, introduces knowledge among the People, and inspires them with a conscious dignity, becoming Freemen. A general emulation takes place, which causes good humour, sociability, good manners, and good morals to be general. That elevation of sentiment, inspired by such a government, makes the common people brave and enterprizing. That ambition which is inspired by it makes them sober, industrious and frugal. You will find among them some elegance, perhaps, but more solidity; a little pleasure, but a great deal of business—some politeness, but more civility. If you compare such a country with the regions of domination, whether Monarchial or Aristocratical, you will fancy yourself in Arcadia or Elysium.

If the Colonies should assume governments separately, they should be left entirely to their own choice of the forms, and if a Continental Constitution should be formed, it should be a Congress, containing a fair and adequate Representation of the Colonies, and its authority should sacredly be confined to these cases, viz. war, trade, disputes between Colony and Colony, the Post-Office, and the unappropriated lands of the Crown, as they used to be called.

These Colonies, under such forms of government, and in such a union, would be unconquerable by all the Monarchies of Europe.

You and I, my dear Friend, have been sent into life, at a time when the greatest lawgivers of antiquity would have wished to have lived. How few of the human race have ever enjoyed an opportunity of making an election of government more than of air, soil, or climate, for themselves or their children. When! Before the present epocha, had three millions of people full power and a fair opportunity to form and establish the wisest and happiest government that human wisdom can contrive? I hope you will avail yourself and your country of that extensive learning and indefatigable industry which you possess, to assist her in the formations of the happiest governments, and the best character of a great People. . . .

SOURCE: John Adams, "Thoughts on Government," in *The Works of John Adams, . . . by his Grandson Charles Francis Adams*, 10 vols. (Boston: Little, Brown and Co., 1856): 4: 193-200.

3. [ANONYMOUS/THOMAS PAINE?]
"FOUR LETTERS ON INTERESTING SUBJECTS"
1776

The most likely author of the "Four Letters" is now considered to be Thomas Paine, who was born in Thetford, Norfolk, England (1737), and he died in New York City (1809. Paine had almost no formal education but was an autodidact who taught himself. Paine left England for America in 1774, just in time to participate in the American Revolution. The views in "Four Letters" of what a constitution is, and particularly its analysis of the British constitution, are consistent with what Paine says of both in Rights of Man *(1791-92). The fourth letter is notable for its distinction between what a constitution is and what a government is. Unlike traditional British constitutional theorists such as William Blackstone, the author of "Four Letters" claims that a constitution and a government are not synonymous. Constitutions, in the new emerging American sense, precede constitutions. The problem with the British constitution is that it is not "fixed." By 1776, American political thinkers were rapidly developing the idea of a written constitution as fundamental law.*

LETTER IV

Among the many publications which have appeared on the subject of political Constitutions, none, that I have seen, have properly defined what is meant by a *Constitution,* that word having been bandied about without any determinate sense being affirmed thereto. A Constitution, and a form of government, are frequently confounded together, and spoken of as synonomous things; whereas they are not only different, but are established for different purposes. All countries have some form of government, but few, or perhaps none, have truly a Constitution. The form of government in England is by a king, lords and commons, but if you ask an Englishman what he means when he speaks of the English Constitution, he is unable to give you any answer. The truth is, the English have no fixed Constitution. The prerogative of the crown, it is true, is under several restrictions, but the legislative power, which includes king, lords and commons, is under none; and whatever acts they pass are laws, be they ever so oppressive or arbitrary. England is likewise defective in Constitution in three other material points, viz. The crown, by virtue of a patent from itself, can increase the number of the lords (one of the legislative branches) at his pleasure. Queen Ann created six in one day, for the purpose of making a majority for carrying a bill then passing, who were afterwards distinguished by the name of the six occasional lords. Lord

Bathurst, the father of the present chancellor, is the only surviving one. The crown can likewise, by a patent, incorporate any town or village, small or great, and empower it to send members to the house of commons, and fix what the precise number of the electors shall be. And an act of the legislative power, that is, an act of king, lords, and commons, can again diminish the house of commons to what number they please, by disfranchising any county, city or town.

It is easy to perceive that individuals by agreeing to erect forms of government, (for the better security of themselves) must give up some part of their liberty for that purpose; and it is the particular business of a Constitution to make out *how much* they shall give up. In this case it is easy to see that the English have no Constitution because they have given up every thing; their legislative power being unlimited without either condition or controul, except in the single instance of trial by Juries. No country can be called *free* which is governed by an absolute power; and it matters not whether it be an absolute royal power or an absolute legislative power, as the consequences will be the same to the people. That England is governed by the latter, no man can deny, there being, as is said before, no Constitution in that country which says to the legislative powers, "Thus far shalt thou go, and no farther." There is nothing to prevent them passing a law which shall give the house of commons power to sit for life, or to fill up the vacancies by appointing others, like the Corporation of Philadelphia. In short, an act of parliament, to use a court phrase, can do any thing but make a man a woman.

A Constitution, when completed, resolves the two following questions: First, What shall the form of government be? And secondly, What shall be its power? And the last of these two is far more material than the first. The Constitution ought likewise to make provision in those cases where it does not empower the legislature to act.

The forms of government are numerous, and perhaps the simplest is the best. The notion of checking by having different houses, has but little weight with it, when inquired into, and in all cases it tends to embarrass and prolong business; besides, what kind of checking is it that one house is to receive from another? or which is the house that is most to be trusted to? They may fall out about forms and precedence, and check one another's honour and tempers, and thereby produce petulances and ill-will, which a more simple form of government would have prevented. That some kind of convenience might now and then arise from having two houses, is granted, and the same may be said of twenty houses; and the question is, whether such a mode would not produce more hurt than good. The more houses the more parties; and perhaps the ill consequence to this country would be, that the landed interest would get into one house, and the commercial interest into the other; and by that means a perpetual and dangerous opposition would be kept up, and no business be got through: Whereas, were there a large, equal and annual representation in one house *only,* the different parties, by being thus banded together, would hear each others arguments, which advantage they cannot have if they sit in different houses. To say, there ought to be two houses, because there are two sorts of interest, is the very reason why there ought to be but one, and *that one* to consist of every sort. The lords and commons in England formerly made but one house; and it is evident, that by separating men you lessen the quantity of knowledge, and increase the difficulties of business. However, let the form of government be what it may, in this, or other provinces, so long as it answers the purpose of the people, and they approve it, they will be happy under it. That which suits one part of the Continent may not in every thing suit another; and when each is pleased, however variously, the matter is ended. No man is a true republican, or worthy of the name, that will not give up his single voice to that of the public; his private opinion he may retain; it is obedience only that is his duty.

The chief convenience arising from two houses is, that the second may sometimes amend small imperfections which would otherwise pass; yet, there is nearly as much chance of their making alterations for the worse as the better; and the supposition that a single house may become arbitrary, can with more reason be said of two, because their strength is greater. Besides, when all the supposed advantages arising from two houses are put together, they do not appear to balance the disadvantage. A division in one house will not retard business, but serves rather to illustrate; but a difference between two houses may produce serious consequences. In queen Ann's reign a quarrel arose between the upper and lower house, which was carried to such a pitch that the nation was under very terrifying apprehensions, and the house of commons was dissolved to prevent worse mischief. A like instance was nearly happening about six years ago, when the members of each house very affrontingly turned one another by force out of doors. The two last bills in the last sessions in England were entirely lost by having two houses; the bill for encreasing liberty of conscience, by taking off the necessity of subscription to the thirty-nine articles, Athanasian creed, etc. after passing the lower house by a very great majority, was thrown out by the upper one; and at the time that the nation was starving with the high price of corn, the bill for regulating the importation and exportation of grain, after passing the lower house, was lost by a *difference* between the two, and when returned from the upper one was thrown on the floor by the commons, and indignantly trampled under foot.—Perhaps most of the Colonies will have two houses, and it will probably be of benefit to have some little difference in the forms of government, as those which do not like one, may reside in another, and by trying different experiments, the best form will the sooner be found out, as the preference at present rests on conjecture.

Government is generally distinguished into three parts, Executive, Legislative and Judicial; but this is more a distinction of words than things. Every king or governor in giving his assent to laws acts legislatively, and not executively: The house of lords in England is both a legislative and judicial body.

In short, the distinction is perplexing, and however we may refine and define, there is no more than two powers in any government, viz. the power to make laws, and the power to execute them; for the judicial power is only a branch of the executive, the Chief of every country being the first magistrate.

A constitution should lay down some permanent ratio, by which the representation should afterwards encrease or decrease with the number of inhabitants; for the right of representation, which is a natural one, ought not to depend upon the will and pleasure of future legislatures. And for the same reason perfect liberty of conscience, security of person against unjust imprisonments, similar to what is called the Habeas Corpus act; the mode of trial in all law and criminal cases; in short, all the great rights which man never mean, nor ever ought, to lose, should be *guaranteed,* not *granted,* by the Constitution, for at the forming a Constitution we ought to have in mind, that whatever is left to be secured by law only, may be altered by another law. That Juries ought to be judges of law, as well as fact, should be clearly described; for though in rare instances Juries may err, it is generally from tenderness, and on the right side. A man cannot be *guilty* of a *good* action, yet if the fact only is to be proved (which is Lord Mansfield's doctrine) and the Jury not empowered to determine in their own minds, whether the fact proved to be done is a crime or not, a man may hereafter be found guilty of going to church or meeting.

There is one circumstance respecting trial by Juries which seems to deserve attention; which is, whether a Jury of Twelve persons, which cannot bring in a verdict unless they are all of one mind, or appear so; or, whether a Jury of not less than Twenty-five, a majority of which shall make a verdict, is the safest to be trusted to? The objections against an Jury of Twelve are, that the necessity of being unanimous prevents the freedom of speech, and causes men sometimes to conceal their own opinions, and follow that of others; that it is a kind of terrifying men into a verdict, and that a strong hearty obstinate man who can bear starving twenty-four or forty-eight hours, will distress the rest into a compliance, that there is no difference, in effect, between hunger and the point of a bayonet, and that under such circumstances a Jury is not, nor can be free. In favour of the latter it is said, that the least majority is thirteen; and the dread of the consequences of disagreeing being removed, men will speak freer, and that justice will thereby have a fairer chance.

It is the part of a Constitution to fix the manner in which the officers of government shall be chosen, and determine the principal outlines of their power, their time of duration, manner of commissioning them, etc. The line, so far as respects their election, seems easy, which is, by the representatives of the people; provincial officers can be chosen no other way, because the whole province cannot be convened, any more than the whole of the Associators could be convened for choosing by election. The mode of choosing delegates for Congress deserves consideration, as they are not officers but legislators. Positive provincial instructions have a tendency to disunion, and, if admitted, will one day or other rend the Continent of America. A continental Constitution, when fixed, will be the best boundaries of Congressional power, and in matters for the general good, they ought to be as free as assemblies. The notion, which some have, of excluding the military from the legislature is unwise, because it has a tendency to make them form a distinct party of their own. Annual elections, strengthened by some kind of periodical exclusion, seem the best guard against the encroachments of power. Suppose the exclusion was triennial, that is, that no person should be returned a member of assembly for more then three succeeding years, nor be capable of being returned again till he had been absent three years. Such a mode would greatly increase the circle of knowledge, make men cautious how they acted, and prevent the disagreeableness of giving offence, by removing some, to make room for others of equal, or perhaps superior, merit. Something of the same kind may be practised respecting Presidents or Governors, not to be eligible after a certain number of returns; and as no person, after filling that rank, can, consistent with character, descend to any other office or employment; and as it may not always happen that the most wealthy are the most capable, some decent provision therefore should be made for them in their retirement, because it is a retirement from the world. Whoever reflects on this, will see many good advantages arising from it.

Modest and decent honorary titles, so as they be neither hereditary, nor convey legislative authority, are of use in a state; they are, when properly conferred, the badges of merit. The love of the public is the chief reward which a generous man seeks, and, surely, if that be an honour, the mode of conferring it must be so likewise.

Next to the forming a good Constitution, is the means of preserving it. If once the legislative power breaks in upon it, the effect will be the same as if a kingly power did it. The Constitution, in either case, will receive its death wound, and "the outward and visible sign," or mere form of government only will remain. "I wish," says Lord Camden, "that the maxim of Machiavel was followed, that of examining a Constitution, at certain periods, according to its first principles; this would correct abuses, and supply defects." The means here pointed out for preserving a Constitution are easy, and some article in the Constitution may provide, that at the expiration of every seven or any other number of years a *Provincial Jury* shall be elected, to enquire if any inroads have been made in the Constitution, and to have power to remove them; but not to make alterations, unless a clear majority of all the inhabitants shall so direct.

Farther observations were intended to have been offered in these letters, but the sudden turn of military affairs hath prevented them; I shall therefore conclude with remarking, that perfection in government, like perfection in all other earthly things, is not to be hoped for. A single house, or a duplication of them, will alike have their evils; and the defect is incurable, being founded in the nature of man, and the instability of things.

SOURCE: Excerpts are from the fourth letter and are reprinted from the original, [Anonymous], "Four Letters on Interesting Subjects," (Philadelphia, PA: Styner and Cist, 1776), pp. 18-24.

4. [ANONYMOUS]
"THE INTEREST OF AMERICA"
1776

In addition to preparing to fight a war and then doing it, the American people also had to design constitutions and construct governments. The New England minutemen were inadequate to fight a winning war against the world's greatest military power. Two fundamental questions confronted America's theorists and constitution-makers: first, who should construct America's constitutions; and second, what was the best form of government? The answer to the first question—which was the most difficult question—shall be taken up in Part II: Creating a Written Constitution as Fundamental Law. Most American theorists agreed on certain fundamental principles and institutions, such as equality, liberty, rights popular sovereignty, republicanism, separation of powers, and written constitutions. The primary question on which they differed, however, concerned the form of government, which was further reduced to this question: who should govern? More specifically, American theorists divided over whether their legislatures should be unicameral or bicameral. The anonymous author of "The Interest of America" was opposed to bicameral legislatures on the grounds that they were unnecessary, created delays, fostered unnecessary rivalries, and instituted an artificial aristocracy that did not reflect the true interests of the America. Instead, he favored a unicameral legislature based on annual elections.

The important day is come, or near at hand, that *America* is to assume a form of Government for herself. We should be very desirous to know what form is best; and that surely is best which is most natural, easy, cheap, and which best secures the rights of the people. We should always keep in mind that great truth, viz: that the good of the people is the ultimate end of civil Government. As we must (some Provinces at least) in a short time assume some new mode of Government, and the matter cannot be deferred so long as to canvass, deliberately weigh, and fully adjust everything that may hereafter appear necessary, we should leave room to alter for the better in time to come. Every Province should be viewed as having a right, either: with or without an application to the Continental Congress, to alter their form of Government in some particulars; and that without being liable to raise a clamour, by some who would be glad to say that it was contrary to the Constitution that they first formed upon; that it was overturning the original plan, and leaving people at uncertainties as to the foundation they are upon, and the like. As the Government is for the people, the people, when properly represented, have a right to alter it for their advantage.

The affair now in view is the most important that ever was before *America*. In my opinion, it is the most important that has been transacted in any nation for some centuries past. If our civil Government is well constructed and well managed, *America* bids fair to be the most glorious State that has ever been on earth. We should now, at the beginning, lay the foundation right. Most, if not all, other Governments have had a corrupt mixture in their very Constitution; they have generally been formed in haste, or out of necessity, or tyrannically, or in a state of ignorance; and, being badly formed, the management of them has been with difficulty. But we have opportunity to form with some deliberation, with free choice, with good advantages for knowledge; we have opportunity to observe what has been right and what wrong in other States, and to profit by them. The plan of *American* Government should, as much as possible, be formed to suit all the variety of circumstances that people may be in—virtuous or vicious, agreeing or contending, moving regularly or convulsed by the intrigues of aspiring men; for we may expect a variety of circumstances in a course of time, and we should be prepared for every condition. We should assume that mode of Government which is most equitable and adapted to the good of mankind, and trust Providence for the event; for *God*, who determines the fate of Governments, is most like to prosper that which is most equitable; and I think there can be no doubt that a well-regulated Democracy is most equitable. An annual of frequent choice of magistrates, who, in a year, or after a few years, are again left upon a level with their neighbours, is most likely to prevent usurpation and tyranny, and most likely to secure the privileges of the people. If rulers know that they shall, in a short term of time, be again out of power, and, it may be, liable to be called to an account for misconduct, it will guard them against maladministration. A truly popular Government has, I believe, never yet been tried in the world. The most remarkable Government that has ever been, viz: the *Roman* Republick, was something near it, but not fully so; and the want of it being fully so, kept a continual contest between the Senate and Plebeians.

America must consist of a number of confederate Provinces, Cantons, Districts, or whatever they may be called. These must be united in a General Congress; but each Province must have a distinct Legislature, and have as much power within itself as possible. The General Congress should not interfere or meddle with Provincial affairs more than needs must. Every Province should be left to do as much within itself as may be; and every Province should allow each County, yea, and each Town, to do as much within themselves as possible. Small bodies manage affairs much easier and cheaper than large ones. If every County and Town manage as much business as may be within themselves, people will be better satisfied, and the Provincial Congress saved much trouble. Our Counties and Towns have heretofore been left to manage many of their own affairs; and it has been a great privilege, and their business has been managed to great advantage. Each County should now choose their own officers, which were heretofore appointed by the Crown. These matters may now be adjusted with much ease. Every Province should be allowed such full power within itself, and receive such advantages by a general union or confederation, that it would choose to continue in that union. The connection of the Provinces should be made to be for the interest of each, and be agreeable to each. This will keep them quiet and peaceable; and nothing will tend so much to this, as to let every Province have as much power and liberty within itself as will consist with the good of the whole. Neither the Continental Congress, nor any other number of men, should assume or use any power or office for their own sake, but for the good of the whole. Let *America* increase ever so much, there must never be any power like a Kingly power; no power used for its own sake, or for the advantage or dignity of any number of men, as distinct from the good of the whole; and while things are thus managed, a general union will be agreeable, and people will not complain.

Notwithstanding every Province should have all possible power within itself, yet some things must be left to the General Congress; as, 1. Making and managing war and making peace. 2. Settling differences between Provinces. 3. Making some maritime laws, or general regulations respecting trade; otherwise one Province might unjustly interfere with another. 4. Ordering a currency for the whole Continent; for it would be best that, as soon as may be, there should be one currency for the whole; the General Congress might order the quota for each Province. 5. The forming of new Provinces. 6. The sale of new lands. 7. Treaties with other nations; consequently some general directions of our *Indian* affairs.

As we are now to assume a new mode of Government, I think it ought properly to be new. Some are for keeping as near the old form of Government in each Province as can well be. But I think it is entirely wrong; it is mistaken policy. It is probable that some who propose it mean well; but I humbly conceive they have not thoroughly considered the thing. Others who propose it may have self-interest at bottom, hoping thereby to retain, or obtain, places of profit or honour. We must come as near a new form of Government as we can, without destroying private property. So far as private property will allow, we must form our Government in each Province just as if we had never any form of Government before. It is much easier to form a new Government than to patch up one partly old and partly new, because it is more simple and natural. I speak chiefly with respect to Legislature. We should by all means avoid several branches of Legislature.

One branch of Legislature is much preferable to more than one, because a plurality causes perpetual contention and waste of time. It was so in *Rome*; it has been so in *Great Britain*; and has been remarkably so in these Provinces in times past. The ever-memorable Congress now in *America* has done business infinitely better than if there had been several orders of Delegates to contest, interrupt, and be a negative one upon another.

A patched Government, consisting of several parts, has been the difficulty, I may call it the disease, of some of the best civil Governments that have been in the world—I mean the *Roman* Republick and the Government of *Great Britain*. Had the *Romans* been a true Democracy, without a Senate, or body different from the Plebeians, they might have avoided those jars and contentions which continually subsisted between those two bodies. Should we admit different branches of Legislature, it might give occasion in time to degenerate into that form of Government, or something like that, which has been so oppressive in our nation. It might open a door for ill-disposed aspiring men to destroy the State. Our having several branches of Legislature heretofore is an argument against, rather than for it, in time to come, because it is a word that not only has been abused, but in its nature tends to abuse. The simplest mode of legislation is certainly best. The *European* nations have, for some centuries past, derived most of their knowledge from the *Greeks* and *Romans*. The *Romans*, especially, have been, in a sort, an example, being excellent in many things. We have been ready to view them so in all things. We are very apt to take in, or imitate, the imperfections as well as the excellencies of those that are excellent. Hence, I suppose; it is that most, if not all, the Republicks in *Europe* have a body of Senators in their form of Government. I doubt not it will be an argument with many, that we in *America* must have something like a Senate, or Council, or Upper House, because the *Romans* and other Republicks have had. But the argument is the other way; it was their imperfection, it was a source of trouble, it was a step towards arbitrary power, and therefore to be avoided. Free Government can better, must better, subsist without it. Different branches of Legislature cause much needless expense, two ways: First, as there are more persons to maintain; and, second, as they waste time, and prolong a session by their contentions. Besides, it is a great absurdity that one branch of a Legislature, that can negative all the rest, should be the principal Executive power in the State. There can be but little chance for proper freedom, where the making and executing the laws of a State lie in the same hand, and that not of the people in general, but of a single person. The Legislative and Executive power in every Province ought to be kept as distinct as possible. Wise, experienced, and publick-spirited persons should be in places of power, and if so, they must be sought out, chosen, and introduced. For this reason there ought not to be a number that are hereditary, for wisdom is not a birthright; nor a number put in place for life, for men's abilities and manners may change. Rulers should be frequently chose to their office. A Provincial Congress is the whole Province met by Representatives; and there is no need of a representative of a King, for we have none; nor can there be need of a Council to represent the House of Lords, for we have not, and hope never shall have, a hereditary nobility, different from the general body of the people; but if we admit different branches of the Legislature, there is danger that there may be in time.

SOURCE: These excerpts are reprinted from "The Interest of America" (1776), in *American Archives: Documents of the Revolutionary Period, 1774-1776*, ed. Peter Force, 4th Ser., (Washington, 1837-56), VI: 840-8

5. CARTER BRAXTON
"AN ADDRESS TO THE CONVENTION OF THE COLONY AND ANCIENT DOMAIN OF VIRGINIA"
1776

Carter Braxton was born on Newington Plantation in King and Queen County, Virginia (1736), and he died in Richmond, Virginia (1797). Braxton was a planter, merchant, politician, founding father, and signer of the Declaration of Independence. He was educated at the College of William and Mary. As a politician, he served in the colonial Virginia House of Burgesses as a leader of the conservative tidewater faction for 14 years, as a delegate to the Continental Congress, in the revolutionary conventions of 1774, 1775, and 1776, and then in the state house of representatives from 1776 to 1785. Braxton was a Patriot and not a Loyalist, but his prescription for government outlined one of the more traditionalist forms of the revolutionary era. Braxton clearly admired the British constitution. He therefore proposed that the governor's term of office be during good behavior, and he proposed that the members of the upper house be elected by members of the lower house and to serve life terms. Braxton's constitutional blueprint imitated the forms and formalities of the British constitution.

When despotism had displayed her banners, and with unremitting ardour and fury scattered her engines of oppression through this wide extended continent, the virtuous opposition of the people to its progress relaxed the tone of government in almost every colony, and occasioned in many instances a total suspension of law. These inconveniencies, however, were natural, and the mode readily submitted to, as there was then reason to hope that justice would be done to our injured country; the same laws, executed under the same authority, soon regain their former use and lustre; and peace, raised on a permanent foundation, bless this our native land.

But since these hopes have hitherto proved delusive, and time, instead of bringing us relief, daily brings forth new proofs of British tyranny, and thereby separates us further from that reconciliation we so ardently wished; does it not become the duty of your, and every other Convention, to assume the reins of government, and no longer suffer the people to live without the benefit of law, and order the protection it affords? Anarchy and riot will follow a continuance of its suspension, and render the enjoyment of our liberties and future quiet at least very precarious.

Presuming that this object will, ere long, engage your attention, and fully persuaded that when it does it will be considered with all the candour and deliberation due to its importance, I have ventured to collect my sentiments on the subject, and in a friendly manner offer them to your consideration. Should they suggest any hints that may tend to improve or embellish the fabric you are about to erect, I shall deem myself happy in having contributed my might to the benefit of a people I esteem, and a country to which I owe every obligation.

Taking for granted, therefore, the necessity of instituting a government capable of affording all the blessings of which the most cruel attempts have been made to deprive us, the first inquiry will be, which of the various forms is best adapted to our situation, and will in every respect most probably answer our purpose.

Various are the opinions of men on this subject, and different are the plans proposed for your adoption. Prudence will direct you to examine them with a jealous eye, and weigh the pretensions of each with care, as well as impartiality. Your, and your children's welfare depends upon the choice. Let it therefore neither be marked by a blind attachment to ancient prejudices on the one hand, or a restless spirit of innovation on the other.

Although all writers agree in the object of government, and admit that it was designed to promote and secure the happiness of every member of society, yet their opinions, as to the systems most productive of this general benefit, have been extremely contradictory. As all these systems are said to move on separate and distinct principles, it may not be improper to analyse them, and by that means shew the manner of their operations.

Government is generally divided into two parts, its mode or form of constitution, and the principle intended to direct it.

The simple forms of government are despotism, monarchy, aristocracy, and democracy. Out of these an infinite variety of combinations may be deduced. The absolute unlimited controul of one man describes despotism, whereas monarchy compels the Sovereign to rule agreeable to certain fundamental laws. Aristocracy vests the sovereignty of a state in a few nobles, and democracy allows it to reside in the body of the people, and is thence called a popular government.

Each of these forms are actuated by different principles. The subjects of an unlimited despotic Prince, whose will is their only rule of conduct, are influenced by the principle of fear. In a monarchy limited by laws the people are insensibly led to the pursuit of honour, they feel an interest in the greatness of their Princes, and, inspired by a desire of glory, rank, and promotion, unite in giving strength and energy to the whole machine. Aristocracy and democracy claim for their principle public virtue, or a regard for the public good independent of private interest.

Let us inquire from which of these several [   ] we should take a cion to ingraft on our wild one, see which is most congenial to our soil, and by the extent and strength of its branches best calculated to shelter the people from the rage of those tempests which often darken the political hemisphere. I will not deny, whatever others may do, that individuals have enjoyed a certain degree of happiness under all these forms. Content, and consequently happiness, depend more on the state of our minds than external circumstances, and some men are satisfied with fewer enjoyments than others. Upon these occasions the inclinations of men, which are often regulated by what they have seen and experienced, ought to be consulted. It cannot be wise to draw them further from their former institutions than obvious reasons and necessity will justify. Should a form of government directly opposite to the ancient one, under which they have been happy, be introduced and established, will they not, on the least disgust, repine at the change, and be disposed even to acts of violence in order to regain their former condition. Many examples in the history of almost every country prove the truth of this remark.

What has been the government of Virginia, and in a revolution how is its spirit to be preserved, are important questions. The better to discuss these points, we should take a view of the constitution of England, because by that model ours was constructed, and under it we have enjoyed tranquillity and security. Our ancestors, the English, after contemplating the various forms of government, and experiencing, as well as perceiving, the defects of each, wisely refused to resign their liberties either to the single man, the few, or the many. They determine to make a compound of each the foundation of their government, and of the most valuable parts of them all to build a superstructure that should surpass all others, and bid defiance to time to injure, or any thing, except national degeneracy and corruption, to demolish.

In rearing this fabric, and connecting its parts, much time, blood, and treasure were expended. By the vigilance, perseverance, and activity of innumerable martyrs, the happy edifice was at length completed under the auspices of the renowned King William in the year 1688. They wisely united the hereditary succession of the Crown with the good behaviour of the Prince; they gave respect and stability to the legislature, by the independence of the Lords, and security, as well as importance to the people, by being parties with their Sovereign in every act of legislation. Here then our ancestors rested from their long and laborious pursuit, and saw many good days in the peaceable enjoyment of the fruit of their labours. Content with having provided against the ills which had befallen them, they seemed to have forgot, that although the seeds of destruction might be excluded from their constitution, they were, nevertheless, to be found in those by whom their affairs were administered.

Time, the improver, as well as destroyer, of all things, discovered to them, that the very man who had wrought their deliverance was capable of pursuing measures leading to their destruction. Much is it to be lamented, that this magnanimous Prince, ascending a throne beset with uncertainty and war, was induced, by the force of both, to invent and practise the art of funding to supply his wants, and create an interest that might support him in possession of his Crown. He succeeded to his wish, and thereby established a monied interest, which was followed by levying of taxes, by a host of tax-gatherers, and a long train of dependents on the Crown. The practice grew into system, till at length the Crown found means to break down those barriers which the constitution had assigned to each branch of the legislature, and effectively destroyed the independence of both Lords and Commons. These breaches, instead of being repaired as soon as discovered, were, by the supineness of the nation permitted to widen by daily practice, till, finally, the influence of the Crown pervaded and overwhelmed the whole people, and gave birth to the many calamities which we now bewail, and for the removal of which the united efforts of America are at this time exerted.

Men are prone to condemn the whole, because a part is objectionable; but certainly it would, in the present case, be more wise to consider, whether, if the constitution was brought back to its original state, and its present imperfections remedied, it would not afford more happiness than any other. If the independence of the Commons could be secured, and the dignity of the Lords preserved, how can a government be better formed for the preservation of freedom? And is there any thing more easy than this? If placemen and pensioners were excluded a seat in either House, and elections made triennial, what danger could be apprehended for prerogative? I have the best authority for asserting, that with these improvements, added to the suppression of boroughs, and giving the people an equal and adequate representation, England would have remained a land of liberty to the latest ages.

Judge of the principle of this constitution by the great effects it has produced. Their code of laws, the boast of Englishmen and of freedom; the rapid progress they have made in trade, in arts and sciences; the respect they commanded from their neighbours, then gaining the empire of the sea; are all powerful arguments of the wisdom of that constitution and government, which raised the people of that island to their late degree of greatness. But though I admire their perfections, I must mourn their faults; and though I would guard against, and cast off their oppression, yet would I retain all their wise maxims, and derive advantage from their mistakes and misfortunes. The testimony of the learned Montesquieu in favour of the English constitution is very respectable. "There is (says he) one nation in the world that has for the direct end of its constitution political liberty." Again he says, "It is not my business to examine whether the English actually enjoy this liberty or not; sufficient it is for my purpose to observe, that it is established by their laws, and I inquire no further."

This constitution, and these laws, have also been those of Virginia, and let it be remembered, that under them she flourished and was happy. The same principles which led the English to greatness animates us. To that principle our laws, our customs, and our manners, are adapted, and it would be perverting all order to oblige us, by a novel government, to give up our laws, our customs, and our manners.

However necessary it may be to shake off the authority of arbitrary British dictators, we ought, nevertheless, to adopt and perfect that system, which

England has suffered to be grossly abused, and the experience of ages has taught us to venerate. This, like almost every thing else, is perhaps liable to objections, and probably the difficulty of adopting a limited monarchy will be largely insisted on. Admit this objection to have weight, and that we cannot in every instance assimulate a government to that, yet no good reason can be assigned why the same principle, or spirit, may not in a great measure be preserved. But, honourable as this spirit is, we daily see it calumniated by advocates for popular governments, and rendered obnoxious to all whom their artifices can influence or delude. The systems recommended to the colonies seem to accord with the temper of the times, and are fraught with all the tumult and riot incident to simple democracy; systems which many think it their interest to support, and without doubt will be industriously propagated among you. The best of these systems exist only in theory, and were never confirmed by the experience, even of those who recommend them. I flatter myself, therefore, that you will not quit a substance actually enjoyed, for a shadow or phantom, by which, instead of being benefited, many have been misled and perplexed.

Let us examine the principles they assign to their government, and try its merits by the unerring standard of truth. In a late pamphlet it is thus stated: The happiness of man, as well as his dignity, consists in virtue; if there be a form of government, then, whose principle is virtue, will not every sober man acknowledge it better calculated to promote the general happiness of society than any other form. Virtue is the principle of a republic, therefore a republic is the best form of government.

The author, with what design I know not, seems to have cautiously blended private with public virtue, as if for the purpose of confounding the two, and thereby recommending his plan under the amiable appearance of courting virtue. It is well known that private and public virtue are materially different. The happiness and dignity of man I admit consists in the practice of private virtues, and to this he is stimulated by the rewards promised to such conduct. In this he acts for himself, and with a view of promoting his own particular welfare. Public virtue, on the other hand, means a disinterested attachment to the public good, exclusive and independent of all private and selfish interest, and which, though sometimes possessed by a few individuals, never characterised the mass of the people in any state. And this is said to be the principle of democratical governments, and to influence every subject of it to pursue such measures as conduce to the prosperity of the whole. A man, therefore, to qualify himself for a member of such a community, must divest himself of all interested motives, and engage in no pursuits which do not ultimately redound to the benefit of society. He must not, through ambition, desire to be great, because it would destroy that equality on which the security of the government depends; nor ought he to be rich, lest he be tempted to indulge himself in those luxuries, which, though lawful, are not expedient, and might occasion envy and emulation. Should a person deserve the esteem of his fellow citizens, and become popular, he must be neglected, if not banished, lest his growing influence disturb the equilibrium. It is remarkable, that neither the justice of Aristides, or the bravery of Themistocles, could shield them from the darts of envy and jealousy; nor are modern times without examples of the same kind.

To this species of government every thing that looks like elegance and refinement is inimical, however necessary to the introduction of manufactures, and the cultivation of arts and sciences. Hence, in some ancient republics, flowed those numberless sumptuary laws, which restrained men to plainness and similarity in dress and diet, and all the mischiefs which attend Agrarian laws, and unjust attempts to maintain their idol equality by an equal division of property.

Schemes like these may be practicable in countries so steril by nature as to afford a scanty supply of the necessaries, and none of the conveniences, of life; but they can never meet with a favourable reception from people who inhabit a country to which Providence has been more bountiful. They will always claim a right of using and enjoying the fruits of their honest industry, unrestrained by any ideal principles of government, and will gather estates for themselves and children without regarding the whimsical impropriety of being richer than their neighbours. These are rights which freemen will never consent to relinquish, and after fighting for deliverance from one species of tyranny, it would be unreasonable to expect they should tamely acquiesce under another.

The truth is, that men will not be poor from choice or compulsion, and these governments can exist only in countries where the people are so from necessity. In all others they have ceased almost as soon as erected, and in many instances been succeeded by despotism, and the arbitrary sway of some usurper, who had before perhaps gained the confidence of the people by eulogiums on liberty, and possessing no property of his own, by most disinterestedly opposing depredations on that of his neighbours. . . .

One of the first staples of our country, you know, is esteemed by many to be one of the greatest luxuries in the world, and I fancy it will be no easy matter to draw you into measures that would exclude its culture and deprive you of the wealth resulting from its exportation.

That I may not tire your patience, I will now proceed to delineate the method in which I would distribute the powers of government, so as to devise the best code of laws, engage their due execution, and secure the liberties of the people. It is agreed by most writers on this subject, that this power should be divided into three parts, each independent of, but having connection with each other. Let the people, in the first place, choose their usual number of Representatives, and let this right return to them every third year.

Let these Representatives when convened, elect a Governor, to continue in authority during his good behavior, of which the two houses of Council of State and Assembly should jointly be the Judges, and by majority of voices supply any vacancy in that office, which may happen by dismission, death, or resignation.

Let the Representatives also choose out of the Colony at large, twenty-four proper persons to constitute a Council of State, who should form a distinct or intermediate branch of the legislature, and hold their places for life, in order that they might possess all the weight, stability and dignity due to the importance of their office. Upon the death or resignation of any of the members let the Assembly appoint another to succeed him.

Let no member of either house, except the Treasurer, hold a post of profit in the government.

Let the Governor have a Privy Council of seven to advise with, tho' they should not be members of either house.

Let the Judges of the Courts of Common Law and Chancery be appointed by the Governor, with the advice of his Privy Council, to hold their offices during their good behaviour, but should be excluded a seat in either house.

Let the Treasurer, Secretary, and other great officers of state be chosen by the lower house, and proper salaries assigned to them as well as to the Judges, &c. &c.

Let all military officers be appointed by the Governor, and all other inferior civil ones.

Let the different Courts appoint their own clerks. The Justices in each county should be paid for their services, and required to meet for the dispatch of business every three months. Let five of them be authorized to form a Court to hear and determine causes, and the others impowered to keep the peace, &c. &c.

These are the outlines of a government which should, I think, preserve the principle of our constitution, and secure the freedom and happiness of the people better than any other.

The Governor will have dignity to command necessary respect and authority, to enable him to execute the laws, without being deterred by the fear of giving offence, and yet be amenable to the other branches of the legislature for every violation of the rights of the people. If this great officer was exposed to the uncertain issue of frequent elections, he would be induced to relax and abate the vigorous execution of the laws whenever such conduct would increase his popularity. Should he, by discharging his duty with impartiality give offence to men of weight and influence, he would be liable to all the opposition, threats, and insults which resentment could suggest; and which few men in such a dependent state would have sufficient resolution to neglect and dispise. Hence it would follow, that the apprehensions of losing his election would frequently induce him to court the favour of the great, at the expense of the duties of his station and the public good. For these, and a variety of other reasons, this office should be held during good behaviour.

The Council of State who are to constitute the second branch of the legislature should be for life. They ought to be well informed of the policy and laws of other states, and therefore should be induced by the permanence of their appointment to devote their time to such studies as may best qualify them for that station. They will acquire firmness from their independency, and wisdom from their reflection and experience, and appropriate both to the good of the state. Upon any disagreement between the Governor and lower house, this body will mediate and adjust such difference, will investigate the propriety of laws, and often propose such as may be of public utility for the adoption of the legislature. Being secluded from offices of profit, they will not be seduced from their duty by pecuniary considerations.

The Representatives of the people will be under no temptation to swerve from the design of their institution by bribery or corruption; all lucrative posts being denied them. And should they on any occasion be influenced by improper motives, the short period of their duration will give their constituents an opportunity of depriving them of power to do injury. The Governor and the members of the Council of State, should be restrained from intermeddling farther in the elections of Representatives, than merely by giving their votes.

The internal government and police of the Colony being thus provided for, the next object of inquiry that presents itself is, how a superintending power over the whole Continent shall be raised, and with what powers invested. Such a power is confessed on all hands to be necessary, as well for the purpose of connecting the Colonies, as for the establishment of many general regulations to which the provincial legislatures will not be competent.

Let a Congress therefore be appointed, composed of members from each Colony in proportion to their number of souls; to convene at any place that may be agreed upon, as often as occasion may require. Let them have power to adjust disputes between Colonies, regulate the affairs of trade, war, peace, alliances, &c. but they should by no means have authority to interfere with the internal police or domestic concerns of any Colony, but confined strictly to such general regulations, as tho' necessary for the good of the whole, cannot be established by any other power. . . .

SOURCE: "Address to the Convention of Virginia, on the subject of Government in general, and recommending a particular form to their consideration: By a Native of the Colony" (1776), in *American Archives: Documents of the Revolutionary Period, 1774-1776*, ed. Peter Force, 4th Ser., (Washington, 1837-56), 6: 748-753.

6. DEMOPHILUS [GEORGE BRYAN?]
"THE GENUINE PRINCIPLES OF THE ANCIENT SAXON, ENGLISH CONSTITUTION"
1776

George Bryan is considered by several scholars of the revolutionary era to be the pseudononymous writer, Demophilus, who penned "The Genuine Principles of the Ancient Saxon, or English Constitution" in 1776. Bryan was born in Dublin, Ireland (1731), and he died in Philadelphia, Pennsylvania (1791). This Irish American came to Philadelphia in 1752. He was a merchant, politician, abolitionist, and Anti-Federalist. In 1776, Bryan was one of the principal authors of the Pennsylvania constitution (along with Timothy Matlack, Dr. Thomas Young, and Benjamin Franklin), which was notable for its unicameral legislature and plural executive. "The Genuine Principles," which draws largely upon Obadiah Hulme's Historical Essay on the English Constitution *(1771) is notable for its rejection of the eighteenth-century British constitution and its support for what the pamphlet called the "ancient saxon" or "English constitution." The distinction in the American mind between these two different constitutions is important. The British constitution, which did not come into existence until after the Glorious Revolution and the unification of the English and Scottish crowns with the Act of Union in 1707, was defined by the principle of parliamentary sovereignty. The English constitution or the pre-Glorious Revolution constitution (also sometimes referred to as the "ancient," "Saxon," or "Gothick" constitution) was, by contrast, a constitution of restraint and defined limits that fixed, enshrined, and protected certain rights and liberties (e.g., no taxation without representation, trial by jury, habeas corpus etc.), fundamental laws, and immutable customs against their infringement by crown or Parliament. The Americans were moving fast beyond their once beloved British constitution and were partly resurrecting a much older notion of what a constitution is or should be.*

INTRODUCTION

As, by the tyranny of George the Third, the compact of allegiance and protection between him and the good people of this Colony is totally dissolved, and the whole power of government is by that means returned to the people at large; it is become absolutely necessary to have this power collected and again reposed in such hands as may be judged most likely to employ it for the common good.

In most states, men have been too careless in the delegation of their governmental power; and not only disposed of it in a very improper manner, but suffered it to continue so long in the same hands, that the *deputies* have, like the King and Lords of Great-Britain, at length become possessors in their own right; and instead of *public servants,* are in fact the *masters* of the public. Our new Republics should use the utmost caution to avoid those fatal errors; and be supremely careful in placing that dangerous power of controlling the actions of individuals, in such a manner that it may not counteract the end for which it was established.

Government may be considered, a *deposite* of the power of society in certain hands, whose business it is to *restrain,* and in some cases to take off such members of the community as disturb the quiet and destroy the security of the honest and peaceable subject. *This government is founded in the nature of man, and is the obvious end of civil society;* "yet such is the thirst of power in most men, that they will sacrifice heaven and earth to wrest it from its foundation; to establish a power in themselves to tyrannize over the persons and properties of others." To prevent this, let every article of the constitution or *sett of fundamental rules* by which even the supreme power of the state shall be governed, be formed by a convention of the delegates of the people, appointed for that express purpose: which constitution shall neither be added to, diminished from, nor altered in any respect by any power besides the power which first framed it. By this means an effectual bar will be opposed to those enterprizing spirits, who have told us with much assurance, that after the people had made their annual or septennial *offering,* they had no more to do with government than their cattle.

A Convention being soon to sit in Philadelphia; I have thought it my duty to collect some sentiments from a certain very scarce book, entitled an Historical Essay on the English Constitution, and publish them, with whatever improving observations our different circumstances may suggest, for the perusal of the gentlemen concerned in the arduous task of framing a constitution.

"That beautiful system, formed, (as Montesquieu says,) in the German woods, was introduced into England about the year four hundred and fifty." The peculiar excellence of this system consisted in its incorporating small parcels of the people into little communities by themselves. These petty states, *held parliaments often;* for whatever concerned them in common, they met together and debated in common; and after due consideration of the matter, they called a vote, and decided the question, by a majority of voices. In these councils every man had a voice, who had a residence of his own in the tithing, (or township) and paid his tax and performed his share of the public duties. This salutary institution, our honorable Conference of Committees has again revived at their late sitting.

To avoid the tumult, which always must attend the hearing and determining civil and criminal cases, by a popular tribunal, they had their executive courts in every township; and still kept the legislative and executive departments separate, in all cases whatsoever.

Among these people we find the origin of the inestimable trial by juries; and I am much mistaken if our present Justices of the Peace, may not also trace their derivation from the same salubrious source. However that may be, one thing is certain, that "they founded their government on the common rights of mankind. They made the elective power of the people the first principle of the constitution, and delegated that power to such men as they could best confide in. But they were curiously cautious in that respect, knowing well the degenerating principles of mankind; that power makes a vast difference in the temper and behaviour of men, and often converts a good man in private life to a tyrant in office. For this reason they never gave up their natural liberty or delegated their power for making laws, to any man for a longer time than one year."

"The object upon which our elective power acts is remarkably different from that of the Romans. Theirs was directed to operate in the election of their chief officers, and particularly their consuls; or those who were vested with the executive authority whom they changed annually. But the senate where the principal power in their state was lodged, was a more fixed body of men; and not subject to the elective power of the people."

"Our Saxon forefathers almost reversed this principle; for they made their wittenagemot or parliament, where the principal power was lodged, annually moveable and entirely subject to the elective power of the people; and gave a more fixed state to the executive authority. This last they continued within a certain sphere of action, prescribed by law; so that it could not operate to the injury of any individual, either in his person or property; and was controllable in all acts of state, by the elective power which they vested annually in their wittenagemot, or parliament."

"The annual exercise of the elective power, was the quintessence, the life and soul of the constitution; and the basis of the whole fabric of their government, from the internal police of the minutest part of the country, to the administration of the government of the whole kingdom. This Saxon institution, formed a perfect model of government; where the natural rights of mankind were preserved, in their full exercise, pure and perfect, as far as the nature of society will admit of."

"It would be something very surprizing to find the people of England continually disputing about the principles and powers, vested in the constituent parts of their government; did we not know that at this day it consists of a mixture of the old, or first establishment, and that which took place at (and since) what is commonly called the conquest, by William the First. These two forms of government, the first founded upon the principles of liberty, and the latter upon the principles of slavery, it is no wonder they are continually at war, one with the other. For the first is grounded upon the natural rights of mankind, in the constant annual exercise of their elective power, and the latter upon the despotic rule of one man. Hence our disputants, drawing their arguments from two principles, widely different, must of course differ in their conclusions."

"Our Saxon forefathers established their government in Britain, before the transactions of mankind were recorded in writing; at least among the northern nations. They therefore handed down to posterity, the principles of their government, by the actual exercise of their rights; which became the ancient usage and custom of the people, and the law of the land. And hence it came to pass, that when this ancient custom and usage ceased to act, the remembrance of the custom ceased with it. We may add to this, that, since the conquest, our arbitrary kings and men of arbitrary principles, have endeavored to destroy the few remaining records, and historical facts that might keep in remembrance a form of government so kind, friendly and hospitable to the human species. It is for these reasons that we have such a scarcity of historical evidence, concerning the principles and manner of conducting the first establishment of our mode of government in this kingdom."

"However, notwithstanding these difficulties, there are many customs, forms, principles and doctrines, that have been handed down to us by tradition; which will serve as so many landmarks, to guide our steps to the foundation of this ancient structure, which, is only buried under the rubbish collected by time, and new establishments. *Whatever is of Saxon establishment is truly constitutional; but whatever is Norman, is heterogeneous to it, and partakes of a tyrannical Spirit.*"

"From these sources it is, that I would endeavor to draw the outlines of this ancient model of government, established in this kingdom by our Saxon forefathers; where it continued to grow and flourish, for six hundred years; 'till it was overwhelmed and destroyed by William the First, commonly called the Conqueror, and lay buried under a load of tyranny for one hundred and forty seven years. When it arose again, like a phoenix from its own ashes in the reign of Henry the Third, by the assistance of many concurrent causes, but principally by the bravery of the English people, under the conduct and intrepidity of our ancient and immortal barons, who restored it, in part, once more to this Isle. And tho' much impaired, maimed, and disfigured, it has stood the admiration of many ages; and still remains *the most noble and ancient monument of Gothic antiquity.*"

It was indeed restored in an impaired condition; as a free constitution must necessarily be, when attempted to be introduced among a people, distinguished by the odious difference of condition of Lord and Vassal.

THE ENGLISH CONSTITUTION

The first establishment of our Constitution, *by the* Saxons, *to what is commonly called the* Norman Conquest, *under the* Heptarchy.

"The first principle of a government that is founded on the natural rights of mankind is the principle of annual election. Liberty and election are in this case synonimous terms; *for where there is no election there can be no liberty.* And therefore the preservation of this elective power, in its full extent, is the preservation of liberty in its fullest extent: and where that is restrained in any degree, liberty is restrained in just the same proportion; and where that is destroyed by any power in a state, whether military or civil, liberty is also destroyed by that power, whether it be lodged in the hands of one man, one hundred or one thousand."

"It is reported by historians that our Saxon forefathers had no kings in their own country, but lived in tribes or small communities, governed by laws of their own making, and magistrates of their own electing; and further, that a number of these communities were united together for their mutual defence and protection. But by what particular bond of union they were united, I know of no historian, that hath given us any information. There were seven tribes of Saxons, that arrived in Britain about the same time, under so many different leaders; but as they had all the same intentions so far as to establish the same form of government, I shall consider them in this respect indiscriminately."

"They first divided the land into small parts, and that divided the inhabitants upon that land, and made them a distinct and separate people from any other. This division they called a tithing. Here they established a government, which was, no doubt the same as that under which they lived in their Mother-Country. They had two sorts of tithings, one called a town tithing, and the other called a rural tithing. These were governed upon the same principles, only thus distinguished; as one is expressive of a town having such a number of inhabitants as to make a tithing of itself; and the other of a tithing situated in the rural part of the kingdom. Thus they went on, as they conquered the country, to divide the land, till they had cut out the whole kingdom into tithings, and established the same form of government in each."

"In this manner they provided for the internal police of the whole country, which they vested in the respective tithings, who annually elected the magistrates that were to administer justice to them, agreeable to the laws and customs they had brought with them from their Mother-Country. And this internal police was so excellent in its nature, that it hath had the encomiums of most authors of our history."

"They had a legislative authority in every tithing, which made laws and regulations for the good government of the tithing. Besides these, they had a court of law, whose jurisdiction was confined to the same limits. All which were created by the elective power of the people, who were resident inhabitants of the tithing; and the right of election, was placed in every man who paid his shot and bore his lot. From hence we may easily perceive, that, under the establishment of these tithings, by reason of their smallness, the natural rights of mankind might very well be preserved in their power by election without any confusion or inconvenience to the inhabitants."

"The first connexion the tithings had with one another, was to form an establishment for the military defence of the country. For this end a number of these tithings were united together, so far as related to their military concerns. This union necessarily created a larger division of the land, equal to the number of tithings that were thus united; and this they called a wapentake or weapontake, and might take in as many tithings as would make a Brigade under a Brigadier General. Here likewise they established a court of council and a court of law, which last was called a wapentake court. In the court of council the chief magistrates of every tithing assembled to elect officers of the militia to their respective command, and regulate all matters relating to the militia; in which, every individual tithing was concerned. The court of law was to enforce these regulations within the jurisdiction." "Let us now consider the third and last division, which they made of the land. This was composed of a certain number of wapentakes, united together; which they called a shire or one complete share or part into which they divided the land. This division completed their system of internal police; by uniting all the tithings within the shire into one body, subject to such laws and regulations as should be made in their shiregemots or shire parliaments; for the benefit and good government of the shire."

"As this division comprehended many tithings and many people, so it had the greatest court of council in England except the high court of parliament; and the chief officer was vested with as high jurisdiction in the shire, as the king in the kingdom."

"They had likewise a court of law, called the shire court; to which, I make no doubt every man might appeal who thought himself injured by the inferior courts in the shire. These divisions in the land, are what I call the skeleton of the constitution which was animated and put in motion by all these establishments."

"We may consider each shire as a complete government; furnished with both a civil and a military power within its own jurisdiction."

"Let us now see by what mode of union, these shires became united together into a kingdom: and it will be found, I apprehend, that they pursued the same principles, which they had used in every other establishment. That is to say, wherever a combined interest was concerned and the people at large were affected by it, the immediate deputies of the people, met together to attend the respective interests of their constituents, and a majority of voices always bound the whole, and determined for any measure, that was supposed to operate for the good of the whole combined body. This meeting of the deputies of the people, was called by the Saxons the wittenagemote, or assembly of the wise men of the nation; which composed their national council and legislative authority."

THE ENGLISH CONSTITUTION

Under the Monarchy

"I have already remarked that a number of the Saxon tribes, while in their own country, were united together for their mutual protection and defence. In like manner was our Heptarchy connected; and their mode of union became a part of the constitution, when the seven kingdoms united together under one king. The matter was simply this: one of the seven kings was always chosen generalissimo over the whole body; and they appointed him a standing council of a certain number of deputies, from each state, without whose advice and concurrence, it is probable he could not act."

"However I do not mean to make any observation upon the powers vested in this standing council; but only to point out that body of men as the origin of our house of lords. Those deputies who composed this great standing council, were appointed to their trust by the joint consent of the king and parliament of the little kingdom from whence they were sent. And when Alfred the great, united the seven kingdoms into one, he undoubtedly, with the approbation of the people, incorporated this great council as a separate branch of the wittenagemote or parliament; so that they still continued to be the king's great council, and a branch of the legislative authority, which they are at this day. In confirmation of which, it is observable, that the consent of the parliament continued necessary for creating a baron of the realm about as low down as Henry the Seventh; which is the only title by which any man can obtain his seat in our House of Lords; and not as Duke, Marquis, Earl, Viscount, &c."

"It is needless to mention that after the union of the seven kingdoms under Alfred, a reduction of the members to serve in parliament became absolutely necessary, because it was then impracticable, by reason of their numbers, for the same members to attend, in one parliament, that used to attend in seven, without such anarchy and confusion as must counteract the end of their meeting."

"Nature herself has confined, or limited the number of men in all societies, that meet together to inform and be informed, by argument and debate, within the natural powers of hearing and speech. So that the question in this case must have been how to reduce the representatives of the people in parliament, to be a convenient number, to transact the business of the nation; and at the same time, to preserve the elective power of the people unhurt? a question of no small difficulty to determine, considering the various interests that were affected by it." *And how was this effected?*

Our historian informs us; "they excluded from this parliament, all the representatives of the rural tithings, as being a body of men the most numerous of any, considered collectively, and yet elected by the fewest people in proportion, which, must be very evident, since the rural part of the kingdom must be more thinly inhabited than the towns. Besides the town tithings or boroughs, where a great number of inhabitants are collected together, upon a small compass of ground, were undoubtedly, the most conveniently situated, for the commodious exercise of the elective power of the people. And the towns, being few in comparison of the rural tithings, and at the same time dispersed over the whole country, were best adapted to receive the regulations they intended to make in their plan of forming the constituent parts of the new parliament."

"Tho' the barons of the realm being great freeholders, carried into parliament the greatest concern for the interest of the rural part of the kingdom; yet not being elective, they were not such a body of men as the constitution, and the safety of the inhabitants of the rural tithings required. And therefore, they constituted shire elections, for two members, to represent the shire in parliament, and those representatives were the origin of our knights of the shire."

"The barons of the realm, and the knights of the shires, I consider as two bodies of men that were substituted, at the establishment of the monarchy, under Alfred the Great, in place of those representatives that used to serve under the Heptarchy for the rural tithings. The alteration that was made with respect to the towns and boroughs was simply this: that all boroughs that used to send one member to the little parliament, to which they belonged, under the Heptarchy, should for the future send two to the great parliament of England."

From the above concise view of the Saxon affairs, it is plain, that in their own country, and for many years after they settled in England, they maintained that natural, wise and equal government, which has deservedly obtained the admiration of every civilized age and country. In their small republics, they often met in council upon their common concerns; and being all equally interested in every question that could be moved in their meetings, they must of course be drawn in to consider, and offer their sentiments of many occasions. It is from the prevalence of this custom among the savages, that they have been enabled to astonish our great lawyers, judges and governors, commissioned to treat with them, by displays of their sublime policy. By Alfred's constitution, all occasions for exercising these talents were cut off from the body of the people: the making and amending of laws, being in a manner entirely referred to that great deliverer and his sublime council, whose wisdom and honesty were implicitly confided in by the whole nation; and at the same time distributive justice, was so uprightly administred by his commissioners of the peace, the men fell into a political stupor, and have never, to this day, thoroughly awakened, to a sense of the necessity there is, to watch over both legislative and executive departments in the state. If they have now and then opened their eyes, it is only to survey, with silent indignation, a state from whence they despair of being able to recover themselves. Fixed establishments on the one hand, rooted habits and prejudices on the other, are not easily got over. Power, like wealth, draws many admirers to its possessor: and tho' all men will confess, that, without a check, it is dangerous in any community, they often flatter themselves, that the *rising* Augustus, having smiled upon them, in his early adventures, they (*in particular*) have nothing to fear from him, and therefore will not oppose him.*

This Colony, having now but one order of freemen in it; and to the honor of Pennsylvania, but very few slaves, it will need but little argument to convince the bulk of an understanding people, that this ancient and justly admired pattern, the old Saxon form of government, will be the best model, that human wisdom, improved by experience, has left them to copy.

To effect which,

Let the first care of our approaching Convention be to incorporate every society of a convenient extent into a Township, which shall be a body politic and corporate by itself, having power of electing annually by ballot a town-clerk to record all the public proceedings of the township, town council &c.— to draw up, sign, and issue warrants by order of the town-council for calling two meetings, and transact all such public business as the laws of the colony shall point out as his duty.—A town council consisting of five or seven respectable men, the major part of whom shall be a quorum, invested with full power to manage the affairs and interest of the town; and to order warrants to be issued for calling annual town meetings on such days as shall be stated for that purpose, by law, and occasionally, on the petition of ten or more freemen of the town, setting forth the cause of the requested meeting.—A town treasurer—a town sealer of weights and measures—assessors—collectors— overseers of the poor—constables—pound keeper—sealer of leather—surveyors of highways—fence viewers—gaugers—and all such other officers as have been or may be found necessary and shall be instituted by the present or any future convention appointed to amend the constitution of this colony.

Approaching that gulph, where all former projectors have found their systems shipwrecked, I shall, with becoming diffidence, propose a method of conducting elections, which I presume will be found a considerable improvement upon Harrington's plan.

After seating all the qualified electors in pews or squares by themselves, let them be numbered, and a box handed round to receive nomination tickets for the officers to be chosen. These tickets being sorted and numbered, let the clerk enter the names of the proposed candidates; beginning with his, who has the highest number of tickets; and thus proceed 'till all are entered. Where there are ties, let one ticket of each be taken and shaken in a hat, to be drawn out in fair lot and registered. Then in this order let the name or names, being first read over distinctly, be proposed by the Moderator, and balloted for by the bean; and if the first name fails of a majority of yeas, let the next in course be put, 'till the choice is made.

To render this mode of voting as fair and convenient as possible, let beans, or balls of opposite colors, be wrapped in small pellets of the same sort of paper, and one of each sort served to every voter. By opening the paper a little, the elector sees the color; returns the paper to its former condition, and drops which he pleases in the bag, first holding it up between his thumb and finger, that the collector may see there is but one; by proceeding in this manner, a corrupt influence can hardly be exercised; which cannot be said of the common custom of balloting. Besides very little writing is needfull: and when the whole meeting is told that white is yea and black nay, every one is alike knowing in the exercise of his elective power, without having occasion to recur to any man for advice or assistance.

For the first election of a governor, deputy-governor, secretary &c. it may be well for the Convention, to send out a nomination to the respective towns or districts; as the present urgency of public affairs requires that no time be lost 'till an established government be erected.

For the future, *as all debates will undoubtedly be held in public,* the consideration of warlike matters being best managed by Committees, the body of the people will soon become acquainted with the true characters of the delegates, and will continue or withdraw their confidence accordingly.

The judges of the supreme judicatory should be nominated by the Governor and executive council, and balloted for by the Assembly.

The *Conservatores,* or justices of the peace should, according to ancient custom be again elected by the districts; and to carry the salutary practice throughout, the justices thus chosen, should, soon after their election, meet at the county town, and ballot for the judges of the county court, the clerk and *solicitor* for the peace, in the county.

All judiciary officers should have moderate salaries; and that they might be encouraged to apply their minds to gain a thorough knowledge of their important business, they should have in their commissions, an estate for life, provided they did not forfeit it by misbehaviour.

Judges of the probate of wills, registers of conveyances, deputy-coroners, and officers of such importance to the people, should be established in every convenient district; it being a great hardship, for people in narrow circumstances, to travel far, to have business of so pressing a nature performed for them.

Sheriffs, coroners, county treasurers, and all such county officers, can be elected no other way, with so much convenience, as to ballot by ticket, in each district, and to send the tickets to the townsmen of the shire-town by a sworn officer, under the seals of the respective moderators, where the votes are taken. And should the tickets, when sorted and numbered, fail to afford any one name, balloted for, a clear majority of votes, that is, that one half, more by one vote, for some certain person, than all the rest; the bench of justices for the whole county being for that purpose summoned by the clerk of that township, should meet, and for that year, supply the place of the officer, thus failing of appointment, by nomination and ballot as before described.

A standing grand jury, conducing much to the peace and good order of society, twenty four members for each county should be annually chosen, in the respective districts, as the representatives; having proper regard to the proportion belonging to each district, to serve for the whole year, and watch over the behaviour of the people.

Traverse juries, should be drawn from a box, furnished annually, with the names of all nonexempt freeholders, written each fairly on a ticket, shaken together, and taken by lot.

Jurors serving one year, should be exempt the two following.

Notwithstanding it may be difficult to find men properly qualified to sustain every office proposed to be established in each district; yet the electors should be supremely careful, never to heap offices or indeed confer more than one on the same person. No governor, counsellor, representative, sheriff, coroner, attorney at law, or clerk of the peace should ever be a justice of the peace. Neither, should any one in the executive departments, civil or military, have a seat in the legislature.

Salaries and fees ought to be *competent:* that able men may not be deterred from accepting them, nor covetous men conceive them a bait. The latter condition of salaries has been the evident ruin of England; while those Commonwealths who have preserved a strict economy in that respect, continue happy and flourishing.

"If we were to select the attributes of good government, we should find them to consist in *wisdom* and *justice.* And if we could divide those virtues, from all bad qualities, in men, and place such men, and such only, to rule over us, we should establish an heaven upon earth. The power of election which our government hath diffused thro' the whole nation, will always produce this happy effect, when left to operate according to its genuine principles. For by dividing the country into small parts, as our tithings were, the character of every man, that was fit to bear an office, was well known amongst his neighbours. And therefore, when the choice of an officer to preside over them was their object of election, the concurrent sentiments of an uninfluenced majority, of a multitude of people, would naturally fall upon those men only, who were most eminent for their wisdom and justice."

The best constructed civil government that ever was devised, having but a poor chance for duration, unless it be defended by arms, against external force as well as internal conspiracies of bad men, it will be the next concern of the convention, to put the colony militia on the most respectable footing.

The Militia is the natural support of a government, *founded on the authority of the people only.*

And to render both the people and the government, perfectly free from any jealousy of each other, it seems proper that the associators should have the choice of all officers immediately commanding them, inclusive of their respective captains—that deputations from a convenient number of companies, consisting both of officers and privates, should ballot for their field officers, and that the legislature should appoint every general officer.

And at length, to come to that dangerous, but necessary engine of state, *a standing army,* whose operations must be conducted with all possible secrecy and dispatch; and for that reason, must be entrusted in few hands; I would propose that a committee of three gentlemen be chosen by joint ballot of the governor, council, and assembly, to be called the committee of war; and to have the conducting of all military affairs, under the direction of the governor and privy council, to whom in matters of great importance, they should always have recourse: but being competent in lesser matters, business would be less subject to delay. This committee being the joint choice of the whole legislature, and by them removeable annually, or at any time, on conviction of misbehaviour, would have a sufficient confidence placed in them, and yet no power that might become dangerous to the liberty of the people.

While all kinds of governmental power reverts annually to the people, there can be little danger of their liberty. Because no maxim was ever more true than that, Where annual election ends, slavery begins. . . .

What is here, faithfully quoted or modestly suggested, is intended to give no offence to any man, or body of men existing. In matters wherein all are concerned, it is the duty of all to give notice of any thing they conceive might be hurtful to the public, if suffered to pass without examination. It is a time when all the sagacity and diligence, all the temper and moderation of this vast Continent, is necessary to separate the *precious* from the *vile.*

We are happy that such plain and salutary paths have been marked out before us. Whatever rubbish has been thrown into them, should be carefully removed, that, like *wisdom's ways,* they may be *pleasant,* and conduct us to a secure and virtuous Peace.

Men entrusted with the formation of civil constitutions, should remember they are *painting for eternity:* that the smallest defect or redundancy in the system they frame may prove the destruction of millions.

Above all things, the greatest care should be taken, that the persons who grant the public money, and should of course have the power of enquiring into its disposal, should have no hand in contracts; or any connection with persons thro' whose hands the public treasure passes. A house of commons should indeed be the guardians of common right, and the interest of the public. Places, pensions and other emoluments, from the public treasury having, for near a century past, been open to British commoners, their power of bringing peculators to account, has been of no use to the oppressed people. They have indeed united with them, and formed such powerful factions as have bid defiance to the whole nation. By this means, the legislative and executive authority, which our wise and virtuous ancestors, carefully kept asunder, are become confounded together, in the hands of the same men. This has principally arisen from another fatal inattention of the people to the usurpations of their deputies, when they took upon them to alter the first principle of the constitution by acts of parliament.

"Upon this foundation, they may mould it into what shape they please; and in the end make us slaves by law. The house of commons are constituted, a body of men, merely passive, with regard to their creation, duration, and dissolution; and therefore have no consent to give to their own duration, even for an hour."

"There cannot be a more dangerous doctrine adopted in a state, than to admit that the legislative authority has a right to alter the constitution."

This shrewd observation needs little to be said in proof of it. For as the constitution limits the authority of the legislature, if the legislature can alter the constitution, they can give themselves what bounds they please.

It is therefore, I beg leave to repeat, that after the approaching Convention has met, and settled the grand outlines of a constitution, let the legislature go on with the affairs of government, without sensible deviation from the obvious meaning of their digest; and whatever inconveniences may be found unprovided for, may be candidly advertised to the public, and amended by another Convention.

THE POWERS OF THE SEVERAL PARTS OF THE LEGISLATURE

The respective powers of the several branches of the Legislature come next into consideration. And it must be confessed, that on this question I find the greatest difference of opinion among the really wise and learned, of any pertaining to our system. Some talk of having two councils, one legislative, and the other executive: some of a small executive council only; which should have nothing to do with framing the laws. Some would have the Governor, an integral part of the legislature: others, only president of the council with a casting vote.

The latter opinion appears to me most consonant to the intentions of wise framers of Governments. The Governor should have a seat in some part of the Legislature, that he might be fully acquainted with the necessity and reasons for passing any bill into a law, and on the other hand, to prevent any one person from possessing too much, or a dangerous power, he should have no more than a casting vote when necessary.

Some are strenuous for only one legislative body namely, the house of representatives: but a council will be found necessary for the following reasons.

An Act, ever so well intended, and in appearance ever so well framed to promote the public good, will notwithstanding, throw the society into confusion, if it can be made appear that it is founded on principles which will not bear examination.

The persons selected to compose a council, are of course always supposed to have a superior degree of acquaintance with the history, laws, and manners of mankind; and by that means they will be more likely to foresee the mischievous consequences, that might follow a proceeding, which at first view did not appear to have any thing dangerous in it, to many honest men, who may however, be very worthy of a seat in the house of representatives.

For on no circumstance does the public peace and prosperity more immediately depend, than on the clearness, fullness and consistency of the laws.

The Governor should be furnished with a small privy council, to afford him their advice and assistance in the executive department; but they should have no share whatever in the Legislature.

In this capacity they should take cognizance of high crimes; such as maladministration of Judges in their offices; being the proper inquest for this purpose—The Assembly and Legislative Council, in like manner to enquire into the conduct of the Governor and privy council, and the cause of complaint being found, a regular trial by the country should determine all causes whatever.

A Council, annually eligible, will endeavor to maintain their seats by the rectitude of their conduct.

To suppose they can *inveterate* themselves, is to suppose that mankind will forget the mischiefs which have overspread the world from the days of Sylla to the present bloody period, from the same tyrannic source.

We should make all prudent provision for posterity, and indeed the most salutary provision we can possibly make for them, is to enable them to provide for themselves; but we ought never to run into one extreme to avoid another.

The last important measure I would propose, is, that, whereas the heat of war in our very neighbourhood, may well be supposed to agitate the minds of the delegates in convention, and render it impossible to have every provision made for the security of our liberties, that cool and continued reflexion would suggest, after the principal parts of the constitution are established, an adjournment might be made to a convenient day; and mean while every man might be invited to give his sentiments freely and discreetly upon any part of the system he might conceive could be altered for the better.

Probably a decennial meeting of delegates, to examine the state of the constitution, and conduct of the government, would not be an imprudent provision for keeping the constitution in health and vigor, by having an opportunity to see that it did not depart from its first principles. This would be effectually holding the supreme power in its *only* safe repository *the hands of* the people.

CONCLUSION

The last and greatest security that men can have for a permanent enjoyment of their rights, is to learn, what they are from their very elements, as they are well explained by Burlamaqui and others; and besides, to learn the art of defending them with their arms.

I, alike discommend a heedless inattention to the concerns of our country and posterity; and a despairing anxiety, grounded on a supposition, that if some particular matters are not settled in just such particular manners, that all will be lost irrecoverably.

This is a day of cool and impartial enquiry. Adversity sobers our spirits and causes us to give each other a patient hearing. We learn from our troubles that each man needs the advice and assistance of his neighbour: and perhaps this is not the most trivial lesson.

The varying circumstances of our situation, have gradually pointed out arrangements already which no man could have foreseen some months ago: those successive improvements which will thence arise, and the advantage of such a communication of sentiments as will accrue from the establishment of frequent town meetings among the people, will give such a new face to the affairs of this colony, and raise up so many able men to improve its internal police; that as arts and manufactures have already made it their peculiar, or at least principal residence, so we trust in God that the principal science that ever rendered mankind happy and glorious, the science of *just* and *equal* government, will shine conspicuous in Pennsylvania.

SOURCE: [Demophilus], "The genuine principles of the ancient Saxon, or English Constitution. Carefully collected from the best authorities; with some observations, on their peculiar fitness, for the united colonies in general, and Pennsylvania in particular." In the digital collection *Evans Early American Imprint Collection:* https://name.umdl.umich.edu/N11656.0001.001. University of Michigan Library Digital Collections. Accessed December 28, 2024.

7. [THEOPHILUS PARSONS]
"THE ESSEX RESULTS"
1778

Theophilus Parsons was born in Newbury, Massachusetts (1750), and he died in Boston, Massachusetts (1813). After graduating from Harvard College and teaching school for three years, Parsons went on to have a distinguished career as a scholar, politician, jurist, and founding father. In 1778, he was a member of the Essex County convention, which was tasked with reviewing the first proposed constitution for Massachusetts drafted by the Massachusetts General Court. He was also a delegate to the second Massachusetts constitutional convention of 1779-1780, and he was a member of the committee of 26 that helped to edit and revise the state constitution penned by John Adams. He also served as a member of the state convention that ratified the federal Constitution in 1788. Parsons ended his career by serving as chief justice of the Supreme Judicial Court of Massachusetts from 1806 to 1813.

"The Essex Result" was Parson's attempt in 1778 to dissuade the citizens of Massachusetts from supporting the proposed state constitution of that year. After the state's legislative body had drafted their constitution, the document was then sent to the town meetings for ratification or rejection. Parson's "Essex Result" was almost certainly the most capacious critique of the proposed constitution, which was eventually rejected. Parson's effort was not simply negative, though. The "Essex Result" effectively laid out the principles and institutions for a new and improved constitution for the Bay state. Among his unique contributions to constitutional theory was Parson's suggestion that that the lower and upper houses of a bicameral legislature should be represent different interests in society. The lower house would represent persons (with their multiplicity of passions, opinions, and interests), and the upper house would represent property. The following extended excerpt from the "Essex Result" does not contain the documents critique of the proposed constitution of 1778.

. . . The reason and understanding of mankind, as well as the experience of all ages, confirm the truth of this proposition, that the benefits resulting to individuals from a free government, conduce much more to their happiness, than the retaining of all their natural rights in a state of nature. These benefits are greater or less, as the form of government, and the mode of exercising the supreme power of the State, are more or less conformable to those principles of equal impartial liberty, which is the property of all men from their birth as the gift of their Creator, compared with the manners and genius of the people, their occupations, customs, modes of thinking, situation, extent of country, and numbers. If the constitution and form of government are wholly repugnant to those principles, wretched are the subjects of that State. They have surrendered a portion of their natural rights, the enjoyment of which was in some degree a blessing, and the consequence is, they find themselves stripped of the remainder. As an anodyne to compose the spirits of these slaves, and to lull them into a passively obedient state, they are told, that tyranny is preferable to no government at all; a proposition which is to be doubted, unless considered under some limitation. Surely a state of nature is more excellent than that, in which men are meanly submissive to the haughty will of an imperious tyrant, whose savage passions are not bounded by the laws of reason, religion, honor, or a regard to his subjects, and the point to which all his movements center, is the gratification of a brutal appetite. As in a state of nature much happiness cannot be enjoyed by individuals, so it has been conformable to the inclinations of almost all men, to enter into a political society so constituted, as to remove the inconveniences they were obliged to submit to in their former state, and, at the same time, to retain all those natural rights, the enjoyment of which would be consistent with the nature of a free government, and the necessary subordination to the supreme power of the state.

To determine what form of government, in any given case, will produce the greatest possible happiness to the subject, is an arduous task, not to be compassed perhaps by any human powers. Some of the greatest geniuses and most learned philosophers of all ages, impelled by their sollicitude to promote the happiness of mankind, have nobly dared to attempt it: and their labours have crowned them with immortality. A Solon, a Lycurgus of Greece, a Numa of Rome are remembered with honor, when the wide extended empires of succeeding tyrants, are hardly important enough to be faintly sketched out on the map, while their superb thrones have long since crumbled into dust. The man who alone undertakes to form a constitution, ought to be an unimpassioned being; one enlightened mind; biassed neither by the lust of power, the allurements of pleasure, nor the glitter of wealth; perfectly acquainted with all the alienable and unalienable rights of mankind; possessed of this grand truth, that all men are born equally free, and that no man ought to surrender any part of his natural rights, without receiving the greatest possible equivalent; and influenced by the impartial principles of rectitude and justice, without partiality for, or prejudice against the interest or professions of any individuals or class of men. He ought also to be master of the histories of all the empires and states which are now existing, and all those which have figured in antiquity, and thereby able to collect and blend their respective excellencies, and avoid those defects which experience hath pointed out. Rousseau, a learned foreigner, a citizen of Geneva, sensible of the importance and difficulty of the subject, thought it impossible for any body of people, to form a free and equal constitution for themselves, in which, every individual should have equal justice done him, and be permitted to enjoy a share of power in the state, equal to what should be enjoyed by any other. Each individual, said he, will struggle, not only to retain all his own natural rights, but to acquire a controul over those of others. Fraud, circumvention, and an union of interest of some classes of people, combined with an inattention to the rights of posterity, will prevail over the principles of equity, justice, and good policy. The Genevans, perhaps the most virtuous republicans now existing, thought like Rousseau. They called the celebrated Calvin to their assistance. He came, and, by their gratitude, have they embalmed his memory.

The freemen inhabiting the territory of the Massachusetts-Bay are now forming a political society for themselves. Perhaps their situation is more favorable in some respects, for erecting a free government, than any other people were ever favored with. That attachment to old forms, which usually embarrasses, has not place amongst them. They have the history and experience of all States before them. Mankind have been toiling through ages for their information; and the philosophers and learned men of antiquity have trimmed their midnight lamps, to transmit to them instruction. We live also in an age, when the principles of political liberty, and the foundation of governments, have been freely canvassed, and fairly settled. Yet some difficulties we have to encounter. Not content with removing our attachment to the old government, perhaps we have contracted a prejudice against some part of it without foundation. The idea of liberty has been held up in so dazzling colours, that some of us may not be willing to submit to that subordination necessary in the freest States. Perhaps we may say further, that we do not consider ourselves united as brothers, with an united interest, but have fancied a clashing of interests amongst the various classes of men, and have acquired a thirst of power, and a wish of domination, over some of the community. We are contending for freedom—Let us all be equally free—It is possible, and it is just. Our interests when candidly considered are one. Let us have a constitution founded, not upon party or prejudice—not one for to-day or to-morrow—but for posterity. Let *Esto perpetua* be it's motto. If it is founded in good policy; it will be founded in justice and honesty. Let all ambitious and interested views be discarded, and let regard be had only to the good of the whole, in which the situation and rights of posterity must be considered: and let equal justice be done to all the members of the community; and we thereby imitate our common father, who at our births, dispensed his favors, not only with a liberal, but with an equal hand.

Was it asked, what is the best form of government for the people of the Massachusetts-Bay? we confess it would be a question of infinite importance: and the man who could truly answer it, would merit a statue of gold to his memory, and his fame would be recorded in the annals of late posterity, with unrivalled lustre. The question, however, must be answered, and let it have the best answer we can possibly give it. Was a man to mention a despotic government, his life would be a just forfeit to the resentments of an affronted people. Was he to hint monarchy, he would deservedly be hissed off the stage, and consigned to infamy. A republican form is the only one consonant to the feelings of the generous and brave Americans. Let us now attend to those principles, upon which all republican governments, who boast any degree of political liberty, are founded, and which must enter into the spirit of a free republican constitution. For all republics are not Free.

All men are born equally free. The rights they possess at their births are equal, and of the same kind. Some of those rights are alienable, and may be parted with for an equivalent. Others are unalienable and inherent, and of that importance, that no equivalent can be received in exchange. Sometimes we shall mention the surrendering of a power to controul our natural rights, which perhaps is speaking with more precision, than when we use the expression of parting with natural rights—but the same thing is intended. Those rights which are unalienable, and of that importance, are called the rights of conscience. We have duties, for the discharge of which we are accountable to our Creator and benefactor, which no human power can cancel. What those duties are, is determinable by right reason, which may be, and is called, a well informed conscience. What this conscience dictates as our duty, is so; and that power which assumes a controul over it, is an usurper; for no consent can be pleaded to justify the controul, as any consent in this case is void. The alienation of some rights, in themselves alienable, may be also void, if the bargain is of that nature, that no equivalent can be received. Thus, if a man surrender all his alienable rights, without reserving a controul over the supreme power, or a right to resume in certain cases, the surrender is void, for he becomes a slave; and a slave can receive no equivalent. Common equity would set aside this bargain.

When men form themselves into society, and erect a body politic or State, they are to be considered as one moral whole, which is in possession of the supreme power of the State. This supreme power is composed of the powers of each individual collected together, and voluntarily parted with by him. No individual, in this case, parts with his unalienable rights, the supreme power therefore cannot controul them. Each individual also surrenders the power of controuling his natural alienable rights, only when the good of the whole requires it. The supreme power therefore can do nothing but what is for the good of the whole; and when it goes beyond this line, it is a power usurped. If the individual receives an equivalent for the right of controul he has parted with, the surrender of that right is valid; if he receives no equivalent, the surrender is void, and the supreme power as it respects him is an usurper. If the supreme power is so directed and executed that he does not enjoy political liberty, it is an illegal power, and he is not bound to obey. Political liberty is by some defined, a liberty of doing whatever is not prohibited by law. The definition is erroneous. A tyrant may govern by laws. The republics of Venice and Holland govern by laws, yet those republics have degenerated into insupportable tyrannies. Let it be thus defined; political liberty is the right every man in the state has, to do whatever is not prohibited by laws, to which he has given his consent. This definition is in unison with the feelings of a free people. But to return—If a fundamental principle on which each individual enters into society is, that he shall be bound by no laws but those to which he has consented, he cannot be considered as consenting to any law enacted by a minority: for he parts with the power of controuling his natural rights, only when the good of the whole requires it; and of this there can be but one absolute judge in the State. If the minority can assume the right of judging, there may then be two judges; for however large the minority may be, there must be another body still larger, who have the same claim, if not a better, to the right of absolute determination. If therefore the supreme power should be so modelled and exerted, that a law may be enacted by a minority, the inforcing of that law upon an individual who is opposed to it, is an act of tyranny. Further, as every individual, in entering into the society, parted with a power of controuling his natural rights equal to that parted with by any other, or in other words, as all the members of the society contributed an equal portion of their natural rights, towards the forming of the supreme power, so every member ought to receive equal benefit from, have equal influence in forming, and retain an equal controul over, the supreme power.

It has been observed, that each individual parts with the power of controuling his natural alienable rights, only when the good of the whole requires it, he therefore has remaining, after entering into political society, all his unalienable natural rights, and a part also of his alienable natural rights, provided the good of the whole does not require the sacrifice of them. Over the class of unalienable rights the supreme power hath no controul, and they ought to be clearly defined and ascertained in a BILL of RIGHTS, previous to the ratification of any constitution. The bill of rights should also contain the equivalent every man receives, as a consideration for the rights he has surrendered. This equivalent consists principally in the security of his person and property, and is also unassailable by the supreme power: for if the equivalent is taken back, those natural rights which were parted with to purchase it, return to the original proprietor, as nothing is more true, than that Allegiance and protection are reciprocal.

The committee also proceeded to consider upon what principles, and in what manner, the supreme power of the state thus composed of the powers of the several individuals thereof, may be formed, modelled, and exerted in a republic, so that every member of the state may enjoy political liberty. This is called by some, *the ascertaining of the political law of the state.* Let it now be called *the forming of a constitution.*

The reason why the supreme governor of the world is a rightful and just governor, and entitled to the allegiance of the universe is, because he is infinitely good, wise, and powerful. His goodness prompts him to the best measures, his wisdom qualifies him to discern them, and his power to effect them. In a state likewise, the supreme power is best disposed of, when it is so modelled and balanced, and rested in such hands, that it has the greatest share of goodness, wisdom, and power, which is consistent with the lot of humanity.

That state, (other things being equal) which has reposed the supreme power in the hands of one or a small number of persons, is the most powerful state. An union, expedition, secrecy and dispatch are to be found only here. Where power is to be executed by a large number, there will not probably be either of the requisites just mentioned. Many men have various opinions: and each one will be tenacious of his own, as he thinks it preferable to any other; for when he thinks otherwise, it will cease to be his opinion. From this diversity of opinions results disunion; from disunion, a want of expedition and dispatch. And the larger the number to whom a secret is entrusted, the greater is the probability of it's disclosure. This inconvenience more fully strikes us when we consider that want of secrecy may prevent the successful execution of any measures, however excellently formed and digested.

But from a single person, or a very small number, we are not to expect that political honesty, and upright regard to the interest of the body of the people, and the civil rights of each individual, which are essential to a good and free constitution. For these qualities we are to go to the body of the people. The voice of the people is said to be the voice of God. No man will be so hardy and presumptuous, as to affirm the truth of that proposition in its fullest extent. But if this is considered as the intent of it, that the people have always a disposition to promote their own happiness, and that when they have time to be informed, and the necessary means of information given them, they will be able to determine upon the necessary measures therefor, no man, of a tolerable acquaintance with mankind, will deny the truth of it. The inconvenience and difficulty in forming any free permanent constitution are, that such is the lot of humanity, the bulk of the people, whose happiness is principally to be consulted in forming a constitution, and in legislation, (as they include the majority) are so situated in life, and such are their laudable occupations, that they cannot have time for, nor the means of furnishing themselves with proper information, but must be indebted to some of their fellow subjects for the communication. Happy is the man, and blessings will attend his memory, who shall improve his leisure, and those abilities which heaven has indulged him with, in communicating that true information, and impartial knowledge, to his fellow subjects, which will insure their happiness. But the artful demagogue, who to gratify his ambition or avarice, shall, with the gloss of false patriotism, mislead his countrymen, and meanly snatch from them the golden glorious opportunity of forming a system of political and civil liberty, fraught with blessings for themselves, and remote posterity, what language can paint his demerit? The execrations of ages will be a punishment inadequate; and his name, though ever blackening as it rolls down the stream of time, will not catch its proper hue.

Yet, when we are forming a Constitution, by deductions that follow from established principles, (which is the only good method of forming one for futurity,) we are to look further than to the bulk of the people, for the greatest wisdom, firmness, consistency, and perseverance. These qualities will most probably be found amongst men of education and fortune. From such men we are to expect genius cultivated by reading, and all the various advantages and assistances, which art, and a liberal education aided by wealth, can furnish. From these result learning, a thorough knowledge of the interests of their country, when considered abstractedly, when compared with the neighbouring States, and when with those more remote, and an acquaintance with its produce and manufacture, and it's exports and imports. All these are necessary to be known, in order to determine what is the true interest of any state; and without that interest is ascertained, impossible will it be to discover, whether a variety of certain laws may be beneficial or hurtful. From gentlemen whose private affairs compel them to take care of their own household, and deprive them of leisure, these qualifications are not to be generally expected, whatever class of men they are enrolled in.

Let all their respective excellencies be united. Let the supreme power be so disposed and ballanced, that the laws may have in view the interest of the whole; let them be wisely and consistently framed for that end, and firmly adhered to; and let them be executed with vigour and dispatch.

Before we proceed further, it must be again considered, and kept always in view, that we are not attempting to form a temporary constitution, one adjusted only to our present circumstances. We wish for one founded upon such principles as will secure to us freedom and happiness, however our circumstances may vary. One that will smile amidst the declensions of European and Asiatic empires, and survive the rude storms of time. It is not therefore to be understood, that all the men of fortune of the present day, are men of wisdom and learning, or that they are not. Nor that the bulk of the people, the farmers, the merchants, the tradesmen, and labourers, are all honest and upright, with single views to the public good, or that they are not. In each of the classes there are undoubtedly exceptions, as the rules laid down are general. The proposition is only this. That among gentlemen of education, fortune and leisure, we shall find the largest number of men, possessed of wisdom, learning, and a firmness and consistency of character. That among the bulk of the people, we shall find the greatest share of political honesty, probity, and a regard to the interest of the whole, of which they compose the majority. That wisdom and firmness are not sufficient without good intentions, nor the latter without the former. The conclusion is, let the legislative body unite them all. The former are called the excellencies that result from an aristocracy; the latter, those that result from a democracy.

The supreme power is considered as including the legislative, judicial, and executive powers. The nature and employment of these several powers deserve a distinct attention.

The legislative power is employed in making laws, or prescribing such rules of action to every individual in the state, as the good of the whole requires, to be conformed to by him in his conduct to the governors and governed, with respect both to their persons and property, according to the several relations he stands in. What rules of action the good of the whole requires, can be ascertained only by the majority, for a reason formerly mentioned. Therefore the legislative power must be so formed and exerted, that in prescribing any rule of action, or, in other words, enacting any law, the majority must consent. This may be more evident, when the fundamental condition on which every man enters into society, is considered. No man consented that his natural alienable rights should be wantonly controuled; they were controulable, only when that controul should be subservient to the good of the whole; and that subserviency, from the very nature of government, can be determined but by one absolute judge. The minority cannot be that judge, because then there may be two judges opposed to each other, so that this subserviency remains undetermined. Now the enacting of a law, is only the exercise of this controul over the natural alienable rights of each member of the state; and therefore this law must have the consent of the majority, or be invalid, as being contrary to the fundamental condition of the original social contract. In a state of nature, every man had the sovereign controul over his own person. He might also have, in that state, a qualified property. Whatever lands or chattels he had acquired the peaceable possession of, were exclusively his, by right of occupancy or possession. For while they were unpossessed he had a right to them equally with any other man, and therefore could not be disturbed in his possession, without being injured; for no man could lawfully dispossess him, without having a better right, which no man had. Over this qualified property every man in a state of nature had also a sovereign controul. And in entering into political society, he surrendered this right of controul over his person and property, (with an exception to the rights of conscience) to the supreme legislative power, to be exercised by the power, *when the good of the whole demanded it*. This was all the right he could surrender, being all the alienable right of which he was possessed. The only objects of legislation therefore, are the person and property of the individuals which compose the state. If the law affects only the persons of the members, the consent of a majority of any members is sufficient. If the law affects the property only, the consent of those who hold a majority of the property is enough. If it affects, (as it will very frequently, if not always,) both the person and property, the consent of a majority of the members, and of those members also, who hold a majority of the property is necessary. If the consent of the latter is not obtained, their interest is taken from them against their consent, and their boasted security of property is vanished. Those who make the law, in this case give and grant what is not theirs. The law, in it's principles, becomes a second stamp act. Lord Chatham very finely ridiculed the British house of commons upon that principle. "You can give and grant, said he, only your own. Here you give and grant, what? The property of the Americans." The people of the Massachusetts-Bay then thought his Lordship's ridicule well pointed. And would they be willing to merit the same? Certainly they will agree in the principle, should they mistake the application. The laws of the province of Massachusetts-Bay adopted the same principle, and very happily applied it. As the votes of proprietors of common and undivided lands in their meetings, can affect only their property, therefore it is enacted, that in ascertaining the majority, the votes shall be collected according to the respective interests of the proprietors. If each member, without regard to his property, has equal influence in legislation with any other, it follows, that some members enjoy greater benefits and powers in legislation than others, when these benefits and powers are compared with the rights parted with to purchase them. For the property-holder parts with the controul over his person, as well as he who hath no property, and the former also parts with the controul over his property, of which the latter is destitute. Therefore to constitute a perfect law in a free state, affecting the persons and property of the members, it is necessary that the law be for the good of the whole, which is to be determined by a majority of the members, and that majority should include those, who possess a major part of the property in the state.

The judicial power follows next after the legislative power; for it cannot act, until after laws are prescribed. Every wise legislator annexes a sanction to his laws, which is most commonly penal, (that is) a punishment either corporal or pecuniary, to be inflicted on the member who shall infringe them. It is the part of the judicial power (which in this territory has always been, and always ought to be, a court and jury) to ascertain the member who hath broken the law. Every man is to be presumed innocent, until the judicial power hath determined him guilty. When that decision is known, the law annexes the punishment, and the offender is turned over to the executive arm, by whom it is inflicted on him. The judicial power hath also to determine what legal contracts have been broken, and what member hath been injured by a violation of the law, to consider the damages that have been sustained, and to ascertain the recompense. The executive power takes care that this recompense is paid.

The executive power is sometimes divided into the external executive, and internal executive. The former comprehends war, peace, the sending and receiving ambassadors, and whatever concerns the transactions of the state with any other independent state. The confederation of the United States of America hath lopped off this branch of the executive, and placed it in Congress. We have therefore only to consider the internal executive power, which is employed in the peace, security and protection of the subject and his property, and in the defence of the state. The executive power is to marshal and command her militia and armies for her defence, to enforce the law, and to carry into execution all the others of the legislative powers.

A little attention to the subject will convince us, that these three powers ought to be in different hands, and independent of one another, and so balanced, and each having that check upon the other, that their independence shall be preserved—If the three powers are united, the government will be absolute, *whether these powers are in the hands of one or a large number.* The same party will be the legislator, accuser, judge and executioner; and what probability will an accused person have of an acquittal, however innocent he may be, when his judge will be also a party.

If the legislative and judicial powers are united, the maker of the law will also interpret it; and the law may then speak a language, dictated by the whims, the caprice, or the prejudice of the judge, with impunity to him— And what people are so unhappy as those, whose laws are uncertain. It will also be in the breast of the judge, when grasping after his prey, to make a retrospective law, which shall bring the unhappy offender within it; and this also he can do with impunity—The subject can have no peaceable remedy— The judge will try himself, and an acquittal is the certain consequence. He has it also in his power to enact any law, which may shelter him from deserved vengeance.

Should the executive and legislative powers be united, mischiefs the most terrible would follow. The executive would enact those laws it pleased to execute, and no others—The judicial power would be set aside as inconvenient and tardy—The security and protection of the subject would be a shadow—The executive power would make itself absolute, and the government end in a tyranny—Lewis the eleventh of France, by cunning and treachery compleated the union of the executive and legislative powers of that kingdom, and upon that union established a system of tyranny. France was formerly under a free government.

The assembly or representatives of the united states of Holland, exercise the executive and legislative powers, and the government there is absolute.

Should the executive and judicial powers be united, the subject would then have no permanent security of his person and property. The executive power would interpret the laws and bend them to his will; and, as he is the judge, he may leap over them by artful constructions, and gratify, with impunity, the most rapacious passions. Perhaps no cause in any state has contributed more to promote internal convulsions, and to stain the scaffold with it's best blood, than this unhappy union. And it is an union which the executive power in all states, hath attempted to form: if that could not be compassed, to make the judicial power dependent upon it. Indeed the dependence of any of these powers upon either of the others, which in all states has always been attempted by one or the other of them, has so often been productive of such calamities, and of the shedding of such oceans of blood, that the page of history seems to be one continued tale of human wretchedness.

The following principles now seem to be established.

1. That the supreme power is limited, and cannot controul the unalienable rights of mankind, nor resume the equivalent (that is, the security of person and property) which each individual receives, as a consideration for the alienable rights he parted with in entering into political society.

2. That these unalienable rights, and this equivalent, are to be clearly defined and ascertained in a BILL of RIGHTS, previous to the ratification of any constitution.

3. That the supreme power should be so formed and modelled, as to exert the greatest possible power, wisdom, and goodness.

4. That the legislative, judicial, and executive powers, are to be lodged in different hands, that each branch is to be independent, and further, to be so ballanced, and be able to exert such checks upon the others, as will preserve it from a dependence on, or an union with them.

5. That government can exert the greatest power when it's supreme authority is vested in the hands of one or a few.

6. That the laws will be made with the greatest wisdom, and best intentions, when men, of all the several classes in the state concur in the enacting of them.

7. That a government which is so constituted, that it cannot afford a degree of political liberty nearly equal to all it's members, is not founded upon principles of freedom and justice, and where any member enjoys no degree of political liberty, the government, so far as it respects him, is a tyranny, for he is controuled by laws to which he has never consented.

8. That the legislative power of a state hath no authority to controul the natural rights of any of its members, unless the good of the whole requires it.

9. That a majority of the state is the only judge when the general good does require it.

10. That where the legislative power of the state is so formed, that a law may be enacted by the minority, each member of the state does not enjoy political liberty. And

11. That in a free government, a law affecting the person and property of it's members, is not valid, unless it has the consent of a majority of the members, which majority should include those, who hold a major part of the property in the state.

It may be necessary to proceed further, and notice some particular principles, which should be attended to in forming the three several powers in a free republican government.

The first important branch that comes under our consideration, is the legislative body. Was the number of the people so small, that the whole could meet together without inconvenience, the opinion of the majority would be more easily known. But, besides the inconvenience of assembling such numbers, no great advantages could follow. Sixty thousand people could not discuss with candor, and determine with deliberation. Tumults, riots, and murder would be the result. But the impracticability of forming such an assembly, renders it needless to make any further observations. The opinions and consent of the majority must be collected from persons, delegated by every freeman of the state for that purpose. Every freeman, who hath sufficient discretion, should have a voice in the election of his legislators. To speak with precision, in every free state where the power of legislation is lodged in the hands of one or more bodies of representatives elected for that purpose, the person of every member of the state, and all the property in it, ought to be represented, because they are objects of legislation. All the members of the state are qualified to make the election, unless they have not sufficient discretion, or are so situated as to have no wills of their own. Persons not twenty one years old are deemed of the former class, from their want of years and experience. The municipal law of this country will not trust them with the disposition of their lands, and consigns them to the care of their parents or guardians. Women what age soever they are of, are also considered as not having a sufficient acquired discretion; not from a deficiency in their mental powers, but from the natural tenderness and delicacy of their minds, their retired mode of life, and various domestic duties. These concurring, prevent that promiscuous intercourse with the world, which is necessary to qualify them for electors. Slaves are of the latter class and have no wills. But are slaves members of a free government? We feel the absurdity, and would to God, the situation of America and the tempers of it's inhabitants were such, that the slave-holder could not be found in the land.

The rights of representation should be so equally and impartially distributed, that the representatives should have the same views, and interests with the people at large. They should think, feel, and act like them, and in fine, should be an exact miniature of their constituents. They should be (if we may use the expression) the whole body politic, with all it's property, rights, and privileges, reduced to a small scale, every part being diminished in just proportion. To pursue the metaphor. If in adjusting the representation of freeman, any ten are reduced into one, all the other tens should be alike reduced: or if any hundred should be reduced to one, all the other hundreds should have just the same reduction. The representation ought also to be adjusted, that it should be the interest of the representatives at all times, to do justice, therefore equal interest among the people, should have equal interest among the body of representatives. The majority of the representatives should also represent a majority of the people, and the legislative body should be so constructed, that every law affecting property, should have the consent of those who hold a majority of the property. The law would then be determined to be for the good of the whole by the proper judge, the majority, and the necessary consent thereto would be obtained: and all the members of the State would enjoy political liberty, and an equal degree of it. If the scale to which the body politic is to be reduced, is but a little smaller than the original, or, in other words, if a small number of freemen should be reduced to one, that is, send one representative, the number of representatives would be too large for the public good. The expences of government would be enormous. The body would be too unwieldy to deliberate with candor and coolness. The variety of opinions and oppositions would irritate the passions. Parties would be formed and factions engendered. The members would list under the banners of their respective leaders: address and intrigue would conduct the debates, and the result would tend only to promote the ambition or interest of a particular part. Such has always been in some degree, the course and event of debates instituted and managed by a large multitude.

For these reasons, some foreign politicians have laid it down as a rule, that no body of men larger than an hundred, would transact business well: and Lord Chesterfield called the British house of commons a mere mob, because of the number of men which composed it.

Elections ought also to be free. No bribery, corruption, or undue influence should have place. They stifle the free voice of the people, corrupt their morals, and introduce a degeneracy of manners, a supineness of temper, and an inattention to their liberties, which pave the road for the approach of tyranny, in all it's frightful forms.

The man who buys an elector by his bribes, will sell him again, and reap a profit from the bargain; and he thereby becomes a dangerous member of society. The legislative body will hold the purse strings, and men will struggle for a place in that body to acquire a share of the public wealth. It has always been the case. Bribery will be attempted, and the laws will not prevent it. All states have enacted severe laws against it, and they have been ineffectual. The defect was in their forms of government. They were not so contrived, as to prevent the practicability of it. If a small corporation can place a man in the legislative body, to bribe will be easy and cheap. To bribe a large corporation would be difficult and expensive, if practicable. In Great-Britain, the representatives of their counties and great cities are freely elected. To bribe the electors there, is impracticable: and their representatives are the most upright and able statesmen in parliament. The small boroughs are bought by the ministry and opulent men; and their representatives are the mere tools of administration or faction. Let us take warning.

A further check upon bribery is, when the corrupter of a people knows not the electors. If delegates were first appointed by a number of corporations, who at a short day were to elect their representatives, these bloodhounds in a state would be at fault. They would not scent their game. Besides, the representatives would probably be much better men—they would be double refined.

But it may be said, the virtuous American would blast with indignation the man, who should proffer him a bribe. Let it now be admitted as a fact. We ask, will that always be the case? The most virtuous states have become vicious. The morals of all people, in all ages, have been shockingly corrupted. The rigidly virtuous Spartans, who banished the use of gold and silver, who gloried in their poverty for centuries, at last fell a prey to luxury and corruption. The Romans, whose intense love to their country, astonishes a modern patriot, who fought the battles of the republic for three hundred years without pay, and who, as volunteers, extended her empire over Italy, were at last dissolved in luxury, courted the hand of bribery, and finally sold themselves as slaves, and prostrated their country to tyrants the most ignominious and brutal. Shall we alone boast an exemption from the general fate of mankind? Are our private and political virtues to be transmitted untainted from generation to generation, through a course of ages? Have we not already degenerated from the pure morals and disinterested patriotism of our ancestors? And are not our manners becoming soft and luxurious, and have not our vices begun to shoot? Would one venture to prophecy, that in a century from this period, we shall be a corrupt luxurious people, perhaps the close of that century would stamp this prophecy with the title of history.

The rights of representation should also be held sacred and inviolable, and for this purpose, representation should be fixed upon known and easy principles; and the constitution should make provision, that recourse should constantly be had to those principles within a very small period of years, to rectify the errors that will creep in through lapse of time, or alteration of situations. The want of fixed principles of government, and a stated regular recourse to them, have produced the dissolution of all states, whose constitutions have been transmitted to us by history.

But the legislative power must not be trusted with one assembly. A single assembly is frequently influenced by the vices, follies, passions, and prejudices of an individual. It is liable to be avaricious, and to exempt itself from the burdens it lays upon it's constituents. It is subject to ambition, and after a series of years, will be prompted to vote itself perpetual. The long parliament in England voted itself perpetual, and thereby, for a time, destroyed the political liberty of the subject. Holland was governed by one representative assembly annually elected. They afterwards voted themselves from annual to septennial; then for life; and finally exerted the power of filling up all vacancies, without application to their constituents. The government of Holland is now a tyranny *though a republic.*

The result of a single assembly will be hasty and indigested, and their judgments frequently absurd and inconsistent. There must be a second body to revise with coolness and wisdom, and to controul with firmness, independent upon the first, either for their creation, or existence. Yet the first must retain a right to a similar revision and controul over the second.

Let us now ascertain some particular principles which should be attended to, in forming the executive power.

When we recollect the nature and employment of this power, we find that it ought to be conducted with vigour and dispatch. It should be able to execute the laws without opposition, and to controul all the turbulent spirits in the state, who should infringe them. If the laws are not obeyed, the legislative power is vain, and the judicial is mere pageantry. As these laws, with their several sanctions, are the only securities of person and property, the members of the state can confide in, if they lay dormant through failure of execution, violence and oppression will erect their heads, and stalk unmolested through the land. The judicial power ought to discriminate the offender, as soon after the commission of the offence, as an impartial trial will admit; and the executive arm to inflict the punishment immediately after the criminal is ascertained. This would have an happy tendency to prevent crimes, as the commission of them would awaken the attendant idea of punishment; and the hope of an escape, which is often an inducement, would be cut off. The executive power ought therefore in these cases, to be exerted with union, vigour, and dispatch. Another duty of that power is to arrest offenders, to bring them to trial. This cannot often be done, unless secrecy and expedition are used. The want of these two requisites, will be more especially inconvenient in repressing treasons, and those more enormous offences which strike at the happiness, if not existence of the whole. Offenders of these classes do not act alone. Some number is necessary to the compleating of the crime. Cabals are formed with art, and secrecy presides over their councils; while measures the most fatal are the result, to be executed by desperation. On these men the thunder of the state should be hurled with rapidity; for if they hear it roll at a distance, their danger is over. When they gain intelligence of the process, they abscond, and wait a more favourable opportunity. If that is attended with difficulty, they destroy all the evidence of their guilt, brave government, and deride the justice and power of the state.

It has been observed likewise, that the executive power is to act as Captain-General, to marshal the militia and armies of the state, and, for her defence, to lead them on to battle. These armies should always be composed of the militia or body of the people. Standing armies are a tremendous curse to a state. In all periods in which they have existed, they have been the scourge of mankind. In this department, union, vigour, secrecy, and dispatch are more peculiarly necessary. Was one to propose a body of militia, over which two Generals, with equal authority, should have the command, he would be laughed at. Should one pretend, that the General should have no controul over his subordinate officers, either to remove them or to supply their posts, he would be pitied for his ignorance of the subject he was discussing. It is obviously necessary, that the man who calls the militia to action, and assumes the military control over them in the field, should previously know the number of his men, their equipments and residence, and the talents and tempers of the several ranks of officers, and their respective departments in the state, that he may wisely determine to whom the necessary orders are to be issued. Regular and particular returns of these requisites should be frequently made. Let it be enquired, are these returns to be made only to the legislative body, or a branch of it, which necessarily moves slow?—Is the General to go to them for information? intreat them to remove an improper officer, and give him another they shall chuse? and in fine is he to supplicate his orders from them, and constantly walk where their leading-strings shall direct his steps? If so, where are the power and force of the militia—where the union—where the dispatch and profound secrecy? Or shall these returns be made to him?—when he may see with his own eyes—be his own judge of the merit, or demerit of his officers—discern their various talents and qualifications, and employ them as the service and defense of his country demand. Besides, the legislative body or a branch of it is local—they cannot therefore personally inform themselves of these facts, but must judge upon trust. The General's opinion will be founded upon his own observations—the officers and privates of the militia will act under his eye: and, if he has it in his power immediately to promote or disgrace them, they will be induced to noble exertions. It may further be observed here, that if the subordinate civil or military executive officers are appointed by the legislative body or a branch of it, the former will become dependent upon the latter, and the necessary independence of either the legislative or executive powers upon the other is wanting. The legislative power will have that undue influence over the executive which will amount to a controul, for the latter will be their creatures, and will fear their creators.

One further observation may be pertinent. Such is the temper of mankind, that each man will be too liable to introduce his own friends and connexions into office, without regarding the public interest. If one man or a small number appoint, their connexions will probably be introduced. If a large number appoint, all their connexions will receive the same favour. The smaller the number appointing, the more contracted are their connexions, and for that reason, there will be a greater probability of better officers, as the connexions of one man or a very small number can fill but a very few of the offices. When a small number of men have the power of appointment, or the management in any particular department, their conduct is accurately noticed. On any miscarriage or imprudence the public resentment lies with weight. All the eyes of the people are converted to a point, and produce that attention to their censure, and that fear of misbehaviour, which are the greatest security the state can have, of the wisdom and prudence of its servants. This observation will strike us, when we recollect that many a man will zealously promote an affair in a public assembly, of which he is but one of a large number, yet, at the same time, he would blush to be thought the sole author of it. For all these reasons, the supreme executive power should be rested in the hands of one or of a small number, who should have the appointment of all subordinate executive officers. Should the supreme executive officer be elected by the legislative body, there would be a dependence of the executive power upon the legislative. Should he be elected by the judicial body, there also would be a dependence. The people at large must therefore designate the person, to whom they will delegate this power. And upon the people, there ought to be a dependence of all the powers in government, for all the officers in the state are but the servants of the people.

We have not noticed the navy-department. The conducting of that department is indisputably in the supreme executive power: and we suppose, that all the observations respecting the Captain-General, apply to the Admiral.

We are next to fix upon some general rules which should govern us in forming the judicial power. This power is to be independent upon the executive and legislative. The judicial power should be a court and jury, or as they are commonly called, the Judges and the jury. The jury are the peers or equals of every man, and are to try all facts. The province of the Judges is to preside in and regulate all trials, and ascertain the law. We shall only consider the appointment of the Judges. The same power which appoints them, ought not to have the power of removing them, not even for misbehavior. That conduct only would then be deemed misbehavior which was opposed to the will of the power removing. A removal in this case for proper reasons, would not be often attainable: for to remove a man from an office, because he is not properly qualified to discharge the duties of it, is a severe censure upon that man or body of men who appointed him—and mankind do not love to censure themselves. Whoever appoints the judges, they ought not to be removable at pleasure, for they will then feel a dependence upon that man or body of men who hath the power of removal. Nor ought they to be dependent upon either the executive or legislative power for their sallaries; for if they are, that power on whom they are thus dependent, can starve them into a compliance. One of these two powers should appoint, and the other remove. The legislative will not probably appoint so good men as the executive, for reasons formerly mentioned. The former are composed of a large body of men who have a numerous train of friends and connexions, and they do not hazard their reputations, which the executive will. It has often been mentioned that where a large body of men are responsible for any measures, a regard to their reputations, and to the public opinion, will not prompt them to use that care and precaution, which such regard will prompt one or a few to make use of. Let one more observation be now introduced to confirm it. Every man has some friends and dependents who will endeavor to snatch him from the public hatred. One man has but a few comparatively, they are not numerous enough to protect him, and he falls a victim to his own misconduct. When measures are conducted by a large number, their friends and connexions are numerous and noisy—they are dispersed through the State—their clamors stifle the execrations of the people, whose groans cannot even be heard. But to resume, neither will the executive body be the most proper judge when to remove. If this body is judge, it must also be the accuser, or the legislative body, or a branch of it, must be—If the executive body complains, it will be both accuser and judge—If the complaint is preferred by the legislative body, or a branch of it, when the judges are appointed by the legislative body, then a body of men who were concerned in the appointment, must in most cases complain of the impropriety of their own appointment.

Let therefore the judges be appointed by the executive body—let their salaries be independent—and let them hold their places during good behaviour—Let their misbehaviour be determinable by the legislative body—Let one branch thereof impeach, and the other judge. Upon these principles the judicial body will be independent so long as they behave well and a proper court is appointed to ascertain their mal-conduct.

The Committee afterwards proceeded to consider the Constitution framed by the Convention of this State. They have examined that Constitution with all the care the shortness of the time would admit. And they are compelled, though reluctantly to say, that some of the principles upon which it is founded, appeared to them inconsonant, not only to the natural rights of mankind, but to the fundamental condition of the original social contract, and the principles of a free republican government. . . .

The committee have now compleated the general outlines of a constitution, which they suppose may be conformable to the principles of a free republican government—They have not attempted the description of the less important parts of a constitution, as they naturally and obviously are determinable by attention to those principles—Neither do they exhibit these general out lines, as the only ones which can be consonant to the natural rights of mankind, to the fundamental terms of the original social contract, and to the principles of political justice; for they do not assume to themselves infallibility. To compleat the task assigned them by this body, this constitution is held up in a general view, to convince us of the practicability of enjoying a free republican government, in which our natural rights are attended to, in which the original social contract is observed, and in which political justice governs; and also to justify us in our objections to the constitution proposed by the convention of this state, which we have taken the liberty to say is, in our apprehension, in some degree deficient in those respects.

To balance a large society on republican or general laws, is a work of so great difficulty, that no human genius, however comprehensive, is perhaps able, by the mere dint of reason and reflection, to effect it. The penetrating and dispassionate judgments of many must unite in this work: experience must guide their labour: time must bring it to perfection: and the feeling of inconveniencies must correct the mistakes which they will probably fall into, in their first trials and experiments.

The plan which the preceeding observations were intended to exhibit in a general view, is now compleated. The principles of a free republican form of government have been attempted, some reasons in support of them have been mentioned, the outlines of a constitution have been delineated in conformity to them, and the objections to the form of government proposed by the general convention have been stated.

. . . The committee are sensible, that the spirit of a free republican constitution, or the moving power which should give it action, ought to be political virtue, patriotism, and a just regard to the natural rights of mankind.

This spirit, if wanting, can be obtained only from that Being, who infused the breath of Life into our first parent. . .

SOURCE: Extracts from Convention of Delegates and Theophilus Parsons. Result of the Convention of Delegates: Holden At Ipswich In the County of Essex, Who Were Deputed to Take Into Consideration the Constitution And Form of Government, Proposed by the Convention of the State of Massachusetts-Bay. (Newbury-Port: Printed and sold by John Mycall, 1778), 8-41, 66-67, 67-68.

PART TWO:

CREATING A WRITTEN CONSTITUTION AS FUNDAMENTAL LAW

1. MASSACHUSETTS CIRCULAR LETTER TO THE COLONIAL LEGISLATURES
FEBRUARY 11, 1768

Written by Samuel Adams and James Otis, Jr. and passed by the Massachusetts House of Representatives in 1768, the Massachusetts Circular Letter was written in response to the recently passed Townshend Acts. The Massachusetts Letter was circulated to the legislatures of the other colonies, where it was favorably received by American Patriots. The Circular Letter is important because it showed how colonial Americans viewed the British constitution, and, more importantly, how they began to develop a new understanding of what a constitution is. The traditional British constitution was simply an assemblage of statutory and common laws along with the forms and formalities of the extant government. The Americans were beginning to see that constitutions should be written, fixed, and grounded in fundamental moral principles. Most importantly, the Massachusetts Circular Letter suggests that constitutions precede governments, not the other way around as was the case with the British constitution.

The House of Representatives of this province have taken into their serious consideration the great difficulties that must accrue to themselves and their constituents by the operation of several Acts of Parliament, imposing duties and taxes on the American colonies.

As it is a subject in which every colony is deeply interested, they have no reason to doubt but your house is deeply impressed with its importance, and that such constitutional measures will be come into as are proper. It seems to be necessary that all possible care should be taken that the representatives of the several assemblies, upon so delicate a point, should harmonize with each other. The House, therefore, hope that this letter will be candidly considered in no other light than as expressing a disposition freely to communicate their mind to a sister colony, upon a common concern, in the same manner as they would be glad to receive the sentiments of your or any other house of assembly on the continent.

The House have humbly represented to the ministry their own sentiments, that his Majesty's high court of Parliament is the supreme legislative power over the whole empire; that in all free states the constitution is fixed, and as the supreme legislative derives its power and authority from the constitution, it cannot overleap the bounds of it without destroying its own foundation; that the constitution ascertains and limits both sovereignty and allegiance, and, therefore, his Majesty's American subjects, who acknowledge themselves bound by the ties of allegiance, have an equitable claim to the full enjoyment of the fundamental rules of the British constitution; that it is an essential, unalterable right in nature, engrafted into the British constitution, as a fundamental law, and ever held sacred and irrevocable by the subjects within the realm, that what a man has honestly acquired is absolutely his own, which he may freely give, but cannot be taken from him without his consent; that the American subjects may, therefore, exclusive of any consideration of charter rights, with a decent firmness, adapted to the character of free men and subjects, assert this natural and constitutional right.

It is, moreover, their humble opinion, which they express with the greatest deference to the wisdom of the Parliament, that the Acts made there, imposing duties on the people of this province, with the sole and express purpose of raising a revenue, are infringements of their natural and constitutional rights; because, as they are not represented in the British Parliament, his Majesty's commons in Britain, by those Acts, grant their property without their consent.

This House further are of opinion that their constituents, considering their local circumstances, cannot, by any possibility, be represented in the Parliament; and that it will forever be impracticable, that they should be equally represented there, and consequently, not at all; being separated by an ocean of a thousand leagues. That his Majesty's royal predecessors, for this reason, were graciously pleased to form a subordinate legislature here, that their subjects might enjoy the unalienable right of a representation; also, that considering the utter impracticability of their ever being fully and equally represented in Parliament, and the great expense that must unavoidably attend even a partial representation there, this House think that a taxation of their constituents, even without their consent, grievous as it is, would be preferable to any representation that could be admitted for them there.

Upon these principles, and also considering that were the right in Parliament ever so clear, yet, for obvious reasons, it would be beyond the rules of equity that their constituents should be taxed on the manufactures of Great Britain here, in addition to the duties they pay for them in England, and other advantages arising to Great Britain, from the Acts of trade, this House have preferred a humble, dutiful, and loyal petition, to our most gracious sovereign, and made such representations to his Majesty's ministers, as they apprehended would tend to obtain redress. They have also submitted to consideration, whether any people can be said to enjoy any degree of freedom if the Crown, in addition to its undoubted authority of constituting a governor, should appoint him such a stipend as it may judge proper, without the consent of the people, and at their expense; and whether, while the judges of the land, and other civil officers, hold not their commissions during good behaviour, their having salaries appointed for them by the Crown, independent of the people, hath not a tendency to subvert the principles of equity, and endanger the happiness and security of the subject.

In addition to these measures, the House have written a letter to their agent which he is directed to lay before the ministry; wherein they take notice of the hardships of the Act for preventing mutiny and desertion, which requires the governor and council to provide enumerated articles for the king's marching troops, and the people to pay the expenses; and also, the commission of the gentlemen appointed commissioners of the customs, to reside in America, which authorizes them to make as many appointments as they think fit, and to pay the appointees what sum they please, for whose malconduct they are not accountable; from whence it may happen that officers of the Crown may be multiplied to such a degree as to become dangerous to the liberty of the people, by virtue of a commission, which does not appear to this House to derive any such advantages to trade as many have supposed.

These are the sentiments and proceedings of this House; and as they have too much reason to believe that the enemies of the colonies have represented them to his Majesty's ministers, and to the Parliament, as factious, disloyal, and having a disposition to make themselves independent of the mother country, they have taken occasion, in the most humble terms, to assure his Majesty, and his ministers, that, with regard to the people of this province, and, as they doubt not, of all the colonies, the charge is unjust. The House is fully satisfied that your assembly is too generous and liberal in sentiment to believe that this letter proceeds from an ambition of taking the lead, or dictating to the other assemblies. They freely submit their opinions to the judgment of others; and shall take it kind in your house to point out to them anything further that may be thought necessary.

This House cannot conclude, without expressing their firm confidence in the king, our common head and father, that the united and dutiful supplications of his distressed American subjects will meet with his royal and favourable acceptance.

SOURCE: Reprinted in its entirety from Harry Alonzo Cushing (ed.), *The Writings of Samuel Adams* (1904-1908), I: 184-188.

2. JOHN ADAMS ON CREATING STATE CONSTITUTIONS AS FUNDAMENTAL LAW

John Adams (1735-1826) spent his post-presidency retirement years reading, thinking, and corresponding with friends. As a central actor in the American Revolution from beginning to end, Adams also devoted a great deal of his time thinking about the causes, nature, and meaning of the Revolution. On October 5, 1802, Adams started to write his autobiography. Naturally, much of his life's story was devoted to his participation in the movement for independence. The selection below is notable because it demonstrates that Adams was one of the first Americans, if not the first (as early as July 1775), to promote the idea of special constitutional conventions distinct from regular legislative bodies as the primary and necessary vehicle by which to draft the revolutionary state constitutions. He believed that republican constitutions should be grounded in the will of the people rather than on the interests of those in power.

SELECTION FROM HIS *AUTOBIOGRAPHY*

It is necessary that I should be a little more particular, in relating the rise and progress of the new government of the States.

On Friday, June 2d, 1775, "The President laid before Congress a letter from the Provincial Convention of Massachusetts Bay, dated May 16th, which was read, setting forth the difficulties they labor under for want of a regular form of government, and as they and the other Colonies are now compelled to raise an army to defend themselves from the butcheries and devastations of their implacable enemies, which renders it still more necessary to have a regular established government, requesting the Congress to favor them with explicit advice respecting the taking up and exercising the powers of civil government, and declaring their readiness to submit to such a general plan as the Congress may direct for the Colonies, or make it their great study to establish such a form of government there as shall not only promote their advantage, but the union and interest of all America."

This subject had engaged much of my attention before I left Massachusetts, and had been frequently the subject of conversation between me and many of my friends,—Dr. Winthrop, Dr. Cooper, Colonel Otis, the two Warrens, Major Hawley, and others, besides my colleagues in Congress,—and lay with great weight upon my mind, as the most difficult and dangerous business that we had to do; (for from the beginning, I always expected we should have more difficulty and danger, in our attempts to govern ourselves, and in our negotiations and connections with foreign powers, than from all the fleets and armies of Great Britain.) It lay, therefore, with great weight upon my mind, and when this letter was read, I embraced the opportunity to open myself in Congress, and most earnestly to entreat the serious attention of all the members, and of all the continent, to the measures which the times demanded. For my part, I thought there was great wisdom in the adage, "when the sword is drawn, throw away the scabbard." Whether we threw it away voluntarily or not, it was useless now, and would be useless forever. The pride of Britain, flushed with late triumphs and conquests, their infinite contempt of all the power of America, with an insolent, arbitrary Scotch faction, with a Bute and Mansfield at their head for a ministry, we might depend upon it, would force us to call forth every energy and resource of the country, to seek the friendship of England's enemies, and we had no rational hope, but from the *Ratio ultima regum et rerum-publicarum.* These efforts could not be made without government, and as I supposed no man would think of consolidating this vast continent under one national government, we should probably, after the example of the Greeks, the Dutch, and the Swiss, form a confederacy of States, each of which must have a separate government. That the case of Massachusetts was the most urgent, but that it could not be long before every other Colony must follow her example. That with a view to this subject, I had looked into the ancient and modern confederacies for examples, but they all appeared to me to have been huddled up in a hurry, by a few chiefs. But we had a people of more intelligence, curiosity, and enterprise, who must be all consulted, and we must realize the theories of the wisest writers, and invite the people to erect the whole building with their own hands, upon the broadest foundation. That this could be done only by conventions of representatives chosen by the people in the several colonies, in the most exact proportions. That it was my opinion that Congress ought now to recommend to the people of every Colony to call such conventions immediately, and set up governments of their own, under their own authority; for the people were the source of all authority and original of all power. These were new, strange, and terrible doctrines to the greatest part of the members, but not a very small number heard them with apparent pleasure, and none more than Mr. John Rutledge, of South Carolina, and Mr. John Sullivan, of New Hampshire.

Congress, however, ordered the letter to lie on the table for further consideration. On Saturday, June 3d, the letter from the convention of the Massachusetts Bay, dated the 16th of May, being again read, the subject was again discussed, and then, *"Resolved,* That a committee of five persons be chosen, to consider the same, and report what in their opinion is the proper advice to be given to that Convention."

The following persons were chosen by ballot, to compose that committee, namely, Mr. J. Rutledge, Mr. Johnson, Mr. Jay, Mr. Wilson, and Mr. Lee. These gentlemen had several conferences with the delegates from our State, in the course of which, I suppose, the hint was suggested, that they adopted in their report.

On Wednesday, June 7th, "On motion, Resolved, That Thursday, the 20th of July next, be observed throughout the twelve United Colonies as a day of humiliation, fasting, and prayer; and that Mr. Hooper, Mr. J. Adams, and Mr. Paine, be a committee to bring in a resolve for that purpose.

"The committee appointed to prepare advice, in answer to the letter from the Convention of Massachusetts Bay, brought in their report, which was read and ordered to lie on the table for consideration.

"On Friday, June 9th. the report of the committee on the letter from the Convention of Massachusetts Bay being again read, the Congress came into the following resolution.

"Resolved, That no obedience being due to the Act of Parliament for altering the charter of the Colony of Massachusetts Bay, nor to a Governor or Lieutenant-Governor who will not observe the directions of, but endeavor to subvert, that charter, the Governor and Lieutenant-Governor of that Colony are to be considered as absent, and their offices vacant; and as there is no Council there, and the inconveniences arising from the suspension of the powers of government are intolerable, especially at a time when General Gage hath actually levied war, and is carrying on hostilities against his Majesty's peaceable and loyal subjects of that Colony; that, in order to conform as near as may be to the spirit and substance of the charter, it be recommended to the Provincial Convention to write letters to the inhabitants of the several places, which are entitled to representation in Assembly, requesting them to choose such representatives, and that the Assembly when chosen do elect Counsellors; and that such assembly or Council exercise the powers of government, until a Governor of His Majesty's appointment will consent to govern the Colony according to its charter.

"Ordered, That the President transmit a copy of the above to the Convention of Massachusetts Bay."

Although this advice was in a great degree conformable to the New York and Pennsylvania system, or in other words, to the system of Mr. Dickinson and Mr. Duane, I thought it an acquisition, for it was a precedent of advice to the separate States to institute governments, and I doubted not we should soon have more occasions to follow this example. Mr. John Rutledge and Mr. Sullivan had frequent conversations with me upon this subject. Mr. Rutledge asked me my opinion of a proper form of government for a State. I answered him that any form that our people would consent to institute, would be better than none, even if they placed all power in a house of representatives, and they should appoint governors and judges; but I hoped they would be wiser, and preserve the English Constitution in its spirit and substance, as far as the circumstances of this country required or would admit. That no hereditary powers ever had existed in America, nor would they, or ought they to be introduced or proposed; but that I hoped the three branches of a legislature would be preserved, an executive, independent of the senate or council, and the house, and above all things, the independence of the judges. Mr. Sullivan was fully agreed with me in the necessity of instituting governments, and he seconded me very handsomely in supporting the argument in Congress. Mr. Samuel Adams was with us in the opinion of the necessity, and was industrious in conversation with the members out of doors, but he very rarely spoke much in Congress, and he was perfectly unsettled in any plan to be recommended to a State, always inclining to the most democratical forms, and even to a single sovereign assembly, until his constituents afterwards in Boston compelled him to vote for three branches. Mr. Cushing was also for one sovereign assembly, and Mr. Paine was silent and reserved upon the subject, at least to me.

Not long after this, Mr. John Rutledge returned to South Carolina, and Mr. Sullivan went with General Washington to Cambridge, so that I lost two of my able coadjutors. But we soon found the benefit of their cooperation at a distance.

On Wednesday, October 18th, the delegates from New Hampshire laid before the Congress a part of the instructions delivered to them by their Colony, in these words:—"We would have you immediately use your utmost endeavors to obtain the advice and direction of the Congress, with respect to a method for our administering justice, and regulating our civil police. We press you not to delay this matter, as its being done speedily will probably prevent the greatest confusion among us."

This instruction might have been obtained by Mr. Langdon, or Mr. Whipple, but I always supposed it was General Sullivan who suggested the measure, because he left Congress with a stronger impression upon his mind of the importance of it, than I ever observed in either of the others. Be this, however, as it may have been, I embraced with joy the opportunity of haranguing on the subject at large, and of urging Congress to resolve on a general recommendation to all the States to call conventions and institute regular governments. I reasoned from various topics, many of which, perhaps, I could not now recollect. Some I remember; as,

1. The danger to the morals of the people from the present loose state of things, and general relaxation of laws and government through the Union.

2. The danger of insurrections in some of the most disaffected parts of the Colonies, in favor of the enemy, or as they called them, the mother country, an expression that I thought it high time to erase out of our language.

3. Communications and intercourse with the enemy, from various parts of the continent could not be wholly prevented, while any of the powers of government remained in the hands of the King's servants.

4. It could not well be considered as a crime to communicate intelligence, or to act as spies or guides to the enemy, without assuming all the powers of government.

5. The people of America would never consider our Union as complete, but our friends would always suspect divisions among us, and our enemies who were scattered in larger or smaller numbers, not only in every State and city, but in every village through the whole Union, would forever represent Congress as divided and ready to break to pieces, and in this way would intimidate and discourage multitudes of our people who wished us well.

6. The absurdity of carrying on war against a king, when so many persons were daily taking oaths and affirmations of allegiance to him.

7. We could not expect that our friends in Great Britain would believe us united and in earnest, or exert themselves very strenuously in our favor, while we acted such a wavering, hesitating part.

8. Foreign nations, particularly France and Spain, would not think us worthy of their attention while we appeared to be deceived by such fallacious hopes of redress of grievances, of pardon for our offences, and of reconciliation with our enemies.

9. We could not command the natural resources of our own country. We could not establish manufactories of arms, cannon, saltpetre, powder, ships, &c., without the powers of government; and all these and many other preparations ought to be going on in every State or Colony, if you will, in the country.

Although the opposition was still inveterate, many members of Congress began to hear me with more patience, and some began to ask me civil questions. "How can the people institute governments?" My answer was, "By conventions of representatives, freely, fairly, and proportionably chosen." "When the convention has fabricated a government, or a constitution rather, how do we know the people will submit to it?" "If there is any doubt of that, the convention may send out their project of a constitution, to the people in their several towns, counties, or districts, and the people may make the acceptance of it their own act." "But the people know nothing about constitutions." "I believe you are much mistaken in that supposition; if you are not, they will not oppose a plan prepared by their own chosen friends; but I believe that in every considerable portion of the people, there will be found some men, who will understand the subject as well as their representatives, and these will assist in enlightening the rest." "But what plan of a government would you advise?" "A plan as nearly resembling the government under which we were born, and have lived, as the circumstances of the country will admit. Kings we never had among us. Nobles we never had. Nothing hereditary ever existed in the country; nor will the country require or admit of any such thing. But governors and councils we have always had, as well as representatives. A legislature in three branches ought to be preserved, and independent judges." "Where and how will you get your governors and councils?" "By elections." "How,—who shall elect?" "The representatives of the people in a convention will be the best qualified to contrive a mode."

After all these discussions and interrogatories, Congress was not prepared nor disposed to do any thing as yet. They must consider farther.

"*Resolved*, That the consideration of this matter be referred to Monday next.

Monday arrived, and Tuesday and Wednesday passed over, and Congress not yet willing to do any thing.

On Thursday, October 26th, the subject was again brought on the carpet, and the same discussions repeated; for very little new was produced. After a long discussion, in which Mr. John Rutledge, Mr. Ward, Mr. Lee, Mr. Gadsden, Mr. Sherman, Mr. Dyer, and some others had spoken on the same side with me, Congress resolved, that a committee of five members be appointed to take into consideration the instructions given to the delegates of New Hampshire, and report their opinion thereon. The members chosen,—Mr. John Rutledge, Mr. J. Adams, Mr. Ward, Mr. Lee, and Mr. Sherman.

Although this committee was entirely composed of members as well disposed to encourage the enterprise as could have been found in Congress, yet they could not be brought to agree upon a report and to bring it forward in Congress, till Friday, November 3d, when Congress, taking into consideration the report of the committee on the New Hampshire instructions, after another long deliberation and debate,—"Resolved, That it be recommended to the Provincial Convention of New Hampshire, to call a full and free representation of the people, and that the representatives, if they think it necessary, establish such a form of government, as in their judgment will best produce the happiness of the people, and most effectually secure peace and good order in the Province, during the continuance of the present dispute between Great Britain and the Colonies."

By this time I mortally hated the words, "Province," "Colonies," and "Mother Country," and strove to get them out of the report. The last was indeed left out, but the other two were retained even by this committee, who were all as high Americans as any in the house, unless Mr. Gadsden should be excepted. Nevertheless, I thought this resolution a triumph, and a most important point gained.

Mr. John Rutledge was now completely with us in our desire of revolutionizing all the governments, and he brought forward immediately some representations from his own State, when "Congress, then taking into consideration the State of South Carolina, and sundry papers relative thereto being read and considered.

"*Resolved*, That a committee of five be appointed to take the same into consideration, and report what in their opinion is necessary to be done. The members chosen, Mr. Harrison, Mr. Bullock, Mr. Hooper, Mr. Chase, and Mr. S. Adams.

On November 4th, "The committee appointed to take into consideration the State of South Carolina, brought in their report, which being read," a number of resolutions passed, the last of which will be found in page 235 of the Journals, at the bottom.

"*Resolved*, That if the Convention of South Carolina shall find it necessary to establish a form of government in that Colony, it be recommended to that Convention to call a full and free representation of the people, and that the said representatives, if they think it necessary, shall establish such a form of government as in their judgment will produce the happiness of the people, and most effectually secure peace and good order in the Colony, during the continuance of the present dispute between Great Britain and the Colonies.

Although Mr. John Rutledge united with me and others, in persuading the committee to report this resolution, and the distance of Carolina made it convenient to furnish them with this discretionary recommendation, I doubt whether Mr. Harrison or Mr. Hooper were, as yet, sufficiently advanced to agree to it. Mr. Bullock, Mr. Chase, and Mr. Samuel Adams, were very ready for it. When it was under consideration, I labored afresh to expunge the words "Colony," and "Colonies," and insert the words "State," and "States," and the word "dispute," to make way for that of "war," and the word "Colonies," for the word "America," or "States," but the child was not yet weaned. I labored, also, to get the resolution enlarged, and extended into a recommendation to the people of all the States, to institute governments, and this occasioned more interrogatories from one part and another of the House. "What plan of government would you recommend?" &c. Here it would have been the most natural to have made a motion that Congress should appoint a committee to prepare a plan of government, to be reported to Congress and there discussed, paragraph by paragraph, and that which should be adopted should be recommended to all the States. But I dared not make such a motion, because I knew that if such a plan was adopted it would be, if not permanent, yet of long duration, and it would be extremely difficult to get rid of it. And I knew that every one of my friends, and all those who were the most zealous for assuming governments, had at that time no idea of any other government but a contemptible legislature in one assembly, with committees for executive magistrates and judges. These questions, therefore, I answered by sporting off hand a variety of short sketches of plans, which might be adopted by the conventions; and as this subject was brought into view in some way or other almost every day, and these interrogatories were frequently repeated, I had in my head and at my tongue's end as many projects of government as Mr. Burke says the Abbé Sieyes had in his pigeon-holes, not however, constructed at such length, nor labored with his-metaphysical refinements. I took care, however, always to bear my testimony against every plan of an unbalanced government.

I had read Harrington, Sidney, Hobbes, Nedham, and Locke, but with very little application to any particular views, till these debates in Congress, and the interrogatories in public and private, turned my thoughts to these researches, which produced the "Thoughts on Government," the

Constitution of Massachusetts, and at length the "Defence of the Constitutions of the United States," and the "Discourses on Davila," writings which have never done any good to me, though some of them undoubtedly contributed to produce the Constitution of New York, the Constitution of the United States, and the last Constitutions of Pennsylvania and Georgia. They undoubtedly, also, contributed to the writings of Publius, called the Federalist, which were all written after the publication of my work in Philadelphia, New York, and Boston. Whether the people will permit any of these Constitutions to stand upon their pedestals, or whether they will throw them all down, I know not. Appearances at present are unfavorable and threatening. I have done all in my power according to what I thought my duty. I can do no more.

SOURCE: John Adams, *Autobiography*, in *The Works of John Adams, Second President of the United States: . . . by his Grandson Charles Francis Adams*, 10 vols. (Boston: Little, Brown and Co., 1856): 3: 12-23.

3. [ANONYMOUS]

"SERIOUS QUESTIONS PROPOSED TO ALL FRIENDS TO THE RIGHTS OF MANKIND, WITH SUITABLE ANSWERS"

1776

Throughout 1776, Pennsylvania was one of the most intellectually and politically engaged provinces and then states to consider the question of constitution-making and political forms. The subjects and then the citizens of Pennsylvania, along with those of Massachusetts, took the lead in thinking about and then developing the processes for establishing new constitutions. First published in The Pennsylvania Evening Post in May 1776, a few months before the drafting of the Pennsylvania constitution, this newspaper article is one of the few written during the revolutionary era in the form of a catechism. The question-and-answer format forces the anonymous author to state in brief and poignant terms the barest essentials of how to create a constitution and the forms and formalities that should govern its structure. The result is a fast-paced and hard-hitting piece that would give Pennsylvania constitution-makers readily accessible talking points. The single most interesting and important principle enunciated by the author of "Serious Questions" is the identification of a special process by which constitutions should be drafted, revised, ratified, and instituted. "Serious Questions" rejects the idea that sitting legislators under the old government should design and build the new constitution. Instead, Pennsylvania's new constitution must be drafted by a special constitutional convention consisting of those men in the province with the "the greatest wisdom and integrity," after which the body must be disbanded immediately and the constitution-makers returned to ordinary life. The drafted constitution must then be published and made available around the state so that every man has the opportunity to see it and comment on it. The original constitutional convention (with a few added members) would then reconvene and amend the proposed constitution, after which time it would become the law of the land. Interestingly, the author of "Serious Questions" also suggests that a special "Committee of Inquiry" be established that would meet every three years to determine if the constitution has been violated in any way. Interestingly, "Serious Questions" was republished in Boston in 1787 as the state was considering whether to ratify the federal constitution.

Serious QUESTIONS proposed to all friends to the rights of mankind, with suitable Answers.

Q. What is government?

A. Certain powers vested by society in public persons for the security, peace and happiness of its members.

Q. What ought a society to do to secure a good government?

A. Any thing. The happiness of man, as an inhabitant of this world, depends entirely upon it.

Q. When ought a new government to be established?

A. When the old becomes impracticable, or dangerous to the rights of the people.

Q. Who ought to form a new constitution of government?

A. The people.

Q. From whom ought public persons to derive their authority to govern?

A. From the people whom they are to govern.

Q. What ought to be the object of government?

A. The welfare of the governed.

Q. How is such a government to be obtained?

A. By forming a constitution which regards men more than things, by framing it in such a manner that the interest of the governours and governed shall ever be the same; and by delegating the powers of government so that the people may always have it in their power to resume them, when abused, without tumult or confusion, and to deliver them to persons more worthy of trust.

Q. Should the officers of the old constitution be entrusted with the power of making a new one when it becomes necessary?

A. No. Bodies of men have the same selfish attachments as individuals, and they will be claiming powers and prerogatives inconsistent with the liberties of the people. Aristocracies will by this means be established, and we shall exchange a bad constitution for a worse, or the tyranny of one for the tyranny of many.

Q. Who ought to have such a trust conferred upon them, as it is the highest and most important which men can delegate?

A. First, Men of the greatest wisdom and integrity, who have as much, if not more, natural than acquired sense and understanding. Secondly, Men who can be under no temptations to frame political distinctions in favour of any class or set of men. Thirdly, Men who the moment the constitution is framed, must descend into the common paths of life, and have as great a chance to feel every defect in the constitution as any man. And lastly, Men who regard not the person of the rich, nor despise the state of the poor, but who prefer justice and equity to all things, and would go any lengths to establish the common rights of mankind on the firmest foundation.

Q. Ought the constitution which a proper number of such persons agree upon to be immediately adopted?

A. No. After agreeing upon a constitution, or form of government, they ought to adjourn for six or nine months, publish the plan, request every man to examine it with the utmost seriousness and attention, make remarks upon it, point out any defects which may appear in it, and offer amendments. Then let the same body of men who framed it, joined by an additional number of new members, meet at the time fixed in their adjournment, canvass the whole again, take the defects pointed out into consideration, and finally agree.—N. B. This frame of government, when agreed upon, should be intituled the Social Compact of the People of —, &c. and should be unalterable in every point, except by a delegation of the same kind of that which originally framed it, appointed for that purpose.

Q. What should be done after this compact is finally agreed upon?

A. The same, or another body of men, should be appointed to draw up what I shall call *a charter of delegation,* being a clear and full description of the quantity and degree of power and authority, with which the society, vests the persons instructed with the power of the society, whether civil or military, legislative, executive or judicial.

Q. Is this all that is necessary to secure a good government?

A. If the legislative be so constituted as never to be able to form an interest of its own separate from the interest of the community at large; if its branches are independent of and balance each other, and all dependant on the people, and if it has the power of calling the executive and judicial branches to account for mal-administration, it might do; but I should propose the addition of a Committee of Inquiry to be chosen every third year, whole authority should extend to the examination of all laws passed within that space of time, to see if any infringed upon the *Social Compact,* to inquire into the application of the public money, and the conduct of all officers whether legislative, executive, or judicial; particularly to see that no branch of the legislature exceed the bounds prescribed to it in the *Charter of Delegation;* to sit in judgment on the delinquent, and they, whom the Committee condemned, should be declared incapable of holding any office of power and trust in the society. This Committee should exist only for six months at most, and should have power to recommend any alteration or amendment of any article in the *Charter of Delegation,* which, by experience, should be found defective or dangerous; which alteration or amendment should be made by a body of men delegated for the purpose, in the same manner as the *Original Compact.* N. B. One article in the original compact should be, that all virtuous men, who believe in a God, should be equally capable of holding any office, for which he was qualified, upon the choice of the people. Nothing but Atheism or open immorality to exclude any man.

Q. Granting the foregoing plan to be just and right, how may it be obtained?

A. By the virtues and unanimity of the people, particularly those who have arms in their hands.

A. Will they be unanimous in establishing a perfectly free government?

A. The people themselves can best answer this question. They began the contest for the sake of freedom, and it is both their duty and interest. Men of sinister views and designs will endeavour to sow divisions. They will lay hold on the bigotry of some, the religious prejudices of others, and the ignorance of a third sort. A few families will endeavour to get all power into their hands, and form an oligarchy or aristocracy. Most nations, who have shaken off royal tyranny, have been enslaved by an aristocracy or oligarchy, which is much worse, purely by leaving the business of framing a constitution to the officers of the old government. They, setting up an interest of their own in opposition to that of the people, formed an aristocracy. For my part I should think it a good precaution to exclude all those who frame the constitution from ever holding any office under it. This should be esteemed so high and sacred a trust, that the man who was thought worthy to frame it, should be forbid ever to degrade himself by holding any office whatever. These things, next to the salvation of our souls, should engage our attention. The first settlers of this province formed a compact with William Penn nearly of this kind, but he artfully got them to give it up. Their will and steady opposition to his encroachments cannot be sufficiently commended. I should expect much from the virtue of their descendants, if they could be persuaded to lay aside groundless fears and jealousies, and heartily to join in correcting and reforming a constitution against the defects of which they have long contended. They have now the only opportunity which, perhaps, will ever be offered them.

SOURCE: [Anonymous], "Serious Questions Proposed to All Friends to the Rights of Mankind in Pennsylvania, with Suitable Answers." *Pennsylvania Evening Post* (Philadelphia, Pennsylvania) II, no. 206, May 16, 1776: 245. *Readex: America's Historical Newspapers.*

4. [ANONYMOUS]
"THE ALARM: OR AN ADDRESS TO THE PEOPLE OF PENNSYLVANIA, ON THE LATE RESOLVE OF CONGRESS, FOR TOTALLY SUPPRESSING ALL POWER AND AUTHORITY DERIVED FROM THE CROWN OF GREAT-BRITAIN."
1776

The American Revolution was a world transformative event. It changed everything in America. Gone were the old charters and colonial governments with their ties to the British crown. In fact, starting in 1774, many colonies found themselves without legally functioning governments. Various governors either resigned or were chased out of office. In many ways, the Americans were in government-less state, or what the seventeenth-century English philosopher, John Locke, described as a "state of nature." As Patrick Henry announced in the Continental Congress in 1774: "Government is dissolved, . . . We are in a State of Nature." In addition to fighting a war, the former colonists had to construct governments to fight the war. But how should they construction their governments, and who should do the designing and constructing? In the spring of 1776, the Continental Congress passed a resolution calling on the separate colonies to write new constitutions for the soon-to-be new states. The obvious choice to construct the new constitutions were the extant revolutionary legislatures, but this solution raised difficult problems. If a formal or informal legislative body were to design and construct a constitution that would suggest that the creating legislature would be superior to its creation, and what a superior may create it may also change or destroy. The anonymous author of "The Alarm," which was published in Philadelphia, argued that constitutions should be drafted by special conventions elected for that purpose and not by a sitting legislature. Over the course of the next few years, the Americans would figure a method by which to make their constitutions a "higher" law not subject to legislative tinkering.

The long continued injuries and insults, which the Continent of America hath sustained from the cruel power of the British Court, and the disadvantages, which the several provinces in the mean time labour under from the want of a permanent form of government, by which they might in a proper constitutional manner of their own, afford protection to themselves, have at length risen to such an height, as to make it appear necessary to the

Honourable Continental Congress to issue a Resolve, recommending it to the several Colonies to take up and establish new governments *on the authority of the people,*" in lieu of those old ones which were established on the authority of the Crown.

This, Fellow Countrymen, is the situation we now stand in, and the matter for your immediate consideration, is simply this: Who are, or who are not, the proper persons to be entrusted with carrying the said Resolve into execution, in what is the most eligible mode of authorizing such persons? for unless they have the full authority of the people for the *especial* purpose, any government modelled by them will not stand.

Men of interested view and dangerous designs may tell you, *The House of Assembly:* But be not deceived by the tinkling of a name, for either such an House does not now exist, or if it does exist, it is by an unconstitutional power, for as the people have not *yet,* by any public act of theirs, transferred to them any new authority necessary to qualify them agreeable to the sense and expression of Congress, which says, "on the Authority of the People," they consequently have none other than what is either immediately derived from, or conveyed to them in consequence of, the royal charter of our enemy, and this, saith the Honourable Congress, *"should be totally suppressed".* Wherefore, in compliance with this advice and recommendation of Congress, it is proposed to enter a public protest, in order to *suppress it,* for legislative bodies of men have no more the power of suppressing the authority they sit by, than they have of creating it, otherwise every legislative body would have the power of suppressing a constitution at will; it is an act which can only be *done to them,* but cannot be done *by them.* Were the present House of Assembly to be suffered by their own *act* to suppress the *old* authority derived from the Crown, they might afterwards suppress the *new* authority received from the people, and thus by continually making and unmaking themselves at pleasure, leave the people at last no right at all. The power from which the new authority is to be derived, is the only power which can properly suppress the old one. Thus, Fellow Countrymen, you are called upon by the standing law of nature and reason, and by the sense of the Honourable Congress, to assert your natural rights, by entering your protest against the authority of the present House of Assembly, in order that a new government, founded "on the authority of the people," may be established.

Until the authority of the Crown, by which the present House of Assembly sits, be suppressed, the House is not qualified to carry the Resolve of Congress, respecting a new government, into execution, and after the House is suppressed, it will be again disqualified, for the want of new authority, for in that case it will be no House at all: Wherefore, both before and after suppression, the present House of Assembly cannot be adequate to the purpose of establishing a new government.

Besides, if a review of the past conduct of the House of Assembly be attended to, it will appear that they are a third time disqualified, in consequence of their own resolve. The unwise and impolitic instructions which they have arbitrarily imposed on the Delegates for this province, and confirmed at their last sitting, forbidding them in the strongest and most positive terms to consent to any change of government, should such be moved for in Congress, amount to a protest against the matter itself contained in the aforesaid resolve of Congress, and have even a reasonable tendency towards disolving the happy union of the colonies, for the Delegates, conceiving themselves bound by those instructions, sat as cyphers in Congress when the loud resolve was passed, declaring that they could not vote thereon, on which ground the term "Assemblies," mentioned in the said resolve of Congress, cannot be applied, as to the purpose of forming new governments, to the Pennsylvania House of Assembly, because it withdrew from the resolve by the neutrality of its Delegates, yet, altho' the Assembly is not included within the resolve itself, as to the exercise of new powers, it is included within the *Preamble* to the resolve, which, without regard to any distinct bodies of men, recommends generally that all the old powers of government be *totally suppressed,* and that new ones be erected on the "authority of the people." And thus far, and no farther, is the Pennsylvania House of Assembly within the sense both of the preamble and the resolve of Congress.

In this situation, what is to be done? The union of the Colonies is not only our glory, but our protection, and altho' the House of Assembly hath outwitted itself, it is no reason that the Province should: Wherefore, in order to restore ourselves to our former Continental rank, which we lost in Congress by not being represented in that resolve; and in order, likewise, that the people of this province may be put into a proper capacity of carrying the said resolve of Congress into execution, we must refer to the second term mentioned therein, viz. *Conventions,* for, even admitting that the present House of Assembly was a proper body, yet, the people may choose which they please, for both are mentioned.

The House of Assembly is a fourth time disqualified by not being sufficiently *wise* for such an important trust. If the aforesaid instructions to the Delegates be examined on the principles of sound reason and policy, they give a very indifferent character of the judgment and wisdom of the House, for, experience hath now taught us, and men of discernment did, at the time of first passing them, foresee that they were unsound in their policy, and would be hurtful in their effects. They are marked with the strongest characters of mischief and ignorance. Yet, they became a precedent to such other provinces as might be induced to believe that the Pennsylvania Assembly, by its central situation for intelligence, was possessed of some secret, which afforded grounds to expect a reconciliation, and under that delusion they likewise issued instructions to the same purpose; and thus, by circulating a false hope, the hands of power were relaxed, and a poisonous prudence was produced in our councils, at a time when a direct contrary spirit ought to have taken place, for if, instead of those instructions, a motion had been made for disclaiming all allegiance to the crown of Britain; and, had proper persons been immediately dispatched to Europe, to have cleared up the character of America from the aspersions which the British court would throw on her, as a pretence for obtaining foreign assistance, and had those persons been properly authorised to have negociated and ratified a treaty of friendship and commerce therewith, there is every reason to believe that we should not only have prevented Britain from obtaining foreign mercenaries, but that we should by this time have had the goods and manufactures of such countries in our stores, and thereby relieved this country from the present scarcity, and saved the poor from the enormous expence of purchasing goods at these present high prices. Thus hath a whole winter, when no molestation could happen to us, been lost and sacrificed thro' the ill policy and ill precedent of the present House of Assembly—Therefore it is no longer worthy of our confidence.

Fifthly—The obligation which the said House of Assembly is under by oaths of allegiance to our enemy again disqualifies them fully and effectually from framing a new government. The members of the said House took those oaths, not as members of the community at large, but as members of the House particularly: Therefore they can only be properly discharged therefrom by ceasing to act in this official character in which, and for which, they took those oaths, besides which, as the new elected members will not now take the oaths, they cannot sit in Assembly with those who have; and those who have, cannot sit as a Convention with those who have not—Therefore the present House, in its present state, has not, nor can have, either the authority of an Assembly or Convention.

Sixthly—The undue influence and partial connexions which many members of the said House are biassed by, render them unfit persons to be trusted with powers to carry the late resolve of Congress into execution; and we have very alarming apprehensions, that a government, modelled by such persons, would be calculated to transfer the good people of this province, like live stock upon a farm, to the proprietaries of the soil. Lord and landlord were never yet united since the world began, and such a government would soon reduce us and our posterity to a state even of animal slavery. The most absolute monarch is supported by revenue *only* and not by revenue and rental both.

Fellow countrymen, it must occur with the fullest force of conviction to every honest, thinking man, that the persons delegated with proper powers to form a plan of government, ought to possess the entire confidence of the people. They should be men having no false bias from old prejudices, no interest distinct or separate from the body of the people; in short, they should be a very different sort of men to what many of the present House of Assembly are. They should be men, likewise, invested with powers to form a plan of government *only,* and not to execute it after it is framed; for nothing can be a greater violation of reason and natural rights, than for men to give authority to themselves: And on this ground, likewise, the House of Assembly is again disqualified.

We have, my Fellow Countrymen, been making shift long enough. It is now high time to come to some settled point, that we may call ourselves a people; for in the present unsettled state of things we are only a decent multitude. Yet, to the honour of this province, to the honour of all America, be it told, so long as the name of America remains, that by the common consent of Citizens, the public peace was preserved inviolate, for nearly three years, *without law*. Perhaps the only instance since the world began.

We are now arrived at a period from which we are to look forward as a *legal people*. The Resolve of Congress, grounded on the justest foundation, hath recommended it to us, to establish a regular plan of *legal government*, and the means which they have recommended for that purpose, are, either by Assemblies or *Conventions*. Conventions, my Fellow Countrymen, are the only proper bodies to form a Constitution, and Assemblies are the proper bodies to make Laws agreeable to that constitution.—This is a just distinction. Let us begin right, and there is no [fear] but, under the providence of God, we shall end well. When the tyrant James the Second, king of Britain, abdicated the government, that is, ran away therefrom, or rather, was driven away by the just indignation of the people, the situation of England was like what America is *now*; and in that state a Convention was chosen, to settle the new or reformed plan of government, before any Parliament could presume to sit; and this is what is distinguished in history by the name of the Revolution.—Here, my Countrymen, is our precedent: A precedent which is worthy of imitation. We need no other—we can have no better. And this precedent is more particularly striking in our situation, because it was concerted between our virtuous ancestors, and the ancestors of those German inhabitants of this and other provinces, who are now incorporated with us in one common stock. Having then a noble precedent before us, let it be our wish to imitate it. The persons who recommend this, are Fellow Citizens with yourselves. They have no private views, no interest to establish for themselves. This aim, end and wish is the happiness of the Community. He who dares say otherwise, let him step forth, and prove it, for, conscious of the purity of our intentions, we challenge the world.

Our present condition may, to many persons, seem more embarrassing than it really is; while, to those who have truly reflected thereon, it appears, that the necessary steps to be taken, in order to extricate ourselves therefrom, and to arrive at a state of legal order, are simple, easy and regular: For the purpose of which, it is proposed, that the Committees of Inspection throughout the several Counties, agreeable to the power they are already invested with, do immediately call a Convention to take charge of the affairs of the province, for we cannot conceive how the House of Assembly can any longer presume to sit, without either breaking through the resolve of Congress, or assuming to themselves arbitrary power. And we do farther propose, that this Convention, when met, so issue out summonses for electing by ballot (of all the freemen throughout the province, including those Germans, or others, who were before disqualified for not having taken oaths of allegiance to our enemy, but are now restored to their natural rights by the late resolve of Congress for suppressing the taking those oaths) a Grand Provincial Convention, consisting at least of One Hundred members, of known and established reputation, for wisdom, virtue and impartiality, without regard to country or profession of religion; whose sole business, when met, shall be to agree upon, and settle a plan of government for this province, which shall secure to every separate inhabitant thereof perfect liberty of conscience, with every civil and legal right and privilege, so that all men, rich and poor, shall be protected in the possession of their peace, property and principles.—And what more can honest men say? We mean well, and under that conscious sanction we implore God and man to help us. The die of this day will cast the fate of posterity in this province. We can no longer confide in the House of Assembly; they have, by a feeble and intimidating prudence held us up as sacrifices to a bloody-minded enemy, they have thrown cold water on the necessary military proceedings of this province and continent, and have been abettors, together with their collegues, in procrastinating the expedition to Canada, which, by that *delay only,* may probably not now succeed.

It is time, and high time, to break off from such men, and to awaken from such unmanly drowsiness: And we have no fear, that as our cause is just, our God will support us against barbarous tyrants, foreign mercenaries, and American traitors.

Having thus clearly stated the case for your consideration, we leave you to the exercise of your own reason, to determine whether the present House of Assembly, under all the disqualification, inconsistencies, prejudices and private interests herein mentioned, is a proper body to be entrusted with the extensive powers necessary for forming or reforming a government agreeable to the Resolve and Recommendation of Congress. Or whether a Convention, chosen fairly and openly for that express purpose, consisting, as has been before mentioned, of at least One Hundred members, of known reputation for wisdom, virtue and impartiality, is not a far more probable, nay the only possible, method for securing the just Rights of the people, and posterity.

SOURCE: [Anonymous], *"The Alarm: or, An address to the people of Pennsylvania, on the late resolve of Congress, for totally suppressing all power and authority derived from the crown of Great-Britain.* Philadelphia,"* Pennsylvania: Printed by Henry Miller, 1776. *Readex: America's Historical Imprint.*

5. Concord Town Meeting Resolutions
October 21, 1776

The great questions confronted by American revolutionary constitution-makers in the years immediately after independence was declared from Great Britain were how their new state constitutions should be designed and constructed and by whom. These questions stumped American revolutionaries for several years. The first revolutionary state constitutions were written and adopted by extra-legal provincial congresses or by revolutionary conventions. The problem with these legislative bodies is that they made both regular laws and now constitutions, which meant that there was little technical difference between an ordinary law regulating hog prices or road construction and a law creating a constitution. This method of constitution-making put the constitutional cart before the horse. In the wake of their bad experience with the British Parliament which claimed to be effectively synonymous with British constitution, American constitution-makers searched for a method or process by which to make their constitutions the creators of and superior to their governments. That method was, remarkably, discovered by ordinary men at a Concord, Massachusetts town meeting (the kind of meeting outlawed by the Massachusetts Government Act of 1774) in 1776. The Concord Resolutions recommended a two-step process by which constitutions would be, first, drafted by special constitutional conventions elected by the people for the soul purpose of designing a government on paper, and then the proposed constitution would be sent to the people for inspection. The Concord Resolutions do not explicitly call for specially elected ratifying conventions to accept or reject the proposed constitution, but they do imply such a process.

At a meeting of the Inhabitents of the Town of Concord being free and twenty one years of age and upward, met by adjournment on the twenty first Day of October 1776 to take into Consideration a Resolve of the Honorable House of Representatives of this State on the 17th of September Last, the Town Resolved as followes------

Resolve 1st. That this State being at Present destitute of a Properly established form of Goverment, it is absolutely necesary that one should be emmediatly formed and established------

Resolved 2 That the Supreme Legislative, either in their Proper Capacity, or in Joint Committee, are by no means a Body proper to form and Establish a Constitution, or form of Government; for Reasons following.

first Because we Conceive that a Constitution in its Proper Idea intends a System of Principles Established to Secure the Subject in the Possession and enjoyment of their Rights and Priviliges, against any Encroachments of the Governing Part------

2d Because the Same Body that forms a Constitution have of Consequence a power to alter it. 3d--Because a Constitution alterable by the Supreme Legislative is no Security at all to the Subject against any Encroachment of the Governing part on any, or on all of their Rights and priviliges. Resolve 3d. That it appears to this Town highly necesary and Expedient that a Convention, or Congress be immediately Chosen, to form and establish a Constitution, by the Inhabitants of the Respective Towns in this State, being free and of twenty one years of age, and upwards, in Proportion as the Representatives of this State formerly ware Chosen; the Convention or Congress not to Consist of a greater number then the House of assembly of this State heretofore might Consist of, Except that each Town and District shall have Liberty to Send one Representative or otherwise as Shall appear meet to the Inhabitants of this State in General

Resolve 4th. that when the Convention, or Congress have formed a Constitution they adjourn for a Short time, and Publish their Proposed Constitution for the Inspection and Remarks of the Inhabitants of this State.

Resolved 5ly. That the Honorable House of assembly of this State be Desired to Recommend it to the Inhabitants of the State to Proceed to Chuse a Convention or Congress for the Purpas abovesaid as soon as Possable.

SOURCE: Oscar Handlin and Mary Handlin, eds. *The Popular Sources of Political Authority: Documents on the Massachusetts Constitution of 1780* (Cambridge, MA: Belknap Press of Harvard University Press, 1966), 152-153. "Concord Town Meeting Resolution". Memo, October 22, 1776. From Teaching American History. https://teachingamericanhistory.org/document/concord-town-meeting-resolution/ (accessed December 28, 2024).

6. THE BIRTHPLACE OF AMERICAN CONSTITUTIONALISM

From the moment that Thomas Gage resigned his position in October 1775 as Great Britain's last royally appointed Governor of Massachusetts, the Bay State did not have a legally functioning government. It did have unofficial or extra-legal legislative bodies to govern the province, but such bodies were not, strictly speaking legal or constitutional. In fact, this state of affairs lasted until ratification of the Massachusetts constitution in 1780. In western Massachusetts, particularly in Berkshire County, the Quarter Sessions courts were closed. A group known as the Berkshire Constitutionalists would not sanction or follow the extra-legal "laws" of the General Court, which, strictly speaking, had no formal authority to enforce its laws. The Berkshire Constitutionalists insisted that only a legally recognized government sanctioned formally by the people could force them to comply its laws. In the first document that follows, representatives from the town of Pittsfield laid out their grievances against the authority of the current "government" in Massachusetts. The Pittsfield representatives insisted that the people are the only true foundation of government, and they drew a sharp distinction between a constitution and legislation. The former, they argued, must precede the latter. In the fall of 1778, the General Court sent an investigating committee to Berkshire County empowered to organize representatives from the local towns in the county to state their grievances. The result was a report written by William Whiting (the second document that follows) arguing that the residents of Massachusetts, including those in Berkshire County, are not in a state of nature but in a state of civil society with a legitimately functioning government that should be obeyed.

TOWN OF PITTSFIELD (BERKSHIRE COUNTY) REPRESENTATIVES
"ADDRESS TO THE COMMITTEE OF THE GENERAL COURT"
NOVEMBER 17, 1778

TO THE HONORABLE COMMITTEE FROM THE GENERAL COURT OF MASSACHUSETTS BAY NOW CONVENED AT PITTSFIELD—

Mr. Chairman, Sir

We whose Names are underwritten indulging some Apprehensions of the Importance of Civil and religious Liberty, the destructive Nature of Tyranny and lawless power, and the absolute necessity of legal Government, to prevent Anarchy and Confusion; have taken this method to indulge our own Feelings and Sentiments respecting the important matters that have for some Time been the Subject of debate in this present Meeting—Political Disquisitions, if managed with Decency, Moderation and Candor are a good preservative against Ignorance and Servility and such a state of perfect Quietude as would endanger the Rights of Mankind united in the Bands of Society. We wish to preserve this Character in what we have now to offer in the Defence of our Constituents in opposing, in times past, the executive Courts of Justice in this County.

We wish with the least Delay to come to the Merits of the cause, and shall now proceed to make those observations on the Nature of Government which are necessary to bring into view the Apprehensions we indulge respecting the present Condition of this state, whether we have a fundamental Constitution or not; and how far we have Government duly organized and how far not: In free States the people are to be considered as the fountain of power. And the social Tie as founded in Compact. The people at large are endowed with alienable and unalienable Rights. Those which are unalienable, are those which belong to Conscience respecting the worship of God and the practice of the Christian Religion, and that of being determined or governed by the Majority in the Institution or formation of Government. The alienable are those which may be delegated for the Common good, or those which are for the common good to be parted with. It is of the unalienable Rights, particularly that of being determined or governed by the Majority on the Institution or formation of Government of which something further is necessary to be considered at this Time. That the Majority should be governed by the Minority on the first Institution of Government is not only contrary to the common apprehensions of Mankind in general, but it contradicts the common Law of Justice and benevolence.

Mankind being in a state of nature equal, the larger Number (Caeteris paribus) is of more worth than the lesser, and the common happiness is to be preferred to that of Individuals. When Men form the social Compact, for the Majority to consent to be governed by the Minority is down right popery in politicks, as submission to him who claims Infallibility, and of being the only Judge of Right and wrong, is popery in Religion. In all free Governments duly organized there is an essential Distinction to be observed between the fundamental Constitution, and Legislation. The fundamental Constitution is the Basis and ground work of Legislation, and ascertains the Rights Franchises, Immunities and Liberties of the people, How and how often officers Civil and military shall be elected by the people, and circumscribing and defining the powers of the Rulers, and so affoarding a sacred Barrier against Tyranny and Despotism. This in antient and corrupt Kingdoms when they have woke out of Slavery to some happy dawnings of Liberty, has been called a Bill of Rights, Magna Charta etc. which must be considered as imperfect Emblems of the Securities of the present grand period. Legislators stand on this foundation, and enact Laws agreeably to it. They cannot give Life to the Constitution: it is the approbation of the Majority of the people at large that gives Life and being to it. This is the foundation of Legislation that is agreeable to true Liberty, it is above the whole Legislature of a free state, it being the foundation upon which the Legislature stands. A Representative Body may form but cannot impose said Constitution upon a free people. The giving Existence to the fundamental Constitution of a free state is a Trust that cannot be delegated. For any rational person to give his vote for another person to aid and assist in forming said Constitution with a view of imposing it on the people without reserving to himself a Right of Inspection Approbation rejection or Amendment, imports, if not impiety, yet real popery in politicks. We could bring many Vouchers for this Doctrine sufficient for our present purpose is the following Extracts from a Noted Writer. In answer to that assertion of another respectable writer that 'The bare Idea of a State without a power some where vested to alter every part of its Laws is the height of political Absurdity.' [Introduction to Blackstone's *Commentaries*, p. 97; note by the editor of *Acts and Resolves*] He remarks upon it, 'A position, which I apprehend, ought to be, in some Measure limited and explained. For if it refers to those particular Regulations, which take place in Consequence of Immemorial Custom, or are enacted by positive Statute, and at the same Time, are subordinate to the fundamental Constitution from which the Legislature itself derives its Authority; it is admitted to be within the power or Trust vested in the Legislature to alter these, pro, Re nata, as the good of Society may require. But this power of Authority of the Legislature to make Alterations cannot be supposed to extend to the Infringement of those essentials Rights and previleges, which are reserved to the Members of a free state at large, as their undoubted Birthright and unalienable property. I say, in every free State there are some Liberties and previleges, which the Society has not given out of their own Hands to their Governors, not even to the Legislature: and to suppose the contrary would be the height of political absurdity; for it is saying that a state is free and not free at the same Time; or which is the same thing, that its Members are possessed of Liberties, of all which they may be divested at the will of the Legislature; that is, they enjoy them during pleasure, but can claim no property in them.

In a word nothing is more certain than that Government in the general nature of it is a Trust in behalf of the people. And there cannot be a Maxim, in my opinion, more ill grounded, than that there must be an arbitrary power lodged somewhere in every Government. If this were true, the different kinds of Government in the world would be more alike, and on a level, than they are generally supposed to be. In our own Government in particular, tho' no one thinks with more respect of the powers which the Constitution hath vested in every branch of the Legislature; yet I must be excused in saying what is strictly true, that the whole Legislature is so far from having an absolute power, that it hath not power in several Cases that might be mentioned.

For instance, their Authority does not extend to making the house of Commons perpetual, or giving that house a power to fill up their own vacancies: the house of Commons being the representatives of all the Commons of England and in that Capassity only a branch of the Legislature; and if they concur in destroying the foundation on which they themselves stand; and if they annihilate the Rights of their Constituents and claim a share in the Legislature upon any other footing than that upon which the Constitution hath given it to them; they subvert the very Trust under which alone they act, and thereby forfeit all their Authority. In short they cannot dispence with any of those essential Rights of the people which it ought to be the great object of Government as it is our Constitution in particular to preserve.'—

These reasonings tend abundantly to evince, that the whole Legislature of any state is insufficient to give Life to the fundamental Constitution of such state, it being the foundation on which they themselves stand and from which alone the Legislature derives its Authority—

May it be considered, further, that to suppose the Representative Body capable of forming and imposing this Compact or Constitution without the Inspection and Approbation Rejection or Amendment of the people at large would involve in it the greatest Absurdity. This would make them greater than the people who send them, this supposes them their own Creators, formers of the foundation upon which they themselves stand. This imparts uncontroulable Dominion over their Constituents for what should hinder them from making such a Constitution as invests them and their successors in office with unlimited Authority, if it be admitted that the Representatives are the people as to forming and imposing the fundamental Constitution of the state upon them without their Approbation and perhaps in opposition to their united sense—In this the very essence of true Liberty consists, viz in every free state the Constitution is adopted by the Majority.

It is needful to be observed that we are not to Judge of true Liberty by other Nations of the Earth, darkness has overspread the Earth, Tyranny Triumphs thro' the world. The Day light of Liberty, only begins to dawn upon these Ends of the Earth. To measure the freedom, the Rights and privileges of the American Empire by those enjoyed by other Nations would be folly.

It is now both easy and natural to apply these reasonings to the present State of Massachusetts Bay. We think it undeniably follows from the preceeding Reasonings that the Compact in this state is not yet formed: when did the Majority of the people at large assent to such Constitution, and what is it? if the Majority of the people of this state have adopted any such fundamental Constitution it is unknown to us and we shall submit to it as we always mean to be governed by the Majority—

Nor will any of those consequences follow on this supposition, that we have no Law, or that the Honorable Council and House of Representatives are Usurpers and Tyrants. Far from it. We consider our case as very Extraordinary. We do not consider this state in all Respects as in a state of Nature tho' destitute of such fundamental Constitution. When the powers of Government were totally dissolved in this state, we esteemed the State Congress as a necessary and useful body of Men suited to our Exigencies and sufficiently authorized to levy Taxes, raise an Army and do what was necessary for our common defence and it is Sir in this Light that we view our present Honorable Court and for these and other reasons *have inculcated* a careful Adherence to their orders. Time will not permit to argue this Matter any longer, for your Honors patience must have been tryed already. These have been some of the reasons we have indulged, and Sentiments we have cultivated respecting a Constitution, and for these Reasons we have been looking forward towards a new Constitution—But we must further add

That a fear of being finally deprived of a Constitution and of being thrown into confusion and divisions by delaying the formation of a new Constitution, has caused our Constituents so early and invariably to oppose the executive Courts—We have feared, we now realize those fears, that upon our submission we shall sink down into a dead Calm and never transmit to posterity a single Right nor leave them the least Knowledge of so fair an Inheritance, as we may now convey to them.—

We and our Constituents have also indulged some fears respecting some of the particular persons appointed for our Rulers least in the future Execution of Law they should execute their own private Resentments, we are willing to hope the best—

We have been ready to consider some of them as indulging an unnatural temper in vilifying and reproaching their own County but we hope they will do better for the future, and that we shall do better, and we wish to give them our confidence.—We are determined to cultivate a spirit of meekness forbearance and Love and to study the Things that shall make for peace and order.

It has appeared to us and those we are appointed to represent that in an early opposition to the executive Courts, such opposition would become general thro' the state, which in our opinion would bring on a new Constitution without Delay. Our hope of which is now very much weakened, and such are the Dissentions of this state that we are now ready to fear we shall never obtain any other than what is called our present Constitution our Apprehensions of which have been already explained—

It is with Gratitude we reflect on the Appointment of this Honorable Committee by the General Court for the purpose of peace Reconciliation and order thro' this County, and their impartial and faithful Execution of their Commission. We are persuaded by the Temper and Moderation exhibited that they will not embibe any prejudices against this County, by what they have seen and heared, and that they will make a Just Representation of our state to the General Court.—

To evince to your Honors our Love of peace Reconciliation and legal Government, and that we have been actuated not by personal Prejudices or

Motives of Ambition, notwithstanding the powerful Reasons we have had for a Suspension of the Executive Courts we are willing to forego our own opinions and if it shall be thought best by our Constituents to submit to the establishment of the Executive Courts in this Country—

SOURCE: *The Acts and Resolves, Public and Private, Province of the Massachusetts Bay* (Boston, MA: Wright and Potter, 1886), 5: 1030-1032.

WILLIAM WHITING
"AN ADDRESS TO THE INHABITANTS OF BERKSHIRE COUNTY, MASS"
1778

. . . I beg leave to present you with a few thoughts on the present unhappy situation of our public affairs; . . .

. . . Let us now weigh the advantages and disadvantages on each side the question, in an even balance; and everyone whose mind is not debased even below that of the most uncultivated savage, must surely prefer a free and equal government to a state of anarchy and confusion. For a civilized people to live, for any considerable time, under a suspension of government, is intollerable: Nothing, therefore, short of the most weighty and important reasons, can justify the people of this county in their present opposition to law and government.

Let us therefore now chiefly attend to those arguments and objections that are urged against the due execution of law, and the powers of government; and if, on the most impartial inquiry, it shall appear dangerous to the just liberties of the people of this county to submit thereto, before a new constitution is formed, I will venture to engage, that the advocates for the immediate execution of law, shall, to a man, join its opposers in their opposition. But should those arguments and objections appear to be insufficient to justify this opposition, we have a right to expect that those persons, on their part, will immediately lay aside their opposition; or, at least, that they will not complain, should the supreme authority of the state take speedy and effectual measures to establish a due course of law in the county. . . .

Let us now, my brethren . . . consider those mighty objections which are so zealously urged against the introduction of law into this county. And I think they may be substantially comprehended in these few words, viz. "We have no constitution of government. And how can we have government without a constitution, or a foundation for it to stand upon?"

Here let me call up your best and most careful attention, while we take a short view of what is termed a state of nature, and afterwards that of civil society.

In a state of nature, each individual has a right, not only to dispose of, order, and direct, his property, his person, and all his own actions, within the bounds of the law of nature, as he thinks fit, but he also has a right in himself, not only to defend, but to judge and to punish the person who shall make any assault or encroachment, either upon his person or property, without asking leave, or depending on the will of any other man, or any set of men whatever.

Now when any number of men enter into a state of society with each other, they resign into the hands of the society, the right they had in a state of nature, of disposing, directing and ordering their own persons and properties, so far as the good of the whole may require it. And as to the right of judging and punishing injuries done to any of the individuals, that is to be wholly given up to the society. Hence, it is obvious, there can be no medium between being in a state of nature, and in a state of civil society.

Again, in all societies of men, united together for mutual aid, support and defense, there exists one supreme, absolute, and rightful judge over the whole; one, who has a right, at all times, to order, direct, and dispose of the persons, actions and properties of the individuals of the community, so far as the good of the community shall require it; and this judge is no other than the majority of the whole.

The great Mr. Locke tells us, "That when men enter into a community, they must give up all the powers necessary for the purposes for which they entered into society, to the majority of the community, and this is done barely by agreeing to enter into political society; which is all the compact there is, or need be, between the individuals to make up a commonwealth. And this is that, and that only, which gives beginning to any lawful government in the world."

Here let it be carefully observed, that when men emerge from a state of nature, and unite in society, in order to form a political government; the first step necessary is, for each individual to give up his alienable natural rights and privileges, to be ordered, directed, and disposed of, as the major part of the community shall think fit; so far as shall be necessary for the good of the whole, of which the majority must be the judges. And this must necessarily take place previous to the community's forming any particular constitution, mode, or form of government whatever: For, to be in a state of society, so far as to be under obligation to obey the rules, and orders prescribed by the major part of the society, is one thing; and for that society to be under any particular constitution or form of government, is another. The latter is necessarily subsequent to the former, and must depend entirely on the pleasure of the supreme judge; that is, the major part of the community, who have an undoubted right to enter upon, or postpone that matter, when, and so long as they see fit; and no individual can, on that account, be justified in withdrawing their allegiance, or refusing to submit to the rules and orders of the society.

Here my brethren, let me call upon you to consider, what an absurd and ridiculous figure those men cut, who cry out vehemently for a *new Constitution*, while, at the same time, by refusing to make that resignation of their alienable rights which is the necessary condition on which men enter into civil society, they positively declare, that they do not even belong to the political society of the State of Massachusetts Bay.

I know some will object, that on the declaration of Independence, all civil government was annihilated; consequently, that we are under no obligation to submit to government, till we have a constitution that we approve of. To which I answer, That even admitting the declaration of Independence did actually annihilate the *Constitution* of the province of the Massachusetts Bay; yet it did not annihilate or materially affect, the union or compact existing among the people: For, as I have already showed, that for a people to be in a state of political society, as to be under indispensable obligation to obey the rules and orders prescribed by the major part of the society, and to be under any particular constitution or form of government, are things entirely distinct, and, that the latter is subsequent to, and wholly dependent on, the former. This, being the case, it follows, that no revolution in, or dissolution of, particular constitutions or forms of government, can absolve the members of the society from their allegiance to the major part of the community. And I can hardly conceive how it is possible for such a society to be dissolved, unless by their being dispersed abroad as the Jews are, so that the will of the major part cannot be, either known or obeyed, or by the usurpation and deadly breath of an absolute tyrant.

It is true, when the majority of a society do not act, or when their will and orders cannot be known to the members; during such suspension, the natural right of defending and protecting himself, reverts back to each individual; and on this principle only, can those salutary mobs, and necessary exertions of the people in the beginning of the present contest, be justified. But after congress and assemblies, composed of the free representatives of the people, had prescribed rules for ordering and conducting the public affairs of the community, whatever has taken place of that sort since, has generally, if not universally, been unnecessary, unwarrantable and seditious.

But should we admit for once, that on the declaration of independence, not only all modes and forms of government were dissolved, but also, that civil society was annihilated at the same time: Yet, as it plainly appears from what has been said, that previous, and in order to the forming of a constitution or mode of government, it is essentially necessary that the people enter into society, and give up their alienable natural rights, and submit to be governed by the major part of the community, I ask, with what face you can pretend to the least colour of right to give your voices in, or to say anything about, a constitution, while you utterly refuse to comply with the necessary preliminaries? This is really no less preposterous than it would be for the savages of the wilderness to run together, and take upon them, in hideous yells, to frame, and enact, a constitution and form of government for the state of Massachusetts Bay.

It is a fact which needs no proof, that whatever state the inhabitants of the Massachusetts Bay might be in at the time independence was declared, they are now in a state of civil society, and (the county of Berkshire excepted) enjoy the blessings of a free and equal government.

And now my brethren, let me ask you this very plain, tho' pertinent and important question, Are you members of the political society of the state of Massachusetts Bay? Or are you not? If you answer in the affirmative; then let me ask you again, why do you refuse to submit to those rules which the community have prescribed? And not only this, but why, by threats and violence, do you deter the servants of the community, in this county, from redressing injuries and insults offered to others, and like the fable of the dog in the manger, neither enjoy the blessings of government yourselves, nor suffer others to enjoy them? Or how will you exculpate yourselves from the charge of being in a state of rebellion against the community?

But should you say that you do not belong to the community, that you do not mean to give up any of your natural rights till you know what constitution you are to be governed by: Then let me tell you, that you must be considered, as being, at best, in a state of nature, and that you can have no right to join, or give your voice in forming a constitution of government.

But perhaps you will say, that you do not act, in this affair, as individuals, but, as a community: For, when the minds of the inhabitants of the county were lately taken upon the expedience or inexpediency of setting up courts, there appeared to be a very great majority against it. Here let me repeat a former question: Are the inhabitants of the county of *Berkshire,* members of the political society of the Massachusetts Bay? Or, are they not? Your conduct, in sending members to the general court, answers this question in the affirmative. A majority of the inhabitants of the county therefore, can be of no more real avail in this matter, than a majority of any particular town, or, than even a majority of any particular family in any particular town in the county. For, it is only a major part of the community that have a right to determine matters of this kind, and they have ordered that courts of sessions be held in this county. The friends of government therefore cannot consider themselves as being, in any measure, included in this vote of the county. The truth of the fact is, that should ninety nine out of an hundred thro the county, vote against law, yet, that hundredth part would, as loyal subjects of the community, have a right to enjoy the benefits of government, and the major part of the community are under absolute obligation, therein to protect and support them. Otherwise the community could have no right to punish them, should they even commit treason against the state: For, no maxim can stand on firmer ground than this, *That protection and allegiance are reciprocal:* and that, *where protection is wanting, allegiance is not due.* Let me entreat you, my brethren, seriously to consider, how shockingly unreasonable, as well as grossly immoral your conduct is, while by threats and violence, you deprive the peaceable and loyal inhabitants of this county, of that inestimable previlege of having their grevances redressed in that ancient and equal way, of tryal by jurors, as well as of all other benefits of a free and lawful government. And all this, upon the most frivolous pretences, as I have already showed, and shall further evince in the course of these observations.

You loudly proclaim yourselves to be *sons of liberty.* Pray, what kind of liberty is it you contend for, against Great Britain? Does not your conduct testify against you, that you contend to the same thing, for which all tyrants contend with each other; viz: that each one may monopolize the whole empire of tyranny to himself? But lest, ere I am aware, I should catch the epidemic disease myself, and a flame of passion, begin to rage in my own breast, I will dismiss this head, and proceed to notice some other objections that are made against the introduction of law into this county. . . .

The plain truth of the case is in fact no other than this,—The inhabitants of the state of Massachusetts Bay, are now in a state of some measure familiar to that which every community must pass through, while they are emerging from a state of nature to that of a free and equal government. They are, at least in a state of civil society, by virtue of a compact or agreement among the people, wherein, as hath been said, every individual hath given up into the hands of the major part of the community, his alienable natural rights, and submitted to be governed by them.

There cannot indeed with propriety, be said to be now, any constitution of government existing in this state, which is designed to be permanent, and to remain for generations to come; but we are now in a proper condition to form one, whenever the major part of the community shall think proper to enter upon so important an undertaking: And then, every individual must submit to such a constitution as the majority shall agree to; though, the larger that majority, the happier it will be. . . .

The truth of the matter is this: On the declaration of independence, the inhabitants of this state, although they considered themselves as being entirely absolved from their allegiance to the powers of Great Britain, and from being any further held by the old constitution than they chose to adopt it; yet they did not think themselves absolved from that mutual compact or union they were in with each other as a civil society, but still considered themselves as being under the government and direction of the major part of the community. Now, in order that society might exercise that degree of government which the peace and safety of the community required, it was also necessary that some particular rule, or form of government should be adopted. Whatever modes and forms therefore, they had been accustomed to from the old charter, and still found would be useful and expedient for a free and independent society, they surely would not be so childish as to deny themselves the benefit of, merely because they were contained in the British charter. . . .

But I must not yet close my address; for the din of a new constitution continually rings in my ears.

For myself, I most heartily wish that we had now such a constitution of government and bill of rights firmly established, as would secure to us and our posterity, all the benefits of a free and equal government, forever: And I will pledge myself that the small abilities and influence I possess, shall be exerted to procure them as soon as possible. At the same time I am fully persuaded that our violent opposition to a due execution of law in this county, is not only groundless, unjust, and exceedingly detrimental to the peace, safety, and welfare of the county; but, will prove the greatest impediment to our ever obtaining such a constitution as we shall be pleased with; for, we hereby lose our influence in the state. We are now considered by the greater part of the people in the state, as being in a kind of political delirium; accordingly they pay but little regard to us. Besides, as hath been observed, we cannot, in justice, claim any right to a share in forming a constitution, so long as, by refusing to submit to the majority, we deny that we belong to the civil community.

Neither do I apprehend it will at all expedite the business of a constitution to threaten the people of this state with a revolt, in case they do not immediately set about a new constitution. Suppose the state to which we apply for their protecting wing, should ask us, why we desire to forsake our parent state and join with strangers? Must not our answer be, because the ancient and extensive state of the Massachusetts Bay are so arbitrary and tyranical, that they will not submit to be governed agreeable to the capricious humor of the county of Berkshire. And will they, knowing our political character, be fond of taking us into their bosoms? Will they not rather reject our suit, under these circumstances, from a just apprehension that we may prove to their community, like the dead fly in the apothecaries precious ointment?

But the word constitution, *like great is Diana,* still sounds in my head. Here, therefore, I must observe, that most of the people are so carried away with this word, as though some magick was contained in it, and under sanction thereof, oppose all law and government are, at the same time, totally ignorant of what is meant by the term, *constitution:* They have affixed an idea to the word, which it by no means admits of. Here then, let us briefly inquire what is meant by a *bill of rights,* and *constitution of government?*

And first, negatively. A bill of rights and constitution of government have no immediate connexion with, or influence in, altering or amending any laws, usages, customs, or modes of proceeding in the general distribution of law among the people as, for instance,—altering laws for the collection of debts, fee bills, regulating the recording of deeds, or transfering the business from county registers to town clerks & c. There is the same door open now for the redress of grievances of this kind (if any such you have) which there will be after the establishment of a new constitution; for these are matters, with which that has nothing to do.

Again, a new constitution will not in the least alter the present mode of proceeding in the different courts of law that are now held in the state. For these are all matters that have no immediate connexion, with a constitution of government.

In order therefore, to a better understanding of this matter, let it be observed, that all mankind are born equally free, and that, by nature, no one is above another;—that when men enter into civil society, they give up, into the hands of the society, many of their natural rights and liberties, to be ordered and directed by the will of the society, which, in a state of nature, could be controlled only by their own wills. Men also possess other natural rights which they cannot divest themselves of, nor give the controul of to any power under heaven. These are called the *unalienable rights of mankind;* and are chiefly the rights of conscience, right of protection & c. Now the design of a bill of rights is to ascertain and clearly describe the rights of conscience, and that security of person and property which the supreme power of the state is bound to protect every individual in the enjoyment of.

A *constitution of government* is that which points out and determines the several branches of authority that shall exist in the state, as, legislative, judicial, and executive, in what manner they shall be appointed,—the kind, and degree of power each branch shall be vested with, and how far they shall be dependent, or independent on each other: It also includes the establishment of general rules for the government of the militia and navy departments; and the whole to be *fixed* and *unalterable,* (unless by the same power which first gave it being) for preventing usurpations, and for the security of future generations; and, as I said before, without any immediate respect to the distribution of law and justice among the people, any otherwise, than as from a tree that grows on a good root, we naturally look for good fruit.

I am sensible that the discription here given of a bill of rights, and constitution of government, is general and concise. All I design by it, is to show that if we had such a bill of rights, and constitution of government now established, this would not remove any of those supposed grievances which I have yet heard complained of in the country of Berkshire; unless the present mode of appointing civil officers be considered as a grievance. And I confess, I see no reason why the inhabitants of this county should be more grieved at this, than the inhabitants of any other part of the state. Should it be thought best to establish some other mode of appointing these officers, this will, doubtless, be duly attended to, whenever the matter of forming a new constitution is taken up. In the meantime, how unbecoming, and arrogant is it, for the inhabitants of this single infant county, to proclaim, as they do by their conduct, that unless the state will immediately comply with their disposition, and form, and content to such a constitution, in all respects, as they approve of, they will continue their revolt from the community? Pray, my brethren, attend seriously to this matter. The business of forming a constitution, is a most weighty and important undertaking and ought not to be gone into by men whose minds are fired with passion, or influenced by prejudice. In a matter of such moment, and in a state so extensive as this, there will necessarily be a great variety of sentiment and opinions: And every particular town and county in the state who differ in sentiment in this important matter, will have, one, as good a right as another, to insist on all the other parts of the community conforming to their plan of government, and to refuse submission to the laws of the state, unless their dispositions are immediately complied with.

And now, my brethren, only consider, how shocking would be the consequences, should your example be followed by all the towns and counties in this state, and through the continent! Instead of being the *United States of America* we should be (I had almost said) the *infinite number of jarring, disunited factions of America!* Our different towns and counties would soon become fields of blood, and exhibit the most dreadful scenes of tumult, violence, and destruction! and our common enemy would have little more to do, than to march through the country and seize on their prey!

Again; is not this the language of our conduct, that the state of Massachusetts Bay is composed of a set of knaves, on the one hand, who are leading the people into slavery, and of fools on the other, who (the county of Berkshire excepted) are suffering themselves to be led by the nose into their snare? And can it be expected that the other counties in the state will feel themselves very much obliged by such a compliment?

As I said before, so say I now again, no person more ardently desires a constitution that shall be acceptable to this county, and to the state in general, than myself: And it grieves me to my heart to meet with such fatal obsticles in the way of it as have now been mentioned. For, as hath been observed, there are, in the state, a great variety of opinions respecting the form of a constitution for this state, as well as to the most proper time for taking up this important business. We shall therefore, never be able to obtain a form of government, till we bring ourselves to such a disposition, that after comparing all those different opinions together, we shall be willing to submit to one that shall be a kind of medium between the whole, and conformable (as near as possible) to the sentiments of the whole. And it is too apparent, that there is not, at present, such a disposition in the inhabitants of this county.

And now, my brethren, from the foregoing observations, I think it evident to a demonstration, that the common cry in this county, *that we have no foundation of government,* is altogether groundless. For, even admitting that we have no particular constitution yet, it hath been shown, that such a constitution is not so essential to government, that there can be no foundation of government without it; but, on the contrary, that a compact or union among the people, by which they agree to submit themselves to be governed by the major part of the community, is itself, a sufficient and substantial foundation of government. And this being the case, how surprising is your conduct, that while you protest to belong to the community, by joining with it in making all the laws and rules for the government thereof, by your representatives, you, at the same time, refuse to submit to those very laws and rules; because, say you, we have no foundation of government. Although the great Mr. Locke tells you, and common sense tells you the same, that this, and this only, is that which can lay a foundation for any lawful government in the world.

I have shown, that the common cry of danger of being enslaved, and again brought under the British yoke of bondage, by introducing (for present convenience) the old constitution, as now practiced upon, is perfectly idle and ridiculous. I have shown that our conduct, in refusing to submit to law, till we have a new form of government established, instead of bringing forward, will have a direct and powerful tendency to retard and embarrass, that desirable and important object.—I have shown, that the people of this county, who at present oppose the due execution of law, have entirely mistook the true meaning and import of the words, *constitution* and form of government. I have shown, that for a people to give up their alienable natural rights, and to agree to be directed by the major part of the society, so far as the good of the whole shall require it, is the only foundation of lawful government; and that this is absolutely necessary, previous to their forming any particular mode of government; and therefore, that as the people of this county refuse to comply with these preliminaries, they do thereby exclude themselves from all just rights to give their voices in forming a constitution.

Notwithstanding the pains I have taken to set these matters in a just point of view, it will be to no good purpose, so long as the people are determined that they will retain all the rights of a state of nature. Let me tell you, my brethren, you cannot retain these rights, and at the same time enjoy the protection of society. It is therefore high time to away with these shocking inconsistencies, in which you have gone on for several years past—pretending to belong to the community of Massachusetts Bay by sending representatives, or rather spies, to the general court, and, at the same time, refusing to obey those laws and rules which they prescribe, unless in some particular instances, wherein they happen to coincide with your fancies! And here I can't but take notice, how shamefully that ancient maxim, *vox populi est vox Dei* (the voice of the people is the voice of God) has been prostituted in this county. When the major part of a free and independent community, by their representatives, declare to the individual members, and the world, their acts and resolutions, this being considered as the greatest power on earth, nothing can more fitly resemble *the voice of God*. But when a small number of individuals, who ought to be members of the society, inflamed with passion (if not with strong drink) collect together for the avowed purpose of opposing the true *vox populi*, let any one say whether their voice is not rather that of blasphemy and treason, than god like.

I shall close my address by repeating my most serious advice to you to act a part more consistent. And as you are now erecting little democracies in several of your towns, you ought to withdraw your representatives from the general assembly of the Massachusetts Bay; for it is highly unreasonable they should sit there as spies. You ought to send them as ambassadors, or commissioners plenipotentiary, and in that character they ought to be received, if received at all, and not as representatives. You ought to send the like officers to the American Congress, and to have your independence confirmed by that august body, before you proceed further in the exercise of your novel governments; otherwise, it is more than possible you may meet with difficulty: For, should you compel anyone to submit to your assumed authority, he will have a right to demand satisfaction, and the state is bound to see him redressed. And you may be assured that the supreme authority of the state will not be easily convinced that those trifling objections against law, which are so easily confused, are sufficient to justify you in setting up independent governments in your several towns, unless you can obtain a ratification of your independence from Congress, which, I dare say, in your most extravagant excursions of fancy, you never once thought of. . . .

SOURCE: Extracts from "An Address to the Inhabitants of the County Berkshire. Respecting their present opposition to civil government" (Hartford, CT: Printed by Watson and Goodwin, 1778), 9-16, 25-27.

Part Three:

Revolutionary State Constitutions

1. THE NEW HAMPSHIRE CONSTITUTION
JANUARY 5, 1776

New Hampshire has the distinction of having created America's first written constitution, and it did so a full six months before the colonies declared their independence from Great Britain. On November 3, 1775, the Continental Congress recommended that the people of New Hampshire, should they so desire, take the steps necessary to draft a constitution and form a temporary government until the conflict with Great Britain had been resolved. To that end, a new provincial congress was elected and on December 27, 1775, a special committee was appointed to draft a constitution. On January 5, 1776, New Hampshire's provincial congress voted on and approved the constitution as it would vote on any other bill. The constitution created a bicameral legislature with a with a House of Representatives (or Assembly) and an upper house called the Council. The congress that drafted the constitution reconstituted itself as the first House of Representatives under the new document. The constitution did not contain a bill or rights, nor did it provide for a chief executive. The New Hampshire constitution was not ratified by the people of the province. In 1784, the state of New Hampshire drafted a new constitution to replace the provincial one.

VOTED, That this Congress take up CIVIL GOVERNMENT for this colony in manner and form following, viz.

WE, the members of the Congress of New Hampshire, chosen and appointed by the free suffrages of the people of said colony, and authorized and empowered by them to meet together, and use such means and pursue such measures as we should judge best for the public good; and in particular to establish some form of government, provided that measure should be recommended by the Continental Congress: And a recommendation to that purpose having been transmitted to us from the said Congress: Have taken into our serious consideration the unhappy circumstances, into which this colony is involved by means of many grievous and oppressive acts of the British Parliament, depriving us of our natural and constitutional rights and privileges; to enforce obedience to which acts a powerful fleet and army have been sent to this country by the ministry of Great Britain, who have exercised a wanton and cruel abuse of their power, in destroying the lives and properties of the colonists in many places with fire and sword, taking the ships and lading from many of the honest and industrious inhabitants of this colony employed in commerce, agreeable to the laws and customs a long time used here.

The sudden and abrupt departure of his Excellency John Wentworth, Esq., our late Governor, and several of the Council, leaving us destitute of legislation, and no executive courts being open to punish criminal offenders; whereby the lives and properties of the honest people of this colony are liable to the machinations and evil designs of wicked men, *Therefore,* for the preservation of peace and good order, and for the security of the lives and properties of the inhabitants of this colony, we conceive ourselves reduced to the necessity of establishing A FORM OF GOVERNMENT to continue during the present unhappy and unnatural contest with Great Britain; PROTESTING and DECLARING that we never sought to throw off our dependence upon Great Britain, but felt ourselves happy under her protection, while we could enjoy our constitutional rights and privileges. And that we shall rejoice if such a reconciliation between us and our parent State can be effected as shall be approved by the CONTINENTAL CONGRESS, in whose prudence and wisdom we confide.

Accordingly pursuant to the trust reposed in us, WE DO Resolve, that this Congress assume the name, power and authority of a house of Representatives or Assembly for the *Colony of New-Hampshire* and that said House then proceed to choose twelve persons, being. reputable freeholders and inhabitants within this colony, in the following manner, viz. five in the county of Rockingham, two in the county of Stratford, two in the county of Hillsborough, two in the county of Cheshire, and one in the county of Grafton, to be a distinct and separate branch of the Legislature by the name of a COUNCIL for this colony, to continue as such until the third Wednesday in December next; any seven of whom to be a quorum to do business. That such Council appoint their President, and in his absence that the senior counsellor preside; that a Secretary be appointed by both branches, who may be a counsellor, or otherwise, as they shall choose:

That no act or resolve shall be valid and put into execution unless agreed to, and passed by both branches of the legislature

That all public officers for the said colony, and each county, for the current year, be appointed by the Council and Assembly, except the several clerks of the Executive Courts, who shall be appointed by the Justices of the respective Courts.

That all bills, resolves, or votes for raising, levying and collecting money originate in the house of Representatives.

That at any session of the Council and Assembly neither branch shall adjourn from any longer time than from Saturday till the next Monday without consent of the other.

And it is further resolved, That if the present unhappy dispute with Great Britain should continue longer than this present year, and the Continental Congress give no instruction or direction to the contrary, the Council be chosen by the people of each respective county in such manner as the Council and house of Representatives shall order.

That general and field officers of the militia, on any vacancy, be appointed by the two houses, and all inferior officers be chosen by the respective companies.

That all officers of the Army be appointed by the two houses, except they should direct otherwise in case of any emergency.

That all civil officers for the colony and for each county be appointed, and the time of their continuance in office be determined by the two houses, except clerks of Courts, and county treasurers, and recorders of deeds.

That a treasurer, and a recorder of deeds for each county be annually chosen by the people of each county respectively; the votes for such officers to be returned to the respective courts of General Sessions of the Peace in the county, there to be ascertained as the Council and Assembly shall hereafter direct.

That precepts in the name of the Council and Assembly, signed by the President of the Council, and Speaker of the house of Representatives, shall issue annually at or before the first day of November, for the choice of a Council and house of Representatives to be returned by the third Wednesday in December then next ensuing, in such manner as the Council and Assembly shall hereafter prescribe.

SOURCE: *The Federal and State Constitutions Colonial Charters, and Other Organic Laws of the States, Territories, and Colonies Now or Heretofore Forming the United States of America*, Compiled and Edited Under the Act of Congress of June 30, 1906 by Francis Newton Thorpe Washington, DC: Government Printing Office, 1909.

2. THE VIRGINIA CONSTITUTION
JUNE 29, 1776

On May 15, 1776, Virginia's provincial congress appointed a committee to draft a declaration of rights and a constitution. A draft declaration of rights was prepared by George Mason and was subsequently read to the provincial congress on May 27, and it was passed unanimously on June 12, 1776. The Virginia assembly then appointed a new committee (led my George Mason, Patrick Henry, Richard Henry Lee, and James Madison) to draft a constitution for the commonwealth, which was passed unanimously on June 29, 1776. The new constitution was notable for its separation of powers between legislative, executive, and judicial branches. The new form of government included a bicameral legislature (i.e., a House of Delegates and a Senate) and Governor or "chief magistrate" as the executive. Judges of the Supreme Court of Appeals were appointed by both houses of the legislature. The Virginia constitution was not ratified by the people of the commonwealth.

The CONSTITUTION or FORM of GOVERNMENT, agreed to and resolved upon by the Delegates and Representatives of the several counties and corporations of Virginia.

I. . . . [T]he government of this country, as formerly exercised under the crown of Great Britain, is TOTALLY DISSOLVED.

We . . . the delegates and representatives of the good people of Virginia, having maturely considered the premises, and viewing with great concern the deplorable condition to which this once happy country must be reduced, unless some regular, adequate mode of civil polity is speedily adopted, and in compliance with a recommendation of the General Congress, do ordain and declare the future form of government of Virginia to be as follows:

The legislative, executive, and judiciary departments, shall be separate and distinct, so that neither exercise the powers properly belonging to the other; nor shall any person exercise the powers of more than one of them at the same time, except that the justices of the county courts shall be eligible to either House of Assembly.

The legislative shall be formed of two distinct branches, who, together, shall be a complete legislature. They shall meet once, or oftener, every year, and shall be called the GENERAL ASSEMBLY OF VIRGINIA. One of these shall be called the HOUSE OF DELEGATES, and consist of two representatives to be chosen for each county, and for the District of West-Augusta, annually, of such men as actually reside in, and are freeholders of the same, or duly qualified according to law, and also of one delegate or representative to be chosen annually for the city of Williamsburg, and one for the borough of Norfolk, and a representative for each of such other cities and boroughs as may hereafter be allowed particular representation by the legislature; but when any city or borough shall so decrease as that the number of persons having right of suffrage therein shall have been for the space of seven years successively less than half the number of voters in some one county in Virginia, such city or borough thenceforward shall cease to send a delegate or representative to the Assembly.

The other shall be called the SENATE, and consist of twenty four members, of whom thirteen shall constitute a House to proceed on business, for whose election the different counties shall be divided into twenty four districts, and each county of the respective district, at the time of the election of its delegates, shall vote for one Senator, who is actually a resident and freeholder within the district, or duly qualified according to law, and is upwards of twenty five years of age; and the sheriffs of each county within five days at farthest after the last county election in the district, shall meet at some convenient place, and from the poll so taken in their respective counties return as a Senator the man who shall have the greatest number of votes in the whole district. To keep up this Assembly by rotation, the districts shall be equally divided into four classes, and numbered by lot. At the end of one year after the general election, the six members elected by the first division shall be displaced, and the vacancies thereby occasioned supplied from such class or division, by new election, in the manner aforesaid. This rotation shall be applied to each division, according to its number, and continued in due order annually.

The right of suffrage in the election of members for both Houses shall remain as exercised at present, and each House shall choose its own speaker, appoint its own officers, settle its own rules of proceeding, and direct writs of election for supplying intermediate vacancies.

All laws shall originate in the House of Delegates, to be approved or rejected by the Senate, or to be amended with the consent of the House of Delegates; except money bills, which in no instance shall be altered by the Senate, but wholly approved or rejected.

A Governor, or chief magistrate, shall be chosen annually, by joint ballot of both Houses, to be taken in each House respectively, deposited in the conference room, the boxes examined jointly by a committee of each house, and the numbers severally reported to them, that the appointments may be entered (which shall be the mode of taking the joint ballot of both Houses in all cases) who shall not continue in that office longer than three years successively, nor be eligible until the expiration of four years after he shall have been out of that office. An adequate, but moderate salary, shall be settled on him during his continuance in office; and he shall, with the advice of a

Council of State, exercise the executive powers of government according to the laws of this commonwealth; and shall not, under any pretense, exercise any power or prerogative by virtue of any law, statute, or custom, of England: But he shall, with the advice of the Council of State, have the power of granting reprieves or pardons, except where the prosecution shall have been carried on by the House of Delegates, or the law shall otherwise particularly direct; in which cases, no reprieve or pardon shall be granted, but by resolve of the House of Delegates.

Either House of the General Assembly may adjourn themselves respectively. The Governor shall not prorogue or adjourn the Assembly during their sitting, nor dissolve them at any time; but he shall, if necessary, either by advice of the Council of State, or on application of a majority of the House of Delegates, call them before the time to which they shall stand prorogued or adjourned.

A Privy Council, or Council of State, consisting of eight members, shall be chosen by joint ballot of both Houses of Assembly, either from their own members or the people at large, to assist in the administration of government. They shall annually choose out of their own members a president, who, in case of the death, inability, or necessary absence of the Governor from the government, shall act as Lieutenant Governor. Four members shall be sufficient to act, and their advice and proceedings shall be entered on record; and signed by the members present (to any part whereof any member may enter his dissent) to be laid before the General Assembly, when called for by them. This Council may appoint their own clerk, who shall have a salary settled by law, and take an oath of secrecy in such matters as he shall be directed by the board to conceal. A sum of money appropriated to that purpose shall be divided annually among the members, in proportion to their attendance; and they shall be incapable, during their continuance in office, of sitting in either House of Assembly. Two members shall be removed by joint ballot of both Houses of Assembly at the end of every three years, and be ineligible for the three next years. These vacancies, as well as those occasioned by death or incapacity, shall be supplied by new elections, in the same manner.

The delegates for Virginia to the Continental Congress shall be chosen annually, or superseded in the mean time by joint ballot of both Houses of Assembly.

The present militia officers shall be continued, and vacancies supplied by appointment of the Governor, with the advice of the Privy Council, or recommendations from the respective county courts; but the Governor and Council shall have a power of suspending any officer, and ordering a court-martial on complaint for misbehavior or inability, or to supply vacancies of officers happening when in actual service. The Governor may embody the militia, with the advice of the Privy Council; and, when embodied, shall alone have the direction of the militia under the laws of the country.

The two Houses of Assembly shall, by joint ballot, appoint Judges of the Supreme Court of Appeals, and General Court, Judges in Chancery, Judges of Admiralty, Secretary, and the Attorney-General, to be commissioned by the Governor, and continue in office during good behavior. In case of death, incapacity, or resignation, the Governor, with the advice of the Privy Council, shall appoint persons to succeed in office, to be approved or displaced by both Houses. These officers shall have fixed and adequate salaries, and, together with all others holding lucrative offices, and all ministers of the Gospel of every denomination, be incapable of being elected members of either House of assembly, or the Privy Council.

The Governor, with the advice of the Privy Council, shall appoint Justices of the Peace for the counties; and in case of vacancies, or a necessity of increasing the number hereafter, such appointments to be made upon the recommendation of the respective county courts. The present acting Secretary in Virginia, and Clerks of all the County Courts, shall continue in office. In case of vacancies, either by death, incapacity, or resignation, a Secretary shall be appointed as before directed, and the Clerks by the respective courts. The present and future Clerks shall hold their offices during good behavior, to be judged of and determined in the General Court. The Sheriffs and Coroners shall be nominated by the respective courts, approved by the Governor, with the advice of the Privy Council, and commissioned by the Governor. The Justices shall appoint Constables, and all fees of the aforesaid officers be regulated by law.

The Governor, when he is out of office, and others offending against the state, either by maladministration, corruption, or other means by which the safety of the state may be endangered, shall be impeachable by the House of Delegates. Such impeachment to be prosecuted by the Attorney-General, or such other person or persons as the House may appoint in the General Court, according to the laws of the land. If found guilty, he or they shall be either for ever disabled to hold any office under government, or removed from such Office *pro tempore*, or subjected to such pains or penalties as the laws shall direct.

If all, or any of the Judges of the General Court, shall, on good grounds (to be judged of by the House of Delegates) be accused of any of the crimes or offences before-mentioned, such House of Delegates may, in like manner, impeach the Judge or Judges so accused, to be prosecuted in the Court of Appeals; and he or they, if found guilty, shall be punished in the same manner as is prescribed in the preceding clause.

Commissions and grants shall run, *In the name of the COMMON-WEALTH of VIRGINIA*, and bear test by the Governor with the seal of the commonwealth annexed. Writs shall run in the same manner, and bear test by the clerks of the several courts. Indictments shall conclude, *Against the peace and dignity of the commonwealth*.

A treasurer shall be appointed annually, by joint ballot of both Houses.

All escheats, penalties, and forfeitures, heretofore going to the king, shall go to the commonwealth, save only such as the legislature may abolish, or otherwise provide for.

The territories contained within the charters erecting the colonies of Maryland, Pennsylvania, North and South Carolina, are hereby ceded, released, and for ever confirmed to the people of those colonies respectively, with all the rights of property, jurisdiction, and government, and all other rights whatsoever which might at any time heretofore have been claimed by Virginia, except the free navigation and use of the rivers Potowmack and Pohomoke, with the property of the Virginia shores or strands bordering on either of the said rivers, and all improvements which have been or shall be made thereon. The western and northern extent of Virginia shall in all other respects stand as fixed by the Charter of King James the first, in the year one thousand six hundred and nine, and by the public treaty of peace between the courts of Great Britain and France in the year one thousand seven hundred and sixty three; unless by act of legislature, one or more territories shall hereafter be laid off, and governments established westward of the Allegheny mountains. And no purchase of land shall be made of the Indian natives but on behalf of the public, by authority of the General Assembly.

In order to introduce this government, the representatives of the people met in Convention shall choose a Governor and Privy Council, also such other officers directed to be chosen by both Houses as may be judged necessary to be immediately appointed. The Senate to be first chosen by the people, to continue until the last day of March next, and the other officers until the end of the succeeding session of Assembly. In case of vacancies, the speaker of either House shall issue writs for new elections.

SOURCE: These excerpts are reprinted from Franci Newton Thorpe (ed.), *The Federal and State Constitutions, Colonial Charters, and other Organic Laws of the States and Territories now or heretofore forming the United States of America*, 7 vols. (Washington: Government Printing Office, 1909), 7: 3815-3819.

3. New Jersey Constitution
July 2, 1776

The last provincial constitution to be passed before the colonies formally declared their independence from Great Britain was New Jersey's. On May 10, 1776, the Continental Congress recommended to all those colonies "where no government sufficient to the exigencies of their affairs have been hitherto established to adopt such Government as shall, in the Opinion of the Representatives of the People, best conduce to the Happiness and Safety of their Constituents in particular and America in general." On June 21, 1776, the New Jersey provincial congress convened and determined that it should follow the recommendation of the Continental Congress and draft a provisional constitution for the soon-to-be state. The congress discussed a draft constitution from June 27 to July 2 and then approved the document by a vote of 26 to 29 two days before the Continental Congress voted to approve the Declaration of Independence. The New Jersey constitution created a bicameral legislature divided between a Legislative Council and a General Assembly, both of which voted annually to elect the Governor. The constitution of New Jersey was not ratified by the people, but it did last sixty-eight years.

WHEREAS all the constitutional authority ever possessed by the kings of Great Britain over these colonies, or their other dominions, was, by compact, derived from the people, and held of them, for the common interest of the whole society; allegiance and protection are, in the nature of things, reciprocal ties; each equally depending upon the other, and liable to be dissolved by the others being refused or withdrawn. And whereas George the Third, king of Great Britain, has refused protection to the good people of these colonies; and, by assenting to sundry acts of the British parliament, attempted to subject them to the absolute dominion of that body; and has also made war upon them, in the most cruel and unnatural manner, for no other cause, than asserting their just rights-all civil authority under him is necessarily at an end, and a dissolution of government in each colony has consequently taken place.

And whereas, In the present deplorable situation of these colonies, exposed to the fury of a cruel and relentless enemy, some form of government is absolutely necessary, not only for the preservation of good order, but also the more effectually to unite the people, and enable them to exert their whole force in their own necessary defence: and as the honorable the continental congress, the supreme council of the American colonies, has advised such of the colonies as have not yet gone into measures, to adopt for themselves, respectively, such government as shall best conduce to their own happiness and safety, and the well-being of America in general:-We, the representatives of the colony of New Jersey, having been elected by all the counties, in the freest manner, and in congress assembled, have, after mature deliberations, agreed upon a set of charter rights and the form of a Constitution, in manner following, viz.

I.   That the government of this Province shall be vested in a Governor, Legislative Council, and General Assembly.

II. That the Legislative Council, and General Assembly, shall be chosen, for the first time, on the second Tuesday in August next; the members whereof shall be the same in number and qualifications as are herein after mentioned; and shall be and remain vested with all the powers and authority to be held by any future Legislative Council and Assembly of this Colony, until the second Tuesday in October, which shall be in the year of our Lord one thousand seven hundred and seventy-seven.

III. That on the second Tuesday in October yearly, and every year forever (with the privilege of adjourning from day to day as occasion may require) the counties shall severally choose one person, to be a member of the Legislative Council of this Colony, who shall be, and have been, for one whole year next before the election, an inhabitant and freeholder in the county in which he is chosen, and worth at least one thousand pounds proclamation money, of real and personal estate, within the same county; that, at the same time, each county shall also choose three members of Assembly; provided that no person shall be entitled to a seat in the said Assembly unless he be, and have been, for one whole year next before the election, an inhabitant of the county he is to represent, and worth five hundred pounds proclamation money, in real and personal estate, in the same county: that on the second Tuesday next after the day of election, the Council and Assembly shall separately meet; and that the consent of both Houses shall be necessary to every law; provided, that seven shall be a quorum of the Council, for doing business, and that no law shall pass, unless there be a majority of all the Representatives of each body personally present, and agreeing thereto. Provided always, that if a majority of the representatives of this Province, in Council and General Assembly convened, shall, at any time or times hereafter, judge it equitable and proper, to add to or diminish the number or proportion of the members of Assembly for any county or counties in this Colony, then, and in such case, the same may, on the principles of more equal representation, be lawfully done; anything in this Charter to the contrary notwithstanding: so that the whole number of Representatives in Assembly shall not, at any time, be less than thirty-nine.

IV. That all inhabitants of this Colony, of full age, who are worth fifty pounds proclamation money, clear estate in the same, and have resided within the county in which they claim a vote for twelve months immediately preceding the election, shall be entitled to vote for Representatives in

Council and Assembly; and also for all other public officers, that shall be elected by the people of the county at large.

V. That the Assembly, when met, shall have power to choose a Speaker, and other their officers; to be judges of the qualifications and elections of their own members; sit upon their own adjournments; prepare bills, to be passed into laws; and to empower their Speaker to convene them, whenever any extraordinary occurrence shall render it necessary.

VI. That the Council shall also have power to prepare bills to pass into laws, and have other like powers as the Assembly, and in all respects be a free and independent branch of the Legislature of this Colony; save only, that they shall not prepare or alter any money bill-which shall be the privilege of the Assembly; that the Council shall, from time to time, be convened by the Governor or Vice-President, but must be convened, at all times, when the Assembly sits; for which purpose the Speaker of the House of Assembly shall always, immediately after an adjournment, give notice to the Governor, or Vice-President, of the time and place to which the House is adjourned.

VII. That the Council and Assembly jointly, at their first meeting after each annual election, shall, by a majority of votes, elect some fit person within the Colony, to be Governor for one year, who shall be constant President of the Council, and have a casting vote in their proceedings; and that the Council themselves shall choose a Vice-President who shall act as such in the absence of the Governor.

VIII. That the Governor, or, in his absence, the Vice-President of the Council, shall have the supreme executive power, be Chancellor of the Colony, and act as captain-general and commander in chief of all the militias and other military force in this Colony; and that any three or more of the Council shall, at all times, be a privy-council, to consult them; and that the Governor be ordinary or surrogate general.

IX. That the Governor and Council, (seven whereof shall be a quorum) be the Court of Appeals, in the last resort, in all clauses of law, as heretofore; and that they possess the power of granting pardons to criminals, after condemnation, in all cases of treason, felony, or other offences.

X. That captains, and all other inferior officers of the militia, shall be chosen by the companies, in the respective counties; but field and general officers, by the Council and Assembly.

XI. That the Council and Assembly shall have power to make the (treat Seal of this Colony, which shall be kept by the Governor, or, in his absence, by the V3ce-President of the Council, to be used by them as occasion may require: and it shall be called, The Great Seal of the Colony of New-Jersey.

XII. That the Judges of the Supreme Court shall continue in office for seven years: the Judges of the Inferior Court of Common Pleas in the several counties, Justices of the Peace, Clerks of the Supreme Court, Clerks of the Inferior Court of Common Pleas and Quarter Sessions, the Attorney-General, and Provincial Secretary, shall continue in office for five years: and the

Provincial Treasurer shall continue in office for one year; and that they shall be severally appointed by the Council and Assembly, in manner aforesaid, and commissioned by the Governor, or, in his absence, the Vice-President of the Council. Provided always, that the said officers, severally, shall be capable of being re-appointed, at the end of the terms severally before limited; and that any of the said officers shall be liable to be dismissed, when adjudged guilty of misbehaviour, by the Council, on an impeachment of the Assembly.

XIII. That the inhabitants of each county, qualified to vote as aforesaid' shall at the title and place of electing their Representatives, annually elect one Sheriff, and one or more Coroners; and that they may re-elect the same person to such offices, until he shall have served three years, but no longer; after which, three years must elapse before the same person is capable of being elected again. When the election is certified to the Governor, or Vice-President, under the hands of six freeholders of the county for which they were elected, they shall be immediately commissioned to serve in their respective offices.

XIV. That the townships, at their annual town meetings for electing other officers, shall choose constables for the districts respectively; and also three or more judicious freeholders of good character, to hear and finally determine all appeals, relative to unjust assessments, in cases of public taxation; which commissioners of appeal shall, for that purpose, sit at some suitable time or times, to be by them appointed, and made know n to the people by advertisements.

XV. That the laws of the Colony shall begin in the following style, viz. " Be it enacted by the Council and General Assembly of this Colony, and it is hereby enacted by authority of the same: " that all commissions, granted by the Governor or Vice-President, shall run thus-" The Colony of New-Jersey to A. B. &c. greeting: " and that all writs shall likewise run in the name of the Colony: and that all indictments shall conclude in the following manner, viz. "Against the peace of this Colony, the government and dignity of the same.

XVI. That all criminals shall be admitted to the same privileges of witnesses and counsel, as their prosecutors are or shall be entitled to.

XVII. That the estates of such persons as shall destroy their own lives, shall not, for that offence, be forfeited; but shall descend in the same manner, as they would have done, had such persons died in the natural way; nor shall any article, which may occasion accidentally the death of any one, be henceforth deemed, a deodand, or in anywise forfeited, on account of such misfortune.

XVIII. That no person shall ever, within this Colony, be deprived of the inestimable privilege of worshipping Almighty God in a manner, agreeable to the dictates of his own conscience; nor, under any presence whatever, be compelled to attend any place of worship, contrary to his own faith and judgment; nor shall any person, within this Colony, ever be obliged to pay tithes, taxes, or any other rates, for the purpose of building or repairing any other church or churches, place or places of worship, or for the maintenance of any minister or ministry, contrary to what he believes to be right, or has deliberately or voluntarily engaged himself to perform.

XIX. That there shall be no establishment of any one religious sect in this Province, in preference to another; and that no Protestant inhabitant of this Colony shall be denied the enjoyment of any civil right, merely on account of his religious principles; but that all persons, professing a belief in the faith of any Protestant sect. who shall demean themselves peaceably under the government, as hereby established, shall be capable of being elected into any office of profit or trust, or being a member of either branch of the Legislature, and shall fully and freely enjoy every privilege and immunity, enjoyed by others their fellow subjects.

XX. That the legislative department of this government may, as much as possible, be preserved from all suspicion of corruption, none of the Judges of the Supreme or other Courts, Sheriffs, or any other person or persons possessed of any post of profit under the government, other than Justices of the Peace, shall be entitled to a seat in the Assembly: but that, on his being elected, and taking his seat, his office or post shall be considered as vacant.

XXI. That all the laws of this Province, contained in the edition lately published by Mr. Allinson, shall be and remain in full force, until altered by the Legislature of this Colony (such only excepted, as are incompatible with this Charter) and shall be, according as heretofore, regarded in all respects, by all civil officers, and others, the good people of this Province.

XXII. That the common law of England, as well as so much of the statute law, as have been heretofore practiced in this Colony, shall still remain in force, until they shall be altered by a future law of the Legislature; such parts only excepted, as are repugnant to the rights and privileges contained in this Charter; and that the inestimable right of trial by jury shall remain confirmed as a part of the law of this Colony, without repeal, forever.

XXIII. That every person, who shall be elected as aforesaid to be a member of the Legislative Council, or House of Assembly, shall, previous to his taking his seat in Council or Assembly, take the following oath or affirmation, viz: "I, A. B., do solemnly declare, that, as a member of the Legislative Council, [or Assembly, as the case may be,] of the Colony of New-Jersey, I will not assent to any law, vote or proceeding, which shall appear to me injurious to the public welfare of said Colony, nor that shall annul or repeal that part of the third section in the Charter of this Colony, which establishes, that the elections of members of the Legislative Council and Assembly shall be annual; nor that part of the twenty-second section in said Charter, respecting the trial by jury, nor that shall annul, repeal, or alter any part or parts of the eighteenth or nineteenth sections of the same."

And any person or persons, who shall be elected as aforesaid, is hereby empowered to administer to the said members the said oath or affirmation.

Provided always, and it is the true intent and meaning of this Congress, that if a reconciliation between Great-Britain and these Colonies should take place, and the latter be taken again under the protection and government of the crown of Britain, this Charter shall be null and void-otherwise to remain firm and inviolable.

SOURCE: These excerpts are reprinted from Franci Newton Thorpe (ed.), *The Federal and State Constitutions, Colonial Charters, and other Organic Laws of the States and Territories now or heretofore forming the United States of America*, 7 vols. (Washington: Government Printing Office, 1909), 7: 2594-2598.

4. DELAWARE STATE CONSTITUTION
SEPTEMBER 20, 1776

Delaware was the first official state after the passage of the Declaration of Independence to draft a constitution. The Delaware General Assembly passed legislation in July 1776 calling for an election to create a convention "to order and declare the future form of Government for the new state." Thus, Delaware was the first state to call for the creation of a special convention for the express purpose of drafting a constitution. The purpose of such a procedure was to elevate the constitution above ordinary acts of legislation. On September 2, 1776, the Delaware constitutional convention appointed a committee of ten to draft a "Declaration of Rights and Fundamental Rules of State," which finished its work by September 11. In the interim, a second committee was formed to draft "a Constitution or System of Government for this State," which was subsequently approved by the plenum on September 20, 1776. Delaware's constitution was bicameral and consisted of an annually elected House of Assembly and an upper house called the Council, which served three-year terms. Delaware's executive authority was vested in a president or Chief Magistrate, who was chosen by a joint ballot of both legislative houses every three years. After the Delaware constitution was approved, the constitutional convention dissolved itself rather than declaring itself the first legislative body under the constitution. The Delaware constitution was not ratified by the people of the state.

THE CONSTITUTION, OR SYSTEM OF GOVERNMENT, AGREED TO AND RESOLVED UPON BY THE REPRESENTATIVES IN FULL CONVENTION OF THE DELAWARE STATE

ARTICLE 1. The government of the counties of New- Castle, Kent and Sussex, upon Delaware, shall hereafter in all public and other writings be called The Delaware State.

ART. 2. The Legislature shall be formed of two distinct branches; they shall meet once or oftener in every year, and shall be called, "The General Assembly of Delaware."

ART. 3. One of the branches of- the Legislature shall be called, "The House of Assembly," and shall consist of seven Representatives to be chosen for each county annually of such persons as are freeholders of the same.

ART. 4. The other branch shall be called "The council," and consist of nine members; three to be chosen for each county at the time of the first election of the assembly, who shall be freeholders of the county for which they are chosen, and be upwards of twenty-five years of age. At the end of one year after the general election, the councillor who had the smallest number of votes in each county shall be displaced, and the vacancies thereby occasioned supplied by the freemen of each county choosing the same or another person at a new election in manner aforesaid. At the end of two years after the first general election, the councillor who stood second in number of votes in each county shall be displaced, and the vacancies thereby occasioned supplied by a new election in manner aforesaid. And at the end of three years from the first general election, the councillor who had the greatest number of votes in each county shall be displaced, and the vacancies thereby occasioned supplied by a new election in manner aforesaid. And this rotation of a councillor being displaced at the end of three years in each county, and his office supplied by a new choice, shall be continued afterwards in due order annually forever, whereby, after the first general election, a councillor will remain in trust for three years from the time of his being elected, and a councillor will be displaced, and the same or another chosen in each county at every election.

ART. 5. The right of suffrage in the election of members for both houses shall remain as exercised by law at present; and each house shall choose its own speaker, appoint its own officers, judge of the qualifications and elections of its own members, settle its own rules of proceedings, and direct writs of election for supplying intermediate vacancies. They may also severally expel any of their own members for misbehavior, but not a second time in the same sessions for the same offence, if reelected; and they shall have all other powers necessary for the legislature of a free and independent State.

ART. 6. All money-bills for the support of government shall originate in the house of assembly, and may be altered, amended, or rejected by the legislative council. All other bills and ordinances may take rise in the house of assembly or legislative council, and may be altered, amended, or rejected by either.

ART. 7. A president or chief magistrate shall be chosen by joint ballot of both houses' to be taken in the house of assembly, and the box examined by the speakers of each house in the presence of the other members, and in case the numbers for the two highest in votes should be equal, then the speaker of the council shall have an additional casting voice, and the appointment of the person who has the majority of votes shall be entered at large on the minutes and journals of each house, and a copy thereof on parchment, certified and signed by the speakers respectively, and sealed with the great seal of the State, which they are hereby authorized to affix, shall be delivered to the person so chosen president, who shall continue in that office three years, and until the sitting of the next general assembly and no longer, nor be eligible until the expiration of three years after he shall have been out of that office. An adequate but moderate salary shall be settled on him during his continuance in office. He may draw for such sums of money as shall be appropriated by the general assembly, and be accountable to them for the same; he may, by and with the advice of the privy council, lay embargoes or prohibit the exportation of any commodity for any time not exceeding thirty days in the recess of the general assembly; he shall have the power of granting pardons or reprieves, except where the prosecution shall be carried on by the house of assembly, or the law shall otherwise direct, in which cases no pardon or reprieve shall be granted, but by a resolve of the house of assembly, and may exercise all the other executive powers of government' limited and restrained as by this constitution is mentioned, and according to the laws of the State. And on his death, inability, or absence from the State, the speaker of the legislative council for the time being shall be vice-president, and in case of his death, inability, or absence from the State, the speaker of the house of assembly shall have the powers of a president, until a new nomination is made by the general assembly.

ART. 8. A privy council, consisting of four members, shall be chosen by ballot, two by the legislative council and two by the house of assembly: *Provided*, That no regular officer of the army or navy in the service and pay of the continent, or of this, or of any other State, shall be eligible; and a member of the legislative council or of the house of assembly being chosen of the privy council, and accepting thereof, shall thereby lose his seat. Three members shall be a quorum, and their advice and proceedings shall be entered of record, and signed by the members present, (to any part of which any member may enter his dissent,) to be laid before the general assembly when called for by them. Two members shall be removed by ballot, one by the legislative council and one by the house of assembly, at the end of two years, and those who remain the next year after, who shall severally be ineligible for the three next years. The vacancies, as well as those occasioned by death or incapacity, shall be supplied by new elections in the same manner; and this rotation of a privy councillor shall be continued afterwards in due order annually forever. The president may by summons convene the privy council at any time when the public exigencies may require, and at such place as he shall think most convenient, when and where they are to attend accordingly.

ART. 9. The president, with the advice and consent of the privy council, may embody the militia, and act as captain-general and commander-in-chief of them, and the other military force of this State, under the laws of the same.

ART. 10. Either house of the General assembly may adjourn themselves respectively. The president shall not prorogue, adjourn, or dissolve the general assembly, but he may, with the advice of the privy council, or on the application of a majority of either house, call them before the time they shall stand adjourned; and the two houses shall always sit at the same time and place, for which purpose immediately after every adjournment the speaker of the house of assembly shall give notice to the speaker of the other house of the time to which the house of assembly stands adjourned.

ART. 11. The Delegates for Delaware to the Congress of the United States of America shall be chosen annually, or superseded in the mean time, by joint ballot of both houses in the general assembly.

ART. 12. The president and general assembly shall by joint ballot appoint three justices of the supreme court for the State, one of whom shall be chief justice, and a judge of admiralty, and also four justices of the courts of common pleas and orphans' courts for each county, one of whom in each court shall be styled "chief justice," (and in case of division on the Ballot the president shall have an additional casting voice,) to be commissioned by the president under the great seal, who shall continue in office during good behavior; and during the time the justices of the said supreme court and courts of common pleas remain in office, they shall hold none other except in the militia. Any one of the justices of either of said courts shall have power, in case of the noncoming of his brethren, to open and adjourn the court. An adequate fixed but moderate salary shall be settled on them during their continuance in office. The president and privy council shall appoint the secretary, the attorney-general, registers for the probate of wills and granting letters of administration, registers in chancery, clerks of the courts of common pleas and orphans' courts, and clerks of the peace, who shall be commissioned as aforesaid, and remain in office during five years, if they behave themselves well; during which time the said registers in chancery and clerks shall not be justices of either of the said courts of which they are officers, but they shall have authority to sign all writs by them issued, and take recognizances of bail. The justices of the peace shall be nominated by the house of assembly; that is to say, they shall name twenty-four persons for each county, of whom the president, with the approbation of the privy council, shall appoint twelve, who shall be commissioned as aforesaid, and continue in office during seven years, if they behave themselves well; and in case of vacancies, or if the legislature shall think proper to increase the number, they shall be nominated and appointed in like manner. The members of the legislative and privy councils shall be justices of the peace for the whole State, during their continuance in trust; and the justices of the courts of common pleas shall be conservators of the peace in their respective counties.

ART. 13. The justices of the courts of common pleas and orphans courts shall have the power of holding inferior courts of chancery, as heretofore, unless the legislature shall otherwise direct.

ART. 14. The clerks of the supreme court shall be appointed by the chief justice thereof, and the recorders of deeds, by the justices of the courts of common pleas for each county severally, and commissioned by the president, under the great seal, and continue in office five years, if they behave themselves well.

ART. 15. The sheriffs and coroners of the respective counties shall be chosen annually, as heretofore; and any person, having served three years as sheriff, shall be ineligible for three years after; and the president and privy council shall have the appointment of such of the two candidates, returned for said offices of sheriff and coroner, as they shall think best qualified, in the same manner that the governor heretofore enjoyed this power.

ART. 16. The general assembly, by joint ballots shall appoint the generals and field-officers, and all other officers in the army or navy of this State; and the president may appoint, during pleasure, until otherwise directed by the legislature, all necessary civil officers not hereinbefore mentioned.

ART. 17. There shall be an appeal from the supreme court of Delaware, in matters of law and equity, to a court of seven persons, to consist of the president for the time being, who shall preside therein, and six others, to be appointed, three by the legislative council, and three by the house of assembly, who shall continue in office during good behavior, and be commissioned by the president, under the great seal; which court shall be styled the " court of appeals," and have all the authority and powers heretofore given by law in the last resort to the King in council, under the old government. The secretary shall be the clerk of this court; and vacancies therein occasioned by death or incapacity, shall be supplied by new elections, in manner aforesaid.

ART. 18. The justices of the supreme court and courts of common pleas, the members of the privy council, the secretary, the trustees of the loan office, and clerks of the court of common pleas, during their continuance in office, and all persons concerned in any army or navy contracts, shall be ineligible to either house of assembly; and any member of either house accepting of any other of the offices herein before mentioned (excepting the office of a justice of the peace) shall have his seat thereby vacated, and a new election shall be ordered.

ART. 19. The legislative council and assembly shall have the power of making the great seal of this State, which shall be kept by the president, or, in his absence, by the vice-president, to be used by them as occasion may require. It shall be called *"The Great Seal of the Delaware State,"* and shall be affixed to all laws and commissions.

ART. 20. Commissions shall run in the name of "The Delaware State," and bear test by the president Writs shall run in the same manner, and bear test in the name of the chief-justice, or justice first named in the commissions for the several courts, and be sealed with the public seals of such courts. Indictments shall conclude, *"Against the peace and dignity of the State."*

ART. 21. In case of vacancy of the offices above directed to be filled by the president and general assembly, the president and privy council may appoint others in their stead until there shall be a new election.

ART. 22. Every person who shall be chosen a member of either house, or appointed to any office or place of trust, before taking his seat, or entering upon the execution of his office, shall take the following oath, or affirmation, if conscientiously scrupulous of taking an oath, to wit: "I, A B. will bear true allegiance to the Delaware State, submit to its constitution and laws, and do no act wittingly whereby the freedom thereof may be prejudiced."

And also make and subscribe the following declaration, to wit: "I, A B. do profess faith in God the Father, and in Jesus Christ His only Son, and in the Holy Ghost, one God, blessed for evermore; and I do acknowledge the holy scriptures of the Old and New Testament to be given by divine inspiration."

And all officers shall also take an oath of office.

ART. 23. The president, when he is out of office, and within eighteen months after, and all others offending against the State, either by maladministration, corruption, or other means, by which the safety of the Commonwealth may be endangered, within eighteen months after the offence committed, shall be impeachable by the house of assembly before the legislative council; such impeachment to be prosecuted by the attorney-general, or such other person or persons as the house of assembly may appoint, according to the laws of the land. If found guilty, he or they shall be either forever disabled to hold any office under government, or removed from office *pro tempore*, or subjected to such pains and penalties as the laws shall direct. And all officers shall be removed on conviction of misbehavior at common law, or on impeachment, or upon the address of the general assembly.

ART. 24. All acts of assembly in force in this State on the 15th day of May last (and not hereby altered, or contrary to the resolutions of Congress or of the late house of assembly of this State) shall so continue, until altered or repealed by the legislature of this State, unless where they are temporary, in which case they shall expire at the times respectively limited for their duration.

ART. 25. The common law of England, as-well as so much of the statute law as has been heretofore adopted in practice in this State, shall remain in force, unless they shall be altered by a future law of the legislature; such parts only excepted as are repugnant to the rights and privileges contained in this constitution, and the declaration of rights, &c., agreed to by this convention.

ART. 26. No person hereafter imported into this State from Africa ought to be held in slavery under any presence whatever; and no negro, Indian, or mulatto slave ought to be brought into this State, for sale, from any part of the world.

ART. 27. The first election for the general assembly of this State shall be held on the List day of October next, at the court-houses in the several counties, in the manner heretofore used in the election of the assembly, except as to the choice of inspectors and assessors, where assessors have not been chosen on the 16th day of September, instant, which shall be made on the morning of the day of election, by the electors, inhabitants of the respective hundreds in each county. At which time the sheriffs and coroners, for the said counties respectively, are to be elected; and the present sheriffs of the counties of Newcastle and Kent may be rechosen to that office until the 1st day of October, A. D. 1779; and the present sheriff for the county of Sussex may be rechosen to that office until the 1st day of October, A. D. 1778, provided the freemen think proper to reelect them at every general election; and the present sheriffs and coroners, respectively, shall continue to exercise their offices as heretofore, until the sheriffs and coroners, to be elected on the said 21st day of October, shall be commissioned and sworn into office. The members of the legislative council and assembly shall meet, for transacting the business of the State, on the 28th day of October next, and continue in office until the 1st day of October, which will be in the year 1777; on which day, and on the 1st day of October in each year forever after, the legislative council, assembly, sheriffs, and coroners shall be chosen by ballot, in manner directed by the several laws of this State, for regulating elections of members of assembly and sheriffs and coroners; and the general assembly shall meet on the 20th day of the same month for the transacting the business of the State; and if any of the said 1st and 20th days of October should be Sunday, then, and in such case, the elections shall be held, and the general assembly meet, the next day following.

ART. 28. To prevent any violence or force being used at the said elections, no person shall come armed to any of them, and no muster of the militia shall be made on that day; nor shall any battalion or company give in their votes immediately succeeding each other, if any other voter, who offers to vote, objects thereto; nor shall any battalion or company, in the pay of the continent, or of this or any other State, be suffered to remain at the time and place of holding the said elections, nor within one mile of the said places respectively, for twenty-four hours before the opening said elections, nor within twenty-four hours after the same are closed, so as in any manner to impede the freely and conveniently carying on the said election: *Provided always*, That every elector may, in a peaceable and orderly manner, give in his vote on the said day of election.

ART. 29. There shall be no establishment of any one religious sect in this State in preference to another; and no clergyman or preacher of the gospel, of any denomination, shall be capable of holding any civil once in this State, or of being a member of either of the branches of the legislature, while they continue in the exercise of the pastorial function.

ART. 30. No article of the declaration of rights and fundamental rules of this State, agreed to by this convention, nor the first, second, fifth, (except that part thereof that relates to the right of suffrage,) twenty-sixth, and twenty-ninth articles of this constitution, ought ever to be violated on any presence whatever. No other part of this constitution shall be altered, changed, or diminished without the consent of five parts in seven of the assembly, and seven members of the legislative council.

SOURCE: These excerpts are reprinted from Franci Newton Thorpe (ed.), *The Federal and State Constitutions, Colonial Charters, and other Organic Laws of the*

States and Territories now or heretofore forming the United States of America, 7 vols. (Washington: Government Printing Office, 1909), 7: 562-568.

In June 1776, 108 delegates of the revolutionary county committees of inspection met for a week-long "Provincial Conference of Committees of the Province of Pennsylvania." The primary purpose of the conference was to arrange for an election to send delegates to a constitutional convention. The conference resolved "that the present Assembly of the Colony is 'not competent to the exigencies of affairs' and that a Provincial Convention ought to be called for inaugurating a form of Colonial government, in compliance with the recommendation of Congress." On July 15, the constitutional convention met with ninety-six delegates and began its work. The first work of the convention was to draft a declaration of rights and then a constitution. The declaration and constitution were both passed by the convention on September 28. The Pennsylvania constitution is notable for its unicameral legislature elected annually, its plural executive (a president elected by the assembly and a twelve-member Supreme Executive Council to serve with the president), and its Council of Censors (elected every seven years) to judge whether the constitution had been violated by the legislature or president. The Pennsylvania constitution was not ratified by the people of the state.

WHEREAS all government ought to be instituted and supported for the security and protection of the community as such, and to enable the individuals who compose it to enjoy their natural rights, and the other blessings which the Author of existence has bestowed upon man; and whenever these great ends of government are not obtained, the people have a right, by common consent to change it, and take such measures as to them may appear necessary to promote their safety and happiness. AND WHEREAS the inhabitants of this commonwealth have in consideration of protection only, heretofore acknowledged allegiance to the king of Great Britain; and the said king has not only withdrawn that protection, but commenced, and still continues to carry on, with unabated vengeance, a most cruel and unjust war against them, employing therein, not only the troops of Great Britain, but foreign mercenaries, savages and slaves, for the avowed purpose of reducing them to a total and abject submission to the despotic domination of the British parliament, with many other acts of tyranny, (more fully set forth in the declaration of Congress) whereby all allegiance and fealty to the said king and his successors, are dissolved and at an end, and all power and authority derived from him ceased in these colonies. AND WHEREAS it is absolutely necessary for the welfare and safety of the inhabitants of said colonies, that they be henceforth free and independent States, and that just, permanent, and proper forms of government exist in every part of them, derived from and founded on the authority of the people only, agreeable to the directions of the honourable American Congress. We, the representatives of the freemen of Pennsylvania, in general convention met, for the express purpose of framing such a government, confessing the goodness of the great Governor of the universe (who alone knows to what degree of earthly happiness mankind may attain, by perfecting the arts of government) in permitting the people of this State, by common consent, and without violence, deliberately to form for themselves such just rules as they shall think best, for governing their future society, and being fully convinced, that it is our indispensable duty to establish such original principles of government, as will best promote the general happiness of the people of this State, and their posterity, and provide for future improvements, without partiality for, or prejudice against any particular class, sect, or denomination of men whatever, do, by virtue of the authority vested in use by our constituents, ordain, declare, and establish, the following Declaration of Rights and Frame of Government, to be the CONSTITUTION of this commonwealth, and to remain in force therein forever, unaltered, except in such articles as shall hereafter on experience be found to require improvement, and which shall by the same authority of the people, fairly delegated as this frame of government directs, be amended or improved for the more effectual obtaining and securing the great end and design of all government, herein before mentioned.

A DECLARATION OF THE RIGHTS OF THE INHABITANTS OF THE COMMONWEALTH OR STATE OF PENNSYLVANIA

I. That all men are born equally free and independent, and have certain natural, inherent and inalienable rights, amongst which are, the enjoying and defending life and liberty, acquiring, possessing and protecting property, and pursuing and obtaining happiness and safety.

II. That all men have a natural and unalienable right to worship Almighty God according to the dictates of their own consciences and understanding: And that no man ought or of right can be compelled to attend any religious worship, or erect or support any place of worship, or maintain any ministry, contrary to, or against, his own free will and consent: Nor can any man, who acknowledges the being of a God, be justly deprived or abridged of any civil right as a citizen, on account of his religious sentiments or peculiar mode of religious worship: And that no authority can or ought to be vested in, or assumed by any power whatever, that shall in any case interfere with, or in any manner controul, the right of conscience in the free exercise of religious worship.

III. That the people of this State have the sole, exclusive and inherent right of governing and regulating the internal police of the same.

IV. That all power being originally inherent in, and consequently derived from, the people; therefore all officers of government, whether legislative or executive, are their trustees and servants, and at all times accountable to them.

V. That government is, or ought to be, instituted for the common benefit, protection and security of the people, nation or community; and not for the particular emolument or advantage of any single man, family, or soft of men, who are a part only of that community, And that the community hath an indubitable, unalienable and indefeasible right to reform, alter, or abolish government in such manner as shall be by that community judged most conducive to the public weal.

VI. That those who are employed in the legislative and executive business of the State, may be restrained from oppression, the people have a right, at such periods as they may think proper, to reduce their public officers to a private station, and supply the vacancies by certain and regular elections.

VII. That all elections ought to be free; and that all free men having a sufficient evident common interest with, and attachment to the community, have a right to elect officers, or to be elected into office.

VIII. That every member of society hath a right to be protected in the enjoyment of life, liberty and property, and therefore is bound to contribute his proportion towards the expence of that protection, and yield his personal service when necessary, or an equivalent thereto: But no part of a man's property can be justly taken from him, or applied to public uses, without his own consent, or that of his legal representatives: Nor can any man who is conscientiously scrupulous of bearing arms, be justly compelled thereto, if he will pay such equivalent, nor are the people bound by any laws, but such as they have in like manner assented to, for their common good.

IX. That in all prosecutions for criminal offences, a man hath a right to be heard by himself and his council, to demand the cause and nature of his accusation, to be confronted with the witnesses, to call for evidence in his favour, and a speedy public trial, by an impartial jury of the country, without the unanimous consent of which jury he cannot be found guilty; nor can he be compelled to give evidence against himself; nor can any man be justly deprived of his liberty except by the laws of the land, or the judgment of his peers.

X. That the people have a right to hold themselves, their houses, papers, and possessions free from search and seizure, and therefore warrants without oaths or affirmations first made, affording a sufficient foundation for them, and whereby any officer or messenger may be commanded or required to search suspected places, or to seize any person or persons, his or their property, not particularly described, are contrary to that right, and ought not to be granted.

XI. That in controversies respecting property, and in suits between man and man, the parties have a right to trial by jury, which ought to be held sacred.

XII. That the people have a right to freedom of speech, and of writing, and publishing their sentiments; therefore the freedom of the press ought not to be restrained.

XIII. That the people have a right to bear arms for the defence of themselves and the state; and as standing armies in the time of peace are dangerous to liberty, they ought not to be kept up; And that the military should be kept under strict subordination to, and governed by, the civil power.

XIV. That a frequent recurrence to fundamental principles, and a firm adherence to justice, moderation, temperance, industry, and frugality are absolutely necessary to preserve the blessings of liberty, and keep a government free: The people ought therefore to pay particular attention to these points in the choice of officers and representatives, and have a right to exact a due and constant regard to them, from their legislatures and magistrates, in the making and executing such laws as are necessary for the good government of the state.

XV. That all men have a natural inherent right to emigrate from one state to another that will receive them, or to form a new state in vacant countries, or in such countries as they can purchase, whenever they think that thereby they may promote their own happiness.

XVI. That the people have a right to assemble together, to consult for their common good, to instruct their representatives, and to apply to the legislature for redress of grievances, by address, petition, or remonstrance.

PLAN OR FRAME OF GOVERNMENT FOR THE COMMONWEALTH OR STATE OF PENNSYLVANIA

SECTION 1. The commonwealth or state of Pennsylvania shall be governed hereafter by an assembly of the representatives of the freemen of the same, and a president and council, in manner and form following-

SECT. 2. The supreme legislative power shall be vested in a house of representatives of the freemen of the commonwealth or state of Pennsylvania.

SECT. 3. The supreme executive power shall be vested in a president and council.

SECT. 4. Courts of justice shall be established in the city of Philadelphia, and in every county of this state.

SECT. 5. The freemen of this commonwealth and their sons shall be trained and armed for its defence under such regulations, restrictions, and exceptions as the general assembly shall by law direct, preserving always to the people the right of choosing their colonels and all commissioned officers under that rank, in such manner and as often as by the said laws shall be directed.

SECT. 6. Every freemen of the full age of twenty-one Years, having resided in this state for the space of one whole Year next before the day of election for representatives, and paid public taxes during that time, shall enjoy the right of an elector: Provided always, that sons of freeholders of the age of twenty-one years shall be intitled to vote although they have not paid taxes.

SECT. 7. The house of representatives of the freemen of this commonwealth shall consist of persons most noted for wisdom and virtue, to be chosen by the freemen of every city and county of this commonwealth respectively. And no person shall be elected unless he has resided in the city or county for which he shall be chosen two years immediately before the said election; nor shall any member, while he continues such, hold any other office, except in the militia.

SECT. 8. No person shall be capable of being elected a member to serve in the house of representatives of the freemen of this commonwealth more than four years in seven.

SECT. 9. The members of the house of representatives shall be chosen annually by ballot, by the freemen of the commonwealth, on the second Tuesday in October forever, (except this present year,) and shall meet on the fourth Monday of the same month, and shall be stiled, The general assembly of the representatives of the freemen of Pennsylvania, and shall have power to choose their speaker, the treasurer of the state, and their other officers; sit on their own adjournments; prepare bills and enact them into laws; judge of the elections and qualifications of their own members; they may expel a member, but not a second time for the same cause; they may administer oaths or affirmations on examination of witnesses; redress grievances; impeach state criminals; grant charters of incorporation; constitute towns, boroughs, cities, and counties; and shall have all other powers necessary for the legislature of a free state or commonwealth: But they shall have no power to add to, alter, abolish, or infringe any part of this constitution.

SECT. 10. A quorum of the house of representatives shall consist of two-thirds of the whole number of members elected; and having met and chosen their speaker, shall each of them before they proceed to business take and subscribe, as well the oath or affirmation of fidelity and allegiance hereinafter directed, as the following oath or affirmation, viz:

I do swear (or affirm) that as a member of this assembly, I will not propose or assent to any bill, vote, or resolution, which stall appear to free injurious to the people; nor do or consent to any act or thing whatever, that shall have a tendency to lessen or abridge their rights and privileges, as declared in the constitution of this state; but will in all things conduct myself as a faithful honest representative and guardian of the people, according to the best of only judgment and abilities.

And each member, before he takes his seat, shall make and subscribe the following declaration, viz:

I do believe in one God, the creator and governor of the universe, the rewarder of the good and the punisher of the wicked. And I do acknowledge the Scriptures of the Old and New Testament to be given by Divine inspiration.

And no further or other religious test shall ever hereafter be required of any civil officer or magistrate in this State.

SECT. 11. Delegates to represent this state in congress shall be chosen by ballot by the future general assembly at their first meeting, and annually forever afterwards, as long as such representation shall be necessary. Any delegate may be superseded at any time, by the general assembly appointing another in his stead. No man shall sit in congress longer than two years successively, nor be capable of reelection for three Years afterwards: and no person who holds any office in the gift of the congress shall hereafter be elected to represent this commonwealth in congress.

SECT. 12. If any city or cities, county or counties shall neglect or refuse to elect and send representatives to the general assembly, two-thirds of the members from the cities or counties that do elect and send representatives, provided they be a majority of the cities and counties of the whole state, when met, shall have all the powers of the general assembly, as fully and amply as if the whole were present.

SECT. 13. The doors of the house in which the representatives of the freemen of this state shall sit in general assembly, shall be and remain open for the admission of all persons who behave decently, except only when the welfare of this state may require the doors to be shut.

SECT. 14. The votes and proceedings of the general assembly shall be printed weekly during their sitting, with the yeas and nays, on any question, vote or resolution, where any two members require it except when the vote is taken by ballot; and when the yeas and nays are so taken every member shall have a right to insert the reasons of his vote upon the minutes, if he desires it.

SECT. 15. To the end that laws before they are enacted may be more maturely considered, and the inconvenience of hasty determinations as much as possible prevented, all- bills of public nature shall be printed for the consideration of the people, before they are read in general assembly the last time for debate and amendment; and, except on occasions of sudden necessity, shall not be passed into laws until the next session of assembly; and for the more perfect satisfaction of the public, the reasons and motives for making such laws shall be fully and clearly expressed in the preambles.

SECT. 16. The stile of the laws of this commonwealth shall be, "Be it enacted, and it is hereby enacted by the representatives of the freemen of the commonwealth of Pennsylvania in general assembly met, and by the authority of the same." And the general assembly shall affix their seal to every bill, as soon as it is enacted into a law, which seal shall be kept by the assembly, and shall be called, The seal of the laws of Pennsylvania, and shall not be used for any other purpose.

SECT. 17. The city of Philadelphia and each county of this commonwealth respectively, shall on the first Tuesday of November in this present year, and on the second Tuesday of October annually for the two next succeeding years, viz. the year one thousand seven hundred and seventy-seven, and the year one thousand seven hundred and seventy-eight, choose six persons to represent them in general assembly. But as representation in proportion to the number of taxable inhabitants is the only principle which can at all times secure liberty, and make the voice of a majority of the people the law of the land; therefore the general assembly shall cause complete lists of the taxable inhabitants in the city and each county in the commonwealth respectively, to be taken and returned to them, on or before the last meeting of the assembly elected in the year one thousand seven hundred and seventy-eight, who shall appoint a representation to each, in proportion to the number of taxables in such returns; which representation shall continue for the next seven years afterwards at the end of which, a new return of the taxable inhabitants shall be made, and a representation agreeable thereto appointed by the said assembly, and so on septennially forever. The wages of-the representatives in general assembly, and all other state charges shall be paid out of the state treasury.

SECT. 18. In order that the freemen of this commonwealth may enjoy the benefit of election as equally as may be until the representation shall commences as directed in the foregoing section, each county at its own choice may be divided into districts, hold elections therein, and elect their representatives in the county, and their other elective officers, as shall be hereafter regulated by the general assembly of this state. And no inhabitant of this state shall have more than one annual vote at the general election for representatives in assembly.

SECT. 19. For the present the supreme executive council of this state shall consist of twelve persons chosen in the follow-in" manner: The freemen of the city of Philadelphia, and of the counties of Philadelphia, Chester, and Bucks, respectively, shall choose by ballot one person for the city, and one for each county aforesaid to serve for three years and no longer, at the time and place for electing representatives in general assembly. The freemen of the counties of Lancaster, York, Cumberland, and Berks, shall, in like manner elect one person for each county respectively, to serve as counsellors for two years and no longer. And the counties of Northampton, Bedford, Northumberland and Westmoreland, respectively, shall, in like manner, elect one person for each county, to serve as counsellors for one year, and no longer. And at the expiration of the time for which each counsellor was chosen to serve, the freemen of the city of Philadelphia, and of the several counties in this state, respectively, shall elect one person to serve as counsellor for three years and no longer; and so on every third year forever. By this mode of election and continual rotation, more men will be trained to public business, there will in every subsequent year be found in the council a number of persons acquainted with the proceedings of the foregoing Years, whereby the business will be more consistently conducted, and moreover the danger of establishing an inconvenient aristocracy will be effectually prevented. All vacancies in the council that may happen by death, resignation, or otherwise, shall be filled at the next general election for representatives in general assembly, unless a particular election for that purpose shall be sooner appointed by the president and council. No member of the general assembly or delegate in congress, shall be chosen a member of the council. The president and vice-president shall be chosen annually by the joint ballot of the general assembly and council, of the members of the council. Any person having served as a counsellor for three successive years, shall be incapable of holding that office for four years afterwards. Every member of the council shall be a justice of the peace for the whole commonwealth, by virtue of his office.

In case new additional counties shall hereafter be erected in this state, such county or counties shall elect a counsellor, and such county or counties shall be annexed to the next neighbouring counties, and shall take rotation with such counties.

The council shall meet annually, at the same time and place with the general assembly.

The treasurer of the state, trustees of the loan office, naval officers, collectors of customs or excise, judge of the admirality, attornies general, sheriffs, and prothonotaries, shall not be capable of a seat in the general assembly, executive council, or continental congress.

SECT. 20. The president, and in his absence the vice-president, with the council, five of whom shall be a quorum, shall have power to appoint and commissionate judges, naval officers, judge of the admiralty, attorney general and all other officers, civil and military, except such as are chosen by the general assembly or the people, agreeable to this frame of government, and the laws that may be made hereafter; and shall supply every vacancy in any office, occasioned by death, resignation, removal or disqualification, until the office can be filled in the time and manner directed by law or this constitution. They are to correspond with other states, and transact business with the officers of government, civil and military; and to prepare such business as may appear to them necessary to lay before the general assembly. They shall sit as judges, to hear and determine on impeachments, taking to their assistance for advice only, the justices of the supreme court. And shall have power to grant pardons and remit fines, in all cases whatsoever, except in cases of impeachment; and in cases of treason and murder, shall have power to grant reprieves, but not to pardon, until the end of the next sessions of assembly; but there shall be no remission or mitigation of punishments on impeachments, except by act of the legislature; they are also to take care that the laws be faithfully executed; they are to expedite the execution of such measures as may be resolved upon by the general assembly; and they may draw upon the treasury for such sums as shall be appropriated by the house: They may also lay embargoes, or prohibit the exportation of any commodity, for any time, not exceeding thirty days, in the recess of the house only: They may grant such licences, as shall be directed by law, and shall have power to call together the general assembly when necessary, before the day to which they shall stand adjourned. The president shall be commander in chief of the forces of the state, but shall not command in person, except advised thereto by the council, and then only so long as they shall approve thereof. The president and council shall have a secretary, and keep fair books of their proceedings, wherein any counsellor may enter his dissent, with his reasons in support of it.

SECT. 21. All commissions shall be in the name, and by the authority of the freemen of the commonwealth of Pennsylvania, sealed with the state seal, signed by the president or vice-president, and attested by the secretary; which seal shall be kept by the council.

SECT. 22. Every officer of state, whether judicial or executive, shall be liable to be impeached by the general assembly, either when in office, or after his resignation or removal for mar-administration: All impeachments shall be before the president or vice-president and council, who shall hear and determine the same.

SECT. 23. The judges of the supreme court of judicature shall have fixed salaries, be commissioned for seven years only, though capable of re-appointment at the end of that term, but removable for misbehaviour at any time by the general assembly; they shall not be allowed to sit as members in the continental congress, executive council, or general assembly, nor to hold any other office civil or military, nor to take or receive fees or perquisites of any kind.

SECT. 24. The supreme court, and the several courts of common pleas of this commonwealth, shall, besides the powers usually exercised by such courts, have the powers of a court of chancery, so far as relates to the perpetuating testimony, obtaining evidence from places not within this state, and the care of the persons and estates of those who are non compos mentis, and such other powers as may be found necessary by future general assemblies, not inconsistent with this constitution.

SECT. 25. Trials shall be by jury as heretofore: And it is recommended to the legislature of this state, to provide by law against every corruption or partiality in the choice, return, or appointment of juries.

SECT. 26. Courts of sessions, common pleas, and orphans courts shall be held quarterly in each city and county; and the legislature shall have power to establish all such other courts as they may judge for the good of the inhabitants of the state. All courts shall be open, and justice shall be impartially administered without corruption or unnecessary delay: All their officers shall be paid an adequate but moderate compensation for their services: And if any officer shall take greater or other fees than the law allows him, either directly or indirectly, it shall ever after disqualify him from holding any office in this state.

SECT. 27. All prosecutions shall commence in the name and by the authority of the freemen of the commonwealth of Pennsylvania; and all indictments shall conclude with these words, "Against the peace and dignity of the same." The style of all process hereafter in this state shall be, The commonwealth of Pennsylvania.

SECT. 28. The person of a debtor, where there is not a strong presumption of fraud, shall not be continued in prison, after delivering Up, bona fide, all his estate real and personal, for the use of his creditors, in such manner as shall be hereafter regulated by law. All prisoners shall be bailable by sufficient sureties, unless for capital offences, when the proof is evident, or presumption great.

SECT. 29. Excessive bail shall not be exacted for bailable oflences: And all fines shall be moderate.

SECT. 30. Justices of the peace shall be elected by the freeholders of each city and county respectively, that is to say, two or more persons may be chosen for each ward, township, or district, as the law shall hereafter direct: And their names shall be returned to the president in council, who shall commissionate one or more of them for each ward, township, or district so returning, for seven years, removable for misconduct by the general assembly. But if any city or county, ward, township, or district in this commonwealth, shall hereafter incline to change the manner of appointing their justices of the peace as settled in this article, the general assembly may make laws to regulate the same, agreeable to the desire of a majority of the freeholders of the city or county, ward, township, or district so applying. No justice of the peace shall sit in the general assembly unless he first resigns his commission; nor shall he be allowed to take any fees, nor any salary or allowance, except such as the future legislature may grant.

SECT. 31. Sheriffs and coroners shall be elected annually in each city and county, by the freemen; that is to say, two persons for each office, one of whom for each, is to be commissioned by the President in council. No person shall continue in the office of sheriff more than three successive years, or be capable of being again elected during four years afterwards. The election shall be held at the same time and place appointed for the election of representatives: And the commissioners and assessors, and other officers chosen by the people, shall also be then and there elected, as has been usual heretofore, until altered or otherwise regulated by the future legislature of this state.

SECT. 32. All elections, whether by the people or in general assembly, shall be by ballot, free and voluntary: And any elector, who shall receive any gift or reward for his vote, in meat, drink, monies, or otherwise, shall forfeit his right to elect for that time, and suffer such other penalties as future laws shall direct. And any person who shall directly or indirectly give, promise, or bestow any such rewards to be elected, shall be thereby rendered incapable to serve for the ensuing year.

SECT. 33. All fees, licence money, fines and forfeitures heretofore granted, or paid to the governor, or his deputies for the support of government, shall hereafter be paid into the public treasury, unless altered or abolished by the future legislature.

SECT. 34. A register's office for the probate of wills and granting letters of administration, and an office for the recording of deeds, shall be kept in each city and county: The officers to be appointed by the general assembly, removable at their pleasure, and to be commissioned by the president in council.

SECT. 35. The printing presses shall be free to every person who undertakes to examine the proceedings of the legislature, or any part of government.

SECT. 36. As every freeman to preserve his independence, (if without a sufficient estate) ought to have some profession, calling, trade or farm, whereby he may honestly subsist, there can be no necessity for, nor use in establishing offices of profit, the usual effects of which are dependence and servility unbecoming freemen, in the possessors and expectants; faction, contention, corruption, and disorder among the people. But if any man is called into public service; to the prejudice of his private affairs, he has a right to a reasonable compensation: And whenever an office, through increase of fees or otherwise, becomes so profitable as to occasion many to apply for it, the profits ought to be lessened by the legislature.

SECT. 37. The future legislature of this state, shall regulate intails in such a manner as to prevent perpetuities.

SECT. 38. The penal laws as heretofore used shall be reformed by the legislature of this state, as soon as may be, and punishments made in some cases less sanguinary, and in general more proportionate to the crimes.

SECT. 39. To deter more effectually from the commission of crimes by continued visible punishments of long duration, and to make sanguinary punishments less necessary; houses ought to be provided for punishing by hard labour, those who shall be convicted of crimes not capital; wherein the criminals shall be imployed for the benefit of the public, or for reparation of injuries done to private persons: And all persons at proper times shall be admitted to see the prisoners at their labour.

SECT. 40. Every officer, whether judicial, executive or military, in authority under this commonwealth, shall take the following oath or affirmation of allegiance, and general oath of office before he enters on the execution of his office.

THE OATH OR AFFIRMATION OF ALLEGIANCE

I do swear (or affirm) that I will be true and faithful to the commonwealth of Pennsylvania: And that I will not directly or indirectly do any act or thing prejudicial or injurious to the constitution or government thereof, as established by the-convention.

THE OATH OR AFFIRMATION OF OFFICE

I-do swear (or affirm) that I will faithfully execute the office of for the of-and will do equal right and justice to all men, to the best of my judgment and abilities, according to law.

SECT. 41. NO public tax, custom or contribution shall be imposed upon, or paid by the people of this state, except by a law for that purpose: And before any law be made for raising it, the purpose for which any tax is to be raised ought to appear clearly to the legislature to be of more service to the community than the money would be, if not collected; which being well observed, taxes can never be burthens.

SECT. 42. Every foreigner of good character who comes to settle in this state, having first taken an oath or affirmation of allegiance to the same, may purchase, or by other just means acquire, hold, and transfer land or other real estate; and after one year's residence, shall be deemed a free denizen thereof, and entitled to all the rights of a natural born subject of this state, except that he shall not be capable of being elected a representative until after two years residence.

SECT. 43. The inhabitants of this state shall have liberty to fowl and hunt in seasonable times on the lands they hold, and on all other lands therein not inclosed; and in like manner to fish in all boatable waters, and others not private property

SECT. 44. A school or schools shall be established in each county by the legislature, for the convenient instruction of youth, with such salaries to the masters paid by the public, as may enable them to instruct youth at low prices: And all useful learning shall be duly encouraged and promoted In one or more universities.

SECT. 45. Laws for the encouragement of virtue, and prevention of vice and immorality, shall be made and constantly kept in force, and provision shall be made for their due execution: And all religious societies or bodies of men heretofore united or incorporated for the advancement of religion or learning, or for other pious and charitable purposes, shall be encouraged and protected in the enjoyment of the privileges, immunities and estates which they were accustomed to enjoy, or could of right have enjoyed, under the laws and former constitution of this state.

SECT. 46. The declaration of rights is hereby declared to be a part of the constitution of this commonwealth, and ought never to be violated on any presence whatever.

SECT. 47. In order that the freedom of the commonwealth may be preserved inviolate forever, there shall be chosen by ballot by the freemen in each city and county respectively, on the second Tuesday in October, in the Year one thousand seven hundred and eighty-three, and on the second

Tuesday in October, in every seventh year thereafter, two persons in each city and county of this state, to be called the COUNCIL OF CENSORS; who shall meet together on the second Monday of November next ensuing their election; the majority of whom shall be a quorum in every case, except as to calling a convention, in which two-thirds of the whole number elected shall agree: And whose duty it shall be to enquire whether the constitution has been preserved inviolate in every part; and whether the legislative and executive branches of government have performed their duty as guardians of the people, or assumed to themselves, or exercised other or greater powers than they are intitled to by the constitution: They are also to enquire whether the public taxes have been justly laid and collected in all parts of this commonwealth, in what manner the public monies have been disposed of, and whether the laws have been duly executed. For these purposes they shall have power to send for persons, papers, and records; they shall have authority to pass public censures, to order impeachments, and to recommend to the legislature the repealing such laws as appear to them to have been enacted contrary to the principles of the constitution. These powers they shall continue to have, for and during the space of one year from the day of their election and no longer: The said council of censors shall also have power to call a convention, to meet within too years after their sitting, if there appear to them an absolute necessity of amending any article of the constitution which may be defective, explaining such as may be thought not clearly expressed, and of adding such as are necessary for the preservation of the rights and happiness of the people: But the articles to be amended, and the amendments proposed, and such articles as are proposed to be added or abolished, shall be promulgated at least six months before the day appointed for the election of such convention, for the previous consideration of the people, that they may have an opportunity of instructing their delegates on the subject.

SOURCE: These excerpts are reprinted from Franci Newton Thorpe (ed.), *The Federal and State Constitutions, Colonial Charters, and other Organic Laws of the States and Territories now or heretofore forming the United States of America*, 7 vols. (Washington: Government Printing Office, 1909), 7: 3084-3092.

6. MARYLAND CONSTITUTION
NOVEMBER 8, 1776

Maryland's provincial congress did not react to the Continental Congress's May 15 recommendation to the states that they form new constitutions and governments until the day before the Declaration of Independence was approved. On July 3, the provincial congress decided that a special constitutional convention should be called "for the express purpose of forming a new Government by the authority of the People only." The problem, however, is that this convention was also assigned the regular tasks of political legislation as well. On August 1, all freemen in the state with property elected delegates for the constitutional convention. On August 14, 1776, Maryland's fifty-three-member constitutional convention met to frame a declaration of rights and a constitution of government. The final declaration of rights and constitution were approved on November 8, 1776. The Maryland constitution was bicameral consisting of a House of Delegates and a Senate. The Governor was chosen annual by a joint session of both legislative houses. The most unique feature of the Maryland constitution was the indirect election of its senate. Voters would elect Senatorial Electors every five years, who in turn would meet to elect the senate. The Maryland constitution was not submitted to the people for ratification.

A DECLARATION OF RIGHTS, AND THE CONSTITUTION AND FORM OF GOVERNMENT AGREED TO BY THE DELEGATES OF MARYLAND, IN FREE AND FULL CONVENTION ASSEMBLED.

A DECLARATION OF RIGHTS

THE parliament of Great Britain, by a declaratory act, having assumed a right to make laws to bind the Colonies in all cases whatsoever, and, in pursuance of Rich claim, endeavoured, by force of arms, to subjugate the United Colonies to an unconditional submission to their will and power, and having at length constrained them to declare themselves independent States, and to assume government under the authority of the people; Therefore we, the Delegates of Maryland, in free and full Convention assembled, taking into our most serious consideration the best means of establishing a good Constitution in this State, for the sure foundation and more permanent security thereof, declare,

I. That all government of right originates from the people, is founded in compact only, and instituted solely for the good of the whole.

II. That the people of this State ought to have the sole and exclusive right of regulating the internal government and police thereof.

III. That the inhabitants of Maryland are entitled to the common law of England, and the trial by Jury, according that law, and to the benefit of such of the English statutes, as existed at the time of their first emigration, and which, by experience, have been found applicable to their local and other circumstances, and of such others as have been since made in England, or Great Britain, and have been introduced, used and practiced by the courts of law or equity; and also to acts of Assembly, in force on the first of June seventeen hundred and seventy-four, except such as may have since expired, or have been or may be altered by facts of Convention, or this Declaration of Rights-subject, nevertheless, to the revision of, and amendment or repeal by, the Legislature of this State: and the inhabitants of Maryland are also entitled to all property, derived to them, from or under the Charter, granted by his Majesty Charles I. to Crecilius Calvert, Baron of Baltimore.

IV. That all persons invested with the legislative or executive powers of government are the trustees of the public, and, as such, accountable for their conduct; wherefore, whenever the ends of government are perverted, and public liberty manifestly endangered, and all other means of redress are ineffectual, the people may, and of right ought, to reform the old or establish a new government. The doctrine of non-resistance, against arbitrary power and oppression, is absurd, slavish, and destructive of the good and happiness of mankind.

V. That the right In the people to participate In the Legislature Is the best security of liberty, and the foundation of all free government; for this purpose, elections ought to be free and frequent, and every man, having property in, a common interest with, and an attachment to the community, ought to have a right of suffrage.

VI. That the legislative, executive and judicial powers of government, ought to be forever separate and distinct from each other.

VII. That no power of suspending laws, or the execution of laws, unless by or derived from the Legislature, ought to be exercised or allowed.

VIII. That freedom of speech and debates, or proceedings in the Legislature, ought not to be impeached in any other court or judicature.

IX. That a place for the meeting of the Legislature ought to be fixed, the most convenient to the members thereof, and to the depository of public records; and the Legislature ought not to be convened or held at any other place, but from evident necessity.

X. That, for redress of grievances, and for amending, strengthening and preserving the laws, the Legislature ought to be frequently convened.

XI. That every man hath a right to petition the Legislature, for the redress of grievances, in a peaceable and orderly manner.

XII. That no aid, charge, tax, fee, or fees, ought to be set, rated, or levied, under any presence, without consent of the Legislature.

XIII. That the levying taxes by the poll is grievous and oppressive, and ought to be abolished; that paupers ought not to be assessed for the support of government; but every other person in the State ought to contribute his proportion of public taxes, for the support of government, according to his actual worth, in real or personal property, within the State; yet fines, duties, or taxes, may properly and justly be imposed or laid, with a political view, for the good government and benefit of the community.

XIV. That sanguinary laws ought to be avoided, as far as is Consistent with the safety of the State: and no law, to inflict cruel and unusual pains and penalties, ought to be made in any case, or at any time hereafter.

XV. That retrospective laws, punishing facts committed before the existence of such laws, and by them only declared criminal, are oppressive, unjust, and incompatible with liberty; wherefore no *ex post facto* law ought to be made.

XVI. That no law, to attains particular persons of treason or felony, ought to be made in any case, or at any time hereafter.

XVII. That every freeman, for any injury done him in his person or property, ought to have remedy, by the course of the law of the land, and ought to have justice and right freely without sale, fully without any denial, and speedily without delay, according to the law of the land.

XVIII. That the trial of facts where they arise, is one of the greatest securities of the lives, liberties and estates of the people.

XIX. That, in all criminal prosecutions, every man hath a right to be informed of the accusation against him; to have a copy of the indictment or charge in due time (if required) to prepare for his defence; to be allowed counsel; to be confronted with the witnesses against him; to have process for his witnesses; to examine the witnesses, for and against him, on oath; and to a speedy trial by an impartial jury, without whose unanimous consent he ought not to be found guilty.

XX. That no man ought to be compelled to give evidence against himself, in a common court of law, or in any other court, but in such cases as have been usually practiced in this State, or may hereafter be directed by the Legislature.

XXI. That no freeman ought to be taken, or imprisoned, or disseized of his freehold, liberties, or privileges, or outlawed, or exiled, or in any manner destroyed, or deprived of his life, liberty, or property, but by the judgment of his peers, or by the law of the land.

XXII. That excessive bail ought not to be required, nor excessive fines imposed, nor cruel or unusual punishments inflicted, by the courts of law.

LX. That all warrants, without oath or affirmation, to search suspected places, or to seize any person or property, are grievous and oppressive; and all general warrants-to search suspected places, or to apprehend suspected persons, without naming or describing the place, or the person in special-are illegal, and ought not to be granted.

XXIV. That there ought to be no forfeiture of any part of the estate of any person, for any crime except murder, or treason against the State, and then only on conviction and attainder.

XXV. That a well-regulated militia is the proper and natural defence of a free government.

XXVI. That standing armies are dangerous to liberty, and ought not to be raised or kept up, without consent of the Legislature.

XXVII. That in all cases, and at all times, the military ought to be under strict subordination to and control of the civil power.

XXVIII. That no soldier ought to be quartered in any house, in time of peace, without the consent of the owner; and in time of war, in such manner only, as the Legislature shall direct,

XXIX. That no person, except regular soldiers, mariners, and marines in the service of this State, or militia when in actual service, ought in any case to be subject to or punishable by martial law.

XXX. That the independency and uprightness of Judges are essential to the impartial administration of Justice, and a great security to the rights and liberties of the people; wherefore the Chancellor and Judges ought to hold commissions during good behaviour; and the said Chancellor and Judges shall be removed for misbehaviour, on conviction in a court of law, and may be removed by the Governor, upon the address of the General Assembly; *Provided*, That two-thirds of all the members of each House concur in such address. That salaries, liberal, but not profuse, ought to be secured to the Chancellor and the Judges, during the continuance of their Commissions, in such manner, and at such times, as the Legislature shall hereafter direct, upon consideration of the circumstances of this State. No Chancellor or Judge ought to hold any other office, civil or military, or receive fees or perquisites of any kind.

XXXI. That a long continuance in the first executive departments of power or trust, is dangerous to liberty; a rotation, therefore, in those departments, is one of the best securities of permanent freedom.

XXXII. That no person ought to hold, at the same time, more shall one office of profit, nor ought any person. In public trust, to receive any present from any foreign prince or state, or from the United States, or any of them, without the approbation of this State.

XXXIII. That, as it is the duty of every man to worship God in such manner as he thinks most acceptable to him; all persons, professing the Christian religion, are equally entitled to protection in their religious liberty; wherefore no person ought by any law to be molested in his person or estate on account of his religious persuasion or profession, or for his religious practice; unless, under colour of religion, any man shall disturb the good order, peace or safety of the State, or shall infringe the laws of morality, or injure others, in their natural, civil, or religious rights; nor ought any person to be compelled to frequent or maintain, or contribute, unless on contract, to maintain any particular place of worship, or any particular ministry; yet the Legislature may, in their discretion, lay a general and equal tax for the support of the Christian religion; leaving to each individual the power of appointing the payment over of the money, collected from him, to the support of any particular place of worship or minister, or for the benefit of the poor of his own denomination, or the poor in general of any particular county: but the churches, chapels, globes, and all other property now belonging to the church of England, ought to remain to the church of England forever. And all acts of Assembly, lately passed, for collecting monies for building or repairing particular churches or chapels of ease, shall continue in force, and be executed, unless the Legislature shall, by act, supersede or repeal the same: but no county court shall assess any quantity of tobacco, or sum of money, hereafter, on the application of any vestrymen or church-wardens; and every encumbent of the church of England, who hath remained in his parish, and performed his duty, shall be entitled to receive the provision and support established by the act, entitled "An act for the support of the clergy of the church of England, in this Province," till the November court of this present year to be held for the county in which his parish shall lie, or partly lie, or for such time as he hate remained in his parish, and performed his duty.

XXXIV. That every gift, sale, or devise of lands, to any minister, public teacher, or preacher of the gospel, as such, or to any religious sect, order or denomination, or to or for the support, use or benefit of, or in trust for, any minister, public teacher, or preacher of the gospel, as such, or any religious sect, order or denomination-and every gift or sale of good-e, or chattels, to go in succession, or to take place after the death of the seller or donor, or to or for such support, use or benefit-and also every devise of goods or chattels to or for the support, use or benefit of any minister, public teacher, or preacher of the gospel, as such, or any religious sect, order, or denomination, without the leave of the Legislature, shall be void; except always any sale, gift, lease or devise of any quantity of land, not exceeding two acres, for a church, meeting, or other house of worship, and for a burying-ground, which shall be improved, enjoyed or used only for such purpose-or such sale, gift, lease, or devise, shall be void.

XXXV. That no other test or qualification ought to be required, on admission to any office of trust or profit, than such oath of support and fidelity to this State, and such oath of office, as shall be directed by this Convention or the Legislature of this State, and a declaration of a belief in the Christian religion.

XXXVI. That the manner of administering an oath to any person, ought to be such, as those of the religious persuasion, profession, or denomination, of which such person is one, generally esteem the most effectual confirmation, by the attestation of the Divine Being. And that the people called Quakers, those called Dunkers, and those called Menonists, holding it unlawful to take an oath on any occasion, ought to be allowed to make their solemn affirmation, in the manner that Quakers 1lave been heretofore allowed to affirm; and to be of the same avail as an oath, in all such cases, as the affirmation of Quakers hath been allowed and accepted within this State, instead of an oath. And further, on such affirmation, warrants to search for stolen goods, or for the apprehension or commitment of offenders, ought to be granted, or security for the peace awarded, and Quakers, Dunkers or Menonists ought also, on their solemn affirmation as aforesaid, to be admitted as witnesses, in all criminal cases not capital.

XXXVII. That the city of Annapolis ought to have all its rights, privileges and benefits, agreeable to its Charter, and the acts of Assembly confirming and regulating the same, subject nevertheless to such alteration as may be made by this Convention, or any future legislature.

XXXVIII. That the liberty of the press ought to be inviolably preserved.

XXXIX. That monopolies are odious, contrary to the spirit of a free government, and the principles of commerce; and ought not to be suffered.

XL. That no title of nobility, or hereditary honours, ought to be granted III this State.

XLI. That the subsisting resolves of this and the several Conventions held for this Colony, ought to be in force as laws, unless altered by this Convention, or the Legislature of this State.

XLII. That this Declaration of Rights, or the Form of Government, to be established by this Convention, or any part or either of them, ought not to be altered, changed or abolished, by the Legislature of this State, but in such manner as this Convention shall prescribe and direct.

This Declaration of Rights was assented to, and passed, in Convention of the Delegates of the freemen of Maryland, begun and held at Annapolis, the 14th day of August, A. D. 1776.

THE CONSTITUTION, OR FORM OF GOVERNMENT

I. THAT the Legislature consist of two distinct branches, a Senate and House of Delegates, which shall be styled, *The General Assembly of Maryland.*

II. That the House of Delegates shall be chosen in the following manner: All freemen, above twenty-one years of age, having a freehold of fifty acres of land, in the county in which they offer to vote, and residing therein-and all freemen, having property in this State above the value of thirty pounds current money, and having resided in the county, in which they offer to vote, one whole year next preceding the election, shall have a right of suffrage, in the election of Delegates for such county: and all freemen, so qualified, shall, en the first Monday of October, seventeen hundred and seventy-seven and on the same day in every year thereafter, assemble in the counties, in which they are respectively qualified to vote, at the court-house, in the said counties; or at such other place as the Legislature shall direct; and, when assembled, they shall proceed to elect, viva voce, four Delegates, for their respective counties, of the most wise, sensible, and discreet of the people, residents in the county where they are to be chosen, one whole year next preceding the election, above twenty-one years of age, and having, in the State, real or personal property above the value of five hundred pounds current money; and upon the final casting of the polls, the four persons who shall appear to have the greatest number of legal votes shall be declared and returned duly elected for their respective counties.

III. That the Sheriff of each county, or, in case of sickness, his Deputy (summoning two Justices of the county, who are required to attend, for the preservation of the peace) shall be the judges of the election, and may adjourn from day to day, if necessary, till the same be finished, so that the whole election shall be concluded in four days; and shall make his return thereof, under his hand, to the Chancellor of this State for the time being.

IV. That all persons qualified, by the charter of the city of Annapolis, to vote for Burgesses, shall, on the same first Monday of October, seventeen hundred and seventy-seven, and on the same day in every year forever thereafter, elect, *viva voce*, by a majority of votes, two Delegates, qualified agreeable to the said charter; that the Mayor, Recorder, and Aldermen of the said city, or any three of them, be judges of the election, appoint the place in the said city for holding the same, and may adjourn from day to day, as aforesaid, and shall make return thereof, as aforesaid: but the inhabitants of the said city shall not be entitled to vote for Delegates for Anne-Arundel county, unless they have a freehold of fifty acres of land in the county distinct from the City.

V. That all persons, inhabitants of Baltimore town, and having the same qualifications as electors in the county, shall, on the same first Monday in October, seventeen hundred and seventy-seven, and on the same day in every year forever thereafter, at such place in the said town as the Judges shall appoint, elect, *viva voce*, by a majority of votes, two Delegates, qualified as aforesaid: but if the said inhabitants of the town shall so decrease, as that a number of persons, having a right of suffrage therein, shall have been, for the space of seven years successively, less than one half the number of voters in some one county in this State, such town shall thenceforward cease to send two Delegates or Representatives to the House of Delegates, until the said town shall have one half of the number of voters in some one county in this State.

VI. That the Commissioners of the said town, or any three or more of them, for the time being, shall be judges of the said election, and may adjourn, as aforesaid, and shall mate return thereof, as aforesaid: but the inhabitants of the said town shall not be entitled to vote for, or be elected, Delegates for Baltimore county: neither shall the inhabitants of Baltimore county, out of the limits of Baltimore town, be entitled to vote for, or be elected, Delegates for the said town.

VII. That on refusal, death, disqualification, resignation, or removal out of this State of any Delegate, or on his becoming Governor, or member of the

Council, a warrant of election shall issue by the Speaker, for the election of another in his place; of which ten days' notice, at least, (excluding the day of notice, and the day of election) shall be given.

VIII. That not less than a majority of the Delegates, with their Speaker (to be chosen by them, by ballot) constitute a House, for the transaction of any business other than that of adjourning.

IX. That the House of Delegates shall judge of the elections and qualifications of Delegates.

X. That the House of Delegates may originate all money bills, propose bills to the Senate, or receive those offered by that body; and assent, dissent, or propose amendments; that they may inquire on the oath of witnesses, into all complaints, grievances, and offences, as the grand inquest of this State; and may commit any person, for any crime, to the public jail, there to remain till he be discharged by due course of law. They may expel any member, for a great misdemeanor, but not a second time for the same cause. They may examine and pass all accounts of the State, relating either to the collection or expenditure of the revenue, or appoint auditors, to state and adjust the same. They may call for all public or official papers and records, and send for persons, whom they may judge necessary in the course of their inquiries, concerning affairs relating to the public interest; and may direct all office bonds (which shall be made payable to the State) to be sued for any breach of duty.

XI. That the Senate may be at full and perfect liberty to exercise their judgment in passing laws-and that they may not be compelled by the House of Delegates, either to reject a money bill, which the emergency of affairs may require, or to assent to some other act of legislation, in their conscience and judgment injurious to the public welfare—the House of Delegates shall not on any occasion, or under any presence annex to, or blend with a money bill, any matter, clause, or thing, not immediately relating to, and necessary for the imposing, assessing, levying, or applying the taxes or supplies, to be raised for the of government, or the current expenses of the State: and to prevent altercation about such bills, it is declared, that no bill, imposing duties or customs for the mere regulation of commerce, or inflicting fines for the reformation of morals, or to enforce the execution of the laws, by which an incidental revenue may arise, shall be accounted a money bill: but every bill, assessing, levying, or applying taxes or supplies, for the support of government, or the current expenses of the State, or appropriating money in the treasury, shall be deemed a money bill.

XII. That the House of Delegates may punish, by imprisonment. Any person who shall be guilty of a contempt in their view, by any disorderly or riotous behaviour, or by threats to, or abuse of their members, or by any obstruction to their proceedings. They may also punish, by imprisonment, any person who shall be guilty of a breach of privilege, by arresting on civil process, or by assaulting any of their members, during their sitting, or on their way to, or return from the House of Delegates, or by any assault of, or obstruction to their officers, in the execution of any order or process, or by assaulting or obstructing any witness, or any other person, attending on, or on their way to or from the House, or by rescuing any person committed by the House: and the Senate may exercise the same power, in similar cases.

XIII. That the Treasurers (one for the western, and another for the eastern shore) and the Commissioners of the Loan Office, may be appointed by the House of Delegates, during their pleasure; and in case of refusal, death, resignation, disqualification, or removal out of the State, of any of the said Commissioners or Treasurers, in the recess of the General Assembly, the governor, with the advice of the Council, may appoint and commission a fit and proper person to such vacant office, to hold the same until the meeting of the next General Assembly.

XIV. That the Senate be chosen in the following manner: All persons, qualified as aforesaid to vote for county Delegates, shall, on the first tidy of September, 1781, and on the same day in every fifth year forever thereafter, elect, *viva voce*, by a majority of votes, two persons for their respective counties (qualified as aforesaid to be elected county Delegates) to be electors of the Senate; and the Sheriff of each county, or, in case of sickness, his Deputy (summoning two Justices of the county, who are required to attend, for the preservation of the peace,) shall hold and be judge of the said election, and make return thereof, as aforesaid. And all persons, qualified as aforesaid, to vote for Delegates for the city of Annapolis and Baltimore town, shall, on the same first Monday of September, 1781, and on the same day in every fifth year forever thereafter, elect, viva voce, by a majority of votes, one person for the said city and town respectively, qualified as aforesaid to be elected a Delegate for the said city and town respectively; the said election to be held in the same manner, as the election of Delegates for the said city and town; the right to elect the said elector, with respect to Baltimore town, to continue as long as the right to elect Delegates for the said town.

XV. That the said electors of the Senate meet at the city of Annapolis, or such other place as shall be appointed for convening the legislature, on the third Monday in September, 1781, and on the same flay in every fifth year forever thereafter, and they, or any twenty-four of them so met, shall proceed to elect, by ballot, either out of their own body, or the people at large, fifteen Senators (nine of whom to be residents on the western, and six to be residents on the eastern shore) men of the most wisdom, experience and virtue, above twenty-five years of age, residents of the State above three whole years next preceding the election, and having real and personal property above the value of one thousand pounds current money.

XVI. That the Senators shall be balloted for, at one and the same time, and out of the gentlemen residents of the western shore, who shall be proposed as Senators, the nine who shall, on striking the ballots, appear to have the greatest numbers in their favour, shall be accordingly declared and returned duly elected: and out of the gentlemen residents of the eastern shore, who shall be proposed as Senators, the six who shall, on striking the ballots, appear to have the greatest number in their favour, shall be accordingly declared and returned duly elected: and if two or more on the same shore shall have an equal number of ballots in their favour, by which the choice shall not be determined on the first ballot, then the electors shall again ballot, before they separate; in which they shall be confined to the persons who on the first ballot shall have an equal number: and they who shall have the greatest number in their favour on the second ballot, shall be accordingly declared and returned duly elected: and if the whole number should not thus be made up, because of an equal number, on the second ballot, still being in favour of two or more persons, then the election shall be determined by lot, between those who have equal numbers; which proceedings of the electors shall be certified under their hands, and returned to the Chancellor for the time being.

XVII. That the electors of Senators shall judge of the qualifications and elections of members of their body; and, on a contested election, shall admit to a seat, as an elector, such qualified person as shall appear to them to have the greatest number of legal votes in his favour.

XVIII. That the electors, immediately on their meeting, and before they proceed to the election of Senators, take such oath of support and fidelity to this State, as this Convention, or the Legislature, shall direct; and also an oath " to elect without favour, affection, partiality, or prejudice, such persons for Senators, as they, in their judgment and conscience, believe best qualified for the office."

XIX. That in case of refusal, death, resignation, disqualification, or removal out of this State, of any Senator, or on his becoming Governor, or a member of the Council, the Senate shall, immediately thereupon, or at their next meeting thereafter, elect by ballot (in the same manner as the electors are above directed to choose Senators) another person in his place, for the residue of the said term of five years.

XX. That not less than a majority of the Senate, with their President (to be chosen by them, by ballot) shall constitute a House, for the transacting any business, other than that of adjourning.

XXI. That the Senate shall judge of the Elections and qualifications of Senators.

XXII. That the Senate may originate any other, except money bills, to which their assent or dissent only shall be given; and may receive any other bills from the House of Delegates, and assent, dissent, or propose amendments.

XXIII. That the General Assembly meet annually, Old the first Monday of November, and if necessary, oftener.

XXIV. That each House shall appoint its own officers, and settle its own rules of proceeding.

XXV. That a person of wisdom, experience, and virtue, shall be chosen Governor, on the second Monday of November, seventeen hundred and seventy-seven, and on the second Monday in every year forever thereafter, by the joint ballot of both Houses (to be taken in each House respectively) deposited in a conference room; the boxes to be examined by a joint committee of both Houses, and the numbers severally reported, that the appointment may be entered; which mode of taking the joint ballot of both Houses shall be adopted in all cases. But if two or more shall have an equal number of ballots in their favour, by which the choice shall not be determined on the first ballot, then a second ballot shall be taken, which shall be confined to the persons who, on the first ballot, shall have had an equal number; and, if the ballots should again be equal between two or more persons, then the election of the Governor shall be determined by lot, between those who have equal numbers: and if the person chosen Governor shall die, resign, move out of the State, or refuse to act, (the-General Assembly sitting) the Senate and House of Delegates shall, immediately thereupon, proceed to a new choice, in manner aforesaid.

XXVI. That the Senators and Delegates, on the second Tuesday of November, 1777, and annually on the second Tuesday of November forever thereafter, elect by Joint ballot (in the same manner as Senators are directed to be chosen) five of the most sensible, discreet, and experienced men, above twenty-five years of age, residents in the State above three years next preceding the election, and having therein a freehold of lands and tenements, above the value of one thousand pounds current money, to be the Council to the Governor, whose proceedings shall be always entered on record, to any part whereof any member may enter his dissent; and their advice, if so required by the Governor, or any member of the Council, shall be given in writing, and signed by the members giving the same respectively: which proceedings of the Council shall be laid before the Senate, or House of Delegates, when called for by them or either of them. The Council may appoint their own Clerk, who shall take such oath of 168upport and fidelity to this State, as this Convention, or the Legislature, shall direct; and of secrecy, in such matters as he shall be directed by the board to keep secret.

XXVII. That the Delegates to Congress, from this State, shall be chosen annually, or superseded in the mean time by the joint ballot of both Houses of Assembly; and that there be a rotation, in such manner, that at least two of the number be annually changed; and no person shall be capable of being a Delegate to Congress for more than three in any term of six years; and no person, who holds any office of profit in the gift of Congress, shall be eligible to sit in Congress; but if appointed to any such office, his seat shall be thereby vacated. That no person, unless above twenty-one years of age, and a resident in the State more than five years next preceding the election, and having real and personal estate in this State above the value of one thousand pounds current money, shall be eligible to sit in Congress.

XXVIII. That the Senators and Delegates, immediately on their annual meeting, and before they proceed to any business, and every person, hereafter elected a Senator or Delegate, before he acts as such, shall take an oath of support and fidelity to this State, as aforesaid; and before the election of a governor, or members of the Council, shall take an oath, " elect without favour, affection, partiality, or prejudice, such person as Governor, or member of the Council, as they, in their judgment and conscience, believe best qualified for the office."

XXIX. That the Senate and Delegates may adjourn themselves respectively: but if the two Houses should not agree on the same time, but adjourn to different days, then shall the Governor appoint and notify one of those days, or some day between, and the Assembly shall then meet and be held accordingly; and he shall, if necessary, by advice of the Council, call them before the time, to which they shall in any manner be adjourned, on giving not less than ten days' notice thereof; but the Governor shall not adjourn the Assembly, otherwise than as aforesaid, nor prorogue or dissolve it, at any time.

XXX. That no person, unless above twenty-five years of age, a resident in this State above five years next preceding the election- and having in the State real and personal property, above the value of five thousand pounds, current money, (one thousand pounds whereof, at least, to be freehold estate) shall be eligible as governor.

XXXI. That the governor shall not continue in that office longer than three years successively, nor be eligible as Governor, until the expiration of four years after he shall have been out of that office.

XXXII. That upon the death, resignation, or removal out of this State, of the Governor, the first named of the Council, for the time being shall act as Governor, and qualify in the same manner; and shall immediately call a meeting of the General Assembly, giving not less than fourteen days' notice of the meeting, at which meeting. A Governor shall be appointed, in manner aforesaid, for the residue of the year.

XXXIII. That the Governor, by and with the advice and consent of the Council, may embody the militia; and, when embodied, shall alone have the direction thereof; and shall also have the direction of all the regular land and sea forces, under the laws of this State, (but he shall not command in person, unless advised thereto by the Council, and then, only so long as they shall approve thereof); and may alone exercise all other the executive powers of government, where the concurrence of the Council is not required, according to the laws of this State; and grant reprieves or pardons for any crime, except in such cases where the law shall otherwise direct; and may, during the recess of the General Assembly, lay embargoes, to prevent the departure of any shipping, or the exportation of any commodities, for any time not exceeding thirty days in any one year-summoning the General Assembly to meet within the time of the continuance of such embargo; and may also order and compel any vessel to ride quarantine, if such vessel, or the port from which she may have come, shall, on strong grounds, be suspected to be infected with the plague; but the Governor shall not, under any presence, exercise any power or prerogative by virtue of any law, statute, or custom of England or Great Britain.

XXXIV. That the members of the Council, or any three or more off them, when convened, shall constitute a board for the transacting of business; that the Governor, for the time being, shall preside in the Council, and be entitled to a vote, on all questions in which the Council shall be divided in opinion; and, in the absence of the Governor, the first named of the Council shall preside; and as such, shall also vote, in all cases, where the other members disagree in their opinion.

XXXV. That, in case of refusal, death, resignation, disqualification, or removal out of the State, of any person chosen a member of the council, the members thereof, immediately thereupon, or at their next meeting thereafter, shall elect by ballot another person (qualified as aforesaid) in his place, for the residue of the Year.

XXXVI. That the Council shall have power to make the Great Seal of this State, which shall be kept by the Chancellor for the time being, and affixed to all laws, commissions, grants, and other public testimonials, as has been heretofore practiced in this State.

XXXVII. That no Senator, Delegate of Assembly, or member of the Council, if he shall qualify as such, shall hold or execute any office of profit, or receive the profits of any office exercised by any other person, during the time for which he shall be elected; nor shall any (governor be capable of holding any other office of profit in this State, while he acts as such. And no person, holding a place of profit or receiving any part of the profits thereof, or receiving the profits or any part of the profits arising on any agency, for the supply of clothing or provisions for the Army or Navy, or holding any office under the United States, or any of them-or a minister, or preacher of the gospel, of any denomination-or any person, employed in the regular land service, or marine, of this or the United States-shall have a seat in the General Assembly or the Council of this State.

XXXVIII. That every Governor, Senator, Delegate to Congress or Assembly, and member of the Council, before he acts as such, shall take an oath " that he will not receive, directly or indirectly at any time, any part of the profits of any office, held by any other person during his acting in his office of Governor, Senator, Delegate to Congress or Assembly, or member of the Council, or the profits or any part of the profits arising on any agency for the supply of clothing or provisions for the Army or Navy."

XXXIX. That if any Senator, Delegate to Congress or Assembly, or member of the Council, shall hold or execute any office of profit, or receive, directly or indirectly, at any time, the profits or any part of the profits of any office exercised by any other person, during his acting as Senator, Delegate to Congress or Assembly, or member of the Council-his seat (on conviction, in a Court of law, by the oath of two credible witnesses) shall be void; and he shall suffer the punishment of wilful and corrupt perjury, or be banished this State forever, or disqualified forever from holding any office or place of trust or profit, as the Court may judge.

XL. That the Chancellor, all Judges, the Attorney-General, Clerks of the General Court, the Clerks of the County Courts, the Registers of the Land Office, and the Registers of Wills, shall hold their commissions during good behaviour, removable only for misbehaviour, on conviction in a Court of law.

XLI. That there be a Register of Wills appointed for each county who shall be commissioned by the Governor, on the joint recommendation of the Senate and House of Delegates; anal that, upon the death, resignation, disqualification, or removal out of the county of any Register of Wills, in the recess of the General Assembly the Governor, with the advice of the Council, may appoint and commission a fit and proper person to such vacant office, to hold the same until the meeting of the General Assembly.

XLII. That Sheriffs shall be elected in each county, by ballot, every third year; that is to say, two persons for the office of Sheriff for each county, the one of whom having the majority of votes, or if both have an equal number, either of them, at the discretion of the Governor, to be commissioned by the Governor for the said office; and having served for three years, such person shall be ineligible for the four years next succeeding; bond with security to be taken every year, as usual; and no Sheriff shall be qualified to act before the same is given. In case of death, refusal, resignation, disqualification, or removal out of the county before the expiration of the three years, the other person, chosen as aforesaid, shall be commissioned by the Governor to execute the said office, for the residue of the said three years, the said person giving bond and security as aforesaid: and in case of his death, refusal, resignation, disqualification, or removal out of the county, before the expiration of the said three years, the Governor, with the advice of the Council, may nominate and commission a fit and proper person to execute the said office for the residue of the said three years, the said person giving bond and security as aforesaid. The election shall be held at the same time and place appointed for the election of Delegates; and the Justices, there summoned to attend for the preservation of the peace, shall be judges thereof, and of the qualification of candidates, who shall appoint a Clerk, to take the ballots. All freemen above the age of twenty-one years, having a freehold of fifty acres of land in the county in which they offer to ballot, and residing therein-and all freemen above the age of twenty-one years, and having property in the State above the value of thirty pounds current money, and having resided in the county in which they offer to ballot one whole year next preceding the election-shall have a right of suffrage. No person to be eligible to the office of Sheriff for a county, but an inhabitant of the said county above the age of twenty-one years, and having real and personal property in the State above the value of one thousand pounds current money. The Justices aforesaid shall examine the ballots; and the two candidates properly qualified, having in each county the majority of legal ballots, shall be declared duly elected for the office of Sheriff, for such county, and returned to the Governor and Council, with a certificate of the number of ballots for each of them.

XLIII. That every person who shall offer to vote for Delegates, or for the election of the Senate, or for the Sheriff, shall (if required by any three persons qualified to vote) before he be permitted to poll, take such oath or affirmation of support and fidelity to this State, as this Convention or the Legislature shall direct.

XLIV. That a Justice of the Peace may be eligible as a Senator, Delegate, or member of the Council, and may continue to act as a Justice of the Peace.

XLV. That no field officer of the militia be eligible as a Senator, Delegate, or member of the Council.

XLVI. That all civil officers, hereafter to be appointed for the several counties of this State, shall have been residents of the county, respectively, for which they shall be appointed, six months next before their appointment; and shall continue residents of their county, respectively, during their continuance in office.

XLVII. That the Judges of the General Court, and Justices of the County Courts, may appoint the Clerks of their respective Courts; and in case of refusal, death, resignation, disqualification,, or removal out of the State, or from their respective shores, of the Clerks of the General Court, or either of them, in the vacation of the said Court- and in case of the refusal, death, resignation, disqualification, or removal out of the county, of any of the said County Clerks, in the vacation of the County Court of which he is Clerk— the Governor, with the advice of the Council, may appoint and commission a fit and proper person to such vacant office respectively, to fold the same until the meeting of the next General Court, or County Court, as the case may be.

XLVIII. That the Governor, for the time being, with the advice and consent of the Council, may appoint the Chancellor, and all Judges and Justices, the Attorney-General, Naval Officers, officers in the regular land and sea service, officers of the militia, Registers of the Land Office, Surveyors, and all other civil officers of government (Assessors, Constables, and Overseers of the roads only excepted) and may also suspend or remove any civil officer who has not a commission, during good behaviour; and may suspend any militia officer, for one month: and may also suspend or remove any regular officer in the land or sea service: and the Governor may remove or suspend any militia officer, in pursuance of the judgment of a Court Martial.

XLIX. That all civil officers of the appointment of the Governor and Council, who do not hold commissions during good behaviour, shall be appointed annually in the third week of November. But if any of them shall be reappointed, they may continue to act, without any new commission or qualification; and every officer, though not reappointed, shall continue to act, until the person who shall be appointed and commissioned in his stead shall be qualified.

L. That the Governor, every member of the Council, and every Judge and Justice, before they act as such, shall respectively take an oath, " That he will not, through favour, affection or partiality vote for any person to office; and that he will vote for such person as, in his judgment and conscience, he believes most fit and best qualified for the office; and that he has not made, nor will make. Any promise or engagement to give his vote or interest in favor of any person."

LI. That there be two Registers of the Land Office, one upon the western, and one upon the eastern shore: that short extracts of the grants and certificates of the land, on the western and eastern shores respectively, be made in separate books, at the public expense, and deposited in the offices of the said Registers, in such manner as shall hereafter be provided by the General Assembly.

LII. That every Chancellor, Judge, Register of Wills, Commissioner of the Loan Office, Attorney-General, Sheriff, Treasurer, Naval Officer, Register of the Land Office, Register of the Chancery Court, and every Clerk of the common law courts, Surveyor and Auditor of the public accounts, before he acts as such, shall take an oath " That he will not directly or indirectly receive any fee or reward, for doing his office of , but what is or shall be allowed by law; nor will, directly or indirectly, receive the profits or any part of the profits of any office held by any other person, and that he does not hold the same office in trust, or for the benefit of any other person."

LIII. That if any Governor, Chancellor, Judge, Register of Wills, Attorney-General, Register of the Land Office, Register of the Chancery Court, or any Clerk of the common law courts, Treasurer, Naval Officer, Sheriff, Surveyor or Auditor of public accounts, shall receive, directly or indirectly, at any time, the profits, or any part of the profits of any office, held by any other person, during his acting in the office to which he is appointed; his election, appointment and commission (on conviction in a court of law by oath of two credible witnesses) shall be void; and he shall suffer the punishment for wilful and corrupt perjury, or be banished this State forever, or disqualified forever from holding any office or place of trust or profit, as the court may adjudge.

LIV. That if any person shall give any bribe, present, or reward, or any promise, or any security for the payment or delivery of any money, or any other thing, to obtain or procure a vote to be Governor, Senator, Delegate to Congress or Assembly, member of the Council, or Judge, or to be appointed to any of the said offices, or to any office of profit or trust, now created or hereafter to be created in this State-the person giving, and the person receiving the same (on conviction in a court of law) shall be forever disqualified to hold any office of trust or profit in this State.

LV. That every person, appointed to any office of profit or trust, shall, before he enters on the execution thereof, take the following oath; to wit :-" I, A. B., do swear, that I do not hold myself bound in allegiance to the King of Great Britain, and that I will be faithful, and bear true allegiance to the State of Maryland; " and shall also subscribe a declaration of his belief in the Christian religion.

LVI. That there be a Court of Appeals, composed of persons of integrity and sound judgment in the law, whose judgment shall be final and conclusive, in all cases of appeal, from the General Court, Court of Chancery, and Court of Admiralty: that one person of integrity and sound judgment in the law, be appointed Chancellor: that three persons of integrity and sound judgment in the law, be appointed judges of the Court now called the Provincial Court; and that the same Court be hereafter called and known by the name of *The General Court*; which Court shall sit on the western and eastern shores, for transacting and determining the business of the respective shores, at such times and places as the future Legislature of this State shall direct and appoint.

LVII. That the style of all laws run thus; *"Be it enacted by the General Assembly of Maryland:"* that all public commissions and grants run thus; *"The State of Maryland,"* &c. and shall be signed by the Governor, and attested by the Chancellor, with the seal of the State annexed-except military commissions, which shall not be attested by the Chancellor or have the seal of the State annexed: that all writs shall run in the same style, and be attesteted, sealed and signed a usual: that all indictments shall conclude, *"Against the peace, government, and dignity of the State."*

LVIII. That all penalties and forfeitures, heretofore going to the King or proprietary, shall go to the State-save only such, as the General Assembly may abolish or otherwise provide for.

LIX. That this Form of Government, and the Declaration of Rights, and no part thereof, shall be altered, changed, or abolished, unless a bill so to alter, change or abolish the same shall pass the General Assembly, and be published at least three months before a new election, and shall be confirmed by the General Assembly, after a new election of Delegates, in the first session after such new election; provided that nothing in this form of government, which relates to the eastern shore particularly, shall at any time hereafter be altered, unless for the alteration and confirmation thereof at least two-thirds of all the members of each branch of the General Assembly shall concur.

LX. That every bill passed by the General Assembly, when engrossed, shall be presented by the Speaker of the House of Delegates, in the Senate, to the Governor for the time being, who shall sign the same, and thereto affix the Great Seal, in the presence of the members of both Houses: every law shall be recorded in the General Court office of the western shore, and in due time printed, published, and certified under the Great Seal, to the several

County Courts, in the same manner as hath been heretofore used in this State.

This Form of Government was assented to, and passed in Convention of the Delegates of the freemen of Maryland, begun and held at the city of Annapolis, the fourteenth of August, A. D. one thousand seven hundred and seventy-six.

SOURCE: These excerpts are reprinted from Franci Newton Thorpe (ed.), *The Federal and State Constitutions, Colonial Charters, and other Organic Laws of the States and Territories now or heretofore forming the United States of America*, 7 vols. (Washington: Government Printing Office, 1909), 7: 1686-1701.

7. NORTH CAROLINA CONSTITUTION
DECEMBER 18, 1776

In August 1776, the North Carolina Council of Safety (the informal body performing governmental actions in the state) announced that elections would be held in October to elect a congress that would serve as congress and constitution-making body. The congress met on November 12 and by December had drafted a declaration of rights and constitution. The North Carolina declaration of rights drew largely from the declarations of Virginia, Pennsylvania, and Maryland. After only three days of discussion, the state had also drafted a constitution, which the congress passed as an ordinary law on December 14. The Declaration of rights was subsequently passed as regular legislation on December 17. The North Carolina constitution created a bicameral legislature, with an annually elected House of Commons and an annually elected Senate. The Governor was elected annually by joint ballot of the House and Senate. The North Carolina constitution was not ratified by the people.

A DECLARATION OF RIGHTS

I. That all political power is vested in and derived from the people only.

II. That the people of this State ought to have the sole and exclusive right of regulating the internal government and police thereof.

III. That no man or set of men are entitled to exclusive or separate emoluments or privileges from the community, but in consideration of public services.

IV. That the legislative, executive, and supreme judicial powers of government, ought to be forever separate and distinct from each other.

V. That all powers of suspending laws, or the execution of laws, by any authority, without consent of the Representatives of the people, is injurious to their rights, and ought not to be exercised.

VI. That elections of members, to serve as Representatives in General Assembly, ought to be free.

VII. That, in all criminal prosecutions, every man has a right to be informed of the accusation against him, and to confront the accusers and witnesses with other testimony, and shall not be compelled to give evidence against himself.

VIII. That no freeman shall be put to answer any criminal charge, but by indictment, presentment, or impeachment.

IX. That no freeman shall be convicted of any crime, but by the unanimous verdict of a jury of good and lawful men, in open court, as heretofore used.

X. That excessive bail should not be required, nor excessive fines imposed, nor cruel or unusual punishments inflicted.

XI. That general warrants -- whereby an officer or messenger may he commanded to search suspected places, without evidence of the fact committed, or to seize any person or persons, not named, whose offences are not particularly described, and supported by evidence -- are dangerous to liberty, and ought not to be granted.

XII. That no freeman ought to be taken, imprisoned, or disseized of his freehold liberties or privileges, or outlawed, or exiled, or in any Manner destroyed, or deprived of his life, liberty, or property, but by the law of the land.

XIII. That every freeman, restrained of his liberty, is entitled to a remedy, to inquire into the lawfulness thereof, and to remove the same, if unlawful; and that such remedy ought not to be denied or delayed.

XIV. That in all controversies at law, respecting property, the ancient mode of trial, by jury, is one of the best securities of the rights of the people, and ought to remain sacred and inviolable.

XV. That the freedom of the press is one of the great bulwarks of liberty, and therefore ought never to he restrained.

XVI. That the people of this State ought not to be taxed, or made subject to the payment of any impost or duty, without the consent of themselves, or their Representatives in General Assembly, freely given.

XVII. That the people have a right to bear arms, for the defence of the State; and, as standing armies, in time of peace, are dangerous to liberty, they ought not to be kept up; and that the military should be kept under strict subordination to, and governed by, the civil power.

XVIII. That the people have a right to assemble together, to consult for their common good, to instruct their Representatives, and to apply to the Legislature, for redress of grievances.

XIX. That all men have a natural and unalienable right to worship Almighty God according to the dictates of their own consciences.

XX. That, for redress of grievances, and for amending and strengthening the laws, elections ought to be often held.

XXI. That a frequent recurrence to fundamental principles is absolutely necessary, to preserve the blessings of liberty.

XXII. That no hereditary emoluments, privileges or honors ought to be granted or conferred in this State.

XXIII. That perpetuities and monopolies are contrary to the genius of a free State, and ought not to be allowed.

XXIV. That retrospective laws, punishing facts committed before the existence of such laws, and by them only declared criminal, are oppressive, unjust, and incompatible with liberty; wherefore no ex post facto law ought to be made.

XXV. The property of the soil, in a free government, being one of the essential rights of the collective body of the people, it is necessary, in order to avoid future disputes, that the limits of the State should be ascertained with precision; and as the former temporary line between North and South Carolina, was confirmed, and extended by Commissioners, appointed by the Legislatures of the two States, agreeable to the order of the late King George the Second, in Council, that line, and that only, should be esteemed the southern boundary of this State as follows: that is to say, beginning on the sea side, at a cedar stake, at or near the mouth of Little River (being the southern extremity of Brunswick county) and running from thence a northwest course, through the boundary house, which stands in thirty-three degrees fifty-six minutes, to thirty-five degrees north latitude; and from thence a west course so far as is mentioned in the Charter of King Charles the Second, to the late Proprietors of Carolina. Therefore all the territories, seas, waters, and harbours, with their appurtenances, lying between the line above described, and the southern line of the State of Virginia, which begins on the sea shore, in thirty-six degrees thirty minutes, north latitude, and from thence runs west, agreeable to the said Charter of King Charles, are the right and property of the people of this State, to be held by them in sovereignty; any partial line, without the consent of the Legislature of this State, at any time thereafter directed, or laid out, in anywise notwithstanding: -- Provided always, That this Declaration of Rights shall not prejudice any nation or nations of Indians, from enjoying such hunting-grounds as may have been, or hereafter shall be, secured to them by any former or future Legislature of this State: -- And provided also, That it shall not be construed so as to prevent the establishment of one or more governments westward of this State, by consent of the Legislature: -- And provided further, That nothing herein contained shall affect the titles or repossessions of individuals holding or claiming under the laws heretofore in force, or grants heretofore made by the late King George the Second, or his predecessors, or the late lords proprietors, or any of them.

THE CONSTITUTION, OR FORM OF GOVERNMENT

WHEREAS allegiance and protection are, in their nature, reciprocal, and the one should of right be refused when the other is withdrawn:

And whereas George the Third, King of Great Britain, and late Sovereign of the British American Colonies, hath not only withdrawn from them his protection, but, by an act of the British Legislature, declared the inhabitants of these States out of the protection of the British crown, and all their property, found upon the high seas, liable to be seized and confiscated to the uses mentioned in the said act; and the said George the Third has also sent fleets and armies to prosecute a cruel war against them, for the purposed reducing the inhabitants of the said Colonies to a state of abject slavery; in consequence whereof, all government under the said King, within the said Colonies, hath ceased, and a total dissolution of government in many of them hath taken place.

And whereas the Continental Congress, having considered the premises, and other previous violation of the rights of the good people of America, have therefore declared, that the Thirteen United Colonies are, of right, wholly absolved from all allegiance to the British crown or any other foreign jurisdiction whatsoever: and that the said Colonies now are, and forever shall be, free and independent States.

Wherefore, in our present state, in order to prevent anarchy and confusion, it becomes necessary that government should be established in this State; therefore we, the Representatives of the freemen of North-Carolina, chosen and assembled in Congress, for the express purpose of framing a Constitution, under the authority of the people, most conducive to their happiness and prosperity, do declare, that a government for this State shall be established, in manner and form following, to wit:

I. That the legislative authority shall be vested in two distinct branches both dependent on the people, to wit, a *Senate* and *House of Commons*.

II. That the Senate shall be composed of Representatives annually chosen by ballot, one for each county in the State.

III. That the House of Commons shall be composed of Representatives annually chosen by ballot, two for each counts and one for each of the towns of Edentown, Newbern, Wilmington, Salisbury, Hillsborough and Halifax.

IV. That the Senate and House of Commons, assembled for the purpose of legislation, shall be denominated, *The General Assembly*.

V. That each member of the Senate shall have usually resided in the county in which he is chosen for one year immediately preceding his election, and for the same time shall have possessed, and continue to possess in the county which he represents, not less than three hundred acres of land in fee.

VI. That each member of the House of Commons shall have usually resided in the county in which he is chosen for one year immediatelv preceding his election, and for six months shall have possessed, and continue to possess, in the county which he represents, not less than one hundred acres of land in fee, or for the term of his own life.

VII. That all freemen, of the age of twenty-one years, who have been inhabitants of any one county within the State twelve months immediately preceding the day of any election and possessed of a freehold within the same county of fifty acres of land for six months next before, and at the day of election, shall be entitled to vote for a member of the Senate.

VIII. That all freemen of the age of twenty-one Years, who have been inhabitants of any one county within this State twelve months immediately preceding the day of any election, and shall have paid public taxes shall be entitled to vote for members of the House of Commons for the county in which he resides.

IX. That all persons possessed of a freehold in any town in this State, having a right of representation and also all freemen who have been inhabitants of any such town twelve mouths next before and at the day of election, and shall have paid public taxes, shall be entitled to vote for a member to represent such town in the House of Commons: -- Provided always, That this section shall not entitle any inhabitant of such town to vote for members of the House of Commons, for the county in which he may reside, nor any freeholder in such county, who resides without or beyond the limits of such town, to vote for a member for said town.

X. That the Senate and House of Commons, when met, shall each have power to choose a speaker and other their officers; be judges of the qualifications and elections of their members; sit upon their own adjournments from day to day, and prepare bills, to be passed into laws. The two Houses shall direct writs of election for supplying intermediate vacancies; and shall also jointly, by ballot, adjourn themselves to any future day and place.

XI. That all bills shall be read three times in each House, before they pass into laws, and be signed by the Speakers of both Houses.

XII. That every person, who shall be chosen a member of the Senate or House of Commons, or appointed to any office or place of trust, before taking his seat, or entering upon the execution of his office, shall take an oath to the State; and all officers shall also take an oath of office.

XIII. That the General Assembly shall, by joint ballot of both houses, appoint Judges of the Supreme Courts of Law and Equity, Judges of Admiralty, and Attorney-General, who shall be commissioned by the Governor, and hold their offices during good behavior.

XIV. That the Senate and House of Commons shall have power to appoint the generals and field-officers of the militia, and all officers of the regular army of this State.

XV. That the Senate and House of Commons, jointly at their first meeting after each annual election, shall by ballot elect a Governor for one year, who shall not be eligible to that office longer than three years, in six successive years. That no person, under thirty years of age, and who has not been a resident in this State above five years, and having, in the State, a freehold in lands and tenements above the value of one thousand pounds, shall be eligible as a Governor.

XIV. That the Senate and House of Commons, jointly, at their first meeting after each annual election, shall by ballot elect seven persons to be a Council of State for one year, who shall advise the Governor in the execution of his office; 2nd that four members shall be a quorum; their advice and proceedings shall be Altered in a journal, to be kept for that purpose only and signed, by the members present; to any part of which, any member present

Nay enter his dissent. And such journal shall he laid before the General Assembly when called for by them.

XVII. That there shall be a seal of this State, which shall be kept by the Governor, and used by him, as occasion may require; and shall be called, *The Great Seal of the State of North Carolina*, and be affixed to all grants and commissions.

XVIII. The Governor. for the time being, shall be captain-general and commander in chief of the militia; and, in the recess of the General Assembly, shall have power, by and with the advice of the Council of State, to embody the militia for the public safety.

XIX. That the Governor, for the tine beings shall have power to draw for and apply such sums of money as shall be voted by the general assembly, for the contingencies of government, and be accountable to them for the same. He also may, by and with the advice of the Council of State, lay embargoes, or prohibit the exportation of any commodity, for any term not exceeding thirty days, at any one time in the recess of the General Assembly; and shall have the power of granting pardons and reprieves, except where the prosecution shall be carried on by the General Assembly, or the law shall otherwise direct; in which case he may in the recess grant a reprieve until the next sitting of the General Assembly; and may exercise all the other executive powers of government, limited and restrained as by this Constitution is mentioned, and according to the laws of the State. And on his death, inability, or absence from the State, the Speaker of the Senate for the time being -- (and in case of his death, inability, or absence from the State, the Speaker of the House of Commons) shall exercise the powers of government after such death, or during such absence or inability of the Governor (or Speaker of the Senate,) or until a new nomination is made by the General Assembly.

XX. That in every case where any officer, the right of whose appointment is by this Constitution vested in the General Assembly, shall, during their recess, die, or his office by other means become vacant, the Governor shall have power, with the advice of the Council of State, to fill up such vacancy, by granting a temporary commission, which shall expire at the end of the next session of the General Assembly

XXI. That the Governor, Judges of the Supreme Court of Law and Equity, Judges of Admiralty, and Attorney-General, shall have adequate salaries during their continuance in office.

XXII. That the General Assembly shall, by joint ballot of both Houses, annually appoint a Treasurer or Treasurers for this State.

XXIII. That the Governor, and other officers, offending against the State, by violating any part of this Constitution, mal-administration, or corruption, may be prosecuted, on the impeachment of the General Assembly, or presentment of the Grand Jury of any court of supreme jurisdiction in this State.

XXIV. That the General Assembly shall, by joint ballot of both Houses, triennially appoint a Secretary for this State.

XXV. That no persons, who heretofore have been, or hereafter may be, receivers of public the monies, shall have a seat in either House of General Assembly, or be eligible to any office in this State, until such person shall have fully accounted for and paid into the treasury all sums for which they may he accountable and liable.

XXVI. That no Treasurer shall have a seat, either in the Senate, House of Commons, or Council of State, during his continuance in that office, or before he shall have finally settled his accounts with the public, for all the monies which may be in his hands at the expiration of his office belonging to the State, and hath paid the same into the hands of the succeeding Treasurer.

XXVII. That no officer in the regular army or navy, in the service and pay of the United States, of this or any other State, nor any contractor or agent for supplying such army or navy with clothing or provisions, shall have a seat either in the Senate, House of Commons, or Council of State, or be eligible thereto: and any member of the Senate, House of Commons, or Council of State, being appointed to and accepting of such office, shall thereby vacate his seat.

XXVIII. That no member of the Council of State shall have a seat, either in the Senate, or House of Commons.

XXIX. That no Judge of the Supreme Court of Law or Equity, or Judge of Admiralty, shall have a seat in the Senate, House of Commons, or Council of State.

XXX. That no Secretary of this State, Attorney-General, or Clerk of any Court of Record, shall have a seat in the Senate, House of Commons, or Council of State.

XXXI. That no clergyman, or preacher of the gospels of any denomination, shall be capable of being a member of either the Senate, House of Commons, or Council of State, while he continues in the exercise of the pastoral function.

XXXII. That no person, who shall deny the being of God or the truth of the Protestant religion, or the divine authority either of the Old or New Testaments, or who shall hold religious principles incompatible with the freedom and safety of the State, shall be capable of holding any office or place of trust or profit in the civil department within this State.

XXXIII. That the Justices of the Peace, within their respective counties in this State, shall in future be recommended to the Governor for the time being, by the Representatives in General Assembly; and the Governor shall commission them accordingly: and the Justices, when so commissioned, shall hold their offices during good behaviour, and shall not be removed from office by the General Assembly, unless for misbehaviour, absence, or inability.

XXXIV. That there shall be no establishment of any one religious church or denomination in this State, in preference to any other; neither shall any person, on any presence whatsoever, be compelled to attend any place of worship contrary to his own faith or judgment, nor be obliged to pay, for the purchase of any glebe, or the building of any house of worship, or for the maintenance of any minister or ministry, contrary to what he believes right, of has voluntarily and personally engaged to perform; but all persons shall be at liberty to exercise their own mode of worship: -- *Provided*, That nothing herein contained shall be construed to exempt preachers of treasonable or seditious discourses, from legal trial and punishment.

XXXV. That no person in the State shall hold mole than one lucrative office, at any one time: -- *Provided*, That no appointment in the militia, or the office of a Justice of the Peace, shall be considered as a lucrative office.

XXXVI. That all commissions and grants shall run in the name of the State of North Carolina, and bear test, and be signed by the Governor. All writs shall run in the same manner and bear test, and be signed by the Clerks of the respective Courts. Indictments shall conclude, *Against the peace and dignity of the estate.*

XXXVII. That the Delegates for this State, to the Continental Congress while necessary, shall be chosen annually by the General Assembly, by ballot; but may be superseded, in the meantime, in the same manner; and no person shall be electoral, to serve in that capacity, for more than three years successively.

XXXVIII. That there shall be a Sheriff, Coroner or Coroners, and Constables, in each county within this State.

XXXIX. That the person of a debtor, where there is not a strong presumption of fraud, shall not be continued in prison, after delivering up, *bona fide*, all his estate real and personal, for the use of his creditors in such manner as shall be hereafter regulated by law. All prisoners shall be bailable by sufficient sureties, unless for capital offences when the proof is evident or the presumption great.

XL. That every foreigner, who comes to settle in this State having first taken an oath of allegiance to the same, may purchase, or, by other means, acquire, hold, and transfer land, or other real estate; and after one year's residence, shall be deemed a free citizen.

XLI. That a school or schools shall be established by the Legislature, for the convenient instruction of youth, with such salaries to the masters, paid by the public, as may enable them to instruct at low prices; and all useful learning shall be duly encouraged, and promoted, in one or more universities.

XLII. That no purchase of lands shall be made of the Indian natives, but on behalf of the public, by authority of the General Assembly.

XLIII. That the future Legislature of this State shall regulate entails, in such a manner as to prevent perpetuities.

XLIV. That the Declaration of Rights is hereby declared to be part of the Constitution of this State, and ought never to be violated, on any presence whatsoever.

XLV. That any member of either House of General Assembly shall have liberty to dissent from, and protest against any act or resolve, which he may think injurious to the public, or any individual, and have the reasons of his dissent entered on the journals.

XLVI. That neither House of the General Assembly shall proceed upon public business, unless a majority of all the members of such House are actually present: and that, upon a motion made and seconded, the yeas and nays, upon any question, shall be taken and entered on the journals; and that the journals of the proceedings of both Houses of the General Assembly shall be printed, and made public, immediately after their adjournment.

This Constitution is not intended to preclude the present Congress from making a temporary provision, for the well ordering of this State, until the General Assembly shall establish government, agreeable to the mode herein before described.

SOURCE: These excerpts are reprinted from Franci Newton Thorpe (ed.), *The Federal and State Constitutions, Colonial Charters, and other Organic Laws of the States and Territories now or heretofore forming the United States of America*, 7 vols. (Washington: Government Printing Office, 1909), 7: 2787-2794.

8. Georgia Constitution
February 5, 1777

On August 8, 1776, Georgia's Council of Safety scheduled elections for a new congress that would serve both as a law-making and a constitution-making body. On January 24, 1777, the Georgia congress appointed a committee to draft a constitution, which was passed and became law on February 4. Rumored to have been written in the evenings at a tavern, the new constitution included featured a unicameral legislature modelled on Pennsylvania's one-chamber assembly. The Governor was elected annually by the legislature out of its own body. The Georgia constitution was not ratified by the people.

Whereas the conduct of the legislature of Great Britain for many years past has been so oppressive on the people of America that of late years they have plainly declared and asserted a right to raise taxes upon the people of America, and to make laws to bind them in all cases whatsoever, without their consent; which conduct, being repugnant to the common rights of mankind, hath obliged the Americans, as freemen, to oppose such oppressive measures, and to assert the rights and privileges they are entitled to by the laws of nature and reason; and accordingly it hath been done by the general consent of all the people of the States of New Hampshire, Massachusetts Bay, Rhode Island, Connecticut, New York, New Jersey, Pennsylvania, the counties of New Castle, Kent, and Sussex on Delaware, Maryland, Virginia, North Carolina, South Carolina, and Georgia, given by their representatives met together in general Congress, in the city of Philadelphia;

And whereas it hath been recommended by the said Congress, on the fifteenth of May last, to the respective assemblies and conventions of the United States, where no government, sufficient to the exigencies of their affairs, hath been hitherto established, to adopt such government as may, in the opinion of the representatives of the people, best conduce to the happiness and safety of their constituents in particular and America in general;

And whereas the independence of the United States of America has been also declared, on the fourth day of July, one thousand seven hundred and seventy-six, by the said honorable Congress, and all political connection between them and the Crown of Great Britain is in consequence thereof dissolved:

We, therefore, the representatives of the people, from whom all power originates, and for whose benefit all government is intended, by virtue of the power delegated to us, do ordain and declare, and it IS hereby ordained and declared, that the following rules and regulations be adopted for the future government of this State:

ARTICLE I. The legislative, executive, and judiciary departments shall be separate and distinct, so that neither exercise the powers properly belonging to the other.

ART. II. The legislature of this State shall be composed of the representatives of the people, as is hereinafter pointed out; and the representatives shall be elected yearly, and every year, on the first Tuesday in December; and the representatives so elected shall meet the first Tuesday in January following, at Savannah, or any other place or places where the house of assembly for the time being shall direct.

On the first day of the meeting of the representatives so chosen, they shall proceed to the choice of a governor, who shall be styled "honorable;" and of an executive council, by ballot out of their own body, viz: two from each county, except those counties which are not yet entitled to send ten members. One of each county shall always attend, where the governor resides, by monthly rotation, unless the members of each county agree for a longer or shorter period. This is not intended to exclude either member attending. The remaining number of representatives shall be called the house of assembly; and the majority of the members of the said house shall have power to proceed on business.

ART. III. It shall be an unalterable rule that the house of assembly shall expire and be at an end, yearly and every year, on the day preceding the day of election mentioned in the foregoing rule.

ART. IV. The representation shall be divided in the following manner: ten members from each county, as is hereinafter directed, except the county of Liberty, which contains three parishes, and that shall be allowed fourteen.

The ceded lands north of Ogechee shall be one county, and known by the name of Wilkes.

The parish of Saint Paul shall be another county, and known by the name of Richmond.

The parish of Saint George shall be another county, and known by the name of Burke.

The parish of Saint Matthew, and the upper part of Saint Philip, above Canouchee, shall be another county, and known by the name of Effingham.

The parish of Christ Church, and the lower part of Saint Philip, below Canouchee, shall be another county, and known by the name of Chatham.

The parishes of Saint John, Saint Andrew, and Saint James shall be another county, and known by the name of Liberty.

The parishes of Saint David and Saint Patrick shall be another county, and known by the name of Glynn.

The parishes of Saint Thomas and Saint Mary shall be another county, and known by the name of Camden.

The port and town of Savannah shall be allowed four members to represent their trade.

The port and town of Sunbury shall be allowed two members to represent their trade.

ART. V. The two counties of Glynn and Camden shall have one representative each, and also they, and all other counties that may hereafter be laid out by the house of assembly, shall be under the following regulations, VIZ: at their first institution each county shall have one member, provided the inhabitants of the said county shall have ten electors; and if thirty, they shall have two; if forty, three; if fifty, four; if eighty, six; if a hundred and upward, ten; at which time two executive councillors shall be chosen from them, as is directed for the other counties.

ART. VI. The representatives shall be chosen out of the residents in each county, who shall have resided at least twelve months in this State, and three months in the county where they shall be elected; except the freeholders of the counties of Glynn and Camden, who are in a state of alarm, and who shall have the liberty of choosing one member each, as specified in the articles of this constitution, in any other county, until they have residents sufficient to qualify them for more; and they shall be of the Protestent religion, and of the age of twenty-one years, and shall be possessed in their own right of two hundred and fifty acres of land, or some property to the amount of two hundred and fifty pounds.

ART. VII. The house of assembly shall have power to make such laws and regulations as may be conducive to the good order and wellbeing of the State; provided such laws and regulations be not repugnant to the true intent and meaning of any rule or regulation contained In this constitution.

The house of assembly shall also have power to repeal all laws and ordinances they find injurious to the people; and the house shall choose its own speaker, appoint its own officers, settle its own rules of proceeding, and direct writs of election for supplying intermediate vacancies, and shall have power of adjournment to any time or times within the year.

ART. VIII. All laws and ordinances shall be three times read, and each reading shall be on different and separate days, except in cases of great necessity and danger; and all laws and ordinances shall be sent to the executive council after the second reading, for their perusal and advice.

ART. IX. All male white inhabitants, of the age of twenty-one years, and possessed in his own right of ten pounds value, and liable to pay tax in this State, or being of any mechanic trade, and shall have been resident six months in this State, shall have a right to vote at all elections for representatives, or any other officers, herein agreed to be chosen by the people at large; and every person having a right to vote at any election shall vote by ballot personally.

ART. X. No officer whatever shall serve any process, or give any other hinderances to any person entitled to vote, either in going to the place of election' or during the time of the said election, or on their returning home from such election; nor shall any military officer, or soldier, appear at any election in a military character, to the intent that all elections may be free and open.

ART. XI. No person shall be entitled to more than one vote, which shall be given in the county where such person resides, except as before excepted; nor shall any person who holds any title of nobility lie entitled to a vote, or be capable of serving as a representative, or hold any post of honor, profit, or trust in this State, whilst such person claims his title of nobility; but if the person shall give up such distinction, in the manner as may be directed by any future legislation, then, and in such case, he shall be entitled to a vote, and represent, as before directed, and enjoy all the other benefits of a free citizen.

ART. XII. Every person absenting himself from an election, and shall neglect to give in his or their ballot at such election, shall be subject to a penalty not exceeding five pounds; the mode of recovery and also the appropriation thereof, to be pointed out and directed by act of the legislature: *Provided, nevertheless,* That a reasonable excuse shall be admitted.

ART. XIII. The manner of electing representatives shall be by ballot, and shall be taken by two or more justices of the peace in each county, who shall provide a convenient box for receiving the said ballots: and, on closing the poll, the ballots shall be compared in public with the list of votes that have been taken, and the majority immediately declared; a certificate of the same being given to the persons elected, and also a certificate returned to the house of representatives.

ART. XIV. Every person entitled to vote shall take the following oath or affirmation, if required, viz: "I, A B. do voluntarily and solemnly swear (or affirm, as the case may be) that I do owe true allegiance to this State, and will support the constitution thereof; so help me God."

ART. XV. Any five of the representatives elected, as before directed, being met, shall have power to administer the following oath to each other; and they, or any other member, being so sworn, shall, in the house, administer the oath to all other members that attend, in order to qualify them to take their seats, viz:

"I, A B. do solemnly swear that I will bear true allegiance to the State of Georgia, and will truly perform the trusts reposed in me; and that I will execute the same to the best of my knowledge, for the benefit of this State, and the support of the constitution thereof, and that I have obtained my election without fraud or bribe whatever; so help me God."

ART. XVI. The continental delegates shall be appointed annually by ballot, and shall have a right to sit, debate, and vote in the house of assembly, and be deemed a part thereof, subject, however, to the regulations contained in the twelfth article of the Confederation of the United States.

ART. XVII. No person bearing any post of profit under this State, or any person bearing any military commission under this or any other State or States, except officers of the militia, shall be elected a representative. And if any representative shall be appointed to any place of profit or military commission, which he shall accept, his seat shall immediately become vacant, and he shall be incapable of reelection whilst holding such office.

By this article it is not to be understood that the office of a justice of the peace is a post of profit.

ART. XVIII. No person shall hold more than one office of profit under this State at one and the same time.

ART. XIX. The governor shall, with the advice of the executive council, exercise the executive powers of government, according to the laws of this State and the constitution thereof, save only in the case of pardons and remission of fines, which he shall in no instance grant; but he may reprieve a criminal, or suspend a fine, until the meeting of the assembly, who may determine therein as they shall Judge fit.

ART. XX. The governor, with the advice of the executive council, shall have power to call the house of assembly together, upon any emergency, before the time which they stand adjourned to.

ART. XXI. The governor, with the advice of the executive council shall fill up all intermediate vacancies that shall happen in offices till the next general election; and all commissions, civil and military, shall be issued by the governor, under his hand and the great seal of the State.

ART. XXII. The governor may preside in the executive council at all times, except when they are taking into consideration and perusing the laws and ordinances offered to them by the house of assembly.

ART. XXIII. The governor shall be chosen annually by ballot, and shall not be eligible to the said office for more than one year out of three, nor shall he hold any military commission under any other State or States.

The governor shall reside at such place as the house of assembly for the time being shall appoint.

ART. XXIV. The governor's oath: "I, A B, elected governor of the State of Georgia, by the representatives thereof, do solemnly promise and swear that I will, during the term of my appointment, to the best of my skill and judgment, execute the said office faithfully and conscientiously' according to law, without favor, affection, or partiality; that I will, to the utmost of my power, support, maintain, and defend the State of Georgia, and the constitution of the same; and use my utmost endeavors to protect the people thereof in the secure enjoyment of all their rights, franchises and privileges; and that the laws and ordinances of the State be duly observed, and that law and justice in mercy be executed in all judgments. And I do further solemnly promise and swear that I will peaceably and quietly resign the government to which I have been elected at the period to which my continuance in the said office is limited by the constitution. And, lastly, I do also solemnly swear that I have not accepted of the government whereunto I am elected contrary to the articles of this constitution; so help me God."

This oath to be administered to him by the speaker of the assembly.

The same oath to be administered by the speaker to the president of the council.

No person shall be eligible to the office of governor who has not resided three years in this State.

ART. XXV. The executive council shall meet the day after their election, and proceed to the choice of a president out of their own body; they shall have power to appoint their own officers and settle their own rules of proceedings.

The council shall always vote by counties, and not individually.

ART. XXVI. Every councillor, being present, shall have power of entering his protest against any measures in council he has not consented to, provided he does it in three days.

ART. XXVII. During the sitting of the assembly the whole of the executive council shall attend, unless prevented by sickness, or some other urgent necessity; and, in that case, a majority of the council shall make a board to examine the laws and ordinances sent them by the house of assembly; and all laws and ordinances sent to the council shall be returned in five days after, with their remarks hereon.

ART. XXVIII. A committee from the council, sent with any proposed amendments to any law or ordinance, shall deliver their reasons for such proposed amendments, sitting and covered; the whole house at that time, except the speaker, uncovered.

ART. XXIX. The president of the executive council, in the absence or sickness of the governor, shall exercise all the powers of the governor.

ART. XXX. When any affair that requires secrecy shall be laid before the governor and the executive council, it shall be the duty of the governor. And he is hereby obliged, to administer the following Oath, viz: "I, A B. do solemnly swear that any business that shall be at this time communicated to the council I will not, in any manner whatever, either by speaking, writing, or otherwise, reveal the same to any person whatever, until leave given by the council, or when called upon by the house of assembly; and all this I swear without any reservation whatever; so help me God."

And the same oath shall be administered to the secretary and other officers necessary to carry the business into execution.

ART. XXXI. The executive power shall exist till renewed as pointed out by the rules of this constitution.

ART. XXXII. In all transactions between the legislative and executive bodies the same shall be communicated by message, to be delivered from the legislative body to the governor or executive council by a committee, and from the governor to the house of assembly by the secretary of the council, and from the executive council by a committee of the said council.

ART. XXXIII. The governor for the time being shall be captains general and commander-in-chief over all the militia, and other military and naval forces belonging to this State.

ART. XXXIV. All militia commissions shall specify that the person commissioned shall continue during good behavior.

ART. XXXV. Every county in this State that has, or hereafter may have, two hundred and fifty men, and upwards, liable to bear arms, shall be formed into a battalion; and when they become too numerous for one battalion, they shall be formed into more, by bill of the legislature; and those counties that have a less number than two hundred and fifty shall be formed into independent companies.

ART. XXXVI. There shall be established in each county a court, to be called a superior court, to be held twice in each year.

On the first Tuesday in March, in the county of Chatham.

The second Tuesday in March, in the county of Effingham.

The third Tuesday in March, in the county of Burke

The fourth Tuesday in March, in the county of Richmond.

The next Tuesday, in the county of Wilkes.

And Tuesday fortnight, in the county of Liberty.

The next Tuesday, in the county of Glynn.

The next Tuesday, in the county of Camden.

The like courts to commence in October and continue as above.

ART. XXXVII. All causes and matters of dispute, between any parties residing in the same county, to be tried within the county.

ART. XXXVIII. All matters in dispute between contending parties residing in different counties shall be tried in the county where the defendant resides, except in cases of real estate, which shall be tried in the county where such real estate lies.

ART. XXXIX. All matters of breach of the peace, felony, murder, and treason against the State to be tried in the county where the same was committed. All matters of dispute, both civil and criminal, in any county where there is not a sufficient number of inhabitants to form a court, shall be tried in the next adjacent county where a court is held.

ART. XL. All causes, of what nature soever, shall be tried in the supreme court, except as hereafter mentioned; which court shall con sist of the chief-justice, and three or more of the justices residing in the county. In case of the absence of the chief-justice, the senior justice on the bench shall act as chief-justice, with the clerk of the county, attorney for the State, sheriff, coroner, constable, and the jurors; and in case of the absence of any of the aforementioned officers, the justices to appoint others in their room *pro tempore*. And if any plaintiff or defendant in civil causes shall be dissatisfied with the determination of the jury, then, and in that case, they shall be at liberty, within three days, to enter an appeal from that verdict, and demand a new trial by a special jury, to be nominated as follows, viz: each party, plaintiff and defendant, shall choose six, six more names shall be taken indifferently out of a box provided for that purpose, the whole eighteen to be summoned, and their names to be put together into the box, and the first twelve that are drawn out, being present, shall be the special jury to try the cause, and from which there shall be no appeal.

ART. XLI. The jury shall be judges of law, as well as of fact, and shall not be allowed to bring in a special verdict; but if all or any of the jury have any doubts concerning points of law, they shall apply to the bench, who shall each of them in rotation give their opinion.

ART. XLII. The jury shall be sworn to bring in a verdict according to lair, and the opinion they entertain of the evidence; provided it be not repugnant to the rules and regulations contained in this constitution.

ART. XLIII. The special jury shall be sworn to bring in a verdict according to law, and the opinion they entertain of the evidence; provided it be not repugnant to justice, equity, and conscience, and the rules and regulations contained in this constitution, of which they shall Judge.

ART. XLIV. Captures, both by sea and land, to be tried in the county where such shall be carried in; a special court to be called by the chief-justice, or in his absence by the then senior justice in the said county, upon application of the captors or claimants, which cause shall be determined within the space of ten days. The mode of proceeding and appeal shall be the same as in the superior courts, unless, after the second trial, an appeal is made to the Continental Congress; and the distance of time between the first and second trial shall not exceed fourteen days; and all maritime causes to be tried in like manner.

ART. XLV. No grand jury shall consist of less than eighteen, and twelve may find a bill.

ART. XLVI. That the court of conscience be continued as heretofore practiced, and that the jurisdiction thereof be extended to try causes not amounting to more than ten pounds.

ART. XLVII. All executions exceeding five pounds, except in the case of a court-merchant, shall be stayed until the first Monday in March; provided security be given for debt and costs.

ART. XLVIII. All the costs attending any action in the superior court shall not exceed the sum of three pounds, and that no cause be allowed to depend in the superior court longer than two terms.

ART. XLIX. Every officer of the State shall be liable to be called to account by the house of assembly.

ART. L. Every county shall keep the public records belonging to the same, and authenticated copies of the several records now in the possession of this State shall be made out and deposited in that county to which they belong.

ART. LI. Estates shall not be entailed; and when a person dies intestate, his or her estate shall be divided equally among their children; the widow shall have a child's share, or her dower, at her option; all other intestates' estates to be divided according to the act of distribution, made in the reign of Charles the Second, unless otherwise altered by any future act of the legislature.

ART. LII. A register of probates shall be appointed by the legislature in every county, for proving wills and granting letters of administration.

ART. LIII. All civil officers in each county shall be annually elected on the day of the general election, except justices of the peace and registers of probates, who shall be appointed by the house of assembly.

ART. LIV. Schools shall be erected in each county, and supported at the general expense of the State, as the legislature shall hereafter point out.

ART. LV. A court-house and jail shall be erected at the public expense in each county, where the present convention or the future legislature shall point out and direct.

ART. LVI. All persons whatever shall have the free exercise of their religion; provided it be not repugnant to the peace and safety of the State; and shall not, unless by consent, support any teacher or teachers except those of their own profession.

ART. LVII. The great seal of this State shall have the following device: on one side a scroll, whereon shall be engraved, "The Constitution of the State of Georgia"; and the motto, *"Pro bono publico."* On the other side, an elegant house, and other buildings, fields of corn, and meadows covered with sheep and cattle; a river running through the same, with a ship under full sail, and the motto, *"Deus nobis haec otia fecit."*

ART. LVIII. No person shall be allowed to plead in the courts of law in this State, except those who are authorized so to do by the house of assembly; and if any person so authorized shall be found guilty of malpractice before the house of assembly, they shall have power to suspend them. This is not intended to exclude any person from that inherent privilege of every *freeman,* the liberty to plead his own cause.

ART. LIX. Excessive fines shall not be levied, not excessive bail demanded.

ART. LX. The principles of the *habeas-corpus* act shall be a part of this constitution.

ART. LXI. Freedom of the press and trial by jury to remain inviolate forever.

ART. LXII. No clergyman of any denomination shall be allowed a seat in the legislature.

ART. LXIII. No alteration shall be made in this constitution without petitions from a majority of the counties, and the petitions from each county to be signed by a majority of voters in each county within this State; at which time the assembly shall order a convention to be called for that purpose, specifying the alterations to be made, according to the petitions preferred to the assembly by the majority of the counties as aforesaid.

Done at Savannah, in convention, the fifth day of February, in the year of our Lord one thousand seven hundred and seventy-seven, and in the first year of the Independence of the United States of America.

SOURCE: These excerpts are reprinted from Franci Newton Thorpe (ed.), *The Federal and State Constitutions, Colonial Charters, and other Organic Laws of the States and Territories now or heretofore forming the United States of America*, 7 vols. (Washington: Government Printing Office, 1909), 7: 777-785.

9. New York Constitution
April 20, 1777

New Yorkers began discussing the need for a written constitution starting in the early months of 1776 before the Continental Congress's May 15 recommendation to the colonies that they adopt new frames of government. Many in the province were reluctant to divert the colony's best minds from fighting a war to drafting a constitution, and many thought the provincial congress was adequate to the task of governing. On May 27, 1776, the New York congress voted overwhelmingly to establish a committee for drafting a constitution. The committee then called on the province to call an election for a new legislative congress with the authority to draft a constitution for the state that would replace the old colonial charter with its ties to the British Crown. The newly elected congress, which met on July 9, 1776, announced on August 1 that it had charged a committee with the responsibility of preparing a bill of rights and a constitution. Due to a British military occupation in New York, the committee did not present a constitution to the congress until March 12, 1777, which was then discussed and approved on April 20. The new constitution was largely drafted by John Jay, Robert R. Livingston, and Gouverneur Morris. The New York constitution had a relatively weak bicameral legislature (an Assembly and Senate) and a relatively strong executive in the form of a governor. One of the most unique features of the empire state constitution was its Council of Revision, a distinct political body with the authority to review and temporarily veto legislation passed by the legislature. The Council of Revision was composed of the governor, chancellor (i.e., the head of the state's court of chancery or equity court), and the justices of the state Supreme Court. The New York constitution was not ratified by the people of New York.

In Convention of the Representatives of this State of New York

Whereas the many tyrannical and oppressive usurpations of the King and Parliament of Great Britain on the rights and liberties of the people of the American colonies had reduced them to the necessity of introducing a government by congresses and committees, as temporary expedients, and to exist no longer than the grievances of the people should remain without redress; And whereas the congress of the colony of New York did, on the thirty-first day of May now last past, resolve as follows, viz:

"Whereas the present government of this colony, by congress and committees, was instituted while the former government, under the Crown of

Great Britain, existed in full force, and was established for the sole purpose of opposing the usurpation of the British Parliament, and was intended to expire on a reconciliation with Great Britain, which it was then apprehended would soon take place, but is now considered as remote and uncertain;

"And whereas many and great inconveniences attend the said mode of government by congress and committees, as of necessity, in many instances, legislative, judicial, and executive popovers have been vested therein, especially since the dissolution of the former government by the abdication of the late governor and the exclusion of this colony from the protection of the King of Great Britain;

"And whereas the Continental Congress did resolve as followeth, to wit:

"'Whereas His Britannic Majesty, in conjunction with the lords and commons of Great Britain, has, by a late act of Parliament, excluded the inhabitants of these united colonies from the protection of his Crown; and whereas no answers whatever to the humble petition of the colonies for redress of grievances end reconciliation with Great Britain has been, or is likely to be, given, but the whole force of that kingdom, aided by foreign mercenaries, is to be exerted for the destruction of the good people of these colonies; and whereas it appears absolutely irreconcilable to reason and good conscience for the people of these colonies now to take the oaths and affirmations necessary for the support of any government under the Crown of Great Britain, and it is necessary that the exercise of every kind of authority under the said Crown should be totally suppressed, and all the popovers of government exerted under the authority of the people of the colonies for the preservation of internal peace, virtue, and good order, as well as for the defense of our lives, liberties, and properties, against the hostile invasions and cruel depredations of our enemies: Therefore,

"'*Resolved*, That it be recommended to the respective assemblies and conventions of the United colonies, where no government sufficient to the exigencies of their affairs has been hitherto established, to adopt such government as shall, in the opinion of the representatives of the people, best conduce to the happiness and safety of their constituents in particular, and America in general.'

"And whereas doubts have arisen whether this congress are invested with sufficient power and authority to deliberate and determine on so important a subject as the necessity of erecting and constituting a new form of government and internal police, to the exclusion of all foreign jurisdiction, dominion, and control whatever; and whereas it appertains of right solely to the people of this colony to determine the said doubts: Therefore

"*Resolved*, That it be recommended to the electors in the several counties in this colony, by election, in the manner and form prescribed for the election of the present congress, either to authorize (in addition to the powers vested in this congress) their present deputies, or others in the stead of their present deputies, or either of them, to take into consideration the necessity and propriety of instituting such new government as in and by the said resolution of the Continental Congress is described and recommended; and if the majority of the counties, by their deputies in provincial congress, shall be of opinion that such new government ought to be instituted and established, then to institute and establish such a government as they shall deem best calculated to secure the rights, liberties, and happiness of the good people of this colony; and to continue in force until a future peace with Great Britain shall render the same unnecessary; and

"*Resolved*, That the said elections in the several counties ought to be had on such day, and at such place or places, as by the committee of each county respectively shall be determined. And it is recommended to the said committees to fix such early days for the said elections as that all the deputies to be elected have sufficient time to repair to the city of New York by the second Monday in July next; on which day all the said deputies ought punctually to give their attendance.

"And whereas the object of the Foregoing resolutions is of the utmost importance to the good people of this colony:

"*Resolved*, That it be, and it is hereby, earnestly recommended to the committees, freeholders, and other electors in the different counties in this colony diligently to carry the same into execution."

And whereas the good people of the said colony, in pursuance of the said resolution, and reposing special trust and confidence in the members of this convention, have appointed, authorized, and empowered them for the purposes, and in the manner, and with the powers in and by the said resolve specified, declared, and mentioned.

And whereas the Delegates of the United American States, in general (Congress convened, did, on the fourth day of July now last past, solemnly publish and declare, in the words following; viz:

"When, in the course of human events, it becomes necessary for one people to dissolve the political bands which have connected them with another, and to assume among the powers of the earth the separate and equal station to which the laws of nature and of nature's God entitle them, a decent respect to the opinions of mankind requires that they should declare the causes which impel them to the separation.

"We hold these truths to be self-evident, that all men are created equal; that they are endowed by their Creator with certain unalienable rights; that among these are, life, liberty, and the pursuit of happiness; that to secure these rights, governments are instituted among men, deriving their just powers from the consent of the governed; that whenever any form of government becomes destructive of these ends, it is the right of the people to alter or to abolish it, and to institute new government, laying its foundation on such principles, and organizing its powers in such form, as to them shall seem most likely to effect their safety and happiness. Prudence, indeed, will dictate that governments long established should not be changed for light and transient causes, and accordingly all experience hath shown that mankind are more disposed to suffer, while evils are sufferable, than to right themselves by abolishing the forms to which they are accustomed. But when a long train of abuses and usurpations; pursuing invariably the same object, evinces a design to reduce them under absolute despotism, it is their right, it is their duty, to throw off such government, and to provide new guards for their future security. Such has been the patient sufferance of these colonies; and such is now the necessity which constrains them to alter their former system of government. The history of the present King of Great Britain is a history of repeated injuries and usurpations, all having in direct object the establishment of an absolute tyranny over these States. To prove this, let facts be submitted to a candid world.

"He has refused his assent to laws, the most wholesome and necessary for the public good.

"He has forbidden his governors to pass laws of immediate and pressing importance, unless suspended in their operation till his assent should be obtained; and when so suspended, he has utterly neglected to attend to them.

"He has refused to pass other laws for the accommodation of large districts of people, unless those people would relinquish the right of representation in the legislature; a right inestimable to them, and formidable to tyrants only.

"He has called together legislative bodies at places unusual, uncomfortable, and distant from the depository of their public records, for the sole purpose of fatiguing them into compliance with his measures.

"He has dissolved representative houses repeatedly, for opposing with manly firmness his invasions on the rights of the people.

"He has refused for a long time, after such dissolutions, to cause others to be elected, whereby the legislative powers, incapable of annihilation, have returned to the people at large, for their exercise; the State remaining in the meantime exposed to all the dangers of invasion from without, and convulsions within.

"He has endeavored to prevent the population of these States; for that purpose obstructing the laws for naturalization of foreigners, refusing to pass others to encourage their migrations hither, and raising the conditions of new appropriations of lands.

"He has obstructed the administration of justice, by refusing his assent to laws for establishing judiciary powers.

"He has made judges dependent on his will alone, for the tenure of their offices, and the amount and payment of their salaries.

"He has erected a multitude of new offices, and sent hither swarms of officers to harass our people and eat out their substance.

"He has kept among us, in times of peace, standing armies, without the consent of our legislatures.

"He has affected to render the military independent of, and superior to, the civil power.

"He has combined with others to subject us to a jurisdiction foreign to our constitution, and unacknowledged by our laws; giving his assent to their acts of pretended legislation:

"For quartering large bodies of troops among us:

"For protecting them, by a mock trial, from punishment for any murders they should commit on the inhabitants of these States:

"For cutting off our trade with all parts of the world:

"For imposing taxes on us without our consent:

"For depriving us, in many cases, of the benefits of trial by jury:

"For transporting us beyond seas, to be tried for pretended offences:

"For abolishing the free system of English laws in a neighboring province, establishing therein an arbitrary government, and enlarging its boundaries, so as to render it at once an example and fit instrument for introducing the same absolute rule into these colonies:

"For taking away our charters, abolishing our most valuable laws, and altering fundamentally the forms of our governments:

"For suspending our own legislatures, and declaring themselves invested with power to legislate for us in all cases whatsoever.

"He has abdicated government here, by declaring us out of his protection, and waging war against us.

"He has plundered our seas, ravaged our coasts, burnt our towns, and destroyed the lives of our people.

"He is at this time transporting large armies of foreign mercenaries to complete the work of death, desolation, and tyranny, already lies on with circumstances of cruelty and perfidy scarcely paralleled in the most barbarous ages, and totally unworthy the head of a civilized nation.

"He has constrained our fellow-citizens, taken captive on the high seas, to bear arms against their country, to become the executioners of their friends and brethren, or to fall themselves by their Lands.

"He has excited domestic insurrections amongst us, and has endeavored to bring on the inhabitants of our frontiers the merciless Indian savages, whose known rule of warfare is an undistinguished destruction of all ages, sexes and conditions.

"In every stage of these oppressions, we have petitioned for redress in the most humble terms. Our repeated petitions have been answered only by repeated injury. A prince whose character is thus marked by every act which may define a tyrant, is unfit to be the ruler of a free people.

Nor have we been wanting in attentions to our British brethren. We have warned them from time to time of attempts by their legislature to extend an unwarrantable jurisdiction over us. We have reminded them of the circumstances of our emigration and settlement here. We have appealed to their native justice and magnanimity, and we have conjured them by the ties of our common kindred to disavow these usurpations, which would inevitably interrupt our connection and correspondence. They too have been deaf to the voice of justice and of consanguinity. We must therefore acquiesce in the necessity which denounces our separation, and hold them as we hold the rest of mankind, enemies in war; in peace, friends.

"We therefore, the Representatives of the United States of America, in general Congress assembled, appealing to the Supreme Judge of the world for the rectitude of our intentions, do, in the name and by the authority of the good people of these colonies, solemnly publish and declare, That these united colonies are, and of right ought to be, free and independent States; that they are absolved from all allegiance to the British Crown, and that all political connection between them and the State of Great Britain is, and ought to be, totally dissolved; and that as free and independent States they have full power to levy war, conclude peace, contract alliances, establish commerce, and to do all other acts and things which independent States may of right do. And for the support of this declaration, with a firm reliance on the protection of Divine Providence, we mutually pledge to each other our lives, our fortunes, and our sacred honor."

And whereas this convention, having taken this declaration into their most serious consideration, did, on the ninth day of July last past, unanimously resolve that the reasons assigned by the Continental Congress for declaring the united colonies free and independent States are cogent and conclusive; and that while we lament the cruel necessity which has rendered that measure unavoidable, we approve the same, and will, at the risk of our lives and fortunes, join with the other colonies in supporting it

By virtue of which several acts, declarations, and proceedings mentioned and contained in the afore-cited resolves or resolutions of the general Congress of the United American States, and of the congresses or conventions of this State, all power whatever therein hath reverted to the people thereof, and this convention hath by their suffrages and free choice been appointed, and among other things authorized to institute and establish such a government as they shall deem best calculated to secure the rights and liberties of the good people of this State, most conducive of the happiness and safety of their constituents in particular, and of America in general.

I. This convention, therefore, in the name and by the authority of the good people of this State, doth ordain, determine, and declare that no authority shall, on any presence whatever, be exercised over the people or members of this State but such as shall be derived from and granted by them.

II. This convention doth further, in the name and by the authority of the good people of this State, ordain, determine, and declare that the supreme legislative power within this State shall be vested in two separate and distinct bodies of men; the one to be called the assembly of the State of New York, the other to be called the senate of the State of New York; who together shall form the legislature, and meet once at least in every year for the despatch of business.

III. And whereas laws inconsistent with the spirit of this constitution, or with the public good, may be hastily and unadvisedly passed: Be it ordained, that the governor for the time being, the chancellor, and the judges of the supreme court, or any two of them, together with the governor, shall be, and hereby are, constituted a council to revise all bills about to be passed into laws by the legislature; and for that purpose shall assemble themselves from time to time, when the legislature shall be convened; for which, nevertheless they shall not receive any salary or consideration, under any presence whatever. And that all bills which have passed the senate and assembly shall, before they become laws, be presented to the said council for their revisal and consideration; and if, upon such revision and consideration, it should appear improper to the said council, or a majority of them, that the said bill should become a law of this State, that they return the same, together with their objections thereto in writing, to the senate or house of assembly (in which soever the same shall have originated) who shall enter the objection sent down by the council at large in their minutes, and proceed to reconsider the said bill. But if, after such reconsideration, two-thirds of the said senate or house of assembly shall, notwithstanding the said objections, agree to pass the same, it shall together with the objections, be sent to the other branch of the legislature, where it shall also be reconsidered, and, if approved by two-thirds of the members present, shall be a law.

And in order to prevent any unnecessary delays, be it further ordained, that if any bill shall not be returned by the council within ten days after it shall have been presented, the same shall be a law, unless the legislature shall, by their adjournment, render a return of the said bill within ten days impracticable; in which case the bill shall be returned on the first day of the meeting of the legislature after the expiration of the said ten days.

IV. That the assembly shall consist of at least seventy members, to be annually chosen in the several counties, in the proportions following, viz:

For the city and county of New York, nine.
The city and county of Albany, ten.
The county of Dutchess, seven.
The county of Westchester, six.
The county of Ulster, six.
The county of Suffolk, five.
The county of Queens, four.
The county of Orange, four.
The county of Kings, two.
The county of Richmond, two.
Tryon County, six.
Charlotte County, four.

Cumberland County, three.

Gloucester County, two.

V. That as soon after the expiration of seven years (subsequent to the termination of the present war) as may be a census of the electors and inhabitants in this State be taken, under the direction of the legislature. And if, on such census, it shall appear that the number of representatives in assembly from the said counties is not justly proportioned to the number of electors in the said counties respectively, that the legislature do adjust and apportion the same by that rule. And further, that once in ever seven years, after the taking of the said first census, a just account of the electors resident in each county shall be taken, and if it shall thereupon appear that the member of electors in any county shall have increased or diminished one or more seventieth parts of the whole number of electors, which, on the said first census, shall be found in this State, the number of representatives for such county shall be increased or diminished accordingly, that is to say, fine representative for every seventieth part as aforesaid.

VI. And whereas an opinion hath long prevailed among divers of the good people of this State that voting at elections by ballot would tend more to preserve the liberty and equal freedom of the people than voting *viva voce*: To the end, therefore, that a fair experiment be made, which of those two methods of voting is to be preferred --

Be it ordained, That as soon as may be after the termination of the present war between the United States of America and Great Britain, an act or acts be passed by the legislature of this State for causing all elections thereafter to be held in this State for senators and representatives in assembly to be by ballot, and directing the manner in which the same shall be conducted. And whereas it is possible that, after all the care of the legislature in framing the said act or acts, certain inconveniences and mischiefs, unforseen at this day, may be found to attend the said mode of electing by ballot:

It is further ordained, That if, after a full and fair experiment shall be made of voting by ballot aforesaid, the same shall be found less conducive to the safety or interest of the State than the method of voting *viva voce*, it shall be lawful and constitutional for the legislature to abolish the same, provided two-thirds of the members present in each house, respectively, shall concur therein. And further, that, during the continuance of the present war, and until the legislature of this State shall provide for the election of senators and representatives in assembly by ballot, the said election shall be made *viva voce*.

VII. That every male inhabitant of full age, who shall have personally resided within one of the counties of this State for six months immediately preceding the day of election, shall, at such election, be entitled to vote for representatives of the said county in assembly; if, during the time aforesaid, he shall have been a freeholder, possessing a freehold of the value of twenty pounds, within the said county, or have rented a tenement therein of the yearly value of forty shillings, and been rated and actually paid taxes to this State: *Provided always*, That every person who now is a freeman of the city of Albany, or who was made a freeman of the city of New York on or before the fourteenth day of October, in the year of our Lord one thousand seven hundred and seventy-five, and shall be actually and usually resident in the said cities, respectively, shall be entitled to vote for representatives in assembly within his said place of residence.

VIII. That every elector, before he is admitted to vote, shall, if required by the returning-officer or either of the inspectors, take an oath, or, if of the people called Quakers, an affirmation, of allegiance to the State.

IX. That the assembly, thus constituted, shall choose their own speaker, be judges of their own members, and enjoy the same privileges, and proceed in doing business in like manner as the assemblies of the colony of New York of right formerly did; and that a majority of the said members shall, from time to time, constitute a house, to proceed upon business.

X. And this convention doth further, in the name and by the authority of the good people of this State, ordain, determine, and declare, that the senate of the State of New York shall consist of twenty-four freeholders to be chosen out of the body of the freeholders; and that they be chosen by the freeholders of this State, possessed of freeholds of the value of one hundred pounds, over and above all debts charged thereon.

XI. That the members of the senate be elected for four years; and, immediately after the first election, they be divided by lot into four classes, six in each class, and numbered one, two, three, and four; that the seats of the members of the first class shall be vacated at the expiration of the first year, the second class the second year, and so on continually; to the end that the fourth part of the senate, as nearly as possible, may be annually chosen.

XII. That the election of senators shall be after this manner: That so much of this State as is now parcelled into counties be divided into four great districts; the southern district to comprehend the city and county of New York, Suffolk, Westchester, Kings, Queens, and Richmond Counties; the middle district to comprehend the counties of Dutchess, Ulster, and Orange; the western district, the city and county of Albany, and Tryon County; and the eastern district, the counties of Charlotte, Cumberland, and Gloucester. That the senators shall be elected by the freeholders of the said districts, qualified as aforesaid, in the proportions following, to wit: in the southern district, nine; in the middle district, six; in the western district, six; and in the eastern district, three. And be it ordained, that a census shall be taken, as soon as may be after the expiration of seven years from the termination of the present war, under the direction of the legislature; and if, on such census, it shall appear that the number of senators is not justly proportioned to the several districts, that the legislature adjust the proportion, as near as may be, to the number of freeholders, qualified as aforesaid, in each district. That when the number of electors, within any of the said districts, shall have increased one twenty-fourth part of the whole number of electors, which. by the said census, shall be found to be in this State, an additional senator shall be chosen by the electors of such district. That a majority of the number of senators to be chosen aforesaid shall be necessary to constitute a senate sufficient to proceed upon business; and that the senate shall, in like manner with the assembly, be the judges of its own members. And be it ordained, that it shall be in the power of the future legislatures of this State, for the convenience and advantage of the good people thereof, to divide the same into such further and other counties and districts as shall to them appear necessary.

XIII. And this convention doth further, in the name and by the authority of the good people of this State, ordain, determine, and declare, that no member of this State shall be disfranchised, or deprived of any the rights or privileges secured to the subjects of this State by this constitution, unless by the law of the land, or the judgment of his peers.

XIV. That neither the assembly or the senate shall have the power to adjourn themselves, for any longer time than two days, without the mutual consent of both.

XV. That whenever the assembly and senate disagree, a conference shall be held, in the preference of both, and be managed by committees, to be by them respectively chosen by ballot. That the doors, both of the senate and assembly, shall at all times be kept open to all persons, except when the welfare of the State shall require their debates to be kept secret. And the journals of all their proceedings shall be kept in the manner heretofore accustomed by the general assembly of the colony of New York; and except such parts as they shall, as aforesaid, respectively determine not to make public be from day to day (if the business of the legislature will permit) published.

XVI. It is nevertheless provided, that the number of senators shall never exceed one hundred, nor the number of the assembly three hundred; but that whenever the number of senators shall amount to one hundred, or of the assembly to three hundred, then and in such case the legislature shall, from time to time thereafter, by laws for that purpose, apportion and distribute the said one hundred senators and three hundred representatives among the great districts and counties of this State, in proportion to the number of their respective electors; so that the representation of the good people of this State, both in the senate and assembly, shall forever remain proportionate and adequate.

XVII. And this convention doth further, in the name and by the authority of the good people of this State, ordain, determine, and declare that the supreme executive power and authority of this State shall be vested in a governor; and that statedly, once in every three years, and as often as the seat of government shall become vacant, a wise and descreet freeholder of this State shall be, by ballot, elected governor, by the freeholders of this State, qualified, as before described, to elect senators; which elections shall be always held at the times and places of choosing representatives in assembly for each respective county; and that the person who hath the greatest number of votes within the said State shall be governor thereof.

XVIII. That the governor shall continue in office three years, and shall, by virtue of his office, be general and commander-in-chief of all the militia, and admiral of the navy of this State; that he shall have power to convene the assembly and senate on extraordinary occasions; to prorogue them from time to time, provided such prorogations shall not exceed sixty days in the space of any one year; and, at his discretion, to grant reprieves and pardons to persons convicted of crimes, other than treason or murder, in which he may suspend the execution of the sentence, until it shall be reported to the legislature at their subsequent meeting; and they shall either pardon or direct the execution of the criminal, or grant a further reprieve.

XIX. That it shall be the duty of the governor to inform the legislature, at every session, of the condition of the State, so far as may respect his department; to recommend such matters to their consideration as shall appear to him to concern its good government, welfare, and prosperity; to correspond with the Continental Congress, and other States; to transact all necessary business with the officers of government, civil and military; to take care that the laws are faithfully executed to the best of his ability; and to expedite all such measures as may be resolved upon by the legislature.

XX. That a lieutenant-governor shall, at every election of a governor, and as often as the lieutenant-governor shall die, resign, or be removed from office, be elected in the same manner with the governor, to continue in office until the next election of a governor; and such lieutenant-governor shall, by virtue of his office, be president of the senate, and, upon an equal division, have a casting voice in their decisions, but not vote on any other occasion. And in case of the impeachment of the governor, or his removal from office, death, resignation, or absence from the State, the lieutenant-governor shall exercise all the power and authority appertaining to the office of governor until another be chosen, or the governor absent or impeached shall return or lie acquitted: *Provided*, That where the governor shall, with the consent of the legislature, be out of the State, in time of war, at the head of a military force thereof, he shall still continue in his command of all the military force of this State both by sea and land.

XXI. That whenever the government shall be administered by the lieutenant-governor, or he shall be unable to attend as president of the senate, the senators shall have power to elect one of their own members to the office of president of the senate, which he shall exercise *pro hac vice*. And if, during such vacancy of the office of governor, the lieutenant-governor shall be impeached, displaced, resign, die, or be absent from the State, the president of the senate shall, in like manner as the lieutenant-governor, administer the government, until others shall be elected by the suffrage of the people, at the succeeding election.

XXII. And this convention doth further, in the name and by the authority of the good people of this State, ordain, determine, and declare, that the treasurer of this State shall be appointed by act of the legislature, to originate with the assembly: *Provided*, that he shall not be elected out of either branch of the legislature.

XXIII. That all officers, other than those who, by this constitution, are directed to be otherwise appointed, shall be appointed in the manner following, to wit: The assembly shall, once in every year, openly nominate and appoint one of the senators from each great district, which senators shall form a council for the appointment of the said officers, of which the governor for the time being, or the lieutenant-governor, or the president of the senate, when they shall respectively administer the government, shall be president and have a casting voice, but no other vote; and with the advice and consent of the said council, shall appoint all the said officers; and that a majority of the said council be a quorum. And further, the said senators shall not be eligible to the said council for two years successively.

XXIV. That all military officers be appointed during pleasure; that all commissioned officers, civil and military, be commissioned by the governor; and that the chancellor, the judges of the supreme court, and first judge of the county court in every county, hold their offices during good behavior or until they shall have respectively attained the age of sixty years.

XXV. That the chancellor and judges of the supreme court shall not, at the same time, hold any other office, excepting that of Delegate to the general Congress, upon special occasions; and that the first Judges of the county courts, in the several counties, shall not, at the same time, hold any other office, excepting that of Senator or Delegate to the general Congress. But if the chancellor, or either of the said judges, be elected or appointed to any other office, excepting as is before excepted, it shall be at his option in which to serve.

XXVI. That sheriffs and coroners be annually appointed; and that no person shall be capable of holding either of the said offices more than four years successively; nor the sheriff of holding any other office at the same time.

XXVII. *And be it further ordained*, That the register and clerks in chancery be appointed by the chancellor; the clerks of the supreme court, by the judges of the said court; the clerk of the court of probate, by the judge of the said court; and the register and marshal of the court of admiralty, by the judge of the admiralty. The said marshal, registers, and clerks to continue in office during the pleasure of those by whom they are appointed as aforesaid.

And that all attorneys, solicitors, and counsellors at law hereafter to be appointed, be appointed by the court, and licensed by the first judge of the court in which they shall respectively plead or practise, and be regulated by the rules and orders of the said courts.

XXVIII. *And be it further ordained*, That where, by this convention, the duration of any office shall not be ascertained, such office shall be construed to be held during the pleasure of the council of appointment: *Provided*, That new commissions shall be issued to judges of the county courts (other than to the first judge) and to justices of the peace, once at the least in every three years.

XXIX. That town clerks, supervisors, assessors, constables, and collectors, and all other officers, heretofore eligible by the people, shall always continue to be so eligible, in the manner directed by the present or future acts of legislature.

That loan officers, county treasurers, and clerks of the supervisors, continue to be appointed in the manner directed by the present or future acts of the legislature.

XXX. That Delegates to represent this State in the general Congress of the United States of America be annually appointed as follows, to wit: The senate and assembly shall each openly nominate as many persons as shall be equal to the whole number of Delegates to be appointed; after which nomination they shall meet together, and those persons named in both lists shall be Delegates; and out of those persons whose names are not on both lists, one-half shall be chosen by the joint ballot of the senators and members of assembly so met together as aforesaid.

XXXI. That the style of all laws shall be as follows, to wit: "*Be it enacted by the people of the State of New York, represented in senate and assembly;*" and that all writs and other proceedings shall run in the name of "The people of the State of New York," and be tested in the name of the chancellor, or chief judge of the court from whence they shall issue.

XXXII. And this convention doth further, in the name and by the authority of the good people of this State, ordain, determine, and declare, that a court shall be instituted for the trial of impeachments, and the correction of errors, under the regulations which shall be established by the legislature; and to consist of the president of the senate, for the time being, and the senators, chancellor, and judges of the supreme court, or the major part of them; except that when an impeachment shall be prosecuted against the chancellor, or either of the judges of the supreme court, the person so impeached shall be suspended from exercising his office until his acquittal; and, in like manner, when an appeal from a decree in equity shall be heard, the chancellor shall inform the court of the reasons of his decree, but shall not have a voice in the final sentence. And if the cause to be determined shall be brought up by writ of error, on a question of law, on a judgment in the supreme court, the judges of that court shall assign the reasons of such their judgment, but shall not have a voice for its affirmance or reversal.

XXXIII. That the power of impeaching all officers of the State, formal and corrupt conduct in their respective offices, be vested in the representatives of the people in assembly; but that it shall always be necessary that two third parts of the members present shall consent to and agree in such impeachment. That previous to the trial of every impeachment, the members of the said court shall respectively be sworn truly and impartially to try and determine the charge in question, according to evidence; and that no judgment of the said court shall be valid unless it be assented to by two third parts of the members then present; nor shall it extend farther than to removal from office, and disqualification to hold or enjoy any place of honor, trust, or profit under this State. But the party so convicted shall be, nevertheless, liable and subject to indictment, trial, judgment, and punishment, according to the laws of the land.

XXXIV. *And it is further ordained*, That in every trial on impeachment, or indictment for crimes or misdemeanors, the party impeached or indicted shall be allowed counsel, as in civil actions.

XXXV. And this convention doth further, in the name and by the authority of the good people of this State, ordain, determine, and declare that such parts of the common law of England, and of the statute law of England and Great Britain, and of the acts of the legislature of the colony of New York, as together did form the law of the said colony on the 19th day of April, in the year of our Lord one thousand seven hundred and seventy-five, shall be and continue the law of this State, subject to such alterations and provisions as the legislature of this State shall, from time to time, make concerning the same. That such of the said acts, as are temporary, shall expire at the times limited for their duration, respectively. That all such parts of the said common law, and all such of the said statutes and acts aforesaid, or parts thereof, as may be construed to establish or maintain any particular denomination of Christians or their ministers, or concern the allegiance heretofore yielded to, and the supremacy, sovereignty, government, or prerogatives claimed or exercised by, the King of Great Britain and his predecessors, over the colony of New York and its inhabitants, or are repugnant to this constitution, be, and they hereby are, abrogated and rejected. And this convention doth further ordain, that the resolves or resolutions of the congresses of the colony of New York, and of the convention of the State of New York, now in force, and not repugnant to the government established by this constitution, shall be considered as making part of the laws of this State; subject, nevertheless, to such alterations and provisions as the legislature of this State may, from time to time, make concerning the same.

XXXVI. *And be it further ordained*, That all grants of lands within this State, made by the King of Great Britain, or persons acting under his authority, after the fourteenth day of October, one thousand seven hundred and seventy-five, shall be null and void; but that nothing in this constitution contained shall be construed to affect any grants of land within this State, made by the authority of the said King or his predecessors, or to annul any charters to bodies-politic by him or them, or any of them, made prior to that day. And that none of the said charters shall be adjudged to be void by reason of any non-user or misuser of any of their respective rights or privileges between the nineteenth day of April, in the year of our Lord one thousand seven hundred and seventy-five and the publication of this constitution. And further, that all such of the officers described in the said charters respectively as, by the terms of the said charters, were to be appointed by the governor of the colony of New York, with or without the advice and consent of the council of the said King, in the said colony, shall henceforth be appointed by the council established by this constitution for the appointment of officers in this State, until otherwise directed by the legislature.

XXXVII. And whereas it is of great importance to the safety of this State that peace and amity with the Indians within the same be at all times supported and maintained; and whereas the frauds too often practiced towards the said Indians, in contracts made for their lands, have, in divers instances, been productive of dangerous discontents and animosities: Be it ordained, that no purchases or contracts for the sale of lands, made since the fourteenth day of October, in the year of our Lord one thousand seven hundred and seventy-five, or which may hereafter be made with or of the said Indians, within the limits of this State, shall be binding on the said Indians, or deemed valid, unless made under the authority and with the consent of the legislature of this State.

XXXVIII. And whereas we are required, by the benevolent principles of rational liberty, not only to expel civil tyranny, but also to guard against that spiritual oppression and intolerance wherewith the bigotry and ambition of weak and wicked priests and princes have scourged mankind, this convention doth further, in the name and by the authority of the good people of this State, ordain, determine, and declare, that the free exercise and enjoyment of religious profession and worship, without discrimination or preference, shall forever hereafter be allowed, within this State, to all mankind: *Provided*, That the liberty of conscience, hereby granted, shall not be so construed as to excuse acts of licentiousness, or justify practices inconsistent with the peace or safety of this State.

XXXIX. And whereas the ministers of the gospel are, by their profession, dedicated to the service of God and the care of souls, and ought not to be diverted from the great duties of their function; therefore, no minister of the gospel, or priest of any denomination whatsoever, shall, at any time hereafter, under any presence or description whatever, be eligible to, or capable of holding, any civil or military office or place within this State.

XL. And whereas it is of the utmost importance to the safety of every State that it should always be in a condition of defence; and it is the duty of every man who enjoys the protection of society to be prepared and willing to defend it; this convention therefore, in the name and by the authority of the good people of this State, doth ordain, determine, and declare that the militia of this State, at all times hereafter, as well in peace as in war, shall be armed and disciplined, and in readiness for service. That all such of the inhabitants of this State being of the people called Quakers as, from scruples of conscience, may be averse to the bearing of arms, be therefrom excused by the legislature; and do pay to the State such sums of money, in lieu of their personal service, as the same; may, in the judgment of the legislature, be worth. And that a proper magazine of warlike stores, proportionate to the number of inhabitants, be, forever hereafter, at the expense of this State, and by acts of the legislature, established, maintained, and continued in every county in this State.

XLI. And this convention doth further ordain, determine, and declare, in the name and by the authority of the good people of this State, that trial by jury, in all cases in which it hath heretofore been used in the colony of New York, shall be established and remain inviolate forever. And that no acts of attainder shall be passed by the legislature of this State for crimes, other than those committed before the termination of the present war; and that such acts shall not work a corruption of blood. And further, that the legislature of this State shall, at no time hereafter, institute any new court or courts, but such as shall proceed according to the course of the common law.

XLII. And this convention doth further, in the name and by the authority of the good people of this State, ordain, determine, and declare that it shall be in the discretion of the legislature to naturalize all such persons, and in such manner, as they shall think proper: *Provided*, All such of the persons so to be by them naturalized, as being born in parts beyond sea, and out of the United States of America, shall come to settle in and become subjects of this State, shall take an oath of allegiance to this State, and abjure and renounce all allegiance and subjection to all and every foreign king, prince, potentate, and State in all matters, ecclesiastical as well as civil.

SOURCE: These excerpts are reprinted from Franci Newton Thorpe (ed.), *The Federal and State Constitutions, Colonial Charters, and other Organic Laws of the States and Territories now or heretofore forming the United States of America*, 7 vols. (Washington: Government Printing Office, 1909), 7: 2623-2638.

10. SOUTH CAROLINA CONSTITUTION
MARCH 19, 1778

The Palmetto state constitution of 1778 was actually South Carolina's second of the revolutionary era. The first constitution—considered at the time to be a temporary expedient—was drafted in March 1776 by the colonies revolutionary Provincial Council. The 1776 frame of government included a bicameral legislature with a General Assembly lower house which elected from its own members the upper house Legislative Council. The two chambers jointly elected the president. In 1778, the state set out to write a permanent constitution to replace the temporary effort of 1776. The new constitution renamed the two houses in its bicameral legislature as the House of Representatives and Senate, which retained their original authority to jointly elect the newly named Governor. The 1778 constitution was not ratified by the people, and it was replaced in 1790 with a new constitution.

Whereas the constitution or form of government agreed to and resolved upon by the freemen of this country, met in congress, the twenty-sixth day of March, one thousand seven hundred and: seventy-six, was temporary only, and suited to the situation of their public affairs at that period, looking forward to an accommodation with Great Britain, an event then desired; and whereas the United Colonies of America have been since constituted independent States, and the political connection heretofore subsisting between them and Great Britain entirely dissolved by the declaration of the honorable the Continental Congress, dated the fourth day of July, one thousand seven hundred and seventy-six, for the many great and weighty reasons therein particularly set forth: It therefore becomes absolutely necessary to frame a constitution suitable to that great event.

Be it therefore constituted and enacted, by his excellency Rawlins Lowndes, esq., president and commander-in-chief in and over the State of South Carolina, by the honorable the legislative council and general assembly, and by the authority of the same:

That the following articles, agreed upon by the freemen of this State, now met in general assembly, be deemed and held the constitution and form of government of the said State, unless altered by the legislative authority thereof, which constitution or form of government shall immediately take place and be in force from the passing of this act, excepting such parts as are hereafter mentioned and specified.

I.   That the style of this country be hereafter the State of South Carolina.

II. That the legislative authority be vested in a general assembly, to consist of two distinct bodies, a senate and house of representatives, but that the
legislature of this State, as established by the constitution or form of government passed the twenty-sixth of March, one thousand and seven hundred
and seventy-six, shall continue and be in full force until the twenty-ninth day
of November ensuing.

III. That as soon as may be after the first meeting of the senate and house
of representatives, and at every first meeting of the senate and house of representatives thereafter, to be elected by virtue of this constitution, they shall
jointly in the house of representatives choose by ballot from among themselves or from the people at large a governor and commander-in-chief, a lieutenant-governor, both to continue for two years, and a privy council, all of
the Protestant religion, and till such choice shall be made the former president or governor and commander-in-chief, and vice-president or lieutenant-
governor, as the case may be, and privy council, shall continue to act as such.

IV. That a member of the senate or house of representatives, being chosen and acting as governor and commander-in-chief or lieutenant-governor,
shall vacate his seat, and another person shall be elected n his room.

V. That every person who shall be elected governor and commander-in-
chief of the State, or lieutenant-governor, or a member of the privy council,
shall be qualified as forthwith; that is to say, the governor and lieutenant-
governor shall have been residents id tills State for ten years, and the members of the privy council five years, preceding their said election, and shall
have in this State a settled plantation or freehold in their and each of their
own right of the value of at least ten thousand pounds currency, clear of debt,
and on being elected they shall respectively take an oath of qualification in
the house of representatives.

VI. That no future governor and commander-in-chief who shall serve
for two years shall be eligible to serve in the said office after the expiration of
the said term until the full end and term of four Years.

VII. That no person in this State shall hold the office of governor thereof,
or lieutenant-governor, and any other office or commission, civil or military,
(except in the militia,) either in this or any other State, or under the authority
of the Continental Congress, at one and the same time.

VIII. That in case of the impeachment of the governor and commander-
in-chief, or his removal from office, death, resignation, or absence from the
State, the lieutenant-governor shall succeed to his office, and the privy council shall choose out of their own body a lieutenant-governor of the State. And
in case of the impeachment of the lieutenant-governor, or his removal from
office death, resignation, or absence from the State, one of the privy council
to be chosen by themselves, shall succeed to his office until a nomination to
those offices respectively, by the senate and house of representatives, for the

remainder of the time for which the officer so impeached, removed from office, dying, resigning, or being absent was appointed.

IX. That the privy council shall consist of the lieutenant-governor for the time being, and eight other members, five of whom shall be a quorum to be chosen as before directed; four to serve for two years, and four for one year, and at the expiration of one year four others shall be chosen in the room of the last four, to serve for two years, and all future members of the privy council shall thenceforward be elected to serve two years, whereby there will be a new election every Year for half the privy council, and a constant rotation established; but no member of the privy council who shall serve for two years shall be eligible to serve therein after the expiration of the said term until the full end and term of four years: Provided always, That no officer of the army or navy in the service of the continent or this State, nor judge of any of the courts of law, shall be eligible, nor shall the father, son, or brother to the governor for the time being be elected in the privy council during his administration. A member of the senate and house of representatives being chosen of the privy council, shall not thereby lose his seat in the senate or house of representatives, unless he be elected lieutenant-governor, in which case he shall, and another person shall be chosen in his stead. The privy council is to advise the governor and commander-in-chief when required, but he shall not be bound to consult them unless directed by law. If a member of the privy council shall die or depart this State during the recess of the general assembly, the privy council shall choose another to act in his room, until a nomination by the senate and house of representatives shall take place. The clerk of the privy council shall keep a regular journal of all their proceedings, in which shall be entered the yeas and nays on every question, and the opinion, with the reasons at large, of anv member who desires it; which journal shall be laid before the legislature when required by either house.

X. That in case of the absence from the seat of government or sickness of the governor and lieutenant-governor, any one of the privy council may be empowered by the governor, under his hand and seal, to act in his room, but such appointment shall not vacate his seat in the senate, house of representatives, or privy council.

XI. That the executive authority be vested in the governor and commander-in-chief, in manner herein mentioned

XII. That each parish and district throughout this State shall on the last Monday in November next and the day followings and on the same days of every succeeding year thereafter, elect by ballot one member of the senate, except the district of Saint Philip and Saint Michael's parishes, Charleston, which shall elect two members; and except also the district between Broad and Saluda Rivers, in three divisions, viz: the Lower district, the Little River district, and the Upper or Spartan district, each of which said divisions shall elect one member; and except the parishes of Saint Matthew and Orange, which shall elect one member; and also except the parishes of Prince George and All Saints, which shall elect one member; and the election of senators for such parishes, respectively, shall, until otherwise altered by the legislature, be at the parish of Prince George for the said parish and the parish of All Saints, and at the parish of Saint Matthew for that parish and the parish of Orange; to meet on the first Monday in January then next, at the seat of government, unless the casualties of war or contagious disorders should render it unsafe to meet there, in which case the governor and commander-in-chief for the time being may, by proclamation, with the advice and consent of the privy council, appoint a more secure and convenient place of meeting; and to continue for two years from the said last Monday in November; and that no person shall be eligible to a seat in the said senate unless he be of the Protestant religion, and hath attained the age of thirty years, and hath been a resident in this State at least five years. Not less than thirteen members shall be a quorum to do business but the president or any three members may adjourn from day to day. No person who resides in the parish or district for which he is elected shall take his seat in the senate, unless he possess a settled estate and freehold in his own right in the said parish or district of the value of two thousand pounds currency at least, clear of debt; and no non-resident shall be eligible to a seat in the said senate unless he is owner of a settled estate and freehold in his own right, in the parish or district where he is elected, of the value of seven thousand pounds currency at least, also clear of debt.

XIII. That on the last Monday in November next and the day following, and on the same days of every second year thereafter, members of the house of representatives shall be chosen, to meet on the first Monday in January then next, at the seat of Government, unless the casualties of war or contagious disorders should render it unsafe to meet there, in which case the governor and commander-in-chief for the time being may, by proclamation, with the advice and consent of the privy council, appoint a more secure-and convenient place of meeting, and to continue for two years from the said last Monday in November. Each parish and district within this State shall send members to the general assembly in the following proportions; that is to say, the parish of Saint Philip and Saint Michael's, Charleston, thirty members; the parish of Christ Church, six members; the parish of Saint John's, in Berkely County, six members; the parish of Saint Andrew, six members; the parish of Saint George, Dorchester, six members; the parish of Saint James, Goose Creek, six members; the parish of Saint Thomas and Saint Dennis, six members; the parish of Saint Paul, six members; the parish of Saint Bartholomew, six members; the parish of Saint Helena, six members; the parish of Saint James, Santee, six members; the parish of Prince George, Winyaw, four members; the parish of All Saints, two members; the parish of Prince Frederick, six members; the parish of Saint John, in Colleton County, six members; the parish of Saint Peter, six members; the parish of Prince William, six members; the parish of Saint Stephen, six members; the district to the eastward of Wateree River, ten members; the district of Ninety-six, ten members;

the district of Saxe Gotha, six members; the district between Broad and Saluda Rivers, in three divisions, viz: the lower district, four members; the Little
River district, four members; the Upper or Spartan district, four members;
the district between Broad and Catawba Rivers, ten members; the district
called the New Acquisition, ten members; the parish of Saint Matthew, three
members; the parish of Orange, three members; the parish of Saint David,
six members; the district between the Savannah River and the North Fork of
Edisto, six members. And the election of the said members shall be conducted as near as may be agreeable to the directions of the present or any
future election act or acts, and where there are no churches or church-wardens in a district or parish, the house of representatives, at some convenient
time before their expiration, shall appoint places of election and persons to
receive votes and make returns. The qualification of electors shall be that
every free white man, and no other person, who acknowledges the being of
a God, and believes in a future state of rewards and punishments, and who
has attained to the age of one and twenty years, and hath been a resident and
an inhabitant in this State for the space of one whole year before the day appointed for the election he offers to give his vote at, and hath a freehold at
least of fifty acres of land, or a town lot, and hath been legally seized and
possessed of the same at least six months previous to such election, or hath
paid a tax the preceding year, or was taxable the present year, at least six
months previous to the said election, in a sum equal to the tax on fifty acres
of land, to the support of this government, shall be deemed a person qualified
to vote for, and shall be capable of electing, a representative or representatives
to serve as a member or members in the senate and house of representatives,
for the parish or district where he actually is a resident, or in any other parish
or district in this State where he hath the like freehold. Electors shall take an
oath or affirmation of qualification, if required by the returning officer. No
person shall be eligible to sit in the house of representatives unless he be of
the Protestant religion, and hath been a resident in this State for three years
previous to his election. The qualification of the elected, if residents in the
parish or district for which they shall be returned, shall be the same as mentioned in the election act, and construed to mean clear of debt. But no non-
resident shall be eligible to a seat in the house of representatives unless he is
owner of a settled estate and freehold in his own right of the value of three
thousand and five hundred pounds currency at least, clear of debt, in the
parish or district for which he is elected.

XIV. That if any parish or district neglects or refuses to elect members,
or if the members chosen do not meet in general assembly, those who do
meet shall have the powers of the general assembly. Not less than sixty-nine
members shall make a house of representatives to do business, but the
speaker or any seven members may adjourn from day to day.

XV. That at the expiration of seven Years after the passing of this constitution, and at the end of every fourteen years thereafter, the representation

of the whole State shall be proportioned in the most equal and just manner according to the particular and comparative strength and taxable property of the different parts of the same regard being always had to the number of white inhabitants and such taxable property.

XVI. That all money bills for the support of government shall originate in the house of representatives, and shall not be altered or amended by the senate, but may be rejected by them, and that no money be drawn out of the public treasury but by the legislative authority of the State. All other bills and ordinances may take rise in the senate or house of representatives, and be altered, amended, or rejected by either. Acts and ordinances having passed the general assembly shall have the great seal affixed to them by a joint committee of both houses, who shall wait upon the governor to receive and return the seal, and shall then be signed by the president of the senate and speaker of the house of representatives, in the senate-house, and shall thenceforth have all the force and validity of a law, and be lodged in the secretary's office. And the senate and house of representatives, respectively, shall enjoy all other privileges Which have at any time been claimed or exercised by the commons house of assembly.

XVII. That neither the senate nor house of representatives shall have power to adjourn themselves for any longer time than three days, without the mutual consent of both. The governor and commander-in-chief shall have no power to adjourn, prorogue, or dissolve them, but may, if necessary, by and with the advice and consent of the privy council, convene them before the time to which they shall stand adjourned. And where a bill hath been rejected by either house, it shall not be brought in again that session, without leave of the house, and a notice of six days being previously given.

XVIII. That the senate and house of representatives shall each choose their respective officers by ballot, without control, and that during a recess the president of the senate and speaker of the house of representatives shall issue writs for filling up vacancies occasioned by death in their respective houses, giving at least three weeks and not more than thirty-five days' previous notice of the time appointed for the election.

XIX. That if any parish or district shall neglect to elect a member or members on the day of election, or in case any person chosen a member of either house shall refuse to qualify and take his seat as such, or die, or depart the State, the senate or house of representatives, as the case may be, shall appoint proper days for electing a member or members in such cases respectively.

XX. That if any member of the senate or house of representatives shall accept any place of emolument, or any commission, (except in the militia or commission of the peace, and except as is excepted in the tenth article,) he shall vacate his seat, and there shall thereupon be a new election; but he shall not be disqualified from serving upon being reelected, unless he is appointed secretary of the State, a commissioner of the treasury, an officer of the customs, register of mesne conveyances, a clerk of either of the courts of justice, sheriff, powder reviewer, clerk of the senate, house of representatives, or privy council, surveyor-general, or commissary of military stores, which officers are hereby declared disqualified from being members either of the senate or house of representatives.

XXI. And whereas the ministers of the gospel are by their profession dedicated to the service of God and the cure of souls, and ought not to be diverted from the great duties of their function, therefore no minister of the gospel or public preacher of any religious persuasion, while he continues in the exercise of his pastoral function, and for two years after, shall be eligible either as governor, lieutenant-governor, a member of the senate, house of representatives, or privy council in this State.

XXII. That the delegates to represent this State in the Congress of the United States be chosen annually by the senate and house of representatives jointly, by ballot, in the house of representatives, and nothing contained in this constitution shall be construed to extend to vacate the seat of any member who is or may be a delegate from this State to Congress as such.

XXIII. That the form of impeaching all officers of the State for mal and corrupt conduct in their respective offices, not amenable to any other jurisdiction, be vested in the house of representatives. But that it shah always be necessary that two-third parts of the members present do consent to and agree in such impeachment. That the senators and such of the judges of this State as are not members of the house of representatives, be a court for the trial of impeachments, under such regulations as the legislature shall establish, and that previous to the trial of every impeachment, the members of the said court shall respectively be sworn truly and impartially to try and determine the charge in question according to evidence, and no judgment of the said court, except judgment of acquittal, shall be valid, unless it shall be assented to by two-third parts of the members then present, and on every trial, as well on impeachments as others, the party accused shall be allowed counsel.

XXIV. That the lieutenant-governor of the State and a majority of the privy council for the time being shall, until otherwise altered by the legislature, exercise the powers of a court of chancery, and there shall be ordinaries appointed in the several districts of this State, to be chosen by the senate and house of representatives jointly by ballot, in the house of representatives, who shall, within their respective districts, exercise the powers heretofore exercised by the ordinary, and until such appointment is made the present ordinary in Charleston shall continue to exercise that office as heretofore.

XXV. That the jurisdiction of the court of admiralty be confined to maritime causes.

XXVI. That justices of the peace shall be nominated by the senate and house of representatives jointly, and commissioned by the governor and commander-in-chief during pleasure. They shall be entitled to receive the fees heretofore established by law; and not acting in the magistracy, they shall not be entitled to the privileges allowed them by law.

XXVII. That all other judicial officers shall be chosen by ballot jointly by the senate and house of representatives, and, except the judges of the court of chancery, commissioned by the governor and commander-in-chief during good behavior, but shall be removed on address of the senate and house of representatives.

XXVIII. That the sheriffs, qualified as by law directed, shall be chosen in like manner by the senate and house of representatives, when the governor, lieutenant-governor, and privy council are chosen, and commissioned by the governor and commander-in-chief, for two years, and shall give security as required by law, before they enter on the execution of their office. No sheriff who shall have served for two years shall be eligible to serve in the said office after the expiration of the said term, until the full end and term of four years, but shall continue in office until such choice be made; nor shall any person be eligible as sheriff in any district unless he shall have resided therein for two years previous to the election.

XXIX. That two commissioners of the treasury, the secretary of the State, the register of mesne conveyances in each district, attorney-general, surveyor-general, powder-receiver, collectors and comptrollers of the customs and waiters, be chosen in like manner by the senate and house of representatives jointly, by ballot, in the house of representatives, and commissioned by the governor and commander-in-chief, for two years; that none of the said officers, respectively, who shall have served for four years, shall be eligible to serve in the said offices after the expiration of the said term, until the full end and term of four years, but shall continue in office until a new choice be made: Provided, That nothing herein contained shall extend to the several persons appointed to the above offices respectively, under the late constitution; and that the present and all future commissioners of the treasury, and powder-receivers, shall each give bond with approved security agreeable to law.

XXX. That all the officers in the army and navy of this State, of and above the rank of captain, shall be chosen by the senate and house of representatives jointly, by ballot in the house of representatives, and commissioned by the governor and commander-in-chief, and that all other officers in the army and navy of this State shall be commissioned by the governor and commander-in-chief.

XXXI. That in case of vacancy in any of the offices above directed to be filled by the senate and house of representatives, the governor and commander-in-chief, with the advice and consent of the privy council, may appoint others in their stead, until there shall be an election by the senate and house of representatives to fill those vacancies respectively

XXXII. That the governor and commander-in-chief, with the advice and consent of the privy council, may appoint during pleasure, until otherwise directed by law, all other necessary officers, except such as are now by law directed to be otherwise chosen.

XXXIII. That the governor and commander-in-chief shall have no power to commence war, or conclude peace, or enter into any final treaty without the consent of the senate and house of representatives.

XXXIV. That the resolutions of the late congress of this State, and all laws now of force here, (and not hereby altered,) shall so continue until altered or repealed by the legislature of this State, unless where they are temporary, in which case they shall expire at the times respectively limited for their duration.

XXXV. That the governor and commander-in-chief for the time being, by and with the advice and consent of the privy council, may lay embargoes or prohibit the exportation of any commodity, for any time not exceeding thirty days, in the recess of the general assembly.

XXXVI. That all persons who shall be chosen and appointed to any office or to any place of trust, civil or military, before entering upon the execution of office, shall take the following oath: " I, A. B., do acknowledge the State of South Carolina to be as free, sovereign, and independent State, and that the people thereof owe no allegiance or obedience to George the Third, King of Great Britain, and I do renounce, refuse, and abjure any allegiance or obedience to him. And I do swear [or affirm, as the case may be] that I will, to the utmost of my power, support, maintain, and defend the said State against the said King George the Third, and his heirs and successors, and his or their abettors, assistants, and adherents, and will serve the said State, in the office of , with fidelity and honor, and according to the best of my skill and understanding: So help me God." —

XXXVII. That adequate yearly salaries be allowed to the public officers of this State, and be fixed by law.

XXXVIII. That all persons and religious societies who acknowledge that there is one God, and a future state of rewards and punishments, and that God is publicly to be worshipped, shall be freely tolerated. The Christian Protestant religion shall be deemed, and is hereby constituted and declared to be, the established religion of this State. That all denominations of Christian Protestants in this State, demeaning themselves peaceably and faithfully, shall enjoy equal religious and civil privileges. To accomplish this desirable purpose without injury to the religious property of those societies of Christians which are by law already incorporated for the purpose of religious worship, and to put it fully into the power of every other society of Christian Protestants, either already formed or hereafter to be formed, to obtain the like incorporation, it is hereby constituted, appointed, and declared that the respective societies of the Church of England that are already formed in this State for the purpose of religious worship shall still continue incorporate and hold the religious property now in their possession. And that whenever fifteen or more male persons, not under twenty-one years of age, professing the

Christian Protestant religion, and agreeing to unite themselves In a society for the purposes of religious worship, they shall, (on complying with the terms hereinafter mentioned,) be, and be constituted a church, and be esteemed and regarded in law as of the established religion of the State, and on a petition to the legislature shall be entitled to be incorporated and to enjoy equal privileges. That every society of Christians so formed shall give themselves a name or denomination by which they shall be called and known in law, and all that associate with them for the purposes of worship shall be esteemed as belonging to the society so called. But that previous to the establishment and incorporation of the respective societies of every denomination as aforesaid, and in order to entitle them thereto, each society so petitioning shall have agreed to and subscribed in a book the following five articles, without which no agreement fir union of men upon presence of religion shall entitle them to be incorporated and esteemed as a church of the established religion of this State:

1st. That there is one eternal God, and a future state of rewards and punishments.

2d. That God is publicly to be worshipped.

3d. That the Christian religion is the true religion

4th. That the holy scriptures of the Old and New Testaments are of divine inspiration, and are the rule of faith and practice.

5th. That it is lawful and the duty of every man being thereunto called by those that govern, to bear witness to the truth.

And that every inhabitant of this State, when called to make an appeal to God as a witness to truth, shall be permitted to do it in that way which is most agreeable to the dictates of his own conscience. And that the people of this State may forever enjoy the right of electing their own pastors or clergy, and at the same time that the State may have sufficient security for the due discharge of the pastoral office, by those who shall be admitted to be clergymen, no person shall officiate as minister of any established church who shall not have been chosen by a majority of the society to which he shall minister, or by persons appointed by the said majority, to choose and procure a minister for them; nor until the minister so chosen and appointed shall have made and subscribed to the following declaration, over and above the aforesaid five articles, viz: "That he is determined by God's grace out of the holy scriptures, to instruct the people committed to his charge, and to teach nothing as required of necessity to eternal salvation but that which he shall be persuaded may be concluded and proved from the scripture; that he will use both public and private admonitions, as well to the sick as to the whole within his cure, as need shall require and occasion shall be given, and that he will be diligent in prayers, and in reading of the same; that he will be diligent to frame and fashion his own self and his family according to the doctrine of Christ, and to make both himself and them, as much as in him lieth, wholesome examples and patterns to the flock of Christ; that he will maintain and set forwards, as much as he can, quietness, peace, and love among all people, and especially among those that are or shall be committed to lids charge. No person shall disturb or molest any religious assembly; nor shall use any reproachful, reviling, or abusive language against any church, that being the certain way of disturbing the peace, and of hindering the conversion of any to the truth, by engaging them in quarrels and animosities, to the hatred of the professors, and that profession which otherwise they might be brought to assent to. To person whatsoever shall speak anything in their religious assembly irreverently or seditiously of the government of this State. No person shall, by law, be obliged to pay towards the maintenance and support of a religious worship that he does not freely join in, or has not voluntarily engaged to support. But the churches, chapels, parsonages, globes, and all other property now belonging to any societies of the Church of England, or any other religious societies, shall remain and be secured to them forever. The poor shall be supported, and elections managed in the accustomed manner, until laws shall be provided to adjust those matters in the most equitable way.

XXXIX. That the whole State shall, as soon as proper laws can be passed for these purposes, be divided into districts and counties, and county courts established.

XL. That the penal laws, as heretofore used, shall be reformed, and punishments made in some cases less sanguinary, and in general more proportionate to the crime.

XLI. That no freeman of this State be taken or imprisoned, or disseized of his freehold, liberties, or privileges, or outlawed, exiled or in any manner destroyed or deprived of his life, liberty, or property, but by the judgment of his peers or by the law of the land.

XLII. That the military be subordinate to the civil power of the State.

XLIII. That the liberty of the press be inviolably preserved.

XLIV. That no part of this constitution shall be altered without notice being previously given of ninety days, nor shall any part of the same be changed without the consent of a majority of the members of the senate and house of representatives.

XLV. That the senate and house of representatives shall not proceed to the election of a governor or lieutenant-governor, until there be a majority of both houses present.

SOURCE: These excerpts are reprinted from Franci Newton Thorpe (ed.), *The Federal and State Constitutions, Colonial Charters, and other Organic Laws of the States and Territories now or heretofore forming the United States of America*, 7 vols. (Washington: Government Printing Office, 1909), 7: 3248-3257.

11. MASSACHUSETTS CONSTITUTION
MARCH 2, 1780

The Massachusetts constitution of 1780 represents the apogee of revolutionary state constitution-making. After the proposed Massachusetts constitution of 1778 (drafted by the General Court) was rejected by the people, political leaders in the state regrouped and attempted to write a new constitution in 1779 with many lessons learned from the mistakes of previous effort. The most important reason for rejecting the 1778 constitution was that it had been drafted by a sitting legislature, which many people in the state, particularly those in the western counties, did not think had the authority to draft and enact a constitution for the state. It was left to Massachusetts to develop a two-step process by which to draft and ratify its constitution. As we saw in the Concord Resolutions of 1776, many people in Massachusetts insisted that their constitution be drafted by a special constitutional convention that would disband immediately after drafting its constitution. By 1779, state leaders developed the second step in the constitutional process, which was the addition of special ratifying conventions in the towns. On June 21, 1779, the Massachusetts House Representatives and the upper house Council announced elections for a constitutional convention that would meet in September. On September 1, the world's first ever constitutional convention met to draft a permanent and fundamental constitution for the Bay state. A drafting committee of thirty-one was appointed, which in turn selected a subcommittee of three (Samuel Adams, James Bowdoin, and John Adams). John Adams was chosen by the subcommittee to work up a first draft, which was accepted with a few revisions. Beginning on October 28, 1779, the plenary convention began examining and debating the proposed constitution, which it did for almost four months. The convention finally agreed on final draft on March 2, 1780. Eighteen hundred copies of the convention's handiwork were then sent to the towns for popular ratification. On October 25, 1780, was considered adopted by the people of Massachusetts and it went into effect.

The constitution is notable for its clear and explicit separation of powers, a bicameral legislature, and a strong executive. The government constructed by Adams was also remarkably democratic: the House of Representatives, Senate, and Governor were all to be elected annually.

The Massachusetts constitution, the last to be written among the original thirteen states, was a model for the framers of the federal Constitution of 1787, and it is the world's oldest written constitution.

A CONSTITUTION OR FRAME OF GOVERNMENT, AGREED UPON BY THE DELEGATES OF THE PEOPLE OF THE STATE OF MASSACHUSETTS BAY

PREAMBLE

The end of the institution, maintenance and administration of government, is to secure the existence of the body-politic; to protect it; and to furnish the individuals who compose it, with the power of enjoying, in safety and tranquillity, their natural rights, and the blessings of life: And whenever these great objects are not obtained, the people have a right to alter the government, and to take measures necessary for their safety, prosperity and happiness.

The body-politic is formed by a voluntary association of individuals: It is a social compact, by which the whole people covenants with each citizen, and each citizen with the whole people, that all shall be governed by certain laws for the common good. It is the duty of the people, therefore, in framing a Constitution of Government, to provide for an equitable mode of making laws, as well as for an impartial interpretation, and a faithful execution of them; that every man may, at all times, find his security in them.

We, therefore, the people of Massachusetts, acknowledging, with grateful hearts, the goodness of the Great Legislator of the Universe, in affording us, in the course of His providence, an opportunity, deliberately and peaceably, without fraud, violence or surprise, of entering into an original, explicit, and solemn compact with each other; and of forming a new Constitution of Civil Government, for ourselves and posterity; and devoutly imploring His direction in so interesting a design, DO agree upon, ordain and establish, the following *Declaration of Rights, and Frame of Government,* as the CONSTITUTION of the COMMONWEALTH of MASSACHUSETTS.

PART THE FIRST: A DECLARATION OF THE RIGHTS OF THE INHABITANTS OF THE COMMONWEALTH OF MASSACHUSETTS

Art. I.--All men are born free and equal, and have certain natural, essential, and unalienable rights; among which may be reckoned the right of enjoying and defending their lives and liberties; that of acquiring, possessing, and protecting property; in fine, that of seeking and obtaining their safety and happiness.

II.--It is the right as well as the duty of all men in society, publicly, and at stated seasons, to worship the SUPREME BEING, the great creator and preserver of the universe. And no subject shall be hurt, molested, or restrained, in his person, liberty, or estate, for worshipping GOD in the manner and season most agreeable to the dictates of his own conscience; or for his religious profession or sentiments; provided he doth not disturb the public peace, or obstruct others in their religious worship.

III.--As the happiness of a people, and the good order and preservation of civil government, essentially depend upon piety, religion and morality; and as these cannot be generally diffused through a community, but by the institution of the public worship of GOD, and of public instructions in piety, religion and morality: Therefore, to promote their happiness and to secure the good order and preservation of their government, the people of this Commonwealth have a right to invest their legislature with power to author- ize and require, and the legislature shall, from time to time, authorize and require, the several towns, parishes, precincts, and other bodies-politic, or religious societies, to make suitable provision, at their own expense, for the institution of the public worship of GOD, and for the support and mainte- nance of public protestant teachers of piety, religion and morality, in all cases where such provision shall not be made voluntarily.

And the people of this Commonwealth have also a right to, and do, in- vest their legislature with authority to enjoin upon all the subjects an attend- ance upon the instructions of the public teachers aforesaid, at stated times and seasons, if there be any on whose instructions they can conscientiously and conveniently attend.

Provided notwithstanding, that the several towns, parishes, precincts, and other bodies-politic, or religious societies, shall, at all times, have the exclusive right of electing their public teachers, and of contracting with them for their support and maintenance.

And all monies paid by the subject to the support of public worship, and of the public teachers aforesaid, shall, if he require it, be uniformly applied to the support of the public teacher or teachers of his own religious sect or denomination, provided there be any on whose instructions he attends: oth- erwise it may be paid towards the support of the teacher or teachers of the parish or precinct in which the said monies are raised.

And every denomination of Christians, demeaning themselves peacea- bly, and as good subjects of the Commonwealth, shall be equally under the protection of the law: And no subordination of any one sect or denomination to another shall ever be established by law.

IV.--The people of this Commonwealth have the sole and exclusive right of governing themselves as a free, sovereign, and independent state; and do, and forever hereafter shall, exercise and enjoy every power, jurisdiction, and right, which is not, or may not hereafter, be by them expressly delegated to the United States of America, in Congress assembled.

V.--All power residing originally in the people, and being derived from them, the several magistrates and officers of government, vested with author- ity, whether legislative, executive, or judicial, are their substitutes and agents, and are at all times accountable to them.

VI.--No man, nor corporation, or association of men, have any other title to obtain advantages, or particular and exclusive privileges, distinct from those of the community, than what arises from the consideration of services rendered to the public; and this title being in nature neither hereditary, nor transmissible to children, or descendants, or relations by blood, the idea of a man born a magistrate, lawgiver, or judge, is absurd and unnatural.

VII.--Government is instituted for the common good; for the protection, safety, prosperity and happiness of the people; and not for the profit, honor, or private interest of any one man, family, or class of men; Therefore the people alone have an incontestible, unalienable, and indefeasible right to institute government; and to reform, alter, or totally change the same, when their protection, safety, prosperity and happiness require it.

VIII.--In order to prevent those, who are vested with authority, from becoming oppressors, the people have a right, at such periods and in such manner as they shall establish by their frame of government, to cause their public officers to return to private life; and to fill up vacant places by certain and regular elections and appointments.

IX.--All elections ought to be free; and all the inhabitants of this Commonwealth, having such qualifications as they shall establish by their frame of government, have an equal right to elect officers, and to be elected, for public employments.

X.--Each individual of the society has a right to be protected by it in the enjoyment of his life, liberty and property, according to standing laws. He is obliged, consequently, to contribute his share to the expense of this protection; to give his personal service, or an equivalent, when necessary: But no part of the property of any individual, can, with justice, be taken from him, or applied to public uses without his own consent, or that of the representative body of the people: In fine, the people of this Commonwealth are not controlable by any other laws, than those to which their constitutional representative body have given their consent. And whenever the public exigencies require, that the property of any individual should be appropriated to public uses, he shall receive a reasonable compensation therefor.

XI.--Every subject of the Commonwealth ought to find a certain remedy, by having recourse to the laws, for all injuries or wrongs which he may receive in his person, property, or character. He ought to obtain right and justice freely, and without being obliged to purchase it; completely, and without any denial; promptly, and without delay; conformably to the laws.

XII.--No subject shall be held to answer for any crime or offence, until the same is fully and plainly, substantially and formally, described to him; or be compelled to accuse, or furnish evidence against himself. And every subject shall have a right to produce all proofs, that may be favorable to him; to meet the witnesses against him face to face, and to be fully heard in his defence by himself, or his council, at his election. And no subject shall be arrested, imprisoned, despoiled, or deprived of his property, immunities, or privileges, put out of the protection of the law, exiled, or deprived of his life, liberty, or estate; but by the judgment of his peers, or the law of the land.

And the legislature shall not make any law, that shall subject any person to a capital or infamous punishment, excepting for the government of the army and navy, without trial by jury.

XIII.--In criminal prosecutions, the verification of facts in the vicinity where they happen, is one of the greatest securities of the life, liberty, and property of the citizen.

XIV.--Every subject has a right to be secure from all unreasonable searches, and seizures of his person, his houses, his papers, and all his possessions. All warrants, therefore, are contrary to this right, if the cause or foundation of them be not previously supported by oath or affirmation; and if the order in the warrant to a civil officer, to make search in suspected places, or to arrest one or more suspected persons, or to seize their property, be not accompanied with a special designation of the persons or objects of search, arrest, or seizure: and no warrant ought to be issued but in cases, and with the formalities, prescribed by the laws.

XV.--In all controversies concerning property, and in all suits between two or more persons, except in cases in which it has heretofore been otherways used and practised, the parties have a right to a trial by jury; and this method of procedure shall be held sacred, unless, in causes arising on the high-seas, and such as relate to mariners wages, the legislature shall hereafter find it necessary to alter it.

XVI.--The liberty of the press is essential to the security of freedom in a state: it ought not, therefore, to be restrained in this Commonwealth.

XVII.--The people have a right to keep and to bear arms for the common defence. And as in time of peace armies are dangerous to liberty, they ought not to be maintained without the consent of the legislature; and the military power shall always be held in an exact subordination to the civil authority, and be governed by it.

XVIII.--A frequent recurrence to the fundamental principles of the constitution, and a constant adherence to those of piety, justice, moderation, temperance, industry, and frugality, are absolutely necessary to preserve the advantages of liberty, and to maintain a free government: The people ought, consequently, to have a particular attention to all those principles, in the choice of their officers and representatives: And they have a right to require of their law-givers and magistrates, an exact and constant observance of them, in the formation and execution of the laws necessary for the good administration of the Commonwealth.

XIX.--The people have a right, in an orderly and peaceable manner, to assemble to consult upon the common good; give instructions to their representatives; and to request of the legislative body, by the way of addresses, petitions, or remonstrances, redress of the wrongs done them, and of the grievances they suffer.

XX.--The power of suspending the laws, or the execution of the laws, ought never to be exercised but by the legislature, or by authority derived from it, to be exercised in such particular cases only as the legislature shall expressly provide for.

XXI.--The freedom of deliberation, speech and debate, in either house of the legislature, is so essential to the rights of the people, that it cannot be the foundation of any accusation or prosecution, action or complaint, in any other court or place whatsoever.

XXII.--The legislature ought frequently to assemble for the redress of grievances, for correcting, strengthening, and confirming the laws, and for making new laws, as the common good may require.

XXIII.--No subsidy, charge, tax, impost, or duties, ought to be established, fixed, laid, or levied, under any pretext whatsoever, without the consent of the people, or their representatives in the legislature.

XXIV.--Laws made to punish for actions done before the existence of such laws, and which have not been declared crimes by preceding laws, are unjust, oppressive, and inconsistent with the fundamental principles of a free government.

XXV.--No subject ought, in any case, or in any time, to be declared guilty of treason or felony by the legislature.

XXVI.--No magistrate or court of law shall demand excessive bail or sureties, impose excessive fines, or inflict cruel or unusual punishments.

XXVII.--In time of peace no soldier ought to be quartered in any house without the consent of the owner; and in time of war such quarters ought not to be made but by the civil magistrate, in a manner ordained by the legislature.

XXVIII.--No person can in any case be subjected to law-martial, or to any penalties or pains, by virtue of that law, except those employed in the army or navy, and except the militia in actual service, but by authority of the legislature.

XXIX.--It is essential to the preservation of the rights of every individual, his life, liberty, property and character, that there be an impartial interpretation of the laws, and administration of justice. It is the right of every citizen to be tried by judges as free, impartial and independent as the lot of humanity will admit. It is therefore not only the best policy, but for the security of the rights of the people, and of every citizen, that the judges of the supreme judicial court should hold their offices as long as they behave themselves well; and that they should have honorable salaries ascertained and established by standing laws.

XXX.--In the government of this Commonwealth, the legislative department shall never exercise the executive and judicial powers, or either of them: The executive shall never exercise the legislative and judicial powers, or either of them: The judicial shall never exercise the legislative and executive powers, or either of them: to the end it may be a government of laws and not of men.

PART THE SECOND: THE FRAME OF GOVERNMENT.

The people, inhabiting the territory formerly called the Province of Massachusetts-Bay, do hereby solemnly and mutually agree with each other, to form themselves into a free, sovereign, and independent body-politic or state, by the name of THE COMMONWEALTH OF MASSACHUSETTS.

CHAPTER I:

THE LEGISLATIVE POWER

SECTION I: THE GENERAL COURT.

Art. I.--The department of legislation shall be formed by two branches, *a Senate* and *House of Representatives:* each of which shall have a negative on the other.

The legislative body shall assemble every year, on the last Wednesday in May, and at such other times as they shall judge necessary; and shall dissolve and be dissolved on the day next preceding the said last Wednesday in May; and shall be styled, The General Court of Massachusetts.

II.--No bill or resolve of the Senate or House of Representatives shall become a law, and have force as such, until it shall have been laid before the Governor for his revisal: And if he, upon such revision, approve thereof, he shall signify his approbation by signing the same. But if he have any objection to the passing of such bill or resolve, he shall return the same, together with his objections thereto, in writing, to the Senate or House of Representatives, in which soever the same shall have originated; who shall enter the objections sent down by the Governor, at large, on their records, and proceed to reconsider the said bill or resolve: But if, after such reconsideration, two thirds of the said Senate or House of Representatives, shall, notwithstanding the said objections, agree to pass the same, it shall, together with the objections, be sent to the other branch of the legislature, where it shall also be reconsidered, and if approved by two thirds of the members present, shall have the force of a law: But in all such cases the votes of both houses shall be determined by yeas and nays; and the names of the persons voting for, or against, the said bill or resolve, shall be entered upon the public records of the Commonwealth.

And in order to prevent unnecessary delays, if any bill or resolve shall not be returned by the Governor within five days after it shall have been presented, the same shall have the force of a law.

III.--The General Court shall forever have full power and authority to erect and constitute judicatories and courts of record, or other courts, to be held in the name of the Commonwealth, for the hearing, trying, and determining of all manner of crimes, offences, pleas, processes, plaints, actions, matters, causes and things, whatsoever, arising or happening within the Commonwealth, or between or concerning persons inhabiting, or residing, or brought within the same; whether the same be criminal or civil, or whether the said crimes be capital or not capital, and whether the said pleas be real, personal, or mixt; and for the awarding and making out of execution thereupon: To which courts and judicatories are hereby given and granted full power and authority, from time to time, to administer oaths or affirmations, for the better discovery of truth in any matter in controversy or depending before them.

IV.--And further, full power and authority are hereby given and granted to the said General Court, from time to time, to make, ordain, and establish, all manner of wholesome and reasonable orders, laws, statutes, and ordinances, directions and instructions, either with penalties or without; so as the same be not repugnant or contrary to this Constitution, as they shall judge to be for the good and welfare of this Commonwealth, and for the government and ordering thereof, and of the subjects of the same, and for the necessary support and defence of the government thereof; and to name and settle annually, or provide by fixed laws, for the naming and settling all civil officers within the said Commonwealth, the election and constitution of whom are not hereafter in this Form of Government otherwise provided for; and to set forth the several duties, powers and limits; of the several civil and military officers of this Commonwealth, and the forms of such oaths or affirmations as shall be respectively administered unto them for the execution of their several offices and places, so as the same be not repugnant or contrary to this Constitution; and to impose and levy proportional and reasonable assessments, rates, and taxes, upon all the inhabitants of, and persons resident, and estates lying, within the said Commonwealth; and also to impose, and levy reasonable duties and excises, upon any produce, goods, wares, merchandize, and commodities whatsoever, brought into, produced, manufactured, or being within the same; to be issued and disposed of by warrant, under the hand of the Governor of this Commonwealth for the time being, with the advice and consent of the Council, for the public service, in the necessary defence and support of the government of the said Commonwealth, and the protection and preservation of the subjects thereof, according to such acts as are or shall be in force within the same.

And while the public charges of government, or any part thereof, shall be assessed on polls and estates, in the manner that has hitherto been practised, in order that such assessments may be made with equality, there shall be a valuation of estates within the Commonwealth taken anew once in every ten years at least, and as much oftener as the General Court shall order.

CHAPTER I

SECTION II: SENATE.

Art. I.--There shall be annually elected by the freeholders and other inhabitants of this Commonwealth, qualified as in this Constitution is provided, forty persons to be Counsellors and Senators for the year ensuing their election; to be chosen by the inhabitants of the districts, into which the Commonwealth may from time to time be divided by the General Court for that purpose: And the General Court, in assigning the numbers to be elected by the respective districts, shall govern themselves by the proportion of the public taxes paid by the said districts; and timely make known to the inhabitants of the Commonwealth, the limits of each district, and the number of Counsellors and Senators to be chosen therein; provided, that the number of such districts shall never be less than thirteen; and that no district be so large as to entitle the same to choose more than six Senators.

And the several counties in this Commonwealth shall, until the General Court shall determine it necessary to alter the said districts, be districts for the choice of Counsellors and Senators, (except that the counties of Dukes County and Nantucket shall form one district for that purpose) and shall elect the following number for Counsellors and Senators, viz:

Suffolk	Six
Essex	Six
Middlesex	Five
Hampshire	Four
Plymouth	Three
Barnstable	One
Bristol	Three
York	Two
Dukes County and Nantucket }	One
Worcester	Five
Cumberland	One
Lincoln	One
Berkshire	Two.

II.--The Senate shall be the first branch of the legislature; and the Senators shall be chosen in the following manner, viz: There shall be a meeting on the first Monday in April annually, forever, of the inhabitants of each town in the several counties of this Commonwealth; to be called by the Selectmen, and warned in due course of law, at least seven days before the first Monday in April, for the purpose of electing persons to be Senators and Counsellors: And at such meetings every male inhabitant of twenty-one years of age and upwards, having a freehold estate within the Commonwealth, of the annual income of three pounds, or any estate of the value of sixty pounds, shall have a right to give in his vote for the Senators for the district of which he is an inhabitant. And to remove all doubts concerning the meaning of the word "inhabitant" in this constitution, every person shall be considered as an inhabitant, for the purpose of electing and being elected into any office, or place within this State, in that town, district, or plantation, where he dwelleth, or hath his home.

The Selectmen of the several towns shall preside at such meetings impartially; and shall receive the votes of all the inhabitants of such towns present and qualified to vote for Senators, and shall sort and count them in open town meeting, and in presence of the Town Clerk, who shall make a fair record in presence of the Selectmen, and in open town meeting, of the name of every person voted for, and of the number of votes against his name; and a fair copy of this record shall be attested by the Selectmen and the Town-Clerk, and shall be sealed up, directed to the Secretary of the Commonwealth for the time being, with a superscription, expressing the purport of the contents thereof, and delivered by the Town-Clerk of such towns, to the Sheriff of the county in which such town lies, thirty days at least before the last Wednesday in May annually; or it shall be delivered into the Secretary's office seventeen days at least before the said last Wednesday in May; and the Sheriff of each county shall deliver all such certificates by him received, into the Secretary's office seventeen days before the said last Wednesday in May.

And the inhabitants of plantations unincorporated, qualified as this Constitution provides, who are or shall be empowered and required to assess taxes upon themselves toward the support of government, shall have the same privilege of voting for Counsellors and Senators, in the plantations where they reside, as town inhabitants have in their respective towns; and the plantation-meetings for that purpose shall be held annually on the same first Monday in April, at such place in the plantations respectively, as the Assessors thereof shall direct; which Assessors shall have like authority for notifying the electors, collecting and returning the votes, as the Selectmen and Town-Clerks have in their several towns, by this Constitution. And all other persons living in places unincorporated (qualified as aforesaid) who shall be assessed to the support of government by the Assessors of an adjacent town, shall have the privilege of giving in their votes for Counsellors and Senators, in the town where they shall be assessed, and be notified of the place of meeting by the Selectmen of the town where they shall be assessed, for that purpose, accordingly.

III.--And that there may be a due convention of Senators on the last Wednesday in May annually, the Governor, with five of the Council, for the time being, shall, as soon as may be, examine the returned copies of such records; and fourteen days before the said day he shall issue his summons to such persons as shall appear to be chosen by a majority of voters, to attend on that day, and take their seats accordingly: Provided nevertheless, that for the first year the said returned copies shall be examined by the President and five of the Council of the former Constitution of Government; and the said President shall, in like manner, issue his summons to the persons so elected, that they may take their seats as aforesaid.

IV.--The Senate shall be the final judge of the elections, returns and qualifications of their own members, as pointed out in the Constitution; and shall, on the said last Wednesday in May annually, determine and declare who are elected by each district, to be Senators, by a majority of votes: And in case there shall not appear to be the full number of Senators returned elected by a majority of votes for any district, the deficiency shall be supplied in the following manner, viz. The members of the House of Representatives, and such Senators as shall be declared elected, shall take the names of such persons as shall be found to have the highest number of votes in such district, and not elected, amounting to twice the number of Senators wanting, if there be so many voted for; and, out of these, shall elect by ballot a number of Senators sufficient to fill up the vacancies in such district: And in this manner all such vacancies shall be filled up in every district of the Commonwealth; and in like manner all vacancies in the Senate, arising by death, removal out of the State, or otherwise, shall be supplied as soon as may be after such vacancies shall happen.

V.--Provided nevertheless, that no person shall be capable of being elected as a Senator, who is not seized in his own right of a freehold within this Commonwealth, of the value of three hundred pounds at least, or possessed of personal estate to the value of six hundred pounds at least, or of both to the amount of the same sum, and who has not been an inhabitant of this Commonwealth for the space of five years immediately preceding his election, and, at the time of his election, he shall be an inhabitant in the district, for which he shall be chosen.

VI.--The Senate shall have power to adjourn themselves, provided such adjournments do not exceed two days at a time.

VII.--The Senate shall choose its own President, appoint its own officers, and determine its own rules of proceeding.

VIII.--The Senate shall be a court with full authority to hear and determine all impeachments made by the House of Representatives, against any officer or officers of the Commonwealth, for misconduct and mal-administration in their offices. But, previous to the trial of every impeachment, the members of the Senate shall respectively be sworn, truly and impartially to try and determine the charge in question, according to evidence. Their judgment, however, shall not extend further than to removal from office and disqualification to hold or enjoy any place of honor, trust, or profit, under this

Commonwealth: But the party, so convicted, shall be, nevertheless, liable to indictment, trial, judgment, and punishment, according to the laws of the land.

IX.--Not less than sixteen members of the Senate shall constitute a quorum for doing business.

CHAPTER I

SECTION III: HOUSE OF REPRESENTATIVES.

Art. I.--There shall be in the Legislature of this Commonwealth, a representation of the people, annually elected, and founded upon the principle of equality.

II.--And in order to provide for a representation of the citizens of this Commonwealth, founded upon the principle of equality, every corporate town, containing one hundred and fifty rateable polls, may elect one Representative: Every corporate town, containing three hundred and seventy-five rateable polls, may elect two Representatives: Every corporate town, containing six hundred rateable polls, may elect three Representatives; and proceeding in that manner, making two hundred and twenty-five rateable polls the mean increasing number for every additional Representative.

Provided nevertheless, that each town now incorporated, not having one hundred and fifty rateable polls, may elect one Representative: but no place shall hereafter be incorporated with the privilege of electing a Representative, unless there are within the same one hundred and fifty rateable polls.

And the House of Representatives shall have power, from time to time, to impose fines upon such towns as shall neglect to choose and return members to the same, agreeably to this Constitution.

The expenses of travelling to the General Assembly, and returning home, once in every session, and no more, shall be paid by the government, out of the public treasury, to every member who shall attend as seasonably as he can, in the judgment of the House, and does not depart without leave.

III.--Every member of the House of Representatives shall be chosen by written votes; and for one year at least next preceding his election shall have been an inhabitant of, and have been seized in his own right of a freehold of the value of one hundred pounds within the town he shall be chosen to represent, or any rateable estate to the value of two hundred pounds; and he shall cease to represent the said town immediately on his ceasing to be qualified as aforesaid.

IV.--Every male person, being twenty-one years of age, and resident in any particular town in this Commonwealth for the space of one year next preceding, having a freehold estate within the same town, of the annual income of three pounds, or any estate of the value of sixty pounds, shall have a right to vote in the choice of a Representative or Representatives for the said town.

V.--The members of the House of Representatives shall be chosen annually in the month of May, ten days at least before the last Wednesday of that month.

VI.--The House of Representatives shall be the Grand Inquest of this Commonwealth; and all impeachments made by them shall be heard and tried by the Senate.

VII.--All money-bills shall originate in the House of Representatives; but the Senate may propose or concur with amendments, as on other bills.

VIII.--The House of Representatives shall have power to adjourn themselves; provided such adjournment shall not exceed two days at a time.

IX.--Not less than sixty members of the House of Representatives shall constitute a quorum for doing business.

X.--The House of Representatives shall be the judge of the returns, elections, and qualifications of its own members, as pointed out in the constitution; shall choose their own Speaker; appoint their own officers, and settle the rules and orders of proceeding in their own house: They shall have authority to punish by imprisonment, every person, not a member, who shall be guilty of disrespect to the House, by any disorderly, or contemptuous behaviour, in its presence; or who, in the town where the General Court is sitting, and during the time of its sitting, shall threaten harm to the body or estate of any of its members, for any thing said or done in the House; or who shall assault any of them therefor; or who shall assault, or arrest, any witness, or other person, ordered to attend the House, in his way in going, or returning; or who shall rescue any person arrested by the order of the House.

And no member of the House of Representatives shall be arrested, or held to bail on mean process, during his going unto, returning from, or his attending, the General Assembly.

XI.--The Senate shall have the same powers in the like cases; and the Governor and Council shall have the same authority to punish in like cases. Provided, that no imprisonment on the warrant or order of the Governor, Council, Senate, or House of Representatives, for either of the above described offences, be for a term exceeding thirty days.

And the Senate and House of Representatives may try, and determine, all cases where their rights and privileges are concerned, and which, by the Constitution, they have authority to try and determine, by committees of their own members, or in such other way as they may respectively think best.

CHAPTER II:

EXECUTIVE POWER

SECTION I: GOVERNOR

Art. I.--There shall be a Supreme Executive Magistrate, who shall be styled, THE GOVERNOR OF THE COMMONWEALTH OF MASSACHU-SETTS; and whose title shall be--HIS EXCELLENCY.

II.--The Governor shall be chosen annually: And no person shall be eligible to this office, unless at the time of his election, he shall have been an inhabitant of this Commonwealth for seven years next preceding; and unless he shall, at the same time, be seized in his own right, of a freehold within the Commonwealth, of the value of one thousand pounds; and unless he shall declare himself to be of the Christian religion.

III.--Those persons who shall be qualified to vote for Senators and Representatives within the several towns of this Commonwealth, shall, at a meeting, to be called for that purpose, on the first Monday of April annually, give in their votes for a Governor, to the Selectmen, who shall preside at such meetings; and the Town Clerk, in the presence and with the assistance of the Selectmen, shall, in open town meeting, sort and count the votes, and form a list of the persons voted for, with the number of votes for each person against his name; and shall make a fair record of the same in the town books, and a public declaration thereof in the said meeting; and shall, in the presence of the inhabitants, seal up copies of the said list, attested by him and the Selectmen, and transmit the same to the Sheriff of the county, thirty days at least before the last Wednesday in May; and the Sheriff shall transmit the same to the Secretary's office seventeen days at least before the said last Wednesday in May; or the Selectmen may cause returns of the same to be made to the office of the Secretary of the Commonwealth seventeen days at least before the said day; and the Secretary shall lay the same before the Senate and the House of Representatives, on the last Wednesday in May, to be by them examined: And in case of an election by a majority of all the votes returned, the choice shall be by them declared and published: But if no person shall have a majority of votes, the House of Representatives shall, by ballot, elect two out of four persons who had the highest number of votes, if so many shall have been voted for; but, if otherwise, out of the number voted for; and make return to the Senate of the two persons so elected; on which, the Senate shall proceed, by ballot, to elect one, who shall be declared Governor.

IV.--The Governor shall have authority, from time to time, at his discretion, to assemble and call together the Counsellors of this Commonwealth for the time being; and the Governor, with the said Counsellors, or five of them at least, shall, and may, from time to time, hold and keep a Council, for the ordering and directing the affairs of the Commonwealth, agreeably to the Constitution and the laws of the land.

V.--The Governor, with advice of Council, shall have full power and authority, during the session of the General Court, to adjourn or prorogue the same to any time the two Houses shall desire; and to dissolve the same on the day next preceding the last Wednesday in May; and, in the recess of the said Court, to prorogue the same from time to time, not exceeding ninety days in any one recess; and to call it together sooner than the time to which it may be adjourned or prorogued, if the welfare of the Commonwealth shall require the same: And in case of any infectious distemper prevailing in the place where the said Court is next at any time to convene, or any other cause happening whereby danger may arise to the health or lives of the members from their attendance, he may direct the session to be held at some other the most convenient place within the State.

And the Governor shall dissolve the said General Court on the day next preceding the last Wednesday in May.

VI.--In cases of disagreement between the two Houses, with regard to the necessity, expediency or time of adjournment, or prorogation, the Governor, with advice of the Council, shall have a right to adjourn or prorogue the General Court, not exceeding ninety days, as he shall determine the public good shall require.

VII.--The Governor of this Commonwealth, for the time being, shall be the commander-in-chief of the army and navy, and of all the military forces of the State, by sea and land; and shall have full power, by himself, or by any commander, or other officer or officers, from time to time, to train, instruct, exercise and govern the militia and navy; and, for the special defence and safety of the Commonwealth, to assemble in martial array, and put in warlike posture, the inhabitants thereof, and to lead and conduct them, and with them, to encounter, repel, resist, expel and pursue, by force of arms, as well as by sea as by land, within or without the limits of this Commonwealth, and also to kill, slay and destroy, if necessary, and conquer, by all fitting ways, enterprizes and means whatsoever, all and every such person and persons as shall, at any time hereafter, in a hostile manner, attempt or enterprize the destruction, invasion, detriment, or annoyance of this Commonwealth; and to use and exercise, over the army and navy, and over the militia in actual service, the law martial, in time of war or invasion, and also in time of rebellion, declared by the legislature to exist, as occasion shall necessarily require; and to take and surprise by all ways and means whatsoever, all and every such person or persons, with their ships, arms, ammunition and other goods, as shall, in a hostile manner, invade, or attempt the invading, conquering, or annoying this Commonwealth; and that the Governor be intrusted with all these and other powers, incident to the offices of Captain-General and Commander-in-Chief, and Admiral, to be exercised agreeably to the rules and regulations of the Constitution, and the laws of the land, and not otherwise.

Provided, that the said Governor shall not, at any time hereafter, by virtue of any power by this Constitution granted, or hereafter to be granted to him by the legislature, transport any of the inhabitants of this Commonwealth, or oblige them to march out of the limits of the same, without their free and voluntary consent, or the consent of the General Court; except so far as may be necessary to march or transport them by land or water, for the defence of such part of the State, to which they cannot otherwise conveniently have access.

VIII.--The power of pardoning offences, except such as persons may be convicted of before the Senate by an impeachment of the House, shall be in the Governor, by and with the advice of Council: But no charter of pardon, granted by the Governor, with advice of the Council, before conviction, shall avail the party pleading the same, notwithstanding any general or particular expressions contained therein, descriptive of the offence, or offences intended to be pardoned.

IX.--All judicial officers, the Attorney-General, the Solicitor-General, all Sheriffs, Coroners, and Registers of Probate, shall be nominated and appointed by the Governor, by and with the advice and consent of the Council; and every such nomination shall be made by the Governor, and made at least seven days prior to such appointment.

X.--The Captains and subalterns of the militia shall be elected by the written votes of the train-band and alarm list of their respective companies, of twenty-one years of age and upwards: The field-officers of Regiments shall be elected by the written votes of the captains and subalterns of their respective regiments: The Brigadiers shall be elected in like manner, by the field officers of their respective brigades: And such officers, so elected, shall be commissioned by the Governor, who shall determine their rank.

The Legislature shall, by standing laws, direct the time and manner of convening the electors, and of collecting votes, and of certifying to the Governor the officers elected.

The Major-Generals shall be appointed by the Senate and House of Representatives, each having a negative upon the other; and be commissioned by the Governor.

And if the electors of Brigadiers, field-officers, captains or subalterns, shall neglect or refuse to make such elections, after being duly notified, according to the laws for the time being, then the Governor, with advice of Council, shall appoint suitable persons to fill such offices.

And no officer, duly commissioned to command in the militia, shall be removed from his office, but by the address of both houses to the Governor, or by fair trial in court martial, pursuant to the laws of the Commonwealth for the time being.

The commanding officers of regiments shall appoint their Adjutants and Quarter-masters; the Brigadiers their Brigade-Majors; and the Major-Generals their Aids: and the Governor shall appoint the Adjutant General.

The Governor, with advice of Council, shall appoint all officers of the continental army, whom by the confederation of the United States it is provided that this Commonwealth shall appoint,--as also all officers of forts and garrisons.

The divisions of the militia into brigades, regiments and companies, made in pursuance of the militia laws now in force, shall be considered as the proper divisions of the militia of this Commonwealth, until the same shall be altered in pursuance of some future law.

XI.--No monies shall be issued out of the treasury of this Common-wealth, and disposed of (except such sums as may be appropriated for the redemption of bills of credit or Treasurer's notes, or for the payment of inter-est arising thereon) but by warrant under the hand of the Governor for the time being, with the advice and consent of the Council, for the necessary defence and support of the Commonwealth; and for the protection and preservation of the inhabitants thereof, agreeably to the acts and resolves of the General Court.

XII.--All public boards, the Commissary-General, all superintending of-ficers of public magazines and stores, be-longing to this Commonwealth, and all commanding officers of forts and garrisons within the same, shall, once in every three months, officially and without requisition, and at other times, when required by the Governor, deliver to him an account of all goods, stores, provisions, ammunition, cannon with their appendages, and small arms with their accoutrements, and of all other public property whatever un-der their care respectively; distinguishing the quantity, number, quality and kind of each, as particularly as may be; together with the condition of such forts and garrisons: And the said commanding officer shall exhibit to the Governor, when required by him, true and exact plans of such forts, and of the land and sea, or harbour or harbours adjacent.

And the said boards, and all public officers, shall communicate to the Governor, as soon as may be after receiving the same, all letters, dispatches, and intelligences of a public nature, which shall be directed to them respec-tively.

XIII.--As the public good requires that the Governor should not be un-der the undue influence of any of the members of the General Court, by a dependence on them for his support--that he should, in all cases, act with freedom for the benefit of the public--that he should not have his attention necessarily diverted from that object to his private concerns--and that he should maintain the dignity of the Commonwealth in the character of its chief magistrate--it is necessary that he should have an honorable stated sal-ary, of a fixed and permanent value, amply sufficient for those purposes, and established by standing laws: And it shall be among the first acts of the Gen-eral Court, after the Commencement of this Constitution, to establish such salary by law accordingly.

Permanent and honorable salaries shall also be established by law for the Justices of the Supreme Judicial Court.

And if it shall be found, that any of the salaries aforesaid, so established, are insufficient, they shall, from time to time, be enlarged, as the General Court shall judge proper.

CHAPTER II

SECTION II. LIEUTENANT-GOVERNOR.

Art. I.--There shall be annually elected a Lieutenant-Governor of the Commonwealth of Massachusetts, whose title shall be HIS HONOR--and who shall be qualified, in point of religion, property, and residence in the Commonwealth, in the same manner with the Governor: And the day and manner of his election, and the qualifications of the electors, shall be the same as are required in the election of a Governor. The return of the votes for this officer, and the declaration of his election, shall be in the same manner: And if no one person shall be found to have a majority of all the votes returned, the vacancy shall be filled by the Senate and House of Representatives, in the same manner as the Governor is to be elected, in case no one person shall have a majority of the votes of the people to be Governor.

II.--The Governor, and in his absence the Lieutenant-Governor, shall be President of the Council, but shall have no vote in Council: And the Lieutenant-Governor shall always be a member of the Council, except when the chair of the Governor shall be vacant.

III.--Whenever the chair of the Governor shall be vacant, by reason of his death, or absence from the Commonwealth, or otherwise, the Lieutenant-Governor, for the time being, shall, during such vacancy, perform all the duties incumbent upon the Governor, and shall have and exercise all the powers and authorities, which by this Constitution the Governor is vested with, when personally present.

CHAPTER II

SECTION III: COUNCIL, AND THE MANNER OF SETTLING ELECTIONS BY THE LEGISLATURE.

Art. I.--There shall be a Council for advising the Governor in the executive part of government, to consist of nine persons besides the Lieutenant-Governor, whom the Governor, for the time being, shall have full power and authority, from time to time, at his discretion, to assemble and call together. And the Governor, with the said Counsellors, or five of them at least, shall and may, from time to time, hold and keep a council, for the ordering and directing the affairs of the Commonwealth, according to the laws of the land.

II.--Nine Counsellors shall be annually chosen from among the persons returned for Counsellors and Senators, on the last Wednesday in May, by the joint ballot of the Senators and Representatives assembled in one room: And in case there shall not be found, upon the first choice, the whole number of nine persons who will accept a seat in the Council, the deficiency shall be made up by the electors aforesaid from among the people at large; and the number of Senators left shall constitute the Senate for the year. The seats of the persons thus elected from the Senate, and accepting the trust, shall be vacated in the Senate.

III.--The Counsellors, in the civil arrangements of the Commonwealth, shall have rank next after the Lieutenant-Governor.

IV.--Not more than two Counsellors shall be chosen out of any one district of this Commonwealth.

V.--The resolutions and advice of the Council shall be recorded in a register, and signed by the members present; and this record may be called for at any time by either House of the Legislature; and any member of the Council may insert his opinion contrary to the resolution of the majority.

VI.--Whenever the office of the Governor and Lieutenant-Governor shall be vacant, by reason of death, absence, or otherwise, then the Council or the major part of them, shall, during such vacancy, have full power and authority, to do, and execute, all and every such acts, matters and things, as the Governor or the Lieutenant-Governor might or could, by virtue of this Constitution, do or execute, if they, or either of them, were personally present.

VII.--And whereas the elections appointed to be made by this Constitution, on the last Wednesday in May annually, by the two Houses of the Legislature, may not be completed on that day, the said elections may be adjourned from day to day until the same shall be completed. And the order of elections shall be as follows; the vacancies in the Senate, if any, shall first be filled up; the Governor and Lieutenant-Governor shall then be elected, provided there should be no choice of them by the people: And afterwards the two Houses shall proceed to the election of the Council.

CHAPTER II

SECTION IV: SECRETARY, TREASURER, COMMISSARY, ETC.

Art. I.--The Secretary, Treasurer and Receiver-General, and the Commissary-General, Notaries-Public, and Naval-Officers, shall be chosen annually, by joint ballot of the Senators and Representatives in one room. And that the citizens of this Commonwealth may be assured, from time to time, that the monies remaining in the public Treasury, upon the settlement and liquidation of the public accounts, are their property, no man shall be eligible as Treasurer and Receiver-General more than five years successively.

II.--The records of Commonwealth shall be kept in the office of the Secretary, who may appoint his Deputies, for whose conduct he shall be accountable, and he shall attend the Governor and Council, the Senate and House of Representatives, in person, or by his deputies, as they shall respectively require.

CHAPTER III:

JUDICIARY POWER

Art. I.--The tenure that all commission officers shall by law have in their offices, shall be expressed in their respective commissions. All judicial officers, duly appointed, commissioned and sworn, shall hold their offices during good behaviour, excepting such concerning whom there is different provision made in this Constitution: Provided, nevertheless, the Governor, with consent of the Council, may remove them upon the address of both Houses of the Legislature.

II.--Each branch of the Legislature, as well as the Governor and Council, shall have authority to require the opinions of the Justices of the Supreme Judicial Court, upon important questions of law, and upon solemn occasions.

III.--In order that the people may not suffer from the long continuance in place of any Justice of the Peace, who shall fail of discharging the important duties of his office with ability or fidelity, all commissions of Justices of the Peace shall expire and become void, in the term of seven years from their respective dates; and, upon the expiration of any commission, the same may, if necessary, be renewed, or another person appointed, as shall most conduce to the well being of the Commonwealth.

IV.--The Judges of Probate of Wills, and for granting letters of administration, shall hold their courts at such places or places, on fixed days, as the convenience of the people shall require. And the Legislature shall, from time to time, hereafter appoint such times and places; until which appointments, the said Courts shall be holden at the times and places which the respective Judges shall direct.

V.--All causes of marriage, divorce and alimony, and all appeals from the Judges of Probate, shall be heard and determined by the Governor and Council until the Legislature shall, by law, make other provisions.

CHAPTER IV:

DELEGATES TO CONGRESS.

The delegates of this Commonwealth to the Congress of the United States, shall, sometime in the month of June annually, be elected by the joint ballot of the Senate and House of Representatives, assembled together in one room; to serve in Congress for one year, to commence on the first Monday in November then next ensuing. They shall have commissions under the hand of the Governor, and the great seal of the Commonwealth; but may be recalled at any time within the year, and others chosen and commissioned, in the same manner, in their stead.

CHAPTER V:

THE UNIVERSITY AT CAMBRIDGE, AND ENCOURAGEMENT OF LITER-ATURE, ETC.

SECTION I: THE UNIVERSITY.

Art. I.--Whereas our wise and pious ancestors, so early as the year one thousand six hundred and thirty six, laid the foundation of Harvard-College, in which University many persons of great eminence have, by the blessing of GOD, been initiated in those arts and sciences, which qualified them for public employments, both in Church and State: And whereas the encouragement of Arts and Sciences, and all good literature, tends to the honor of God, the advantage of the Christian religion, and the great benefit of this, and the other United States of America--It is declared, That the PRESIDENT AND FELLOWS OF HARVARD-COLLEGE, in their corporate capacity, and their successors in that capacity, their officers and servants, shall have, hold, use, exercise and enjoy, all the powers, authorities, rights, liberties, privileges, immunities and franchises, which they now have, or are entitled to have, hold, use, exercise and enjoy: And the same are hereby ratified and confirmed unto them, the said President and Fellows of Harvard-College, and to their successors, and to their officers and servants, respectively, forever.

II.--And whereas there have been at sundry times, by divers persons, gifts, grants, devises of houses, lands, tenements, goods, chattels, legacies and conveyances, heretofore made, either to Harvard-College in Cambridge, in New-England, or to the President and Fellows of Harvard-College, or to the said College, by some other description, under several charters successively: IT IS DECLARED, That all the said gifts, grants, devises, legacies and conveyances, are hereby forever confirmed unto the President and Fellows of Harvard-College, and to their successors, in the capacity aforesaid, according to the true intent and meaning of the donor or donors, grantor or grantors, devisor or devisors.

III.--And whereas by an act of the General Court of the Colony of Massachusetts-Bay, passed in the year one thousand six hundred and forty-two, the Governor and Deputy-Governor, for the time being, and all the magistrates of that jurisdiction, were, with the President, and a number of the clergy in the said act described, constituted the Overseers of Harvard-College: And it being necessary, in this new Constitution of Government, to ascertain who shall be deemed successors to the said Governor, Deputy-Governor and Magistrates: IT IS DECLARED, That the Governor, Lieutenant-

Governor, Council and Senate of this Commonwealth, are, and shall be deemed, their successors; who, with the President of Harvard-College, for the time being, together with the ministers of the congregational churches in the towns of Cambridge, Watertown, Charlestown, Boston, Roxbury, and Dorchester, mentioned in the said act, shall be, and hereby are, vested with all the powers and authority belonging, or in any way appertaining to the Overseers of Harvard-College; PROVIDED, that nothing herein shall be construed to prevent the Legislature of this Commonwealth from making such alterations in the government of the said university, as shall be conducive to its advantage, and the interest of the republic of letters, in as full a manner as might have been done by the Legislature of the late Province of the Massachusetts-Bay.

Chapter V

Section II: The Encouragement of Literature, etc.

Wisdom, and knowledge, as well as virtue, diffused generally among the body of the people, being necessary for the preservation of their rights and liberties; and as these depend on spreading the opportunities and advantages of education in the various parts of the country, and among the different orders of the people, it shall be the duty of legislators and magistrates, in all future periods of this Commonwealth, to cherish the interests of literature and the sciences, and all seminaries of them; especially the university at Cambridge, public schools, and grammar schools in the towns; to encourage private societies and public institutions, rewards and immunities, for the promotion of agriculture, arts, sciences, commerce, trades, manufactures, and a natural history of the country; to countenance and inculcate the principles of humanity and general benevolence, public and private charity, industry and frugality, honesty and punctuality in their dealings; sincerity, good humour, and all social affections, and generous sentiments among the people.

Chapter VI:

Oaths and Subscriptions; Incompatibility of and Exclusion from Offices; Pecuniary Qualifications; Commissions; Writs; Confirmation of Laws; Habeas Corpus; The Enacting Style; Continuance of Officers; Provision for a future Revisal of the Constitution, etc.

Art I.--Any person chosen Governor, Lieutenant-Governor, Counsellor, Senator, or Representative, and accepting the trust, shall, before he proceed to execute the duties of his place or office, make and subscribe the following declaration, viz.--

"I, A. B. do declare, that I believe the Christian religion, and have a firm persuasion of its truth; and that I am seized and possessed, in my own right, of the property required by the Constitution as one qualification for the office or place to which I am elected."

And the Governor, Lieutenant-Governor, and Counsellors, shall make and subscribe the said declaration, in the presence of the two Houses of Assembly; and the Senators and Representatives first elected under this Constitution, before the President and five of the Council of the former Constitution, and, forever afterwards, before the Governor and Council for the time being.

And every person chosen to either of the places or offices aforesaid, as also any person appointed or commissioned to any judicial, executive, military, or other office under the government, shall, before he enters on the discharge of the business of his place or office, take and subscribe the following declaration, and oaths or affirmations, viz.--

"I, A. B. do truly and sincerely acknowledge, profess, testify and declare, that the Commonwealth of Massachusetts is, and of right ought to be, a free, sovereign and independent State; and I do swear, that I will bear true faith and allegiance to the said Commonwealth, and that I will defend the same against traitorous conspiracies and all hostile attempts whatsoever: And that I do renounce and adjure all allegiance, subjection and obedience to the King, Queen or Government of Great Britain, (as the case may be) and every other foreign power whatsoever: And that no foreign Prince, Person, Prelate, State or Potentate, hath, or ought to have, any jurisdiction, superiority, preeminence, authority, dispensing or other power, in any matter, civil, ecclesiastical or spiritual, within this Commonwealth; except the authority and power which is or may be vested by their Constituents in the Congress of the United States: And I do further testify and declare, that no man or body of men hath or can have any right to absolve or discharge me from the obligation of this oath, declaration or affirmation; and that I do make this acknowledgment, profession, testimony, declaration, denial, renunciation and abjuration, heartily and truly, according to the common meaning and acceptation of the foregoing words, without any equivocation, mental evasion, or secret reservation whatsoever. So help me GOD."

"I, A. B. do solemnly swear and affirm, that I will faithfully and impartially discharge and perform all the duties incumbent on me as; according to the best of my abilities and understanding, agreeably to the rules and regulations of the Constitution, and the laws of this Commonwealth." "So help me GOD."

Provided always, that when any person, chosen or appointed as afore-said, shall be of the denomination of the people called Quakers, and shall decline taking the said oaths, he shall make his affirmation in the foregoing form, and subscribe the same, omitting the words *"I do swear," "and adjure," "oath or," "and abjuration,"* in the first oath; and in the second oath, the words *"swear and;"* and in each of them the words "*So help me* GOD;" sub-joining instead thereof, *"This I do under the pains and penalties of perjury."*

And the said oaths or affirmations shall be taken and subscribed by the Governor, Lieutenant Governor, and Counsellors, before the President of the Senate, in the presence of the two Houses of Assembly; and by the Sena-tors and Representatives first elected under this Constitution, before the President and five of the Council of the former Constitution; and forever af-terwards before the Governor and Council for the time being: And by the residue of the officers aforesaid, before such persons and in such manner as from time to time shall be prescribed by the Legislature.

II.--No Governor, Lieutenant Governor, or Judge of the Supreme Judi-cial Court, shall hold any other office or place, under the authority of this Commonwealth, except such as by this Constitution they are admitted to hold, saving that the Judges of the said Court may hold the offices of Justices of the Peace through the State; nor shall they hold any other place or office, or receive any pension or salary from any other State or Government or Power whatever.

No person shall be capable of holding or exercising at the same time, within this State, more than one of the following offices, viz:--Judge of Pro-bate--Sheriff--Register of Probate--or Register of Deeds--and never more than any two offices which are to be held by appointment of the Governor, or the Governor and Council, or the Senate, or the House of Representatives, or by the election of the people of the State at large, or of the people of any county, military offices and the offices of Justices of the Peace excepted, shall be held by one person.

No person holding the office of Judge of the Supreme Judicial Court--Secretary--Attorney General--Solicitor General--Treasurer or Receiver Gen-eral--Judge of Probate--Commissary General--President, Professor, or In-structor of Harvard College--Sheriff--Clerk of the House of Representatives--Register of Probate--Register of Deeds--Clerk of the Supreme Judicial Court--Clerk of the Inferior Court of Common Pleas--or Officer of the Cus-toms, including in this description Naval Officers--shall at the same time have a seat in the Senate or House of Representatives; but their being chosen or appointed to, and accepting the same, shall operate as a resignation of their seat in the Senate or House of Representatives; and the place so vacated shall be filled up.

And the same rule shall take place in case any judge of the said Supreme Judicial Court, or Judge of Probate, shall accept a seat in Council; or any Counsellor shall accept of either of those offices or places.

And no person shall ever be admitted to hold a seat in the Legislature, or any office of trust or importance under the Government of this Commonwealth, who shall, in the due course of law, have been convicted of bribery or corruption in obtaining an election or appointment.

III.--In all cases where sums of money are mentioned in this Constitution, the value thereof shall be computed in silver at six shillings and eight pence per ounce: And it shall be in the power of the Legislature from time to time to increase such qualifications, as to property, of the persons to be elected to offices, as the circumstances of the Commonwealth shall require.

IV.--All commissions shall be in the name of the Commonwealth of Massachusetts, signed by the Governor, and attested by the Secretary or his Deputy, and have the great seal of the Commonwealth affixed thereto.

V.--All writs, issuing out of the clerk's office in any of the Courts of law, shall be in the name of the Commonwealth of Massachusetts: They shall be under the seal of the Court from whence they issue: They shall bear test of the first Justice of the Court to which they shall be returnable, who is not a party, and be signed by the clerk of such court.

VI.--All the laws which have heretofore been adopted, used and approved in the Province, Colony or State of Massachusetts Bay, and usually practiced on in the Courts of law, shall still remain and be in full force, until altered or repealed by the Legislature; such parts only excepted as are repugnant to the rights and liberties contained in this Constitution.

VII.--The privilege and benefit of the writ of *habeas corpus* shall be enjoyed in this Commonwealth in the most free, easy, cheap, expeditious and ample manner; and shall not be suspended by the Legislature, except upon the most urgent and pressing occasions, and for a limited time not exceeding twelve months.

VII.--The enacting style, in making and passing all acts, statutes and laws, shall be--"Be it enacted by the Senate and House of Representatives, in General Court assembled, and by the authority of the same."

IX.--To the end there may be no failure of justice or danger arise to the Commonwealth from a change of the Form of Government--all officers, civil and military, holding commissions under the government and people of Massachusetts Bay in New-England, and all other officers of the said government and people, at the time this Constitution shall take effect, shall have, hold, use, exercise and enjoy all the powers and authority to them granted or committed, until other persons shall be appointed in their stead: And all courts of law shall proceed in the execution of the business of their respective departments; and all the executive and legislative officers, bodies and powers shall continue in full force, in the enjoyment and exercise of all their trusts, employments and authority; until the General Court and the supreme and executive officers under this Constitution are designated and invested with their respective trusts, powers and authority.

X.--In order the more effectually to adhere to the principles of the Constitution, and to correct those violations which by any means may be made therein, as well as to form such alterations as from experience shall be found necessary--the General Court, which shall be in the year of our Lord one thousand seven hundred and ninety-five, shall issue precepts to the Selectmen of the several towns, and to the Assessors of the unincorporated plantations, directing them to convene the qualified voters of their respective towns and plantations for the purpose of collecting their sentiments on the necessity or expediency of revising the Constitution, in order to amendments.

And if it shall appear by the returns made, that two thirds of the qualified voters throughout the State, who shall assemble and vote in consequence of the said precepts, are in favor of such revision or amendment, the General Court shall issue precepts, or direct them to be issued from the Secretary's office to the several towns, to elect Delegates to meet in Convention for the purpose aforesaid.

The said Delegates to be chosen in the same manner and proportion as their Representatives in the second branch of the Legislature are by this Constitution to be chosen.

XI.--This form of government shall be enrolled on parchment, and deposited in the Secretary's office, and be a part of the laws of the land--and printed copies thereof shall be prefixed to the book containing the laws of this Commonwealth, in all future editions of the said laws.

SOURCE: These excerpts are reprinted from Franci Newton Thorpe (ed.), *The Federal and State Constitutions, Colonial Charters, and other Organic Laws of the States and Territories now or heretofore forming the United States of America*, 7 vols. (Washington: Government Printing Office, 1909), 7: 1888-1922.

PART FOUR:

CONSTITUTIONAL SECOND THOUGHTS

1. BENJAMIN RUSH
"OBSERVATIONS ON THE PRESENT GOVERNMENT OF PENNSYLVANIA "
1777

Benjamin Rush was born on his father's farm north of Philadelphia in the province of Pennsylvania, British America (1746), and he died in Philadelphia, state of Pennsylvania in the United States (1813). He attended the College of New Jersey (Princeton), graduating when he was fifteen. He then enrolled at the University of Edinburgh, where he received the degree of Doctor of Medicine. Rush was a member of the Continental Congress that passed the Declaration of Independence, and he also served in the War of Independence as Military Surgeon. Rush went on to become a physician, politician, social reformer, educator, politician, revolutionary patriot, and founding father. In later years, he was a professor of chemistry and medicine at the College of Philadelphia (now University of Pennsylvania). In 1812, Rush reconciled his two old friends, John Adams and Thomas Jefferson, who had not communicated with each other in many years. In his "Observations on the Present Government of Pennsylvania," Rush delivered a stinging critique of the new Pennsylvania constitution, which placed too much power in its unicameral legislature. Rush's principal argument claimed that the unicameral legislature, rather than being inherently democratic created a powerful new aristocracy that would eventually acquire absolute power and overwhelm the executive and judiciary. Rush was a proponent of what he called a "compound" legislature, by which he meant a bicameral legislature.

LETTER I

EVERY free government should consist of three parts, viz. I. A BILL OF RIGHTS. II. A CONSTITUTION, And III. LAWS.

1. The BILL OF RIGHTS should contain the great principles of *natural* and *civil liberty*. It should be unalterable by any human power.
2. The CONSTITUTION is the executive part of the Bill of Rights. It should contain the division and distribution of the power of the people.—The modes and forms of making laws, of executing justice, and of transacting business: Also the limitation of power, as to time and jurisdiction. It should be unalterable by the legislature, and should be changed only by a representation of the people, chosen for that purpose.

III. LAWS are the executive part of a constitution. They cease to be binding whenever they transgress the principles of Liberty, as laid down in the Constitution and Bill of Rights.

Let us now apply these principles to the Bill of Rights, Constitution and Laws of Pennsylvania. But previous to my entering upon this task, I beg leave to declare, that I am not led to it by a single party or personal prejudice; on the contrary, I honour most of the friends of the present government as the warmest Whigs among us, and I am proud of numbering several of the gentlemen who were concerned in making, and in attempting to execute the government, among my particular friends.

1. The Bill of Rights has confounded *natural* and *civil* rights in such a manner as to produce endless confusion in society.

2. The Constitution in the gross is exceptionable in the following particulars:

3. No regard is paid in it to the ancient habits and customs of the people of Pennsylvania in the distribution of the supreme power of the state, nor in the forms of business, or in the stile of the Constitution. The suddenness of the late revolution, the attachment of a large body of the people to the old Constitution of the state, and the general principles of human nature made an attention to ancient forms and prejudices a matter of the utmost importance to this state in the present controversy with Great-Britain. Of so much consequence did the wise Athenians view the force of ancient habits and customs in their laws and government, that they punished all *strangers* with death who interfered in their politics. They well knew the effects of novelty upon the minds of the people, and that a more fatal stab could not be given to the peace and safety of their state than by exposing its laws and government to frequent or *unnecessary* innovations.

4. The Constitution is wholly repugnant to the principles of action in man, and has a direct tendency to check the progress of genius and virtue in human nature. It supposes perfect equality, and an equal distribution of property, wisdom and virtue, among the inhabitants of the state.

5. It comprehends many things which belong to a Bill of Rights, and to Laws, and which form no part of a Constitution.

6. It is contrary, in an important article, to the Bill of Rights. By the second article of the Bill of Rights, "no man can be abridged of any *civil* right, who acknowledges the being of a GOD;" but by the Constitution, no man can take his seat in the Assembly, who does not "acknowledge the Scriptures of the Old and New Testament to be given by divine inspiration."

7. It is deficient in point of perspicuity and method. Instead of reducing the legislative, executive and judicial parts of the constitution,

with their several powers and forms of business, to distinct heads, the whole of them are jumbled together in a most unsystematic manner.

8. It fixes all these imperfections upon the people for seven years, by precluding them from the exercise of their own power to remove them at any other time, or in any other manner than by a septennial convention, called by a Council of Censors.

III. The laws and proceedings of the Assembly of Pennsylvania are in many particulars contrary to the constitution. Only one half of the Members took the oath of allegiance, prescribed in the tenth section of the constitution. The Speaker of the House issued writs for the election of Members of Assembly and of Counsellors, notwithstanding this power is lodged, by the 19th section of the constitution, *only* in the President and Council. Two gentlemen were appointed Members of Congress, who held offices under the Congress, which is expressly forbidden in the 11th section of the constitution. The constitution requires further in the 40th section, that every military officer should take the oath of allegiance, before he enters upon the execution of his office; but the Assembly have dispensed with this oath in their Militia Law. The 15th section of the constitution declares, that no law shall be passed, unless it be previously published for the consideration of the People; but the Assembly passed all the laws of their late session, without giving the People an opportunity of seeing them, till they were called upon to obey them. These proceedings of the Assembly lead to one, and perhaps to all the three following conclusions: First, That the Assembly have violated the principles of the constitution; secondly, that the constitution is so formed, that it could not be executed by the Assembly, consistent with the safety of the State; lastly, that none of their laws are binding, inasmuch as they are contrary to the superior and radical laws of the constitution. These considerations are all of a most alarming nature. Farewel to Liberty, when the sacred bulwarks of a constitution can be invaded by a legislature! And if the constitution cannot be executed in all its parts, without endangering the safety of the State, and if all our late; laws must be set aside in a court of justice, because they were not assented to by the People, previous to their being enacted, is it not high time for the People to unite and form a more effectual, and more practicable system of government?—

If strict justice should poise the scale in the trial of tory property, I can easily foresee from the virtue of the People, on which side the beam would turn; but it becomes us to reflect, that all trials for forfeited property must be held in courts of *written* law, and the flaws of our constitution and laws are so wide, that the most gigantic Tory criminal might escape through them.

Letter II

I SHALL now proceed to say a few words upon particular parts of the Constitution.

In the second section, "the supreme legislature is vested in a *'single'* House of Representatives of the Freemen of the Commonwealth." By this section we find, that the supreme, absolute, and uncontrouled power of the whole State is lodged in the hands of *one body* of men. Had it been lodged in the hands of one man, it would have been less dangerous to the safety and liberties of the community. Absolute power should never be trusted to man. It has perverted the wisest heads, and corrupted the best hearts in the world. I should be afraid to commit my property, liberty and life to a body of angels for one whole year. The Supreme Being alone is qualified to possess supreme power over his creatures. It requires the wisdom and goodness of a Deity to controul, and direct it properly.

In order to shew the extreme danger of trusting all the legislative power of a State to a single representation, I shall beg leave to transcribe a few sentences from a letter, written by Mr. JOHN ADAMS, to one of his friends in North-Carolina, who requested him to favour him with a plan of government for that State above a twelve-month ago. This illustrious Citizen, who is second to no man in America, in an inflexible attachment to the liberties of this country, and to republican forms of government, writes as follows,

"I think a people cannot be *long free*, nor *ever* happy, whose government is in one Assembly. My reasons for this opinion are as follow,

1. "A single Assembly is liable to all the vices, follies and frailties of an individual,—subject to fits of humour,—starts of passions, flights of enthusiasm,—partialities of prejudice, and consequently productive of hasty results and absurd judgments. All these errors ought to be corrected, and defects supplied by some controuling power.

2. "A single Assembly is apt to be avaricious, and in time will not scruple to exempt itself from burdens, which it will lay, without compunction, upon its constituents.

3. "A single Assembly is apt to grow ambitious, and after a time will not hesitate to vote itself perpetual. This was one fault of the long parliament, but more remarkably of Holland, whose Assembly first voted themselves from *annual* to *septennial*, then for *life*, and after a course of years, that all vacancies happening by death or otherwise, should be filled by *themselves*, without any application to constituents at all.

4. "Because a single Assembly possessed of all the powers of government would make arbitrary laws for their own interest, and adjudge all controversies in their own favor."

If any thing could be necessary upon this subject, after such an authority, I might here add, that Montesquieu—Harrington—Milton—Addison—Price—Bolingbroke, and others, the wisest statesmen, and the greatest friends to Liberty in the world, have left testimonies upon record of the extreme folly and danger of a people's being governed by a single legislature. I shall content myself with the following extract from the last of those authors.

The sentiments correspond exactly with those of our countryman before-mentioned.

"By simple forms of government, I mean such as lodge the whole supreme power, absolutely and without controul, either in a single person, or in the principal persons of the community, or in the whole body of the people. Such governments are governments of arbitrary will, and therefore of all imaginable absurdities the most absurd. They stand in direct opposition to the sole motive of submission to any government whatsoever; for if men quit the State, and renounce the rights of nature, (one of which is, to be sure, that of being governed by their own will) they do this, that they may not remain exposed to the arbitrary will of other men, the weakest to that of the strongest, the few to that of the many. Now, in submitting to any single form of government whatever, they establish what they mean to avoid, and for fear of being exposed to arbitrary will sometimes, they choose to be governed by it always. These governments do not only degenerate into tyranny; they are tyranny in their very institution; and they who submit to them, are slaves, not subjects, however the supreme power may be exercised; for tyranny and slavery do not so properly consist in the stripes that are given and received, as in the power of giving them at pleasure, and the necessity of receiving them, whenever and for whatever they are inflicted."

I might go on further and shew, that all the dissentions of Athens and Rome, so dreadful in their nature, and so fetal in their consequences, originated in single Assemblies possessing all the power of those commonwealths; but this would be the business of a volume, and not of a single essay.—I shall therefore pass on, to answer the various arguments that have been used in Pennsylvania, in support of a single legislature.

1. We are told, that the perfection of every thing consists in its simplicity,—that all mixtures in government are impurities, and that a single legislature is perfect, because it is simple.—To this I answer, that we should distinguish between simplicity in principles, and simplicity in the application of principles to practice. What can be more simple than the principles of mechanics, and yet into how many thousand forms have they been tortured by the ingenuity of man. A few simple elementary bodies compose all the matter of the universe, and yet how infinitely are they combined in the various forms and substances which they assume in the animal, vegetable, and mineral kingdoms. In like manner a few simple principles enter into the composition of all free governments. These principles are perfect security for property, liberty and life; but these principles admit of extensive combinations, when reduced to practice:—Nay more, they require them. A despotic government is the most simple government in the world, but instead of affording security to property, liberty or life, it obliges us to hold them all on the simple will of a capricious sovereign. I maintain therefore, that all governments are

safe and free in proportion as they are compounded in a certain degree, and on the contrary, that all governments are dangerous and tyrannical in proportion as they approach to simplicity.

2. We are told by the friends of a single legislature, that there can be no danger of their becoming tyrannical, since they must partake of all the burdens they lay upon their constituents. Here we forget the changes that are made upon the head and heart by arbitrary power, and the cases that are recorded in history of *annual* Assemblies having refused to share with their constituents in the burdens which they had imposed upon them. If every elector in Pennsylvania is capable of being elected an assembly-man, then agreeably to the sixth section of the constitution, it is possible for an Assembly to exist who do not possess a single foot of property in the State, and who can give no other evidence of a common interest in, or attachment to, the community than having paid "public taxes," which may mean poor-taxes. Should this be the case, (and there is no obstacle in the constitution to prevent it) surely it will be in the power of such an Assembly to draw from the State the whole of its wealth in a few years, without contributing any thing further towards it than their proportion of the trifling tax necessary to support the poor.—But I shall shew in another place equal dangers from another class of men, becoming a majority in the Assembly.

3. We are told of instances of the House of Lords, in England, checking the most salutary laws, after they had passed the House of Commons, as a proof of the inconvenience of a compound legislature. I believe the fact to be true, but I deny its application in the present controversy. The House of Lords, in England, possess privileges and interests, which do not belong to the House of Commons. Moreover they derive their power from the crown and not from the people. No wonder therefore they consult their own interests, in preference to those of the People. In the State of Pennsylvania we wish for a council, with *no one* exclusive privilege, and we disclaim every idea of their possessing the smallest degree of power, but what is derived from the *annual* suffrages of the People, A body thus chosen could have no object in view but the happiness of their constituents. It is remarkable in Connecticut, that the legislative council of that State has in no one instance made amendments, or put a negative upon the acts of their Assembly, in the course of above one hundred years, in which both have not appeared to the people in a few months to have been calculated to promote their liberty and happiness.

4. We are told, that the Congress is a single legislature, therefore a single legislature is to be preferred to a compound one.—The objects of legislation in the Congress relate only to peace and war, alliances, trade, the Post-Office, and the government of the army and navy.

They never touch the liberty, property, nor life of the individuals of any State in their resolutions, and even in their ordinary subjects of legislation, they are liable to be checked by *each* of the Thirteen States.

5. We have been told, that a legislative council or governor lays the foundation for aristocratical and monarchical power in a community. However ridiculous this objection to a compound legislature may appear, I have more than once heard it mentioned by the advocates for a single Assembly. Who would believe, that the same fountain of pure water should send forth, at the same time, wholesome and deadly streams? Are not the Council and Assembly both formed alike by the *annual* breath of the people? But I will suppose, that a legislative Council aspired after the honors of hereditary titles and power, would they not be *effectually* checked by the Assembly?

I cannot help commending the zeal that appears in my countrymen against the power of a King or a House of Lords. I concur with them in all their prejudices against hereditary titles, honour and power. History is little else than a recital of the follies and vices of kings and noblemen, and it is because I dread so much from them, that I wish to exclude them forever from Pennsylvania, for notwithstanding our government has been called a simple democracy, I maintain, that a foundation is laid in it for the most complete aristocracy that ever existed in the world.

In order to prove this assertion, I shall promise two propositions, which have never been controverted: First, where there is wealth, there will be power; and, secondly, the rich have always been an over-match for the poor in all contests for power.

These truths being admitted, I desire to know what can prevent our single representation being filled, in the course of a few years, with a majority of rich men? Say not, the people will not choose such men to represent them. The influence of wealth at elections is irresistible. It has been seen and felt in Pennsylvania, and I am obliged in justice to my subject to say, that there are poor men among us as prepared to be influenced, as the rich are prepared to influence them. The fault must be laid in both cases upon human nature. The consequence of a majority of rich men getting into the legislature is plain. Their wealth will administer fuel to the love of arbitrary power that is common to all men. The present Assembly have furnished them with precedents for breaking the Constitution. Farewel now to annual elections! Public emergencies will sanctify the most daring measures. The clamours of their constituents will be silenced with offices, bribes or punishments. An aristocracy will be established, and Pennsylvania will be inhabited like most of the countries in Europe, with only two sorts of animals, tyrants and slaves.

It has often been said, that there is but one rank of men in America, and therefore, that there should be only one representation of them in a government. I agree, that we have no artificial distinctions of men into noblemen and commoners among us, but it ought to be remarked, that superior degrees of industry and capacity, and above all, commerce, have introduced inequality of property among us, and these have introduced natural distinctions of rank in Pennsylvania, as certain and general as the artificial distinctions of men in Europe. This will ever be the case while commerce exists in this country. The men of middling property and poor men can never be safe in a mixed representation with the men of over-grown property. Their liberties can only be secured by having exact bounds prescribed to their power, in the fundamental principles of the Constitution. By a representation of the men of middling fortunes in one house, their *whole* strength is collected against the influence of wealth. Without such a representation, the violent efforts of individuals to oppose it would be divided and broken, and would want that system, which alone would enable them to check that lust for dominion which is always connected with opulence. The government of Pennsylvania therefore has been called most improperly a government for poor men. It carries in every part of it a poison to their liberties. It is impossible to form a government more suited to the nations and interests of rich men.

6. But says the advocate for a single legislature, if one of the advantages of having a Legislative Council arises from the Counsellors possessing more wisdom than the Assembly, why may not the mentors of the Council be thrown into the Assembly, in order to instruct and enlighten them? If sound reasoning always prevailed in popular Assemblies, this objection to a Legislative Council might have some weight. The danger in this case would be, that the Counsellors would partake of the passions and prejudices of the Assembly, by taking part in their debates; or, if they did not, that they would be so inconsiderable in point of numbers, that they would be constantly outvoted by the members of the Assembly.

7. But would you suffer twenty or thirty men in a Legislative Council to controul seventy or eighty in an Assembly? Yes, and that for two reasons: First, I shall suppose that they will consist of men of the most knowledge and experience in the State: Secondly, that their obligations to wisdom and integrity will be much stronger than the Assembly's can be, because fewer men will be answerable for unjust or improper proceedings at the bar of the public. But I beg pardon of my readers for introducing an answer to an objection to a small number of men controuling the proceedings of a greater. The friends of the present Constitution of Pennsylvania cannot urge this objection with any force, for in the 47th section of the Constitution I find twenty-four men called a COUNCIL of CENSORS, invested with a supreme and *uncontrouled* power to revise and to censure all the laws and proceedings of not a single Assembly, but of all the Assemblies that shall exist for seven years, which Assemblies may contain the united wisdom of five hundred and four Assembly-men.

They are moreover, invested with more wisdom than the Convention that is to be chosen by their recommendation; for this Convention, which is to consist of seventy-two men, is to make no *one* alteration in the Constitution but what was suggested to them by the Council of Censors. I can easily conceive, that two houses consisting of an unequal number of members, both viewing objects through the same medium of time and place, may agree in every thing essential, and disagree in matters only of doubtful issue to the welfare of the state; but I am sure, a body of twenty-four men fating in judgment upon the proceedings of a body of men defunct in their public capacity seven years before them, cannot fail of committing the most egregious mistakes from the obscurity which time, and their ignorance of a thousand facts and reasonings must throw upon all their deliberations. But more of the arbitrary power of the Censors hereafter.

8.	We are told that the state of Pennsylvania has always been governed by a single legislature, and therefore, that part of our Constitution is not an innovation. There is a short way of confuting this assertion by pronouncing it without any foundation. The Governor always had a negative power upon our laws, and was a distinct branch of our legislature. It is true, he sometimes exercised his power to the disadvantage of the people; for he was the servant of a King who possessed an interest distinct from that of his people, and in some cases the Governor himself possessed an interest incompatible with the rights of the people. God forbid that ever we should see a resurrection of his power in Pennsylvania, but I am obliged to own, that I have known instances in which the *whole* have thanked him for the interposition of his negative and amendments upon the acts of the Assembly. Even the Assembly themselves have acknowledged the justice of his conduct upon these occasions, by condemning in their cooler hours their own hasty, and ill-digested resolutions.

9.	But why all these arguments in favor of checks for the Assembly. The Constitution (says the single legislative-man) has provided no less than four for them. First, Elections will be annual. Secondly, The doors of the Assembly are to be always open. Thirdly, All laws are to be published for the consideration and assent of the people: And, Fourthly, The Council of Censors will punish, by their censures, all violations of the Constitution, and the authors of bad laws. I shall examine the efficacy of each of these checks separately.

I hope, for the peace of the state, that we shall never see a body of men in power more attached to the present Constitution than the present Assembly, and if, with all their affection for it, they have broken it in many articles, it is reasonable to suppose that future Assemblies will use the same freedoms with it. They may, if they chuse, abolish annual elections. They may tell their constituents that elections draw off the minds of the people from necessary labour; or, if a war should exist, they may shew the impossibility of holding elections when there is a chance of the militia being called into the field to oppose a common enemy: Or lastly, they may fetter elections with oaths in such a manner as to exclude nine-tenths of the electors from voting. Such stratagems for perpetual power will never want men nor a *society* of men to support them; for the Assembly possesses such a plenitude of power from the influence of the many offices of profit and honour that are in their gift, that they may always promise themselves support from a great part of the state. But I will suppose that no infringement is ever made upon annual elections. In the course of even one year a single Assembly may do the most irreparable mischief to a state. Socrates and Barnevelt were both put to death by Assemblies that held their powers at the election of the people. The same Assemblies would have shed oceans of tears to have recalled those illustrious citizens to life again, in less than half a year after they imbrued their hands in their blood.

I am highly pleased with having the doors of our Assembly kept constantly open; but how can this check the proceedings of the Assembly, none but a few citizens of the town or county, where the Assembly sits, or a few travelling strangers, can ever attend or watch them?

I shall take no notice of the delays of business, which must arise from publishing all laws for the consideration and assent of the people; but I beg to be informed *how long* they must be published before they are passed? For I take it for granted, that each county has a right to equal degrees of time to consider of the laws. In what manner are they to be circulated? How are the sentiments of the people, scattered over a county fifty or sixty miles in extent, to be collected? Whether by ballot, or by voting in a tumultuary manner? These are insurmountable difficulties in the way of the people at *large* acting as a check upon the Assembly. But supposing an attempt should be made to restrain the single legislature in this manner, are we sure the disapprobation of the people would be sufficient to put a negative upon improper or arbitrary laws? Would not the Assembly, from their partiality to their own proceedings, be apt to pass over the complaints of the people in silence? to neglect or refuse to enter their petitions or remonstrances upon their Journals? or to raise the hue and cry of a fostered junto upon them, as "*tories*" or "*apostate whigs*," or "*an aristocratic faction?*"

To talk of the Council of Censors, as a check upon the Assembly, is to forget that a man or a body of men may deceive, rob, and enslave the public for seven years, and then may escape the intended efficacy of the censures of the Council by death, or by flying into a neighbouring state.

10. We are informed that a single legislature was supported in the Convention by Dr. Franklin, and assented to by Mr. Rittenhouse; gentlemen distinguished for their uncommon abilities, and deservedly dear for their virtues to every lover of human nature. The only

answer, after what has been said, that I shall give to this argument, is, that Divine Providence seems to have permitted them to *err* upon this subject, in order to console the world for the very great superiority they both possess over the rest of mankind in every thing else, except the science of government.

Thus have I answered all the arguments that ever I have heard offered in favour of a single legislature, and I hope, silenced all the objections that have been made to a double representation of the people. I might here appeal further to the practice of our courts of law in favour of repeated deliberations and divisions. In a free government, the most inconsiderable portion of our liberty and property cannot be taken from us, without the judgment of two or three courts; but, by the Constitution of Pennsylvania, the whole of our liberty and property, and even our lives, may be taken from us, by the hasty and passionate decision of a single Assembly.

I shall conclude my observations upon this part of the Constitution, by summing up the advantages of a compound or double legislature.

1. There is the utmost *freedom* in a compound legislature. The decisions of two legislature bodies cannot fail of coinciding with the wills of a great majority of the community.
2. There is *safety* in such a government, in as much as each body possesses a free and independant power, so that they mutually check ambition and usurpation in each other.
3. There is the greatest *wisdom* in such a government. Every act being obliged to undergo the revision and amendments of two bodies of men, is necessarily strained of every mixture of folly, passion, and prejudice.
4. There is the longest *duration* of freedom in such a government.
5. There is the most *order* in such a government. By order, I mean obedience to laws, subordination to magistrates, civility and decency of behaviour, and the contrary of every thing like mobs and factions.
6. Compound governments are most agreeable to *human nature,* inasmuch as they afford the greatest scope for the expansion of the powers and virtues of the mind. Wisdom, learning, experience, with the most extensive benevolence; the most unshaken firmness, and the utmost elevation of soul, are all called into exercise by the opposite and different duties of the different representations of the people.

LETTER III

THE powers of government have been very justly divided into legislative, executive and judicial. Having discussed the legislative power of the government of Pennsylvania, I shall proceed now to consider the executive and judicial.

It is agreed on all hands that the executive and judicial powers of government should be *wholly independant* of the legislative. The authors of the

Pennsylvania Constitution *seem* to have given their sanction to this opinion, by separating those powers from the powers of the Assembly.—It becomes us to enquire whether they have made them so independant of the Assembly as to give them the free exercise of their own judgments.

The insignificant figure the President and Council make in the Constitution from not having a negative upon the laws of the Assembly, alone would soon have destroyed their authority and influence in the State. But the authors of the Constitution have taken pains to throw the whole power of the Council at once into the hands of the Assembly, by rendering the former dependant upon the latter in the two following particulars.

1.   The President is chosen by the joint ballot of the Assembly and Council. The Assembly being to the Council, in point of numbers, as five are to one, of course chuse the President. Each member will expect in his turn to fill the first chair in the State, and hence the whole Council will yield themselves up to the will of the Assembly.

2.   The salaries of the President and of each of the Counsellors are fixed by the Assembly. This will necessarily render them dependant upon them. It is worthy of notice here, that a rotation is established in the 19th section of the Constitution, to "prevent the danger of an inconvenient aristocracy."—From what abuse of power can this aristocracy arise? Are they not the creatures of the Assembly? But there is a magic terror in the sound of a Counsellor. Call a man an Assemblyman, or a Censor, and he becomes an innocent creature, though you invest him with the despotism of an eastern monarch. If the Council are dependant upon the Assembly, it follows of course that the Judges, who are appointed by the Council, are likewise dependant upon them. But in order more fully to secure their dependance upon the will of the Assembly, they are obliged to hold their salaries upon the tenure of their will. In vain do they hold their commissions for seven years. This is but the shadow of independance. They cannot live upon the air, and their absolute dependance upon the Assembly gives that body a transcendent influence over all the courts of law in the State. Here then we have discovered the legislative, executive and judicial powers of the State all blended together.—The liberty, the property and life of every individual in the State are laid prostrate by the Constitution at the feet of the Assembly. This combination of powers in one body has in all ages been pronounced a tyranny. To live by one man's will became the cause of all men's misery; but better, far better, would it be to live by the will of one man, than to live, or rather to die, by the will of a body of men. Unhappy Pennsylvania! Methinks I see the scales of justice broken in thy courts.—I see the dowry of the widow and the portion of the orphans unjustly taken from them, in order to gratify the avarice of some demagogue who rules the Assembly by his eloquence and

arts.—I see the scaffolds streaming with the blood of the wisest and best men in the State.—I see the offices of government—But the prospect is too painful, I shall proceed to take notice of some other parts of the Constitution.

It was not sufficient to contaminate justice at its fountain, but its smallest streams are made to partake of impurity by the Convention. In the section of the Constitution "all Justices of the Peace are to be elected by the freeholders of each city and county." The best observations that can be made on this part of the Constitution is to inform the public, that not above one half the people of the State chose magistrates agreeable to the laws of the Assembly for that purpose; that more than one half of those that were chosen have refused to accept of commissions, and that many of those who act are totally disqualified from the want of education or leisure for the office.—It has been said often, and I wish the saying was engraven over the doors of every statehouse on the Continent, that "all power is *derived* from the people," but it has never yet been said that all power is *seated* in the people. Government supposes and requires a delegation of power: It cannot exist without it. And the idea of making the people at large judges of the qualifications necessary for magistrates, or judges of laws, or checks for Assemblies proceeds upon the supposition that mankind are all alike wise, and just, and have equal leisure. It moreover destroys the necessity for all government. What man ever made himself his own attorney? And yet this would not be more absurd than for the people at *large* to pretend to give up their power to a set of rulers, and afterwards reserve the right of making and of judging of all their laws themselves. Such a government is a monster in nature. It contains as many Governors, Assemblymen, Judges and Magistrates as there are freemen in the State, all exercising the same powers and at the same time. Happy would it be for us, if this monster was remarkable only for his absurdity; but, alas! he contains a tyrant-in his bowels. All history shews us that the people soon grow weary of the folly and tyranny of one another. They prefer one to many matters, and stability to instability of slavery. They prefer a Julius Caesar to a Senate, and a Cromwell to a perpetual parliament.

I cannot help thinking a mistake lays rather in words than ideas when we talk of the rights of the people. Where is the difference between my chusing a Justice of Peace, and my chusing an Assemblyman and a Counsellor, by whose joint suffrages a Governor is chosen, who appoints a Justice for me? I am still the first link of the sacred chain of the power of the State. But are there no cases in which I may be bound by acts of a single, or of a body of magistrates in the State, whom I have had no hand in chusing? Yes, there are. Here then I am bound contrary to the principles of liberty (which consist in a man being governed by men chosen by himself), whereas if all the magistrates in the State were appointed by the Governor, or executive part of the State, it would be impossible for me to appear before the bar of a magistrate any where who did not derive his power *originally* from me.

By the 5th section all militia officers below the rank of a Brigadier General are to be chosen by the people. Most of the objections that have been mentioned against magistrates being chosen by the people, apply with equal force against the people's chusing their military officers. By the militia law of this State we find the soldier ceases to be commanded by the officer of his choice as soon as he comes in the field. He might as well be commanded by an officer of another State as by one of his own State, for whom he did not vote. Had he been appointed by the executive power of the government, he might have looked upon him originally as the creature of his own power, and might have claimed his care in the camp, from his influence at elections, in moving those springs in government, from which he derived his commission. But the unsuitableness of this part of the Constitution to the genius of the people of Pennsylvania, will appear in the strongest point of light, from attending to the two following facts: 1st: Most of the irregularities committed by the militia, that were in service last year, were occasioned by that laxity of discipline, which was introduced and kept up by officers holding their commissions by the breath of the people: And 2dly, Above one half of the State have refused or neglected to chuse officers, agreeably to the recommendation of the Assembly.—And even in many of those places, where elections for officers have been held, Colonels have been chosen by forty and Captains and Subalterns by only four or five votes.

In the 22d section of the Constitution it is said, "every officer of the state, whether judicial or executive, shall be liable to be impeached by the General Assembly, before the President and Council, either when in office or after his resignation or removal for maladministration." Why is a man in this case to be deprived of a trial by jury? and what is the reason that no *time* is *fixed* for the commencement of this impeachment after resignation or removal for maladministration? A judicial or military officer may be innocent, and yet, from the delay of his trial for six or seven years, he may be deprived by death or otherways of the vouchers of his innocence. Woe to the man that ever holds one of the high offices of the State of Pennsylvania! He must ever, after his resignation, hold his life at the pleasure of the orator who rules the Assembly. The least mark of disrespect shewn to him, or to any of the Assembly, rouses the Constitution and laws of his country against him; and perhaps, after an interval of twenty or thirty years conscious integrity, his grey hairs are dragged with sorrow to the grave. Let not this be thought to be too high a picture of this part of the Constitution of Pennsylvania. It is a picture of human nature in similar circumstances, in every age and country. Men possessed of unlimited and uncontrouled power are beasts of prey.

But, is there no power lodged in the Constitution to alter these imperfections? Has our Convention monopolized all the wisdom of succeeding years, so as to preclude any improvements being made in the infant science of government? Must we groan away our lives in a patient submission to all the evils in the Constitution which have been described? Let the 47th and last section of the Constitution answer these questions. By this section it is declared, that after the expiration of seven years, there shall "be chosen two men from each city and county, (a majority of whom shall be a quorum in every case, except as to *calling a Convention*) who shall be called a Council of Censors, and who shall have power to call a Convention within two years after their fitting, if there appears to them an absolute necessity of amending any article of the Constitution which may be defective, explaining such as may be thought not clearly expressed, and of adding such as are necessary for the preservation of the rights and happiness of the people." From this paragraph it is evident, that the Constitution was thought to be the perfection of human wisdom, and that the authors of it intended that it should last forever. Every section of the Constitution, I believe, was determined by a *majority* of the Members of the Convention, and in the 12th section of the Constitution we find, that if only two-thirds of the people concur in the execution of it, the members of Assembly chosen by them, are to "possess all the powers of the General Assembly as fully and amply as if the whole were present." This is strictly agreeable to the principles of good government; but, why are these principles to be trampled upon, when the great question is to be agitated, whether the Constitution shall be altered? For, unless every county and city in the State concur in electing Censors, and unless *two thirds* of them agree in calling a Convention, there is no possibility of obtaining an alteration of a single article of the Constitution. If the Assembly had not taught us that it was neither treason nor perjury to break the Constitution, I am sure it would have remained inviolate for ever; for I am persuaded that several of the counties would have refused to have chosen Censors. But suppose they had, if only one short of *two thirds* of them refused to agree in the measure, we could have no Convention. The minority would give laws to a majority. A solecism in government! But there is no end to the tyranny and absurdity of our Constitution.

But the Council of Censors have not yet finished their business. They are empowered by the Constitution "to enquire, whether the *Constitution* has been preserved *inviolate* in *every* part? and whether the legislative and executive branches of government have performed their duty, as guardians of the people; or assumed to themselves, or exercised *other* or greater powers than they are entitled to by the Constitution: They are also to enquire, whether the public taxes have been justly laid and collected in all parts of this commonwealth;—in what manner the public monies have been disposed of, and whether the laws have been duly executed: For these purposes they shall have power to send for persons, papers and records; they shall have authority to pass public censures, and to recommend to the legislature, the repealing such laws as appear to them to have been enacted contrary to the principles of the Constitution: These powers they shall continue to have for, and during the space of one year, from the day of their election, and no longer."

Is this the commission of the Grand Turk? or is it an extract from an act of the British Parliament, teeming with vengeance against the liberties of America?—No.—It is an epitome of the powers of the Council of Censors established by the late Convention of Pennsylvania. Innocence has nothing to fear from justice, when it flows through the regular channels of law; but where is the man who can ensure himself a moment's safety from a body of men invested with absolute power for one whole year to censure and condemn, without judge or jury, every individual in the State. I shall suppose the Council to consist of a majority of those Members of Assembly, who took the oath of allegiance to the Constitution, and who voted, that no officer should be excused from taking it, who accepted of a militia-commission under the authority of this State. I shall suppose them assembled for the business of their office. The work of an age is to be performed in a single year.—Methinks I see such of those worthy gentlemen as are living, who, for the sake of union, consented to dispense with the oath of allegiance to the Constitution, led like criminals to their bar.—I hear peals of wrath denounced against them. I see those virtuous gentlemen, who composed the Executive Council in the year 1777, summoned to appear at their tribunal, to answer for their having abdicated the duties of their office, by an adjournment, at a time when the State was threatened with an invasion. In vain they plead, that the Constitution had invested them with no power for the defence of the State. Their names and their families are branded with infamy by a "public censure." I see hundreds and thousands coming, one after another, before the Council, to be censured for refusing to chuse magistrates and militia-officers, agreeably to the laws of the Assembly. But who are they who are dragged with so much violence to the inquisitorial tribunal? They are a number of citizens who prayed for some alterations to be made in the Constitution. In vain they plead the obligations of reason and conscience against submitting to the government. In vain they plead their zeal and services in the common cause of America. It is all to no purpose. They recommend to the Assembly to impeach them for high treason. They are condemned as traitors, and the streets swim with their blood.—Good heavens! where was the mild genius of Pennsylvania, when this part of the Constitution obtained the assent of the Convention?—Spirit of liberty, whither waft thou sled?—

But perhaps the Constitution has provided a remedy for its defects, without the aid of the Council of Censors? No—this cannot be done; for every Member of Assembly, before he takes his seat, is obliged, by the 10th section of the Constitution, to swear that he will not "do nor consent to any act whatever, that shall have a tendency to lessen or abridge their rights and privileges as declared *in the Constitution of this State*," as also, "that he will not directly or indirectly do or consent to any act or thing prejudicial or injurious to the Constitution or Government thereof, as *established by the Convention*," agreeably to the 40th section of the Constitution. These oaths of infallibility and passive obedience to the form of the Constitution, effectually preclude every man, who holds an office under it, from attempting to procure the least amendment in any part of it. It is a mere quibble upon words to say, that a man may mend the Constitution, without "doing any thing prejudicial or injurious to it." The Convention did not intend any such construction to be put upon their oaths, and hence we find in the introduction to the Constitution, they "declare the frame of government to be the Constitution of this commonwealth, and to remain in force therein *for ever, unaltered*, except in such articles as shall hereafter, upon experience, be found to require improvement, and which shall, by the same authority of the people fairly delegated, as this *frame of government* directs, be amended and improved." Now we know, that the frame of government forbids the least amendment being made in the Constitution in any other than by the recommendation of a Council of Censors.

Had the Constitution appeared to me to have been unexceptionable in every part, and had it been the result of the united wisdom of men and angels, I would not have taken an oath of passive obedience to it, for seven or nine years. The constant changes in human affairs, and in the dispositions of a people, might render occasional alterations, in that time, necessary in the most perfect Constitution. But to take an oath of allegiance to a Constitution,—full of experiments,—a Constitution that was indeed a new thing under the sun,—that had never been tried in some of its parts in *any* country,—and that had produced misery in other of its parts in *every* country,—I say to swear to support or even to submit, for seven or nine years, to such a Constitution, is to trifle with all morality, and to dishonour the sacred name of GOD himself.

What would you think of a man, who would consent to shut his eyes, and swallow a quantity of food that had never before been tasted by a human creature, and swear at the same time, that if it should disorder him in ever so great a degree, he would take nothing to relieve him for eight and forty hours? Such a man would be wife, compared with the man who takes an oath of allegiance to the Constitution of Pennsylvania.

It is to no purpose to talk here of the many excellent articles in the Bill of Rights; such as religious toleration,—the habeas corpus act,—trials by juries,—the rotation of office, &c. None of them can flourish long in the neighbourhood of a single Assembly, and a Council of Censors possessing all the powers of the State.—These inestimable privileges in the Constitution of Pennsylvania resemble a tree loaded with the most luscious fruit, but surrounded with thorns, in such a manner, as to be for ever inaccessible to the hungry traveller.

Perhaps, while the government is upon its good behaviour, and while the passions of the State are directed against a cruel and common enemy, we may not experience all the calamities that have been demonstrated to flow from the Constitution.—But the revolution of a few years, and the return of peace, will most certainly render Pennsylvania, under her present Constitution, the most miserable spot upon the surface of the globe.

I believe all the Members of the late Convention were true Whigs, and aimed sincerely at forming a free and happy government: But, I am sure, that if Filmar and Hobbes had sat among them, they could not have formed a government more destructive of human happiness; nor could Lord North or General Howe have formed one more destructive of union and vigour, in our public affairs, than the present Constitution of Pennsylvania.

It is one thing to understand the *principles*, and another thing to understand the *forms* of government. The former are simple; the latter are difficult and complicated. There is the same difference between principles and forms in all other sciences. Who understood the principles of mechanics and optics better than Sir Isaac Newton? and yet Sir Isaac could not for his life have made a watch or a microscope. Mr. Locke is an oracle as to the *principles*, Harrington and Montesquieu are oracles as to the *forms* of government.

LETTER IV

A Question very naturally arises from taking a review of the tyranny of the government of Pennsylvania, What measures shall be taken to amend them? There can be but two answers to this question. 1st. To submit to the Constitution for the present, till a peace with Great-Britain will give us leisure to make a better; or, 2dly, to call a Convention immediately for the purpose of making a new Constitution. I believe the State is divided only about these two things; for the party who believe the government to be a *good* one, is too inconsiderable to be noticed in this place.

1. I beg leave to offer a few objections to our *submitting* to the Constitution, and shall endeavour, II. to obviate the objections that have been made to the immediate calling of a Convention, for the purpose of altering and amending it.

2. There is the utmost danger to the State of Pennsylvania to a temporary submission to the Constitution from the following causes, 1. The government is a tyranny. The moment we submit to it we become slaves. We hold every thing dear to us in society upon the tenure of the will of a single man in a single Assembly. Perhaps the mark of the beast may not be fixed immediately upon us, but the contract is made, and we are sold, together with our posterity, the hewers of wood and drawers of water for ever. 2. The Constitution cannot be executed in part without being *broken*. Now there cannot be a more dangerous precedent in a free country, than a legislature violating in a single article even the *forms* of a Constitution. 3. The present government will not draw forth the wisdom nor strength of the State, nor afford that assistance to our States which is expected from us in the present Great Britain. Wise and good men every where in the government. The militia law is only partially executed; justice open

for the sequestration or confiscation of Tory property; and, lastly, we shall never be able under the present government to contribute our share towards sinking the Continental debt by taxes. There is not force enough in the *whole* State to draw taxes from a single county against their consent. Alas! we are the brink of ruin. Our State has lifted a knife to her throat, and is about to undo herself by a hasty and ill-judged exercise of her own power. Our enemies are exulting, and our friends are weeping over our alarming situation. Our ancestors look down, and our posterity look up to us for a happier Constitution. We are engaged with our Sister States in 2 bloody and expensive war. The liberty of the whole world is the price for which we fight. Human nature looks to us to avenge the mighty ills she has suffered from the tyrants of the old world. She has already dropped a tear of joy upon the prospect of recovering among us her first and original dignity. A *good government* is an engine not less necessary to ensure us success in these glorious purposes than ammunition and *fire-arms*. The way of duty is plain. Let a Convention be chosen, to alter and amend the government. This measure alone will restore vigor and union to Pennsylvania. Say not, my dear countrymen, THIS IS NOT THE TIME, THE ENEMY ARE AT OUR GATES, LET US FIRST REPEL THEM. Look at our militia on a field day— see the attempts of the friends to the Constitution to open our courts—hear the complaints and murmurs of the people. They all proclaim that NOW is the time for altering our Constitution. No confusion can arise from It. The gentlemen in the opposition declare their determination to support the present Assembly in the execution of every law necessary for the safety and defence of the State, and above all in the execution of the militia and test laws. They have no interest unconnected with yours. They see with the same distress as you do the Tories triumphing in our disunion. Be not deceived. The Tories are not enemies to the present government; they enjoy the benefits of its weakness, and there is good authority to say they have *secretly* helped to carry it into execution. Let us beware of being imposed upon by the popular cry of the *necessity of the times*. When the Dissenters in Virginia and South Carolina prayed for the abolition of the Episcopal establishment in those States, the High-Churchmen acknowledged that their demands were just, but said, that *this was not the time* for attending to them, and that such a change in the government would throw all things into confusion. The demands were notwithstanding complied with, and an union unparalleled in former times was immediately produced in those Spates. When a declaration of independence last summer appeared to be the only measure that could save America, the Tories and moderate men acknowledged the justice of our separation from

Great-Britain, but said, "This is not the time." The event shewed that the time was come, for, exclusive of the advantages we have gained from it in foreign Courts, it served to precipitate the timid, the doubtful and the disaffected characters from their mixture with the real Whigs, and although it lessened the numbers in the opposition, it added to their strength by producing union and decision among them. To delay justice (has been emphatically said) is to deny it. In like manner to *delay* liberty is to *take* it away.

The Convention of New-York formed their government within the reach of the thunder of the enemy's cannon, and while one half of their State was in their possession. Is our situation more dangerous than it was last year? The members of the late Convention were chosen on a day when the Associators of the whole State were in motion. The Constitution was made while above 5000 of them were in the field. The sense of the people was not *asked* upon the subject of the Constitution; but it was *given* in the most public manner. No more than 1500 freemen voted for its being executed, for that number only took the oath of allegiance to the Constitution at the election in October. Let us talk no more then of the "*necessity of the times.*" This is the State apology at St. James's for all the crimes of the present reign and for all the savages and bloodshed we have witnessed in America. The State of Massachusetts Bay are preparing for an invasion; they expect General Burgoyne every hour in their harbours with a powerful army, and yet in a Boston paper, of the 5th of May, I find the following resolution of their Assembly and Council,

STATE OF MASSACHUSETTS BAY.

In the HOUSE of REPRESENTATIVES, May 5, 1777.

"*Resolved*, That it be, and hereby is recommended to the several towns and places in this State, impowered by the laws thereof, to send Members to the General Assembly, that, at their next election of a Member or Members to represent them, they make choice of men, in whose integrity and abilities they can place the greatest confidence; and, in addition to the common and ordinary powers of representation, instruct them in one with the Council, to form such a Constitution of Government, as they shall judge best calculated to promote the happiness of this State; and when compleated, to cause the same to be printed in all the *Boston* News-Papers, and also in Hand-Bills, one of which to be transmitted to the Selectmen of each town, or the Committee of each plantation, to be by them laid before their respective towns or plantations, at a regular meeting of the inhabitants thereof, to be called for that purpose; in order to its being, by each town and plantation, duly considered. And a return of their approbation or disapprobation to be made into the Secretary's Office of this State, at a reasonable time to be fixed on by the General Court, specifying the numbers present in such meeting, voting for, and those voting against the same: And if, upon a fair examination of the said returns by the General Court, or such Committee as they shall appoint for that purpose, it shall appear, that the said Form of Government is approved of by at least two thirds of those who are free, and twenty one years of age, belonging to this State, and present in the several meetings, then the General Court shall be impowered to establish the same as the Constitution and Form of Government of the State of *Massachusetts Bay*, according to which the inhabitants thereof shall be governed in all succeeding generations, unless the same shall be altered by their own express direction, or that of at least two thirds of them. And it is further recommended to the Selectmen of the several towns, in the return of their precepts for the choice of Representatives, to signify their having considered this Resolve, and their doings thereon."

But further, recollect, my dear countrymen, our conduct upon reading the resolution of the Honourable Congress of the 15th of May, 1776. We seized it as a Warrant that proclaimed liberty to us and our posterity for ever. It was said by some people at that time, "Let the Assembly execute that resolution;" but we spurned the advice, and we acted like men. We said, that the "Assembly was not chosen by a majority of votes in the State," owing to the inequality of our representation, and that they wanted the "confidence of the people." We thought nothing then of the loss of time occasioned by the meeting of a Conference of Committees, to settle the mode and time of chusing a Convention. The delay of months, the distractions of the State, and the danger of an invasion, were thought to be trifling when compared with the prospect of a good Constitution, that should *immediately* collect and exert the Whig strength of the State.

Thus have I finished my observations upon the Constitution of Pennsylvania. I have taken notice only of its most essential defects, and have aimed to discuss them with candour. The occasional remarks upon the proceedings of the Assembly, are to be charged entirely to the faults of the Constitution.— I believe the gentlemen in power have nothing in view but the freedom and independance of the State; and such has been the zeal and integrity of many of them in the pursuit of those great objects, that it gives me pain to reflect, that I have been obliged to differ from them in the best means of obtaining them. . . .

SOURCE: "Observations upon the present government of Pennsylvania. . . ." In the digital collection *Evans Early American Imprint Collection*. https://name.umdl.umich.edu/N12353.0001.001. University of Michigan Library Digital Collections. Accessed December 24, 2024.

2. THOMAS JEFFERSON
DRAFT OF CONSTITUTION FOR VIRGINIA
(BEFORE JUNE 13, 1776)

Thomas Jefferson was born in Albemarle County in Virginia (1743), and he died on his plantation estate at Monticello (1826). Jefferson was a planter, lawyer, architect, political philosopher, politician, statesman, diplomat, second vice-president of the United States, third president (1801-1809), and founding father. He attended the College of William and Mary, where he was introduced to the great Enlightenment philosophers of the seventeenth and eighteenth centuries. Jefferson is, of course, best known as the principal author of the Declaration of Independence. In June 1776, the young Virginian was in Philadelphia as a delegate from Virginia to the Continental Congress. At virtually the same that he was writing a draft of the Declaration of Independence, Jefferson also found the time to write a draft constitution for Virginia. Jefferson's draft is notable for its clear statement promoting separation of powers and a bicameral legislature. The most unique feature of Jefferson's draft constitution was its inclusion of a clause which provided the people the ability to alter or repeal the constitution through the calling of county conventions.

A *Bill* for new-modelling the form of Government and for establishing the Fundamental principles thereof in future.

Whereas George Guelf king of Great Britain and Ireland and Elector of Hanover, heretofore entrusted with the exercise of the kingly office in this government hath endeavored to pervert the same into a detestable and insupportable tyranny; . . .

Be it therefore enacted by the authority of the people that the said, George Guelf be, and he hereby is deposed from the kingly office within this government and absolutely divested of all it's rights, powers, and prerogatives: and that he and his descendants and all persons acting by or through him, and all other persons whatsoever shall be and forever remain incapable of the same: and that the said office shall henceforth cease and never more either in name or substance be re-established within this colony.

And be it further enacted by the authority aforesaid that the following fundamental laws and principles of government shall henceforth be established.

The Legislative, Executive and Judiciary offices shall be kept forever separate; no person exercising the one shall be capable of appointment to the others, or to either of them.

LEGISLATIVE

Legislation shall be exercised by two separate houses, to wit a house of Representatives, and a house of Senators, which shall be called the General Assembly of Virginia.

HOUSE. OF REPRESENTATIVES

The sd house of Representatives shall be composed of persons chosen by the people annually on the [1st day of October] and shall meet in General assembly on the [1st day of November] following and so from time to time on their own adjournments, or at any time when summoned by the Administrator and shall continue sitting so long as they shall think the publick service requires.

Vacancies in the said house by death or disqualification shall be filled by the electors under a warrant from the Speaker of the said house.

ELECTORS

All male persons of full age and sane mind having a freehold estate in [one fourth of an acre] of land in any town, or in [25] acres of land in the country, and all elected persons resident in the colony who shall have paid scot and lot to government the last [two years] shall have right to give their vote in the election of their respective representatives. And every person so qualified to elect shall be capable of being elected, provided he shall have given no bribe either directly or indirectly to any elector, and shall take an oath of fidelity to the state and of duty in his office, before he enters on the exercise thereof. During his continuance in the said office he shall hold no public pension nor post of profit, either himself, or by another for his use.

The number of Representatives for each county or borough shall be so proportioned to the numbers of it's qualified electors that the whole number of representatives shall not exceed [300] nor be less than [125.] for the present there shall be one representative for every [ ] qualified electors in each county or borough: but whenever this or any future proportion shall be likely to exceed or fall short of the limits beforementioned, it shall be again adjusted by the house of representatives.

The house of Representatives when met shall be free to act according to their own judgment and conscience.

SENATE

The Senate shall consist of not less than [15] nor more than [50] members who shall be appointed by the house of Representatives. One third of them shall be removed out of office by lot at the end of the first [three] years and their places be supplied by a new appointment; one other third shall be removed by lot in like manner at the end of the second [three] years and their places be supplied by a new appointment; after which one third shall be removed annually at the end of every [three] years according to seniority. When once removed, they shall be forever incapable of being re-appointed to that house. Their qualifications shall be an oath of fidelity to the state, and of duty in their office, the being [31] years of age at the least, and the having given no bribe directly or indirectly to obtain their appointment. While in the senatorial office they shall be incapable of holding any public pension or post of profit either themselves, or by others for their use.

The judges of the General court and of the High court of Chancery shall have session and deliberative voice, but not suffrage in the house of Senators.

The Senate and the house of representatives shall each of them have power to originate and amend bills; save only that bills for levying money bills shall be originated and amended by the representatives only: the assent of both houses shall be requisite to pass a law.

The General assembly shall have no power to pass any law inflicting death for any crime, excepting murder, & such those offences in the military service for which they shall think punishment by death absolutely necessary: and all capital punishments in other cases are hereby abolished. Nor shall they have power to prescribe torture in any case whatever: nor shall there be power anywhere to pardon crimes or to remit fines or punishments: nor shall any law for levying money be in force longer than [ten years] from the time of its commencement.

[Two thirds] of the members of either house shall be a Quorum to proceed to business.

EXECUTIVE

The executive powers shall be exercised in manner following.

ADMINISTRATOR

One person to be called the [Administrator] shall be annually appointed by the house of Representatives on the second day of their first session, who after having acted [one] year shall be incapable of being again appointed to that office until he shall have been out of the same [three] years.

DEPUTY ADMINISTRATOR

Under him shall be appointed by the same house and at the same time, a Deputy-Administrator to assist his principal in the discharge of his office, and to succeed, in case of his death before the year shall have expired, to the whole powers thereof during the residue of the year.

The administrator shall possess the power formerly held by the king: save only that, he shall be bound by acts of legislature tho' not expressly named;

> he shall have no negative on the bills of the Legislature;
>
> he shall be liable to action, tho' not to personal restraint for private duties or wrongs;
>
> he shall not possess the prerogatives;
>
> of dissolving, proroguing or adjourning either house of Assembly;
>
> of declaring war or concluding peace;
>
> of issuing letters of marque or reprisal;
>
> of raising or introducing armed forces, building armed vessels, forts or strongholds;
>
> of coining monies or regulating their values;
>
> of regulating weights and measures;
>
> of erecting courts, offices, boroughs, corporations, fairs, markets, ports, beacons, lighthouses, seamarks.
>
> of laying embargoes, or prohibiting the exportation of any commodity for a longer space than [40] days.
>
> of retaining or recalling a member of the state but by legal process pro delicto vel contractu.
>
> of making denizens.
>
> of pardoning crimes, or remitting fines or punishments.
>
> of creating dignities or granting rights of precedence.

But these powers shall be exercised by the legislature alone, and excepting also those powers which by these fundamentals are given to others, or abolished.

Privy Council

A Privy council shall be annually appointed by the house of representatives whose duties it shall be to give advice to the Administrator when called on by him. With them the Deputy Administrator shall have session and suffrage.

Delegates

Delegates to represent this colony in the American Congress shall be appointed when necessary by the house of Representatives. After serving [one] year in that office they shall not be capable of being re-appointed to the same during an interval of [one] year.

Treasurer

A Treasurer shall be appointed by the house of Representatives who shall issue no money but by authority of both houses.

ATTORNEY GENERAL

An Attorney general shall be appointed by the house of Representatives

HIGH SHERIFFS, &C.

High Sheriffs and Coroners of counties shall be annually elected by those qualified to vote for representatives: and no person who shall have served as high sheriff [one] year shall be capable of being re-elected to the said office in the same county till he shall have been out of office [five] years.

Other Officers

All other Officers civil and military shall be appointed by the Administrator; but such appointment shall be subject to the negative of the Privy council, saving however to the Legislature a power of transferring to any other persons the appointment of such officers or any of them.

JUDICIARY

The Judiciary powers shall be exercised
    First, by County courts and other inferior jurisdictions:
    Secondly, by a General court & a High court of Chancery:
    Thirdly, by a Court of Appeals.

COUNTY COURTS, &C.

The judges of the county courts and other inferior jurisdictions shall be appointed by the Administrator, subject to the negative of the privy council. They shall not be fewer than [five] in number. Their jurisdictions shall be defined from time to time by the legislature: and they shall be removable for misbehavior by the court of Appeals.

GENL. COURT AND HIGH CT. OF CHANCERY

The Judges of the General court and of the High court of Chancery shall be appointed by the Administrator and Privy council. If kept united they shall be [5] in number, if separate, there shall be [5] for the General court & [3] for the High court of Chancery. The appointment shall be made from the faculty of the law, and of such persons of that faculty as shall have actually exercised the same at the bar of some court or courts of record within this colony for [seven] years. They shall hold their commissions during good behavior, for breach of which they shall be removable by the court of Appeals. Their jurisdiction shall be defined from time to time by the Legislature.

COURT OF APPEALS

The Court of Appeals shall consist of not less than [7] nor more than [11] members, to be appointed by the house of Representatives: they shall hold their offices during good behavior, for breach of which they shall be removable by an act of the legislature only. Their jurisdiction shall be to determine finally all causes removed before them from the General Court or High Court of Chancery, or of the county courts or other inferior jurisdictions for misbehavior: [to try impeachments against high offenders lodged before them by the house of representatives for such crimes as shall hereafter be precisely defined by the Legislature, and for the punishment of which, the said legislature shall have previously prescribed certain and determinate pains.] In this court the judges of the General court and High court of Chancery shall have session and deliberative voice, but no suffrage.

JURIES

All facts in causes whether of Chancery, Common, Ecclesiastical, or Marine law, shall be tried by a jury upon evidence given viva voce, in open court: but where witnesses are out of the colony or unable to attend through sickness or other invincible necessity, their deposition may be submitted to the credit of the jury.

FINES, &C.

All Fines or Amercements shall be assessed, & Terms of imprisonment for Contempts & Misdemeanors shall be fixed by the verdict of a Jury.

PROCESS

All Process Original & Judicial shall run in the name of the court from which it issues.

QUORUM

Two thirds of the members of the General court, High court of Chancery, or Court of Appeals shall be a Quorum to proceed to business.

RIGHTS, PRIVATE AND PUBLIC

LANDS

Unappropriated or Forfeited lands shall be appropriated by the Administrator with the consent of the Privy council.

Every person of full age neither owning nor having owned [50] acres of land, shall be entitled to an appropriation of [50] acres or to so much as shall make up what he owns or has owned [50] acres in full and absolute dominion. And no other person shall be capable of taking an appropriation.

Lands heretofore holden of the crown in fee simple, and those hereafter to be appropriated shall be holden in full and absolute dominion, of no superior whatever.

No lands shall be appropriated until purchased of the Indian native proprietors; nor shall any purchases be made of them but on behalf of the public, by authority of acts of the General assembly to be passed for every purchase specially.

The territories contained within the charters erecting the colonies of Maryland, Pennsylvania, North and South Carolina, are hereby ceded, released, & forever confirmed to the people of those colonies respectively, with all the rights of property, jurisdiction and government and all other rights whatsoever which might at any time heretofore have been claimed by this colony. The Western and Northern extent of this country shall in all other respects stand as fixed by the charter of until by act of the Legislature one or more territories shall be laid off Westward of the Alleghaney mountains for new colonies, which colonies shall be established on the same fundamental laws contained in this instrument, and shall be free and independent of this colony and of all the world.

Descents shall go according to the laws Gavelkind, save only that females shall have equal rights with males.

SLAVES

No person hereafter coming into this county shall be held within the same in slavery under any pretext whatever.

NATURALIZATION

All persons who by their own oath or affirmation, or by other testimony shall give satisfactory proof to any court of record in this colony that they propose to reside in the same [7] years at the least and who shall subscribe the fundamental laws, shall be considered as residents and entitled to all the rights of persons natural born.

RELIGION

All persons shall have full and free liberty of religious opinion; nor shall any be compelled to frequent or maintain any religious institution.

ARMS

No freeman shall be debarred the use of arms [within his own lands].

STANDING ARMIES

There shall be no standing army but in time of actual war.

FREE PRESS

Printing presses shall be free, except so far as by commission of private injury cause may be given of private action.

FORFEITURES

All Forfeitures heretofore going to the king, shall go the state; save only such as the legislature may hereafter abolish.

WRECKS

The royal claim to Wrecks, waifs, strays, treasure-trove, royal mines, royal fish, royal birds, are declared to have been usurpations on common right.

SALARIES

No Salaries or Perquisites shall be given to any officer but by some future act of the legislature. No salaries shall be given to the Administrator, members of the legislative houses, judges of the court of Appeals, judges of the County courts, or other inferior jurisdictions, Privy counsellors, or Delegates to the American Congress: but the reasonable expences of the Administrator, members of the house of representatives, judges of the court of Appeals, Privy counsellors, & Delegates for subsistence while acting in the duties of their office, may be borne by the public, if the legislature shall so direct.

QUALIFICATIONS

No person shall be capable of acting in any office Civil, Military [or Ecclesiastical] The Qualifications of all not otherwise directed, shall be an oath of fidelity to state and the having given no bribe to obtain their office who shall have given any bribe to obtain such office, or who shall not previously take an oath of fidelity to the state.

None of these fundamental laws and principles of government shall be repealed or altered, but by the personal consent of the people on summons to meet in their respective counties on one and the same day by an act of Legislature to be passed for every special occasion: and if in such county meetings the people of two thirds of the counties shall give their suffrage for any particular alteration or repeal referred to them by the said act, the same shall be accordingly repealed or altered, and such repeal or alteration shall take it's place among these fundamentals and stand on the same footing with them, in lieu of the article repealed or altered.

The laws heretofore in force in this colony shall remain in force, except so far as they are altered by the foregoing fundamental laws, or so far as they may be hereafter altered by acts of the Legislature.

SOURCE: Extracts taken from "Draft Constitution for Virginia 1776," Yale Law School, The Avalon Project: https://avalon.law.yale.edu/18th_century/jeffcons.asp

3. THOMAS JEFFERSON
SELECTION FROM *NOTES ON THE STATE OF VIRGINIA*
1785

Virginia's revolutionary state constitution was drafted by George Mason and adopted in June 1776. Like all the other state constitutions drafted between 1776 and 1780, the Virginia constitution was an experiment conducted during a perilous time when the colonies were preparing for war and about to declare their independence from Great Britain. Not surprisingly, none of the constitutions were without various flaws. During his time as Governor of Virginia (1779-1781), Jefferson saw firsthand the vices of the Virginia constitution. In the following selection from his Notes on the State of Virginia *first published in 1785, Jefferson identified six principal flaws in the Virginia constitution: 1) too many ordinary citizens were unrepresented in the legislature; 2) representation in the legislature was unequal between districts and regions in the state: 3) the interests and principles of the House of Delegates and the Senate were too similar; 4) too much power—legislative, executive, and judicial—was concentrated in the legislative body; 5) the constitution, because it had been written by an ordinary legislative body, could be changed or suspended at the will of any sitting legislature; and 6) the assembly had the power of determining its own quorum, which could be reduced to the rule of a few (an oligarchy) or even one (a dictator). Jefferson concluded his critique of the Virginia constitution by suggesting that it could fixed by calling a convention to "amend its defects."*

QUERY XIII: *The constitution of the State and its several charters?*

. . . In each state separately a new form of government was established. Of ours particularly the following are the outlines. The executive powers are lodged in the hands of a governor, chosen annually, and incapable of acting more than three years in seven. He is assisted by a council of eight members. The judiciary powers are divided among several courts, as will be hereafter explained. Legislation is exercised by two houses of assembly, the one called the house of delegates, composed of two members from each county, chosen annually by the citizens, possessing an estate for life in 100 acres of uninhabited land, or 25 acres with a house on it, or in a house or lot in some town: the other called the Senate, consisting of 24 members, chosen quadrennially by the same electors, who for this purpose are distributed into 24 districts. The concurrence of both houses is necessary to the passage of a law. They have the appointment of the governor and council, the judges of the superior courts, auditors, attorney general, treasurer, register of the land office, and delegates to congress. As the dismemberment of the state had never had its confirmation, but, on the contrary, had always been the subject of protestation and complaint, that it might never be in our own power to raise scruples on that subject, or to disturb the harmony of our new confederacy, the grants to Maryland, Pennsylvania and the two Carolinas were ratified.

This constitution was formed when we were new and unexperienced in the science of government. It was the first, too, which was formed in the whole United States. No wonder then that time and trial have discovered very capital defects in it.

1. The majority of the men in the state, who pay and fight for its support, are unrepresented in the legislature, the roll of freeholders entitled to vote not including generally the half of those on the roll of the militia, or of the tax-gatherers.

2. Among those who share the representation, the shares are very unequal. Thus the county of Warwick, with only one hundred fighting men, has an equal representation with the county of Loudon, which has 1746. So that every man in Warwick has as much influence in the government as 17 men in Loudon. But lest it should be thought that an equal interspersion of small among large counties, through the whole state, may prevent any danger of injury to particular parts of it, we will divide it into districts, and shew the proportions of land, of fighting men, and of representation in each:

Between the sea - coast and falls of the rivers	11,205	19,012	71	12
Between the falls of the rivers and Blue Ridge of mountains	18,759	18,828	46	8
Between the Blue Ridge and the Alleghany	11,911	7,673	16	2
Between the Alleghany and Ohio	79,650	4,458	16	2
Total	121,525	49,971	149	24

An inspection of this table will supply the place of commentaries on it. It will appear at once that nineteen thousand men, living below the falls of the rivers, possess half of the senate, and want four members only of possessing a majority of the house of delegates; a want more than supplied by the vicinity of their situation to the seat of government, and of course the greater degree of convenience and punctuality with which their members may and will attend in the legislature. These nineteen thousand, therefore, living in one part of the country, give law to upwards of thirty thousand living in another, and appoint all their chief officers executive and judiciary. From the difference of their situation and circumstances, their interests will often be very different.

3. The senate is, by its constitution, too homogenous with the house of delegates. Being chosen by the same electors, at the same time, and out of the same subjects, the choice falls of course on men of the same description. The purpose of establishing different houses of legislation is to introduce the influence of different interests or different principles. Thus in Great Britain it is said their constitution relies on the house of commons for honesty, and the lords for wisdom; which would be a rational reliance, if honesty were to be bought with money, and if wisdom were hereditary. In some of the American States, the delegates and senators are so chosen, as that the first represent the persons, and the second the property of the State. But with us, wealth and wisdom have equal chance for admission into both houses. We do not, therefore, derive from the separation of our legislature into two houses, those benefits which a proper complication of principles is capable of producing, and those which alone can compensate the evils which may be produced by their dissensions.

4. All the powers of government, legislative, executive, and judiciary, result to the legislative body. The concentrating these in the same hands is precisely the definition of despotic government. It will be no alleviation that these powers will be exercised by a plurality of hands, and not by a single one. 173 despots would surely be as oppressive as one. Let those who doubt it turn their eyes on the republic of Venice. As little will it avail us that they are chosen by ourselves. An *elective despotism* was not the government we fought for, but one which should not only be founded on free principles, but in which the powers of government should be so divided and balanced among several bodies of magistracy, as that no one could transcend their legal limits, without being effectually checked and restrained by the others. For this reason that convention, which passed the ordinance of government laid its foundation on this basis, that the legislative, executive and judiciary departments should be separate and distinct, so that no person should exercise the powers of more than one of them at the same time. But no barrier was provided between these several powers. The judiciary and executive members were left dependent on the legislative, for their subsistence in office, and some of them for their continuance in it. If therefore the legislature assumes executive and judiciary powers, no opposition is likely to be made; nor, if made, can it be effectual; because in that case they may put their proceedings into the form of an act of assembly, which will render them obligatory on the other branches. They have accordingly in many instances, decided rights which should have been left to judiciary controversy: and the direction of the executive, during the whole time of their session, is becoming habitual and familiar. And this is done with no ill intention. The views of the present

members are perfectly upright. When they are led out of their regular province, it is by art in others, and inadvertence in themselves. And this will probably be the case for some time to come. But it will not be a very long time. Mankind soon learn to make interested uses of every right and power which they possess, or may assume. The public money and public liberty, intended to have been deposited with three branches of magistracy, but found inadvertently to be in the hands of one only, will soon be discovered to be sources of wealth and dominion to those who hold them; distinguished, too, by this tempting circumstance, that they are the instrument, as well as the object, of acquisition. With money we will get men, said Cæsar, and with men we will get money. Nor should our assembly be deluded by the integrity of their own purposes, and conclude that these unlimited powers will never be abused, because themselves are not disposed to abuse them. They should look forward to a time, and that not a distant one, when a corruption in this, as in the country from which we derive our origin, will have seized the heads of government, and be spread by them through the body of the people; when they will purchase the voices of the people, and make them pay the price. Human nature is the same on every side of the Atlantic, and will be alike influenced by the same causes. The time to guard against corruption and tyranny, is before they shall have gotten hold of us. It is better to keep the wolf out of the fold, than to trust to drawing his teeth and talons after he shall have entered. To render these considerations the more cogent, we must observe in addition:

5. That the ordinary legislature may alter the constitution itself. On the discontinuance of assemblies, it became necessary to substitute in their place some other body, competent to the ordinary business of government, and to the calling forth the powers of the State for the maintenance of our opposition to Great Britain. Conventions were therefore introduced, consisting of two delegates from each county, meeting together and forming one house, on the plan of the former house of Burgesses, to whose places they succeeded. These were at first chosen anew for every particular session. But in March 1775, they recommended to the people to choose a convention, which should continue in office a year. This was done, accordingly, in April 1775, and in the July following that convention passed an ordinance for the election of delegates in the month of April annually. It is well known, that in July 1775, a separation from Great Britain and establishment of republican government, had never yet entered into any person's mind. A convention, therefore, chosen under that ordinance, cannot be said to have been chosen for the purposes which certainly did not exist in the minds of those who passed it. Under this ordinance, at the annual election in April 1776, a convention for the year was chosen. Independance, and the establishment of a new form of government, were not even yet the objects of the people at large. One extract from the pamphlet called Common sense had appeared in the Virginia papers in February, and copies of the pamphlet itself had got in a few

hands.[1] But the idea had not been opened to the mass of the people in April, much less can it be said that they had made up their minds in its favor. So that the electors of April 1776, no more than the legislators of July 1775, not thinking of independance and a permanent republic, could not mean to vest in these delegates powers of establishing them, or any authorities other than those of the ordinary legislature. So far as a temporary organization of government was necessary to render our opposition energetic, so far their organization was valid. But they received in their creation no powers but what were given to every legislature before and since. They could not, therefore, pass an act transcendent to the powers of other legislatures. If the present assembly pass an act, and declare it shall be irrevocable by subsequent assemblies, the declaration is merely void, and the act repealable, as other acts are. So far, and no farther authorized, they organized the government by the ordinance entituled a Constitution or Form of government. It pretends to no higher authority than the other ordinance of the same session; it does not say that it shall be perpetual; that it shall be unalterable by other legislatures; that it shall be transcendent above the powers of those who they knew would have equal power with themselves. Not only the silence of the instrument is a proof they thought it would be alterable, but their own practice also; for this very convention, meeting as a House of Delegates in General assembly with the Senate in the autumn of that year, passed acts of assembly in contradiction of their ordinance of government; and every assembly from that time to this has done the same. I am safe therefore in the position that the constitution itself is alterable by the ordinary legislature. Though this opinion seems founded on the first elements of common sense, yet is the contrary maintained by some persons. I. Because, say they, the conventions were vested with every power necessary to make effectual opposition to Great Britain. But to complete this argument, they must go on, and say further, that effectual opposition could not be made to Great Britain without establishing a form of government perpetual and unalterable by the legislature; which is not true. An opposition which at some time or other was to come to an end, could not need a perpetual institution to carry it on: and a government amendable as its defects should be discovered, was likely to make effectual resistance, as one that should be unalterably wrong. Besides, the assemblies were as much vested with all powers requisite for resistance as the Conventions were. If therefore these powers included that of modelling the form of government in the one case, they did so in the other. The assemblies then as well as the conventions may model the government; that is, they may alter the ordinance of government. 2. They urge that if the convention had meant that this instrument should be alterable, as their other ordinances were, they would have called it an ordinance; but they have called it a *constitution,* which *ex vi termini,* means "an act above the power of the ordinary legislature." I answer that *constitutio, constitutum, statutum, lex,* are convertible terms. "*Constitutio* dicitur jus quod a principe conditur." "*Constitutum,* quod ab imperatoribus rescriptum statutumve est." "*Statutum,* idem quod lex." Calvini Lexicon juridicum. *Constitution* and *statute* were originally terms of the[1] civil law, and from thence introduced by Ecclesiastics into the English law. Thus in the statute 25 Hen. VIII. c. 19, §. 1, "*Constitutions* and *ordinances*" are used as synonimous. The term *constitution* has many other significations in physics and politics; but in Jurisprudence, whenever it is applied to any act of the legislature, it invariably means a statue, law, or ordinance, which is the present case. No inference then of a different meaning can be drawn from the adoption of this title: on the contrary, we might conclude that, by their affixing to it a term synonimous with ordinance or statute, they meant it to be an ordinance or statute. But of what consequence is their meaning, where their power is denied? If they meant to do more than they had power to do, did this give them power? It is not the name, but the authority which renders an act obligatory. Lord Coke says, 'an article of the statute, 11. R. II. c. 5. that no person should attempt to revoke any ordinance then made, is repealed, for that such restraint is against the jurisdiction and power of the parliament.' 4. inst. 42. and again, 'though divers parliaments, have attempted to restrain subsequent parliaments, yet could they never effect it; for the latter parliament hath ever power to abrogate, suspend, qualify, explain, or make void the former in the whole or in any part thereof, notwithstanding any words of restraint, prohibition, or penalty, in the former; for it is a maxim in the laws of the parliament, 'quod leges posteriores priores contrarias abrogant.' 4. inst. 43.—To get rid of the magic supposed to be in the word *constitution,* let us translate it into its definition as given by those who think it above the power of the law; and let us suppose the convention, instead of saying, 'We the ordinary legislature, establish a *constitution,*' had said, 'We the ordinary legislature, establish an act *above the power of the ordinary legislature.*' Does not this expose the absurdity of the attempt? 3. But, say they, the people have acquiesced, and this has given it an authority superior to the laws. It is true that the people did not rebel against it: and was that a time for the people to rise in rebellion? Should a prudent acquiescence, at a critical time, be construed into a confirmation of every illegal thing done during that period? Besides, why should they rebel? At an annual election they had chosen delegates for the year, to exercise the ordinary powers of legislation, and to manage the great contest in which they were engaged. These delegates thought the contest would be best managed by an organized government. They therefore, among others, passed an ordinance of government. They did not presume to call it perpetual and unalterable. They well knew they had no power to make it so; that our choice of them had been for no such purpose, and at a time when we could have no such purpose in contemplation. Had an unalterable form of government been meditated, perhaps we should have chosen a different set of people. There was no cause then for the people to rise in rebellion. But to what dangerous lengths will this argument lead? Did the acquiescence of the colonies under the various acts of power exercised by Great Britain in our infant state, confirm these acts, and so far invest them with the authority of the people as to render them unalterable, and our present resistance wrong? On every unauthoritative exercise of power by the legislature must the people rise in rebellion, or their silence be construed into a surrender of that power to them? If so, how many rebellions should we have had already? One certainly for every session of assembly. The other states in the union have been of opinion that to render a form of government unalterable by ordinary acts of assembly, the people must delegate persons with special powers. They have accordingly chosen special conventions to form and fix their governments. The individuals then who maintain the contrary opinion in this country, should have the modesty to suppose it possible that they may be wrong, and the rest of America right. But if there be only a possibility of their being wrong, if only a plausible doubt remains of the validity of the ordinance of government, is it not better to remove that doubt by placing it on a bottom which none will dispute? If they be right we shall only have the unnecessary trouble of meeting once in convention. If they be wrong, they expose us to the hazard of having no fundamental rights at all. True it is, this is no time for deliberating on forms of government. While an enemy is within our bowels, the first object is to expel him. But when this shall be done, when peace shall be established, and leisure given us for intrenching within good forms, the rights for which we have bled, let no man be found indolent enough to decline a little more trouble for placing them beyond the reach of question. If anything more be requisite to produce a conviction of the expediency of calling a convention at a proper season to fix our form of government, let it be the reflection:

6. That the assembly exercises a power of determining the quorum of their own body which may legislate for us. After the establishment of the new form they adhered to the *Lex majoris partis,* founded in common law as well as common right. It is the natural law of every assembly of men, whose numbers are not fixed by any other law. They continued for some time to require the presence of a majority of their whole number, to pass an act. But the British parliament fixes its own quorum; our former assemblies fixed their own quorum; and one precedent in favor of power is stronger than an hundred against it. The house of delegates, therefore, have lately voted that, during the present dangerous invasion, forty members shall be a house to proceed to business. They have been moved to this by the fear of not being able to collect a house. But this danger could not authorize them to call that a house which was none; and if they may fix it at one number, they may at another, till it loses its fundamental character of being a representative body. As this vote expires with the present invasion, it is probable the former rule will be permitted to revive; because at present no ill is meant. The power, however, of fixing their own quorum has been avowed, and a precedent set. From forty it may be reduced to four, and from four to one; from a house to a committee, from a committee to a chairman or speaker, and thus an oligarchy or

monarchy be substituted under forms supposed to be regular. '*Omnia mala exempla ex bonis orta sunt; sed ubi imperium ad ignaros aut minus bonos pervenit, novum illud exemplum ab dignis et idoneis ad indignos et non idoneos fertur.*' When, therefore, it is considered, that there is no legal obstacle to the assumption by the assembly of all the powers legislative, executive, and judiciary, and that these may come to the hands of the smallest rag of delegation, surely the people will say, and their representatives, while yet they have honest representatives, will advise them to say, that they will not acknowledge as laws any acts not considered and assented to by the major part of their delegates.

In enumerating the defects of the constitution, it would be wrong to count among them what is only the error of particular persons. In December 1776, our circumstances being much distressed, it was proposed in the house of delegates to create a *dictator,* invested with every power legislative, executive, and judiciary, civil and military, of life and of death, over our persons and over our properties: and in June 1781,again under calamity, the same proposition was repeated, and wanted a few votes only of being passed.— One who entered into this contest from a pure love of liberty, and a sense of injured rights, who determined to make every sacrifice, and to meet every danger, for the re-establishment of those rights on a firm basis, who did not mean to expend his blood and substance for the wretched purpose of changing this master for that, but to place the powers of governing him in a plurality of hands of his own choice, so that the corrupt will of no one man might in future oppress him, must stand confounded and dismayed when he is told, that a considerable portion of that plurality had meditated the surrender of them into a single hand, and, in lieu of a limited monarch, to deliver him over to a despotic one! How must he[1] find his efforts and sacrifices abused and baffled, if he may still, by a single vote, be laid prostrate at the feet of one man! In God's name, from whence have they derived this power? Is it from our ancient laws? None such can be produced. Is it from any principle in our new constitution expressed or implied? Every lineament of that expressed or implied, is in full opposition to it. Its fundamental principle is, that the state shall be governed as a commonwealth. It provides a republican organization, proscribes under the name of *prerogative* the exercise of all powers undefined by the laws; places on this basis the whole system of our laws; and by consolidating them together, chooses that they shall be left to stand or fall together, never providing for any circumstances, nor admitting that such could arise, wherein either should be suspended; no, not for a moment. Our antient laws expressly declare, that those who are but delegates themselves shall not delegate to others powers which require judgment and integrity in their exercise. Or was this proposition moved on a supposed right in the movers, of abandoning their posts in a moment of distress? The same laws forbid the abandonment of that post, even on ordinary occasions; and much more a transfer of their powers into other hands and other forms, without consulting the people. They never admit the idea that these, like sheep or cattle, may be given from hand to hand without an appeal to their own will.— Was it from the necessity of the case? Necessities which dissolve a government, do not convey its authority to an oligarchy or a monarchy. They throw back, into the hands of the people, the powers they had delegated, and leave them as individuals to shift for themselves. A leader may offer, but not impose himself, nor be imposed on them. Much less can their necks be submitted to his sword, their breath be held at his will or caprice. The necessity which should operate these tremendous effects should at least be palpable and irresistible. Yet in both instances, where it was feared, or pretended with us, it was belied by the event. It was belied, too, by the preceding experience of our sister states, several of whom had grappled through greater difficulties without abandoning their forms of government. When the proposition was first made, Massachusets had found even the government of committees sufficient to carry them through an invasion. But we at the time of that proposition, were under no invasion. When the second was made, there had been added to this example those of Rhode-Island, New-York, New-Jersey, and Pennsylvania, in all of which the republican form had been found equal to the task of carrying them through the severest trials. In this state alone did there exist so little virtue, that fear was to be fixed in the hearts of the people, and to become the motive of their exertions, and the principle of their government? The very thought alone was treason against the people; was treason against mankind in general; as rivetting forever the chains which bow down their necks by giving to their oppressors a proof, which they would have trumpeted through the universe, of the imbecility of republican government, in times of pressing danger, to shield them from harm. Those who assume the right of giving away the reins of government in any case, must be sure that the herd, whom they hand on to the rods and hatchet of the dictator, will lay their necks on the block when he shall nod to them. But if our assemblies supposed such a resignation in the people, I hope they mistook their character. I am of opinion, that the government, instead of being braced and invigorated for greater exertions under their difficulties, would have been thrown back upon the bungling machinery of county committees for administration, till a convention could have been called, and its wheels again set into regular motion. What a cruel moment was this for creating such an embarrassment, for putting to the proof the attachment of our countrymen to republican government! Those who meant well, of the advocates for this measure, (and most of them meant well, for I know them personally, had been their fellow-labourers in the common cause, and had often proved the purity of their principles,) had been seduced in their judgment by the example of an antient republic, whose constitution and circumstances were fundamentally different. They had sought this precedent in the history of Rome, where alone it was to be found, and where at length, too, it had proved fatal. They had taken it from a republic rent by the most bitter factions and tumults, where the

government was of a heavy-handed unfeeling aristocracy, over a people fe-
rocious, and rendered desperate by poverty and wretchedness; tumults
which could not be allayed under the most trying circumstances, but by the
omnipotent hand of a single despot. Their constitution, therefore, allowed a
temporary tyrant to be erected, under the name of a Dictator; and that temporary tyrant, after a few examples, became perpetual. They misapplied this
precedent to a people mild in their dispositions, patient under their trial,
united for the public liberty, and affectionate to their leaders. But if from the
constitution of the Roman government there resulted to their Senate a power
of submitting all their rights to the will of one man, does it follow that the
assembly of Virginia have the same authority? What clause in our constitution has substituted that of Rome, by way of residuary provision, for all cases
not otherwise provided for? Or if they may step ad libitum into any other
form of government for precedents to rule us by, for what oppression may
not a precedent be found in this world of the bellum omnium in omnia?
Searching for the foundations of this proposition, I can find none which may
pretend a colour of right or reason, but the defect before developed, that
there being no barrier between the legislative, executive, and judiciary departments, the legislature may seize the whole: that having seized it, and possessing a right to fix their own quorum, they may reduce that quorum to one,
whom they may call a chairman, speaker, dictator, or by any other name they
please.—Our situation is indeed perilous, and I hope my countrymen will be
sensible of it, and will apply, at a proper season, the proper remedy; which is
a convention to fix the constitution, to amend its defects, to bind up the several branches of government by certain laws, which, when they transgress,
their acts shall become nullities; to render unnecessary an appeal to the people, or in other words a rebellion, on every infraction of their rights, on the
peril that their acquiescence shall be construed into an intention to surrender those rights.

SOURCE: Andrew A. Lipscomb and Albert Ellery Bergh, ed., *The Works of
Thomas Jefferson*, Memorial Edition, 20 vols., (Washington, DC: Thomas Jefferson Memorial Association, 1903), 2:159-178.

4. THOMAS JEFFERSON
DRAFT OF A CONSTITUTION FOR VIRGINIA
1783

In 1783, anticipating that Virginia would either scrap or revise its 1776 constitution, Thomas Jefferson took up his pen and drafted a new constitution for his state in 1783. Printed as an appendix to the Notes on the State of Virginia, *this new draft constitution offered a new frame of government without the defects of the 1776 constitution. The 1783 constitution provided for broad-based suffrage and equitable representation, corresponding to the number electors in each district. Jefferson's constitution called for triennial elections for the House of Delegates instead of annually, and he lengthened the term of office for senators from one to six years. Jefferson also gave his Governor more independence (no doubt reflecting his own recent experience as Governor) by increasing the executive's term of office to a single five-year term. Jefferson's 1783 draft constitution omitted a bill of rights. In line with the growing American movement to create written constitutions as fundamental law, Jefferson's proposed constitution prohibited the legislature from infringing on the constitution. Jefferson was a constitutionalist first and a republican second.*

It is known to you and to the world that the government of Great Britain, with which the American states were not long since connected, assumed over them an authority which to some of them appeared unwarrantable and oppressive; that they endeavoured to enforce this authority by arms, and that the states of New Hampshire, Massachusets, Rhode island, Connecticut, New York, New Jersey, Pennsylvania, Delaware, Maryland, Virginia, North Carolina, South Carolina and Georgia, considering resistance, with all it's train of horrors, as a lesser evil than abject submission, closed in the appeal to arms. It hath pleased the sovereign disposer of all human events, to give to this appeal an issue favourable to the rights of these states, to enable them to reject for ever all dependance on a government which had shewn itself so capable of abusing the trusts reposed in it, and to obtain from that government a solemn and explicit acknowlegement that we are free, sovereign and independant states. During the progress of that war through which we had to labour for the establishment of our rights, the legislature of the commonwealth of Virginia found it necessary to establish a form of government for preventing anarchy and pointing our efforts to the two important objects of war against our invaders and peace and happiness among ourselves. But this, like all other their acts of legislation, being subject to be changed by subsequent legislatures, possessing equal powers with themselves, it has been thought expedient that it should receive those amendments which time and trial have suggested, and be rendered permanent by a power superior to that of the ordinary legislature. The General assembly therefore of this state recommended it to the good people thereof to chuse delegates to meet in General convention with powers to form a constitution of government for them, to which all laws present and future shall be subordinate; and in compliance with this recommendation they have thought proper to make choice of us, and to vest us with powers for this purpose.

We therefore the Delegates chosen by the said good people of this state for the purpose aforesaid, and now assembled in General convention do, in execution of the authority with which we are invested, establish the following Constitution of government for the said state of Virginia.

The said state shall hereafter for ever be governed as a Commonwealth.

The Legislative, Executive, and Judiciary departments shall be separate and distinct, so that no person, or collection of persons of any one of them shall exercise any power properly belonging to either of the others, except in the instances hereinafter expressly permitted.

The Legislature shall consist of two distinct branches, the concurrence of both of which expressed on three several readings, shall be necessary to the passage of a law. One of these branches shall be called the House of Delegates, the other the Senate, and both together the General Assembly.

Delegates for the General assembly shall be chosen on the Monday preceding the 25th. day of December which shall be in the year 178 and thenceforwards triennially. But if an election cannot be concluded on that day, it may be adjourned from day to day till it can be concluded.

The number of delegates shall be so proportioned to the number of qualified electors in the whole state hat they shall never exceed 300. nor be fewer than 100. <For the> Whenever such excess or deficiency shall take place, the house of delegates so deficient or excessive, shall, notwithstanding this continue in being during its legal term; but they shall during that term, re-adjust the proportion so as to bring their number within the limits beforementioned at the ensuing election. If any county be reduced in it's qualified electors below the number necessary to send one delegate, let it be annexed to some adjoining county.

For the election of Senators, let the several counties be allotted by the <legislature> Senate from time to time into such and so many districts as they shall find best, and let each county at the time of electing it's delegates chuse Senatorial electors, qualified as themselves are, and four in number for each delegate their county is entitled to send, who shall convene and conduct themselves in such manner as the legislature shall direct with the Senatorial electors from the other counties of their district, and then chuse by ballot one Senator for every six delegates which their district is entitled to chuse. Let the Senatorial districts be divided into two classes, one of which shall be dissolved at the first ensuing general election of Delegates, the other at the next and so on alternately for ever.

All free male citizens of full age and sane mind, who for one year before shall have been resident in the county, or shall through the whole of that time have possessed therein real property of the value of or shall for the same time have been enrolled in the militia, and no others, shall have right to vote for delegates for the said county, *<and persons of the same description qualified by the like residence, property, or military condition within the district shall have right to vote for Senatorial>* and for Senatorial electors for the district. They shall give in their votes personally and by balot.

The General assembly shall meet at the place to which they shall have last adjourned themselves on the 14th. day after the day of the election of Delegates, *<and so annually on that day till the period of their dissolution. The Governor shall have pow>* and thenceforward at any other time or place on their own adjournment. But if they shall at any time adjourn for more than one year, such adjournment shall be void and they shall meet on that day twelve-month. Neither house without the concurrence of the other shall adjourn for more than one week, nor to any other place than the one at which they are sitting. The Governor shall also have power, with the advice of the council of state, to call them at any other time to the same place, or to a different one where that shall have become since the last adjournment, dangerous from an enemy or from infection.

A majority of either house shall be a Quorum and shall be requisite for doing business: but any smaller numbers which from time to time shall be thought expedient by the respective houses, shall be sufficient to call for and to punish their non-attending members and to adjourn themselves for any time not exceeding one week.

The members during their attendance on General assembly and for so long a time before and after as shall be necessary for travelling to and from the same shall be privileged from all personal restraint and assault, and shall have no other privilege whatsoever. They shall receive during the same time daily wages in gold or silver equal to the value of two bushels of wheat. This value shall be deemed one dollar by the bushel till the year 1790. in which and in every tenth year thereafter the General court at their first sessions in the year shall cause a special jury of the most respectable merchants and farmers to be summoned to declare what shall have been the averaged value of wheat during the last ten years; which averaged value shall be the measure of wages for the ten subsequent years.

Of this General assembly the Treasurer, Attorney General, Register, Ministers of the Gospel, officers of the regular armies of this state or of the United states, persons receiving salaries or emoluments from any power foreign to our Confederacy, *<persons>* those who *<shall>* are not resident in the counties for which they are chosen Delegates or districts for which they are chosen Senators, persons who shall have committed treason, felony or such other crime as would subject them to infamous punishment or who shall have been convicted by due course of law of bribery or corruption in endeavouring to procure an election to the said assembly, shall be incapable of being members. All others not herein elsewhere excluded who may elect, shall be capable of being elected thereto, and none else.

Any member of the said assembly accepting any office of profit under this state, or the United states, or any of them shall thereby vacate his seat, but shall be capable of being re-elected.

Vacancies occasioned by such disqualifications, by death, or otherwise, shall be supplied by the electors on a writ from the Speaker of the respective house.

The General assembly shall not have power to infringe this constitution; to abridge the civil rights of any person on account of his religious belief; to restrain him from professing and supporting that belief, or to compel him to contributions, other than those he shall himself have stipulated, for the support of that or any other: to ordain death for any crime but treason or murder, or offences in the military line: to pardon or give a power of pardoning persons duly convicted of treason or felony, but instead thereof they may substitute one or two new trials and no more: to pass laws for punishing actions done before the existence of such laws: to pass any bill of attainder, <or other law declaring any person guilty> of treason or felony: to prescribe torture in any case: nor to permit the introduction of any more slaves to reside in this state, or the continuance of slavery beyond the generation which shall be living on the 31st. day of December 1800; all persons born after that day being hereby declared free.

The General assembly shall have power to sever from this state all of any part of it's territory Westward of the Ohio or of the meridian of the mouth of the Great Kanhaway, and to cede to Congress 100 square miles in any other part of this state, exempted from the jurisdiction and government of this state so long as Congress shall hold their sessions therein or in any territory adjacent thereto which may be ceded to them by any other state.

They shall have power to appoint the Speakers of their respective houses, Treasurer, Auditors, Attorney general, Register [all General officers of the military] their own clerks, and serjeants <and doorkeep> and no other officers, except where in other parts of this constitution such appointment is expressly given them.

The Executive powers shall be exercised by a Governor who shall be chosen by joint balot of both houses of assembly, and when chosen shall remain in office five years, and be ineligible a second time. During his term he shall hold no other office or emolument under this state or any other state or power whatsoever. By Executive powers we mean no reference to those powers exercised under our former government by the crown as of it's prerogative; nor that these shall be the standard of what may or may not be deemed the rightful powers of the Governor. We give him those powers only which are necessary to carry into execution the laws, and which are not in their nature [either legislative or] Judiciary. The application of this idea must be left to reason. We do however expressly deny him the praerogative powers of erecting courts, offices, boroughs, corporations, fairs, markets, ports, beacons, lighthouses, and seamarks; of laying embargoes, of establishing precedence, of retaining within the state or recalling to it any citizen thereof, and of making denizens, except so far as he may be authorized from time to time by the legislature to exercise any of these powers. The powers of declaring war and concluding peace, of contracting alliances, of issuing letters of marque and reprisal, of raising or introducing armed forces, of building armed vessels, forts or strongholds, of coining money or regulating it's value, of regulating weights and measures, <*so far as they are or may be*> we leave to be exercised under the authority of the Confederation; but in all cases respecting them which are out of the said confederation, they shall be exercised by the Governor under the regulation of such laws as the legislature may think it expedient to pass.

The whole military of the state, whether regular or militia, shall be subject to his directions; but he shall leave the execution of those directions to the General officers [appointed by the legislature.]

His salary shall be fixed by the legislature at the session of assembly in which he shall be appointed, and before such appointment be made; or if it be not then fixed, it shall be the same which his next predecessor in office was entitled to. In either case he may demand it quarterly out of any money which shall be in the public treasury, and it shall not be in the power of the legislature to give him less or more, either during his continuance in office, or after he shall have gone out of it. The lands, houses, and other things appropriated to the use of the Governor, shall remain to his use, during his continuance in office.

A Council of State shall be chosen by joint balot of both houses of assembly, who shall hold their offices [during good behavior, 7. years and be ineligible a second time,] and who, while they shall be of the said council shall hold no other office or emolument under this state or any other state or power whatsoever. Their duty shall be to attend and advise the Governor when called on by him, and their advice in any case shall be a sanction to him. They shall also have power and it shall be their duty to meet at their own will and to give their advice, tho' not required by the Governor, in cases where they shall think the public good calls for it. Their advice and proceedings shall be entered in books to be kept for that purpose and shall be signed as approved or disapproved by the members present. These books shall be laid before either house of assembly when called for by them. The said council shall consist of eight members for the present: but their numbers may be increased or <*diminished*> reduced by the legislature whenever they shall think it necessary; provided such reduction be made only as the appointments become vacant by death, resignation, disqualification, or regular deprivation. A majority of their actual number <*shall be a Quorum*> and not fewer shall be a Quorum. They shall be allowed for the present 500.£ each by the year, payable quarterly out of any money which shall be in the public treasury. Their salary however may be increased or abated from time to time at the discretion of the legislature; provided such increase or abatement shall not by any ways or means be made to affect either then or at any future time any one of those then actually in office. At the end of each quarter their salary shall be divided into equal portions by the number of days on which during that quarter a council has been held, or required by the governor or their own adjournment, and one of those portions shall be withheld from each member for every of the said days which without cause allowed good by the board he failed to attend, or departed before adjournment without their leave <of the board>. If no board should have been held during the quarter there shall be no deduction.

They shall annually chuse a President who shall preside in council in the absence of the governor, and who in case of his <death> office becoming vacant by death or otherwise shall have authority to exercise all his functions, till a new appointment be made, as he shall also in any interval during which the Governor shall declare himself unable to attend to the duties of his office.

The Judiciary powers shall be exercised by County courts and such other inferior courts as the legislature shall think proper to erect, and by four Superior courts, to wit, a court of Admiralty, a General court of common law, a High court of Chancery and court of Appeals.

The judges of the High Court of Chancery, General court and Court of Admiralty shall be four in number each, to be appointed by joint balot of both houses of assembly, and to hold their offices during good behavior. While they continue judges they shall hold no other office or emolument under this state or any other state or power whatsoever, except that they may be delegated to Congress, receiving no additional allowance.

These judges assembled together shall constitute the Court of Appeals.

A majority of the members of either of these courts, and not fewer, shall be a Quorum; but in the court of Appeals nine members shall be necessary to do business. Any smaller numbers however may be authorized by the legislature to adjourn their respective courts.

They shall be allowed for the present 500.£ each by the year, paiable quarterly out of any money which shall be in the public treasury. Their salaries however may be increased or abated from time to time at the discretion of the legislature: provided such increase or abatement shall not by any ways or means be made to affect, either then or at any future time, any one of those then actually in office. At the end of each quarter their salary shall be divided into equal portions by the number of days on which during that quarter their respective courts sat, or should have sat, and one of these portions shall be withheld from each member for every of the said days <he failed to attend> which without cause allowed good by his court, he failed to attend or departed before adjournment without their leave. If no court should have been held during the quarter there shall be no deduction.

There shall moreover be a court of Impeachments to consist of three members of the Council of state, one of each of the Superior courts of Chancery, Common law, and Admiralty, two members of the House of Delegates and one of the Senate, to be chosen by the body respectively of which they are. Before this court any <*one*> member of the three branches <*of government may impeach any member of the other two for any cause sufficient to remove him from his office; and the only sentence they shall have authority to give*> of government, that is to say, the Governor, any member of the Council, of the two houses of legislature or of the Superior courts may be impeached by the Governor the Council, or either of the said houses or courts for <*any sufficient*> such misbehavior in office as would be sufficient to remove him therefrom: and the only sentence they shall have authority to pass shall be that of deprivation and future incapacity of office. Seven members shall be requisite to make a court and two thirds of those present must concur in the sentence. The offences cognisable by this court shall be cognisable by no other, and they shall be judges of fact as well as law.

The Justices or judges of the inferior courts already erected, or hereafter to be erected shall be appointed by the Governor on advice of the Council of state, and shall hold their offices during good behavior or the existence of their court. For breach of the good behavior they shall be tried according to the laws of the land before the court of Appeals, who shall be judges of the fact as well as of the law. The only sentence they shall have authority to pass shall be that of deprivation and future incapacity of office, and two thirds of the members present must concur in the sentence.

All courts shall appoint their own clerks, who shall hold their offices during good behavior or the existence of their court: they shall also appoint all other their attending officers to continue during their pleasure. Clerks appointed by the Superior courts shall be removeable by their respective courts: those to be appointed by other courts shall have been previously examined and certified to be duly qualified by some two members of the General court and shall be removeable for breach of the good behavior by the court of Appeals only, who shall be judges of the fact as well as of the law, [and] two thirds of the members present must concur in the sentence.

The justices or judges of the inferior courts may be members of the legislature.

The judgment of no inferior court shall be final in any civil case of greater value than 50. bushels of wheat as last rated in the General court for settling the allowance to the members of the General assembly, nor in any case of treason, felony, or other crime which would subject the party to infamous punishment.

In all <*courts except that of Impeachment and that of Appeals in the particular cases before specified*> causes depending before any court, other than those of Impeachments, of Appeals and Military courts facts [put in issue] shall be tried by jury, and <*the*> in all courts whatever witnesses shall give their testimony viv voce in open court wherever their attendance can be procured; and all parties shall be allowed Counsel and compulsory process for their witnesses.

Fines, amercements and terms of imprisonment left indefinite by the law other than for Contempts shall be fixed by the jury triers of the offence.

The Governor, two Counsellors of state, and a judge from each of the Superior courts of Chancery, Common law and Admiralty, shall be a council to revise all bills which shall have passed both houses of assembly; in which council the Governor, when present, shall preside. Every bill, before it becomes law, shall be presented to this council, who shall have a right to advise it's rejection, returning the *<same>* bill with their advice and reasons in writing to the house in which *<said bill>* it originated, who shall proceed to reconsider the said bill. But if after such reconsideration two thirds of the house shall be of opinion the bill should pass finally, they shall pass and send it with the advice and written reasons of the said council of revision to the other house, wherein if two thirds also shall be of opinion it should pass finally, it shall thereupon become law: otherwise it shall not.

<A bill rejected on advice of the Council of revision may again be brought in during the same session of Assembly with such alterations as will render it conformable to their advice.>

If any bill presented to the said Council be not within one week (exclusive of the day of presenting it) returned by them with their advice of rejection and reasons to the house wherein it originated, or to the clerk of the said house in case of it's adjournment over the expiration of the week, it shall be law from the *<time of such>* expiration of the week and shall then be demandeable by the clerk of the house of Delegates to be filed of record in his office.

The bills which they approve, *<or on which they omit to decide within the week before limited,>* shall become law from the time of such approbation *<or week's omission,>* and shall then be returned to or demandeable by the clerk of the House of Delegates to be filed of record in his office.

A bill rejected on advice of the Council of revision may again be *<brought on>* proposed during the same session of Assembly with such alterations as will render it conformable to their advice.

The members of the said Council of revision shall be appointed from time to time by the board or court of which they respectively are. Two of the Executive and two of the Judiciary members shall be requisite to do business. And to prevent the evils of non-attendance, the board and courts may at any time name all or so many as they will of their members in the particular order in which they would chuse the duty of attendance to devolve from preceding to subsequent members, the preceding failing to attend. They shall have additionally for their services in this council the same allowance as members of assembly have.

The Confederation is made a part of this constitution, subject to such future alterations as shall be agreed to by the legislature of this and by all the other confederating states. The Delegates to Congress shall be five in number. They shall be appointed by joint balot of both houses *<of assembly and shall hold this office till revoked by the joint will of both the said houses, or until their incapacitation under the Confederation>* of assembly for any term not exceeding one year, subject to be recalled at any time within the term by joint vote of both the said houses. They may at the same time be members of the Legislative or Judiciary departments.

<Every citizen> The benefits of the writ of Habeas corpus shall be extended by the legislature to every person within this state and without fee, and shall be so facilitated that no person may be detained in prison more than ten days after he shall have demanded and been refused such writ by the judge appointed by law, or if none be appointed, then by any judge of a superior court; nor more than ten days after such writ shall have been served on the person detaining him and no order given on due examination for his remandment or discharge.

The Military shall be subordinate to the civil power.

Printing presses shall be subject to no other restraint than liableness to legal prosecution for false *<hoods>* facts printed and published.

Any two of the three branches of government concurring in opinion, each by the voices of two thirds of their whole existing number, that a Convention is necessary for altering this Constitution or correcting breaches of it, they shall be authorized to issue writs to every county for the election of so many delegates as they are authorized to send to the General assembly, which elections shall be held and writs returned as the laws shall have provided in the cases of elections of Delegates to assembly, mutatis mutandis, and the said delegates shall meet at the usual place of holding assemblies three months after the date of such writs, and shall be acknoleged to have equal powers with this present Convention. The said writs shall be signed by all the members approving of the same.

To introduce this government the following special and temporary provision is made.

This Convention having been *<assemb>* authorized only to amend those laws which constituted the form of government, no general dissolution of the whole system of laws can be supposed to have taken place; but all laws in force at the meeting of this Convention and not inconsistent with this Constitution, remain in full force, subject *<however>* to alterations by the ordinary legislature.

The present General assembly shall continue till the Monday preceding the 25th. day of December in this present year. The several counties shall then, by their electors qualified as provided by this constitution, elect delegates which for the present shall be in number one for every militia of the said county according to the latest returns in possession of the Governor, and shall also chuse Senatorial electors in proportion thereto, which Senatorial electors shall meet on the 7th. day after the day of their election at the court house of that county of their present district which would stand first in an Alphabetical arrangement of their counties, and shall chuse Senators in the proportion fixed by this Constitution.

The elections and returns shall be conducted in all circumstances not hereby particularly prescribed by the same persons and under the same form and circumstances as prescribed by the present laws in elections of Senators and Delegates of assembly. The said Senators and Delegates shall constitute the first General assembly of the new government, and shall specially apply themselves to the procuring an exact return from every county of the number of it's qualified electors, and to the settlement of the number of Delegates to be elected for the ensuing General assembly.

The present governor shall continue in office to the end of the term for which he was elected.

All other officers of every kind shall continue in office as they would have done had their appointment been under this constitution, and new ones, where new are hereby called for, shall be appointed by the authority to which such appointment is referred. One of the present judges of the General court, he consenting thereto, shall by joint ballot of both houses of assembly at their first meeting be transferred to the High court of Chancery.

SOURCE: "Jefferson's Draft of a Constitution for Virginia, [May–June 1783]," *Founders Online,* National Archives, https://founders.archives.gov/documents/Jefferson/01-06-02-0255-0004.

5. JAMES MADISON TO CALEB WALLACE
A CONSTITUTION FOR KENTUCKY
AUGUST 23, 1785

James Madison was born in Port Conway, Virginia (1751), and he died in Montpellier, Virginia (1836). Madison was an American revolutionary, patriot, statesmen, diplomat, and founding father who served as the fourth president of the United States from 1809 to 1817. He is best known to history as the "Father of the Constitution" for the leading role he played in drafting the Constitution and the Bill of Rights.

On July 12, 1785, Caleb Wallace, an old friend of Madison's from Princeton and now living on the frontier in the Kentucky District, sent his former classmate a letter asking for advice on how to draft a constitution for the new territory, which was then petitioning Virginia for statehood. (The Kentucky territory was under Virginia's control.) At the time, Madison chaired the committee appointed by the Virginia Assembly to review Kentucky's request. Wallace asked Madison if he would "be so kind as to favour me with such a Form of Government as you would wish to live under when you come." On August 23, the Virginian replied with a rough constitutional blueprint that he described as "my ideas toward a constitution of Government for the State in embryo." Some of the state constitutions had been in existence for almost a decade when Madison wrote to Wallace in 1785 and with the knowledge of those experiences in mind, he offered several interesting ideas to his friend. Madison's blueprint is first organized around a separation of the legislative, executive, and judicial powers of government. His greatest complaint against many of the state constitutions concerned the instability and injustice of the laws passed by their legislatures. Madison therefore proposed a bicameral legislature that would include a senate "constituted on such principles as will give wisdom and steadiness to legislation." Madison also seemed very concerned with finding certain constitutional mechanisms and institutions that would preserve the integrity of the constitution into the distant future. Madison strongly supported New York's Council of Revision, and he was open to Pennsylvania's Council of Censors.

Your favour of the 12th. of July was safely deliverd to me by Mr. Craig. I accept with pleasure your propos'd exchange of Western for Eastern intelligence and though I am a stranger to parental ties can sufficiently con[c]ieve the happiness of which they are a source to congratulate you on Your possession of two fine sons & a Daughter. I do not smile at the Idea of transplanting myself into your wilderness. Such a change of my abode is not indeed probable. Yet I have no local partialities which can keep me from any place which promises the greatest real advantages but If such a removal was not even possible I should nevertheless be ready to communicate, as you desire my Ideas towards a constitution of Government for the State in embryo. I pass over the general policy of the measure which calls for such a provision. It has been unanimously embraced by those who being most interested in it must have but consider'd it, & will I dare say be with equal unanimity acceded to by the other party which is to be consulted. I will first offer some general remarks on the Subject, & then answer your several queries.

1. *The Legislative department* ought by all means, as I think to include a Senate constituted on such principles as will give *wisdom* and steadiness to legislation. The want of these qualities is the grievance complained of in all our republics. The want of *fidelity* in the administration of power having been the grievance felt under most Governments, and by the American States themselves under the British Government. It was natural for them to give too exclusive an attention to this primary attribute. The Senate of Maryland with a few amendments is a good model. Trial has I am told verified the expectations from it. A Similar one made a part of our constitution as it was originally proposed but the inexperience & jealousy of our then Councils, rejected it in favour of our present Senate a worse could hardly have been substituted & yet bad as it is, it is often a useful bitt in the mouth of the house of Delegates. Not a single Session passes without instances of sudden resolutions by the latter of which they repent in time to intercede privately with the Senate for their Negative. For the other branch models enough may be found. Care ought however to be taken against its becoming to numerous, by fixing the number which it is never to exceed. The quorum, wages, and privileges of both branches ought also to be fixed. A majority seems to be the natural quorum. The wages of the members may be made payable for   years to come in the medium value of wheat, for   years preceeding as the same shall from period to period be rated by a respectable Jury appointed for that purpose by the Supreme Court. The privileges of the members ought not in my opinion to extend beyond an exemption of their persons and equipage from arrests during the time of their actual Service. If it were possible it would be well to define the extent of the Legislative power but the nature of it seems in many respects to be indefinite. It is very practicable however to enumerate the essential exceptions. The Constitution may expresly restrain them from medling with religion—from abolishing Juries from taking away the Habeus corpus—from forcing a citizen to give evidence against himself, from controuling the press, from enacting retrospective laws at least in criminal cases, from abridging the right of suffrage, from seizing private property for public use without paying its full Valu[e] from licensing the importation of Slaves, from infringing the Confederation &c &c.

As a further security against fluctuating & indegested laws the Constitution of New York has provided a Council of Revision. I approve much of such an institution & believe it is considerd by the most intelligent citizens of that state as a valuable safeguard both to public interests & to private rights. Another provision has been suggested for preserving System in Legislative proceedings which to some may appear still better. It is that a standing commtee composed of a few select & skilful individuals should be appointed to prepare bills on all subjects which they may judge proper to be submitted to the Legislature at their meetings & to draw bills for them during their Sessions. As an antido[te] both to the jealousy & danger of their acquiring an improper influence they might be made incapable of holding any other Office Legislative, Executive, or Judiciary. I like this Suggestion so much, that I have had thoughts of proposing it to our Assembly, who give almost as many proofs as they pass laws of their need of some such Assistance.

2 *The Executive Department* Though it claims the 2d place is not in my estimation entitled to it by its importance all the great powers which are properly executive being transferd to the Fœderal Government. I have made up no final opinion whether the first Magistrate should be chosen by the Legislature or the people at large or whether the power should be vested in one man assisted by a council or in a council of which the President shall be only primus inter pares.5 There are examples of each in the U. States and probably advantages & disadvantages attending each. It is material I think that the number of members should be small & that their Salaries should be either unalterable by the Legislature or alterable only in such manner as will not affect any individual in place. Our Executive is the worst part of a ba[d] Constitution. The Members of it are dependant on the Legislature not only for their wages but for their reputation and therefore are not likely to withstand usurpations of that branch; they are besides too numerous and expensive, their organization vaugue & perplexed & to crown the absurdi[ty] some of the members may without any new appointment continue in Office for life contrary to one of Articles of the Declaration of Right[s.]

3d *The Judiciary Department* merits every care. Its efficacy is Demonstrated in G. Brittain where it maintains private Right against all the corruptions of the two other departments & gives a reputation to the whole Government which it is not in itself entitled to. The main points to be attended to are 1. that the Judges should hold their places during good behavior. 2. that their Salaries should be either fixed like the wages of the Representatives or not be alterable so as to affect the Individuals in Office. 3 that their Salaries be liberal. The first point is obvious: without the second the independance aimed at by the first will be Ideal only: without the 3d. the bar will be superior to the bench which destroys all security for a Systematick administration of Justice. After securing these essential points I should think it unadvisable to descend so far into detail as to bar any future Modification of this department which experience may recommend. An enumeration of the principal courts with power to the Legislature to Institute inferior Courts may suffice. The Admiralty business can never be extensive in your situation and may be refer'd to one of the other Courts. With regard to a Court of Chancery as distinct from a Court of Law, the reasons of Lord Bacon on the affirmative side outweigh in my Judgment those of Lord Kaims on the other side.6 Yet I should think it best to leave this important question to be decided by future lights without tying the hands of the Legislature one way or the other. I consider our county courts as on a bad footing and would never myself consent to copy them into another constitution.

All the States seem to have seen the necessity of providing for Impeachments but none of them to have hit on an unexceptionable Tribunal. In some the trial is referd to the Senate in others to the Executive, in others to the Judiciary department. It has been suggested that a tribunal composed of members from each Department would be better than either and I entirely concur in their opinion. I proceed next to your queries.

1 "Whether is a representation according to number, or property, or in a joint proportion to both the most Safe? or is a representation by counties preferable to a more equitable mode that will be difficult to adjust?" Under this question may be consider'd 1. the right of Suffrage. 2 the mode of suffrage. 3 the plan of representation. As to the 1. I think the extent which ought to be given to this right a matter of great delicacy and of critical Importance. To restrain it to the landholders will in time exclude too great a proportion of citizens; to extend it to all citizens without regard to property, or even to all who possess a pittance may throw too much power into hands which will either abuse it themselves or sell it to the rich who will abuse it. I have thought it might be a good middle course to narrow this right in the choice of the least popular, & to enlarge it in that of the more popular branch of the Legislature. There is an example of this Distinction in N. Carolina if in none of the States.7 How it operates or is relished by the people I cannot say. It would not be surprising if in the outset at least it should offend the sense of equallity which re[i]gns in a free Country. In a general vein I see no reason why the rights of property which chiefly bears the burden of Government & is so much an object of Legislation should not be respected as well as personal rights in the choice of Rulers. It must be owned indeed that property will give influence to the holder though it should give him no legal priviledges and will in generall be safe on that as well as other Accounts, expecially if the business of Legislation be guarded with the provisions hinted at. 2 as to the mode of suffrage I lean strongly to that of the ballott, notwithstanding the objections which be against it. It appears to me to be the only radical cure for those arts of Electioneering which poison the very fountain of Liberty. The States in which the Ballott has been the Standing mode are the only instances in which elections are tolerably chaste and those arts in disgrace. If it should be thought improper to fix this mode by the constitution I should think it at least necessary to avoid any constitutional bar to a future adoption

of it. 3 By the plan of representation I mean 1. the classing of the Electors 2 the proportioning of the representatives to each class. The first cannot be otherwise done than by geographical description as by Counties. The second may easily be done in the first instance either by comprizing within each county an equal number of electors; or by proportioning the number of representatives of each county to its number of electors. The dificulty arises from the disproportionate increase of electors in different Counties. There seem to be two methods only by which the representation can be equalized from time to time. The 1 is to change the bounds of the counties. The 2d to change the number of representatives allotted to them respectavely, as the former would not only be most troublesome & expensive, but would involve a variety of other adjustments. The latter method is evidently the best. Examples of a Constitutional provision for it exists in several of the States. In some it is to be executed periodically in others pro re nata. The latter seems most accurate and very practicable. I have already intimated the propriety of fixing the number of representatives which ought never to be exceeded. I should suppose 150 or even 100 might safely be made the ne plus ultra for Kentuckey.

2 "Which is to be preferd an Anual, Trienniel, or Septennial Succession to Offices or frequent elections without limitations in choice or that the Officers when chosen should continue quamdiu se bene gesserint?" The rule ought no doubt to be different in the different Departments of power. For one part of the Legislature Annual Elections will I suppose be held indispensably though some of the ablest Statesmen & soundest Republicans in the U States are in favour of triennial. The great danger in departing from Annual elextions in this case lies in the want of some other natural term to limit the departure. For the other branch 4 or 5 Years may be the period. For neither branch does it seem necessary or proper to prohibit an indefinite reeligibility. With regard to the Executive if the elections be frequent & particularly, if made as to any member of it by the people at large a reeligibility cannot I think be objected to. If they be unfrequent, a temporary or perpetual incapacitation according to the degree of unfrequency at least in the case of the first Magistrate may not be amiss. As to the Judiciary department enough has been said & as to the Subordinate officers civil & Military, nothing need be said more than that a regulation of their appointments may under a few restrictions be safely trusted to the Legislature.

3. "How far may the same person with propriety be employed in the different departments of Government in an infant Country where the counsel of every individual may be needed?["] Temporary deviations from fundamental principles are always more or less dangerous. When the first pretext fails, those who become interested in prolonging the evil will rarely be at a loss for other pretexts. The first precedent too familiarizes the people to the irregularity, lessens their veneration for those fundamental principles, & makes them a more easy prey to Ambition & self Interest. Hence it is that abuses of every kind when once established have been so often found to

perpetuate themselves. In this caution I refer chiefly to an improper mixture of the three great departments within the State. A Delegation to Congress is I conceive compatible with either.

4 "Should there be a periodical review of the Constitution? Nothing appears more eligible in theory nor has sufficient trial perhaps been yet made to condemn it in practise. Pensylvania has alone adopted the expedient. Her citizens are much divided on the subject of their constitution in general & probably on this part of it in particular I am inclind to think though am far from being certain, that it is not a favourite part even with those who are fondest of their Constitution. Another plan has been thought of which might perhaps Succeed better and would at the same time be a safeguard to the equilibrium of the constituent Departments of Government. This is that a Majority of any two of the three departments should have authority to call a plenipotentiary convention whenever they may think their constitutional powers have been Violated by the other Department or that any material part of the Constitution needs amendment. In your situation I should think [it] both imprudent & indecent not to leave a door open for at least one revision of your first Establishment; imprudent because you have neither the same resources for supporting nor the same lights for framing a good establishment now as you will have 15 or 20 Years hence; indecent because an handfull of early sett[l]ers ought not to preclude a populous Country from a choice of the Government under which they & their Posterity are to live. Should your first Constitution be made thus temporary the objections against an intermediate union of officers will be proportionably lessen'd. Should a revision of it not be made thus necessary & certain there will be little probability of its being ever revised. Faulty as our Constitution is as well with regard to the Authority which formed it as the manner in which it is formed the Issue of an experiment has taught us the difficulty of amending it; & Although the issue might have proceeded from the unseasonableness of the time yet it may be questioned whether at any future time the greater depth to which it will have stricken its roots will not counterballance any more auspicious circumstances for overturning it.

5 & 6 "Or will it be better unalterably to fix some leading Principles in Government and make it consistant for the Legislature to introduce such changes in lessor matters as may become expedient? can censors be provided that will impartially point out differences in the Constitutions & the Violations that may happen.["] Answers on these points may be gatherd from what has been already said.

I have been led to offer my sentiments in this loose forms rather than to attempt a delineation of such a plan of Government as would please myself not only by my Ignorance of many local circumstances & opinions which must be consulted in such a work but also by the want of sufficient time for it. At the recei[p]t of your letter I had other employment and what I now write is in the midst of preparations for a Journey of business which will carry me as far as Philadelphia at least & on which I shall set out in a day or two. I am sorry that it is not in my power to give you some satisfactory information concerning the Mississippi. A Minister from Spain has been with Congress for some time & is authorised as I understand to treat on what ever subjects may concern the two nations. If any explanations or propositions have passed between him & the Minister of Congress, they are as yet on the list of Cabinett Secrets. As soon as any such shall be made public & come to my knowledge I shall take the first opportunity of transmitting them.

SOURCE: James Madison from Caleb Wallace, 25 September 1785," *Founders Online,* National Archives, https://founders.archives.gov/documents/Madison/01-08-02-0192.

6. JAMES MADISON
"OBSERVATIONS ON THE 'DRAUGHT OF A CONSTITUTION FOR VIRGINIA'"
1788

Because of the critical role he played in the drafting of the federal Constitution in the summer of 1787 and its subsequent ratification over the course of the next year, James Madison became known as the "Father of the Constitution." Madison's old Princetonian classmates, particularly those living in the Kentucky district which was still searching for a good constitution and statehood, called on their old friend again for advice about on how to design and construct a constitution. Three years after his 1785 exchange with Caleb Wallace, Madison received a letter on August 26, 1788, from John Brown, a political leader of the Kentucky district and another old Princetonian. As Kentucky again weighed plans for statehood, Brown wrote to Madison soliciting advice on a frame of government. Specifically, Brown asked Madison for his assessment of Jefferson's 1783 draft constitution for Virginia. Madison's October 15 response could best be described as respectfully critical of his fellow Virginian's constitutional model, which he considered to be a flawed model for Virginia or Kentucky. The Jefferson plan was, according to Madison, too democratic and too localist. Madison preferred a six-year term for senators as compared to Jefferson's two-year term because he thought the senate should represent experience, steadfastness, and wisdom over against "occasional impetuosities" of the lower house. He also thought the senate should represent the "interest of the whole society" rather than the competing and diverse interests of different localities. In the name of "liberty" and "justice," Madison was concerned that various post-revolutionary state assemblies had violated the "rights of property." Interestingly, following New York's constitution, Madison proposed a Council of Revision to determine whether laws passed by the legislature were unconstitutional. Madison had proposed unsuccessfully something like a Council of Revision for the federal Constitution. That he would continue to support the idea suggests that Madison was first and foremost a constitutionalist before he was a republican.

REMARKS ON MR. JEFFERSON'S DRAUGHT OF A CONSTITUTION

SENATE

The term of two years is too short. Six years are not more than sufficient. A Senate is to withstand the occasional impetuosities of the more numerous branch. The members ought therefore to derive a firmness from the tenure of their places. It ought to supply the defect of knowledge and experience incident to the other branch, there ought to be time given therefore for attaining the qualifications necessary for that purpose. It ought finally to maintain that system and steadiness in public affairs without which no Government can prosper or be respectable. This cannot be done by a body undergoing a frequent change of its members. A Senate for six years will not be dangerous to liberty. On the contrary it will be one of its best guardians. By correcting the infirmities of popular Government, it will prevent that disgust agst. that form which may otherwise produce a sudden transition to some very different one. It is no secret to any attentive & dispassionate observer of the pol: Situation of the U. S. that the real danger to republican liberty has lurked in that cause.

The appointment of Senators by districts seems to be objectionable. A spirit of *locality*2 is inseparable from that mode. The evil is fully displayed in the County representations; the members of which are everywhere observed to lose sight of the aggregate interests of the Community, and even to sacrifice them to the interests or prejudices of their respective constituents. In general these local interests are miscalculated. But it is not impossible for a measure to be accomodated to the particular interests of every County or district, when considered by itself, and not so, when considered in relation to each other and to the whole State; in the same manner as the interests of individuals may be very different in a State of nature and in a Political Union. The most effectual remedy for the local biass is to impress on the minds of the Senators an attention to the interest of the whole Society by making them the choice of the whole Society, each citizen voting for every Senator. The objection here is that the fittest characters would not be sufficiently known to the people at large.3 But in free Governments, merit and notoriety of character are rarely separated, and such a regulation would connect them more and more together. Should this mode of election be on the whole not approved, that established in Maryland presents a valuable alternative. The latter affords perhaps a greater security for the selection of merit. The inconveniences chargeable on it are two: first that the Council of electors favors cabal. Against this the shortness of its existence is a good antidote. Secondly that in a large State the meeting of the Electors must be expensive if they be paid, or badly attended if the service be onerous. To this it may be answered that in a case of such vast importance, the expence which could not be great, ought to be disregarded. Whichever of these modes may be preferred, it cannot be amiss so far to admit the plan of districts as to restrain the choice to persons residing in different parts of the State. Such a regulation will produce a diffusive confidence in the Body, which is not less necessary than the other means of rendering it useful. In a State having large towns which can easily unite their votes the precaution would be essential to an immediate choice by the people at large. In Maryland no regard is paid to residence. And what is remarkable vacancies are filled by the Senate itself. This last is an obnoxious expedient and cannot in any point of view have much effect. It was probably meant to obviate the trouble of occasional meetings of the Electors. But the purpose might have been otherwise answered by allowing the unsuccessful candidates to supply vacancies according to the order of their standing on the list of votes, or by requiring provisional appointments to be made along with the positive ones. If an election by districts be unavoidable and the ideas here suggested be sound, the evil will be diminished in proportion to the extent given to the districts, taking two or more Senators from each district.

ELECTORS

The first question arising here is how far property ought to be made a qualification. There is a middle way to be taken which corresponds at once with the Theory of free government and the lessons of experience. A freehold or equivalent of a certain value may be annexed to the right of vot[in]g for Senators, & the right left more at large in the election of the other House. Examples of this distinction may be found in the Constitutions of several States, particularly if I mistake not, of North Carolina & N. York. This middle mode reconciles and secures the two cardinal objects of Government, the rights of persons, and the rights of property. The former will be sufficiently guarded by one branch, the latter more particularly by the other. Give all power to property; and the indigent [will] be oppressed. Give it to the latter and the effect may be transposed. Give a defensive share to each and each will be secure. The necessity of thus guarding the rights of property was for obvious reasons unattended to in the commencement of the Revolution. In all the Governments which were considered as beacons to republican patriots & lawgivers, the rights of persons were subjected to those of property. The poor were sacrificed to the rich. In the existing state of American population, & American property [,] the two classes of rights were so little discriminated that a provision for the rights of persons was supposed to include of itself those of property, and it was natural to infer from the tendency of republican laws, that these different interests would be more and more identified. Experience and investigation have however produced more correct ideas on this subject. It is now observed that in all populous countries, the smaller part only can be interested in preserving the rights of property. It must be foreseen that America, and Kentucky itself will by degrees arrive at this State of Society; that in some parts of the Union a very great advance is already made towards it. It is well understood that interest leads to injustice as well when the opportunity is presented to bodies of men, as to individuals; to an interested majority in a republic, as to the interested minority of any other form of Government. The time to guard agst. this danger is at the first forming of the Constitution, and in the present state of population when the bulk of the people have a sufficient interest in possession or in prospect to be attached to the rights of property, without being insufficiently attached to the rights of persons. Liberty not less than justice pleads for the policy here recommended. If *all* power be suffered to slide into hands not interested in the rights of property which must be the case whenever a majority fall under that description, one of two things cannot fail to happen; either they will unite against the other description and become the dupes & instruments of ambition, or their poverty & independence will render them the mercenary instruments of wealth. In either case liberty will be subverted; in the first by a despotism growing out of anarchy, in the second, by an oligarchy founded on corruption.

The second question under this head is whether the ballot be not a better mode than that of voting viva voce. The comparative experience of the States pursuing the different modes is in favor of the first. It is found less difficult to guard against fraud in that, than against bribery in the other.

EXCLUSIONS

Does not the exclusion of Ministers of the Gospel as such violate a fundamental principle of liberty by punishing a religious profession with the privation of a civil right? Does it not violate another article of the plan itself which exempts religion from the cognizance of Civil power? Does it not violate justice by at once taking away a right and prohibiting a compensation for it. And does it not in fine violate impartiality by shutting the door agst the Ministers of one religion and leaving it open for those of every other.

The re-eligibility of members after accepting offices of profit is so much opposed to the present way of thinking in America that any discussion of the subject would probably be a waste of time.

LIMITS OF POWER

It is at least questionable whether death ought to be confined to "Treason and murder." It would not therefore be prudent to tie the hands of Government in the manner here proposed. The prohibition of pardon, however specious in theory would have practical consequences, which render it inadmissible. A single instance is a sufficient proof. The crime of treason is generally shared by a number, and often a very great number. It would be politically if not morally wrong to take away the lives of all, even if every individual were equally guilty. What name would be given to a severity which made no distinction between the legal & the moral offence—between the deluded multitude, and their wicked leaders. A second trial would not avoid the difficulty; because the oaths of the jury would not permit them to hearken to any voice but the inexorable voice of the law.

The power of the Legislature to appoint any other than their own officers departs too far from the Theory which requires a separation of the great

Depts of Government. One of the best securities against the creation of un-necessary offices or tyrannical powers, is an exclusion of the authors from all share in filling the one, or influence in the execution of the others. The proper mode of appointing to offices will fall under another head.

EXECUTIVE GOVERNOUR

An election by the Legislature is liable to insuperable objections. It not only tends to faction intrigue and corruption, but leaves the Executive under the influence of an improper obligation to that department. An election by the people at large, as in this 10 & several other States—or by Electors as in the appointment of the Senate in Maryland, or indeed by the people through any other channel than their legislative representatives, seems to be far prefera-ble. The ineligibility a second time, though not perhaps without advantages, is also liable to a variety of strong objections. It takes away one powerful mo-tive to a faithful & useful administration, the desire of acquiring that title to a re-appointment. By rendering a periodical change of men necessary, it dis-courages beneficial undertakings which require perseverance and system, or, as frequently happened in the Roman Consulate, either precipitates or pre-vents the execution of them. It may inspire desperate enterprizes for the at-tainment of what is not attainable by legitimate means. It fetters the judgment and inclination of the Community; and in critical moments would either produce a violation of the Constitution, or exclude a choice which might be essential to the public safety. Add to the whole, that by putting the Executive Magistrate in the situation of the tenant of an unrenewable lease, it would tempt him to neglect the constitutional rights of his department, and to con-nive at usurpations by the Legislative department, with which he may con-nect his future ambition or interest.

The clause restraining the first Magistrate from the immediate com-mand of the military force would be made better by excepting cases in which he should receive the sanction of the two branches of the Legislature.

COUNCIL OF STATE

The following variations are suggested. 1. The election to be made by the people immediately, or thro' some other medium than the Legislature. 2. A distributive choice should perhaps be secured as in the case of the Senate. 3 instead of an ineligibility a second time, a rotation as in the federal Senate, with an abrdgmt. of the term to be substituted.

The appointment to offices is, of all the functions of Republican & per-haps every other form of Government, the most difficult to guard against abuse. Give it to a numerous body, and you at once destroy all responsibility, and create a perpetual source of faction and corruption. Give it to the Exec-utive wholly, and it may be made an engine of improper influence and favor-itism. Suppose the power were divided thus: let the Executive alone make all the subordinate appointments; and the Government and Senate as in the Federal Constitution, those of the superior order. It seems particularly fit that the Judges, who are to form a distinct department should owe their offices partly to each of the other departments rather than wholly to either.

JUDICIARY

Much detail ought to [be] avoided in the constitutional regulation of this department, that there may be room for changes which may be demanded by the progressive changes in the state of our population. It is at least doubtful whether the number of Courts, the number of Judges, or even the boundaries of Jurisdiction ought to be made unalterable but by a revisal of the Constitution. The precaution seems no otherwise necessary than as it may prevent sudden modifications of the establishment, or addition of obsequious Judges, for the purpose of evading the checks of the Constitution & giving effect to some sinister policy of the Legislature. But might not the same object be otherwise attained? By prohibiting, for example, any innovations in those particulars without the consent of that department: or without the annual sanction of two or three successive assemblies; over & above the other pre-requisites to the passage of a law.

The model here proposed for a Court of Appeals is not recommended by experience. It is found as might well be presumed that the members are always warped in their appellate decisions by an attachment to the principles and jurisdiction of their respective Courts & still more so by the previous decision on the case removed by appeal. The only effectual cure for the evil, is to form a Court of Appeals, of distinct and select Judges. The expence ought not be admitted as an objection. 1. because the proper administration of Justice is of too essential a nature to be sacrificed to that consideration. 2. The number of inferior Judges might in that case be lessened. 3. The whole department may be made to support itself by a judicious tax on law proceedings.

The excuse for non-attendance would be a more proper subject of enquiry somewhere else than in the Court to which the party belonged. Delicacy, mutual connivance &c. would soon reduce the regulation to mere form; or if not, it might become a disagreeable source of little irritations among the members. A certificate from the local Court or some other local authority where the party might reside or happen to be detained from his duty, expressing the cause of absence as well as that it was judged to be satisfactory, might be safely substituted. Few Judges would improperly claim their wages, if such a formality stood in the way. These observations are applicable to the Council of State.

A Court of Impeachments is among the most puzzling articles of a republican Constitution; and it is far more easy to point out defects in any plan, than to supply a cure for them. The diversified expedients adopted in the Constitutions of the several States prove how much the compilers were embarrassed on this subject. The plan here proposed varies from all of them; and is perhaps not less than any a proof of the difficulties which pressed the ingenuity of its author. The remarks arising on it are 1. that it seems not to square with reason, that the right to impeach should be united to that of trying the impeachment, & consequently in a proportional degree, to that of sharing in the appointment of, or influence on the Tribunal to which the trial may belong. 2. As the Executive & Judiciary would form a majority of the Court, and either have a right to impeach, too much might depend on a combination of these departments. This objection would be still stronger, if the members of the Assembly were capable as proposed of holding offices, and were amenable in that capacity to the Court. 3. The H. of Delegates and either of those departments could appt. a majority of the Court. Here is another danger of combination, and the more to be apprehended as that branch of the Legislation wd. also have the right to impeach, a right in their hands of itself sufficiently weighty; and as the power of the Court wd. extend to the head of the Ex. by whose independence the constitutional rights of that department are to be secured against Legislative usurpations. 4. The dangers in the two last cases would be still more formidable; as the power extends not only to deprivation; but to future incapacity of office. In the case of all officers of sufficient importance to be objects of factious persecution, the latter branch of power is in every view of a delicate nature. In that of the Chief Magistrate, it seems inadmissible, if he be chosen by the Legislature; and much more so, if immediately by the people themselves. A temporary incapacitation is the most that cd. be properly authorised.

The 2 great desiderata in a Court of impeachments are 1. impartiality. 2. respectability—the first in order to a right—the second in order to a satisfactory decision. These characteristics are arrived at in the following modification—Let the Senate be denied the right to impeach. Let ⅓ of the members be struck out, by alternate nominations of the prosecutors & party impeached; the remaining ⅔ to be the *Stamen* of the Court. When the House of Delegates impeach, let the Judges or a certain proportion of them—and the Council of State be associated in the trial. When the Governor or Council impeaches, let the Judges only be associated: When the Judges impeach let the Council only be associated. But if the party impeached by the House of Delegates be a member of the Executive or Judiciary let that of which he is a member not be associated. If the party impeached belong to one & be impeached by the other of these branches, let neither of them be associated, the decision being in this case left with the Senate alone or if that be thought exceptionable, a few members might be added by the H. of Ds. ⅔ of the Court should in all cases be necessary to a conviction, & the chief Magistrate *at least* should be exempt from a sentence of perpetual if not of temporary incapacity. It is extremely probable that a critical discussion of this outline may discover objections which do not occur. Some do occur; but appear not to be greater than are incident to any different modification of the Tribunal.

The establishment of trials by Jury & viva voce testimony in *all* cases and in *all* Courts, is to say the least a delicate experiment; and would most probably be either violated, or be found inconvenient.

COUNCIL OF REVISION

A revisionary power is meant as a check to precipitate, to unjust, and to unconstitutional laws. These important ends would it is conceived be more effectually secured, without disarming the Legislature of its requisite authority, by requiring bills to be separately communicated to the Executive & Judiciary depts. If either of these objects, let ⅔, if both ¾ of each House be necessary to overrule the objection; and if either or both protest against a bill as violating the Constitution, let it moreover be suspended, notwithstanding the overruling proportion of the Assembly, until there shall have been a subsequent election of the H. of Ds. and a repassage of the bill by ⅔ or ¾ of both Houses, as the case may be. It sd. not be allowed the Judges or the Ex to pronounce a law thus enacted, unconstitutional & invalid.

In the State Constitutions & indeed in the Federal one also, no provision is made for the case of a disagreement in expounding them; and as the Courts are generally the last in making their decision, it results to them, by refusing or not refusing to execute a law, to stamp it with its final character. This makes the Judiciary Dept paramount in fact to the Legislature, which was never intended, and can never be proper.

The extension of the Habeas Corpus to the cases in which it has been usually suspended, merits consideration at least. If there be emergences which call for such a suspension, it can have no effect to prohibit it, because the prohibition will assuredly give way to the impulse of the moment; or rather it will have the bad effect of facilitating other violations that may be less necessary. The Exemption of the press from liability in every case for *true facts*, is also an innovation and as such ought to be well considered. This essential branch of liberty is perhaps in more danger of being interrupted by local tumults, or the silent awe of a predominant party, than by any direct attacks of Power

---

SOURCE: "Observations on Jefferson's Draft of a Constitution for Virginia, [ca. 15 October] 1788," *Founders Online*, National Archives, https://founders.archives.gov/documents/Madison/01-11-02-0216.

PART FIVE:

REVOLUTIONARY REFORM

1. THOMAS JEFFERSON
SELECTION FROM NOTES ON THE STATE OF VIRGINIA
1785

Thomas Jefferson (1743-1826) wrote Notes on the State of Virginia *in response to a series of questions posed by François Barbé-Marbois (secretary of the French delegation in Philadelphia), who was collecting information about the American states. Jefferson completed a first draft of* Notes *in 1781 and then revised the book in 1782 and 1783. The book was first published anonymously in Paris in 1785 when Jefferson was serving the United States as a trade representative, and it was published in London in 1787.* Notes on the State of Virginia *is divided in twenty-three chapters or "queries" that examine Virginia's geography, topography, geology, natural resources, climate, native peoples and their languages, history, laws, customs, economy, and institutions. Jefferson's discussion of Virginia's plants and animals was in response to the views of the Comte de Buffon, whose multi-volume* Histoire Naturelle *(1749-1804) claimed that plant, animal, and human life would degenerate in the New World. The selections below are taken from the "queries" XIV and XVII on the laws and religion of Virginia. Jefferson's discussion of slavery in Query XIV has been moved to Part Six.*

QUERY XIV: *The administration of justice and the description of the laws?*

The state is divided into counties. In every county are appointed magistrates, called justices of the peace, usually from eight to thirty or forty in number, in proportion to the size of the county, of the most discreet and honest inhabitants. They are nominated by their fellows, but commissioned by the governor, and act without reward. These magistrates have jurisdiction both criminal and civil. If the question before them be a question of law only, they decide on it themselves; but if it be a fact, or of fact and law combined, it must be referred to a jury. In the latter case, of a combination of law and fact, it is usual for the jurors to decide the fact, and to refer the law arising on it to the decision of the judges. But this division of the subject lies with their discretion only. And if the question relate to any point of public liberty, or if it be one of those in which the judges may be suspected of bias, the jury undertake to decide both law and fact. If they be mistaken, a decision against right, which is casual only, is less dangerous to the state, and less afflicting to the loser, than one which makes part of a regular and uniform system. In truth, it is better to toss up cross and pile in a cause, than to refer it to a judge whose mind is warped by any motive whatever, in that particular case. But the common sense of twelve honest men gives still a better chance of just decision, than the hazard of cross and pile. These judges execute their process by the sheriff or coroner of the county, or by constables of their own appointment. If any free person commit an offence against the commonwealth, if it be below the degree of felony, he is bound by a justice to appear before their court, to answer it on indictment or information. If it amount to felony, he is committed to jail; a court of these justices is called; if they on examination think him guilty, they send him to the jail of the general court, before which court he is to be tried first by a grand jury of 24, of whom 13 must concur in opinion; if they find him guilty, he is then tried by a jury of 12 men of the county where the offence was committed, and by their verdict, which must be unanimous, he is acquitted or condemned without appeal. If the criminal be a slave, the trial by the county court is final. In every case, however, except that of high treason, there resides in the governor a power of pardon. In high treason the pardon can only flow from the general assembly. In civil matters these justices have jurisdiction in all cases of whatever value, not appertaining to the department of the admiralty. This jurisdiction is twofold. If the matter in dispute be of less value than 4⅙ dollars, a single member may try it at any time and place within his county, and may award execution on the goods of the party cast. If it be of that or greater value, it is determinable before the county court, which consists of four at the least of those justices and assembles at the court-house of the county on a certain day in every month. From their determination, if the matter be of the value of ten pounds sterling, or concern the title or bounds of lands, an appeal lies to one of the superior courts.

There are three superior courts, to wit, the high court of chancery, the general court, and court of admiralty. The first and second of these receive appeals from the county courts, and also have original jurisdiction, where the subject of controversy is of the value of ten pounds sterling, or where it concerns the title or bounds of lands. The jurisdiction of the admiralty is original altogether. The high court of chancery is composed of three judges, the general court of five, and the court of admiralty of three. The two first hold their sessions at Richmond at stated times, the chancery twice in the year, and the general court twice for business civil and criminal, and twice more for criminal only. The court of admiralty sits at Williamsburg whenever a controversy arises.

There is one supreme court, called the court of appeals, composed of the judges of the three superior courts, assembling twice a year at stated times at Richmond. This court receives appeals in all civil cases from each of the superior courts, and determines them finally. But it has no original jurisdiction.

If a controversy arise between two foreigners of a nation in alliance with the United States, it is decided by the Consul for their State, or, if both parties chuse it, by the ordinary courts of justice. If one of the parties only be such a foreigner, it is triable before the courts of justice of the country. But if it shall have been instituted in a county court, the foreigner may remove it into the general court, or court of chancery, who are to determine it at their first sessions, as they must also do if it be originally commenced before them. In cases of life and death, such foreigners have a right to be tried by a jury, the one-half foreigners, the other natives.

All public accounts are settled with a board of auditors, consisting of three members appointed by the general assembly, any two of whom may act. But an individual, dissatisfied with the determination of that board, may carry his case into the proper superior court.

A description of the laws.

The general assembly was constituted, as has been already shown, by letters-patent of March the 9th, 1607, in the 4th year of the reign of James the first. The laws of England seem to have been adopted by consent of the settlers, which might easily enough be done whilst they were few and living all together. Of such adoption, however, we have no other proof than their practice till the year 1661, when they were expressly adopted by an act of the assembly, except so far as 'a difference of condition' rendered them inapplicable. Under this adoption, the rule, in our courts of judicature was, that the common law of England, and the general statutes previous to the 4th of James, were in force here; but that no subsequent statutes were, *unless we were named in them*, said the judges and other partisans of the crown, but *named or not named*, said those who reflected freely. It will be unnecessary to attempt a description of the laws of England, as that may be found in English publications. To those which were established here, by the adoption of the legislature, have been since added a number of acts of assembly passed during the monarchy, and ordinances of convention and acts of assembly enacted since the establishment of the republic. The following variations from the British model are perhaps worthy of being specified:

Debtors unable to pay their debts, and making faithful delivery of their whole effects, are released from confinement, and their persons forever discharged from restraint for such previous debts: but any property they may afterwards acquire will be subject to their creditors.

The poor, unable to support themselves, are maintained by an assessment on the titheable persons in their parish. This assessment is levied and administered by twelve persons in each parish, called vestrymen, originally chosen by the housekeepers of the parish, but afterwards filling vacancies in their own body by their own choice. These are usually the most discreet farmers, so distributed through their parish, that every part of it may be under the immediate eye of some one of them. They are well acquainted with the details and œconomy of private life, and they find sufficient inducements to execute their charge well, in their philanthropy, in the approbation of their neighbors, and the distinction which that gives them. The poor who have neither property, friends, nor strength to labour, are boarded in the houses of good farmers, to whom a stipulated sum is annually paid. To those who are able to help themselves a little, or have friends from whom they derive some succours, inadequate however to their full maintenance, supplementary aids are given which enable them to live comfortably in their own houses, or in the houses of their friends. Vagabonds without visible property or vocation, are placed in work houses, where they are well clothed, fed, lodged, and made to labour. Nearly the same methods of providing for the poor prevails through all our states; and from Savannah to Portsmouth you will seldom meet a beggar. In the larger towns, indeed, they sometimes present themselves. These are usually foreigners, who have never obtained a settlement in any parish. I never yet saw a native American begging in the streets or highways. A subsistence is easily gained here: and if, by misfortunes, they are thrown on the charities of the world, those provided by their own country are so comfortable and so certain, that they never think of relinquishing them to become strolling beggars. Their situation too, when sick, in the family of a good farmer, where every member is emulous to do them kind offices, where they are visited by all the neighbors, who bring them the little rarities which their sickly appetites may crave, and who take by rotation the nightly watch over them, when their condition requires it, Is without comparison better than in a general hospital, where the sick, the dying and the dead are crammed together in the same rooms, and often in the same beds. The disadvantages, inseparable from general hospitals, are such as can never be counterpoised by all the regularities of medicine and regimen. Nature and kind nursing save a much greater proportion in our plain way, at a smaller expense, and with less abuse. One branch only of hospital institution is wanting with us; that is a general establishment for those laboring under difficult cases of chirurgery. The aids of this art are not equivocal. But an able chirurgeon cannot be had in every parish. Such a receptacle should therefore be provided for those patients: but no others should be admitted.

Marriages must be solemnized either on special licence, granted by the first magistrate of the county, on proof of the consent of the parent or guardian of either party under age, or after solemn publication, on three several Sundays, at some place of religious worship, in the parishes where the parties reside. The act of solemnization may be by the minister of any society Christians, who shall have been previously licensed for this purpose by the court of the county. Quakers and Menonists however are exempted from all these conditions, and marriage among them is to be solemnized by the society itself.

A foreigner of any nation, not in open war with us, becomes naturalized by removing to the state to reside, and taking an oath of fidelity: and thereupon acquires every right of a native citizen: and citizens may divest themselves of that character, by declaring, by solemn deed, or in open court, that they mean to expatriate themselves, and no longer to be citizens of this state.

Conveyances of land must be registered in the court of the county wherein they lie, or in the general court, or they are void, as to creditors, and subsequent purchasers.

Slaves pass by descent and dower as lands do. Where the descent is from a parent, the heir is bound to pay an equal share of their value in money to each of his brothers and sisters.

Slaves, as well as lands, were entailable during the monarchy; but, by an act of the first republican assembly, all donees in tail, present and future, were vested with the absolute dominion of the entailed subject.

Bills of exchange, being protested, carry 10 per cent. Interest from their date.

No person is allowed, in any other case, to take more than five per centum per annum simple interest for the loan of moneys.

Gaming debts are made void, and monies actually paid to discharge such debts (if they exceed 40 shillings) may be recovered by the payer within three months, or by any other person afterwards.

Tobacco, flour, beef, pork, tar, pitch, and turpentine must be inspected by persons publicely appointed before they can be exported.

The erecting iron-works and mills is encouraged by many privileges; with necessary cautions however to prevent their dams from obstructing the navigation of the water courses. The general assembly have on several occasions shewn a great desire to encourage the opening the great falls of James and Patowmac rivers. As yet, however, neither of these have been effected.

The laws have also descended to the preservation and improvement of the races of useful animals, such as horses, cattle, deer; to the extirpation of those which are noxious, as wolves, squirrels, crows, blackbirds; and to the guarding our citizens against infectious disorders, by obliging suspected vessels coming into the state, to perform quarantine, and by regulating the conduct of persons having such disorders within the state.

The mode of acquiring lands, in the earliest times of our settlement, was by petition to the general assembly. If the lands prayed for were already cleared of the Indian title, and the assembly thought the prayer reasonable, they passed the property by their vote to the petitioner. But if they had not yet been ceded by the Indians, it was necessary that the petitioner should previously purchase their right. This purchase the assembly verified, by inquiries of the Indian proprietors; and being satisfied of its reality and fairness, proceeded further to examine the reasonableness of the petition, and its consistence with policy; and according to the result either granted or rejected the petition. The company also sometimes, though very rarely, granted lands, independently of the general assembly. As the colony increased, and individual applications for land multiplied, it was found to give too much occupation to the general assembly to inquire into and execute the grant in every special case. They therefore thought it better to establish general rules, according to which all grants should be made, and to leave to the governor the execution of them, under these rules. This they did by what have been usually called the land laws, amending them from time to time, as their defects were developed. According to these laws, when an individual wished a portion of unappropriated land, he was to locate and survey it by a public officer, appointed for that purpose: its breadth was to bear a certain proportion to its length: the grant was to be executed by the governor: and the lands were to be improved in a certain manner, within a given time. From these regulations there resulted to the state a sole and exclusive power of taking conveyances of the Indian right of soil; since, according to them an Indian conveyance alone could give no right to an individual, which the laws would acknowledge. The state, or the crown, thereafter, made general purchases of the Indians from time to time, and the governor parcelled them out by special grants, conformed to the rules before described, which it was not in his power, or in that of the crown, to dispense with. Grants, unaccompanied by their proper legal circumstances, were set aside regularly by *scire facias,* or by bill in Chancery. Since the establishment of our new government, this order of things is but little changed. An individual, wishing to appropriate to himself lands still unappropriated by any other, pays to the public treasurer a sum of money proportioned to the quantity he wants. He carries the treasurer's receipt to the auditors of public accompts, who thereupon debit the treasurer with the sum, and order the register of the land-office to give the party a warrant for his land. With this warrant from the register, he goes to the surveyor of the county where the land lies on which he has cast his eye. The Surveyor lays it off for him, gives him its exact description, in the form of a certificate, which certificate he returns to the land-office, where a grant is made out, and is signed by the governor. This vests in him a perfect dominion in his lands, transmissible to whom he pleases by deed or will, or by descent to his heirs, if he die intestate.

Many of the laws which were in force during the monarchy being relative merely to that form of government, or inculcating principles inconsistent with republicanism, the first assembly which met after the establishment of the commonwealth, appointed a committee to revise the whole code, to reduce it into proper form and volume, and report it to the assembly. This work has been executed by three gentlemen, and reported; but probably will not be taken up till a restoration of peace shall leave to the legislature leisure to go through such a work.

The plan of the revisal was this. The common law of England, by which is meant that part of the English law which was anterior to the date of the oldest statutes extant, is made the basis of the work. It was thought dangerous to attempt to reduce it to a text: it was therefore left to be collected from the usual monuments of it. Necessary alterations in that, and so much of the whole body of the British statutes, and of acts of assembly, as were thought proper to be retained, were digested into 126 new acts, in which simplicity of style was aimed at, as far as was safe. The following are the most remarkable alterations proposed:

To change the rules of descent, so as that the lands of any person dying intestate shall be divisible equally among all his children, or other representatives, in equal degree.

To make slaves distributable among the next of kin, as other movables.

To have all public expences, whether of the general treasury, or of a parish or county, (as for the maintenance of the poor, building bridges, courthouses, &c.,) supplied by assessments on the citizens, in proportion to their property.

To hire undertakers for keeping the public roads in repair, and indemnify individuals through whose lands new roads shall be opened.

To define with precision the rules whereby aliens should become citizens, and citizens make themselves aliens.

To establish religious freedom on the broadest bottom. . . .

The revised code further proposes to proportion crimes and punishments. This is attempted in the following scale:

    I. Crimes whose punishment extends to *Life*.

        1. High treason. Death by hanging. Forfeiture of lands and goods to the commonwealth.

        2. Petty treason. Death by hanging. Dissection. Forfeiture of half the lands and goods to the representatives of the party slain.

        3. Murder.

            1. By poison. Death by poison. Forfeiture of one-half, as before.

            2. In duel. Death by hanging. Gibbeting, if the challenger. Forfeiture of one-half as before, unless it be the party challenged, then the forfeiture is to the commonwealth.

            3. In any other way. Death by hanging. Forfeiture of one-half as before.

        4. Manslaughter. The second offence is murder.

    II. Crimes whose punishment goes to *Limb*.

        1. Rape . . . Dismemberment.

        2. Sodomy . . . Dismemberment.

        3. Maiming . . . Retaliation, and the forfeiture of half of the lands and goods to the sufferer.

        4. Disfiguring . . . Retaliation, and the forfeiture of half of the lands and goods to the sufferer.

III. Crimes punishable by *Labour*.

1. Manslaughter, 1st offence.	Labor VII. Years for the public.	Forfeiture of half, as in murder.
2. Counterfeiting money.	Labor VI. Years.	Forfeiture of lands and goods to the commonwealth.
3. Arson	Labor V. years.	Reparation threefold.
4. Asportation of vessels.		
5. Robbery.	Labor IV. Years.	Reparation double.
6. Burglary.		
7. House-breaking.	Labor III. Years.	Reparation.
8. Horse-stealing.		
9. Grand larceny.	Labor II. Years.	Reparation. Pillory.
10. Petty larceny.	Labor I. year.	Reparation. Pillory.
11. Pretensions to witchcraft, &c.	Ducking.	Stripes.
12. Excusable homicide.	To be pitied, not punished.	
13. Suicide.		
14. Apostacy. Heresy.		

Pardon and privilege of clergy are proposed to be abolished; but if the verdict be against the defendant, the court in their discretion may allow a new trial. No attainder to cause a corruption of blood, or forfeiture of dower. Slaves guilty of offences punishable in others by labour, to be transported to Africa, or elsewhere, as the circumstances of the time admit, there to be continued in slavery. A rigorous regimen proposed for those condemned to labour.

Another object of the revisal is, to diffuse knowledge more generally through the mass of the people. This bill proposes to lay off every country into small districts of five or six miles square, called hundreds and in each of them to establish a school for teaching, reading, writing, and arithmetic. The tutor to be supported by the hundred, and every person in it entitled to send their children three years gratis, and as much longer as they please, paying for it. These schools to be under a visitor who is annually to chuse the boy of best genius in the school, of those whose parents are too poor to give them further education, and to send him forward to one of the grammar schools, of which twenty are proposed to be erected in different parts of the country, for teaching Greek, Latin, geography, and the higher branches of numerical arithmetic. Of the boys thus sent in any one year, trial is to be made at the grammar schools one or two years, and the best genius of the whole selected, and continued six years, and the residue dismissed. By this means twenty of the best geniuses will be raked from the rubbish annually, and be instructed, at the public expence, so far as the grammar schools go. At the end of six years instruction, one half are to be discontinued (from among whom the grammar schools will probably be supplied with future masters); and the other half, who are to be chosen for the superiority of their parts and disposition, are to be sent and continued three years in the study of such sciences as they shall chuse, at William and Mary college, the plan of which is proposed to be enlarged, as will be hereafter explained, and extended to all the useful sciences. The ultimate result of the whole scheme of education would be the teaching all the children of the State reading, writing, and common arithmetic; turning out ten annually, of superior genius, well taught in Greek, Latin, geography, and the higher branches of arithmetic; turning out ten others annually, of still superior parts, who, to those branches of learning, shall have added such of the sciences as their genius shall have them led to; the furnishing to the wealthier part of the people convenient schools at which their children may be educated at their own expence.—The general objects of this law are to provide an education adapted to the years, to the capacity, and the condition of every one, and directed to their freedom and happiness. Specific details were not proper for the law. These must be the business of the visitors entrusted with its execution. The first stage of this education being the schools of the hundreds, wherein the great mass of the people will receive their instruction, the principal foundations of future order will be laid here. Instead, therefore, of putting the Bible and Testament into the hands of the

children at an age when their judgments are not sufficiently matured for religious inquiries, their memories may here be stored with the most useful
facts from Grecian, Roman, European, and American history. The first elements of morality too may be instilled into their minds; such as, when further developed as their judgments advance in strength, may teach them how
to work out their own greatest happiness, by shewing them that it does not
depend on the condition of life in which chance has placed them, but is always the result of a good conscience, good health, occupation, and freedom
in all just pursuits.—Those whom either the wealth of their parents or the
adoption of the state shall destine to higher degrees of learning, will go on to
the grammar schools, which constitute the next stage, there to be instructed
in the languages. The learning Greek and Latin, I am told, is going into disuse
in Europe. I know not what their manners and occupations may call for: but
it would be very ill-judged in us to follow their example in this instance.
There is a certain period of life, say from eight to fifteen or sixteen years of
age, when the mind like the body is not yet firm enough for laborious and
close operations. If applied to such, it falls an early victim to premature exertion; exhibiting, indeed, at first, in these young and tender subjects, the
flattering appearance of their being men while they are yet children, but end-
ing in reducing them to be children when they should be men. The memory
is then most susceptible and tenacious of impressions; and the learning of
languages being chiefly a work of memory, it seems precisely fitted to the
powers of this period, which is long enough too for acquiring the most useful
languages, antient and modern. I do not pretend that language is science. It
is only an instrument for the attainment of science. But that time is not lost
which is employed in providing tools for future operation: more especially
as in this case the books put into the hands of the youth for this purpose may
be such as will at the same time impress their minds with useful facts and
good principles. If this period be suffered to pass in idleness, the mind becomes lethargic and impotent, as would the body it inhabits if unexercised
during the same time. The sympathy between body and mind during their
rise, progress and decline, is too strict and obvious to endanger our being
misled while we reason from the one to the other.—As soon as they are of
sufficient age, it is supposed they will be sent on from the grammar schools
to the university, which constitutes our third and last stage, there to study
those sciences which may be adapted to their views.—By that part of our
plan which prescribes the selection of the youths of genius from among the
classes of the poor, we hope to avail the state of those talents which nature
has shown as liberally among the poor as the rich, but which perish without
use, If not sought for and cultivated.—But of all the views of this law none is
more important, none more legitimate, than that of rendering the people the
safe, as they are the ultimate, guardians of their own liberty. For this purpose
the reading in the first stage, where *they* will receive their whole education,
is proposed, as has been said, to be chiefly historical. History, by apprising

them of the past, will enable them to judge of the future; it will avail them of the experience of other times and other nations; it will qualify them as judges of the actions and designs of men; it will enable them to know ambition under every disguise it may assume; and knowing it, to defeat its views. In every government on earth is some trace of human weakness, some germ of corruption and degeneracy, which cunning will discover, and wickedness insensibly open, cultivate and improve. Every government degenerates when trusted to the rulers of the people alone. The people themselves therefore are its only safe depositories. And to render even them safe, their minds must be improved to a certain degree. This indeed is not all that is necessary, though it be essentially necessary. An amendment of our constitution must here come in aid of the public education. The influence over government must be shared among all the people. If every individual which composes their mass participates of the ultimate authority, the government will be safe; because the corrupting the whole mass will exceed any private resources of wealth; and public ones cannot be provided but by levies on the people. In this case every man would have to pay his own price. The government of Great Britain has been corrupted, because but one man in ten has a right to vote for members of parliament. The sellers of the government, therefore, get nine-tenths of their price clear. It has been thought that corruption Is restrained by confining the right of suffrage to a few of the wealthier of the people: but it would be more effectually restrained by an extension of that right to such members as would bid defiance to the means of corruption.

Lastly, it is proposed, by a bill in this revisal, to begin a public library and gallery, by laying out a certain sum annually in books, paintings, and statues.

QUERY XVII: *The different religions received into that State?*

The first settlers in this country were emigrants from England, of the English church, just at a point of time when it was flushed with complete victory over the religious of all other persuasions. Possessed, as they became, of the powers of making, administering and executing the laws, they shewed equal intolerance in this country with their Presbyterian brethren, who had emigrated to the northern government. The poor Quakers were flying from persecution in England. They cast their eyes on these new countries as asylums of civil and religious freedom; but they found them free only for the reigning sect. Several acts of the Virginia assembly of 1659, 1662, and 1693, had made it penal in parents to refuse to have their children baptized; had prohibited the unlawful assembling of Quakers; had made it penal for any master of a vessel to bring a Quaker into the state; had ordered those already here, and such as should come thereafter, to be imprisoned till they should abjure the country; provided a milder punishment for their first and second return, but death for their third; had inhibited all persons from suffering their meetings in or near their houses, entertaining them individually, or disposing of books which supported their tenets. If no capital execution took place here, as did in New-England, it was not owing to the moderation of the church, or spirit of the legislature, as may be inferred from the law itself; but to historical circumstances which have not been handed down to us. The Anglicans retained full possession of the country about a century. Other opinions began then to creep in, and the great care of the government to support their own church, having begotten an equal degree of indolence in its clergy, two thirds of the people had become dissenters at the commencement of the present revolution. The laws indeed were still oppressive on them, but the spirit of the one party had subsided into moderation, and of the other had risen to a degree of determination which commanded respect.

The present state of our laws on the subject of religion is this. The convention of May 1776, in their declaration of rights, declared it to be a truth, and a natural right, that the exercise of religion should be free; but when they proceeded to form on that declaration the ordinance of government, instead of taking up every principle declared in the bill of rights, and guarding it by legislative sanction, they passed over that which asserted our religious rights, leaving them as they found them. The same convention, however, when they met as a member of the general assembly in October 1776, repealed all *acts of parliament* which had rendered criminal the maintaining any opinions in matters of religion, the forbearing to repair to church, and the exercising any mode of worship; and suspended the laws giving salaries to the clergy, which suspension was made perpetual in October 1779. Statutory oppressions in religion being thus wiped away, we remain at present under those only imposed by the common law, or by our own acts of assembly. At the common law, *heresy* was a capital offence, punishable by burning. Its definition was left to the ecclesiastical judges, before whom the conviction was, till the statute of the 1 El. C. 1. Circumscribed it, by declaring that nothing should be deemed heresy but what had been so determined by authority of the canonical scriptures, or by one of the four first general councils, or by some other council having for the grounds of their declaration the express and plain words of the scriptures. Heresy, thus circumscribed, being an offence at the common law, our act of assembly of October 1777, c. 17 gives cognizance of it to the general court, by declaring that the jurisdiction of that court shall be general in all matters at the common law. The execution is by the writ *De hæretico comburendo*. By our own act of assembly of 1705, c. 30, if a person brought up in the Christian religion denies the being of a God, or the trinity, or asserts there are more Gods than one, or denies the Christian religion to be true, or the scriptures to be of divine authority, he is punishable on the first offence by incapacity to hold any office or employment ecclesiastical, civil, or military; on the second by disability to sue, to take any gift or legacy, to be guardian, executor or administrator, and by three years imprisonment, without bail. A father's right to the custody of his own children being founded in law on his right of guardianship, this being taken away, they may of course be severed from him and put, by the authority of a court, into more orthodox hands. This is a summary view of that religious slavery under which a people have been willing to remain who have lavished their lives and fortunes for the establishment of their civil freedom. The error seems not sufficiently eradicated, that the operations of the mind, as well as the acts of the body, are subject to the coercion of the laws. But our rulers can have authority over such natural rights, only as we have submitted to them. The rights of conscience we never submitted, we could not submit. We are answerable for them to our God. The legitimate powers of government extend to such acts only as are injurious to others. But it does me no injury for my neighbor to say there are twenty gods, or no god. It neither picks my pocket nor breaks my leg. If it be said his testimony in a court of justice cannot be relied on, reject it then, and be the stigma on him. Constraint may make him worse by making him a hypocrite, but it will never make him a truer man. It may fix him obstinately in his errors, but will not cure them. Reason and free inquiry are the only effectual agents against error. Give a loose to them, they will support the true religion by bringing every false one to their tribunal, to the test of their investigation. They are the natural enemies of error, and of error only. Had not the Roman government permitted free inquiry, Christianity could never have been introduced. Had not free inquiry been indulged, at the æra of the reformation, the corruptions of Christianity could not have been purged away. If it be restrained now, the present corruptions will be protected, and new ones encouraged. Was the government to prescribe to us our medicine and diet, our bodies would be in such keeping as our souls are now. Thus in France the emetic was once forbidden as a medicine, and the potatoe as an article of food. Government is just as infallible, too, when it fixes systems in physics. Galileo was sent to the inquisition for affirming that the earth was a sphere; the government had declared it to be as flat as a trencher, and Galileo was obliged to abjure his error. This error however at length prevailed, the earth became a globe, and Descartes declared it was whirled round its axis by a vortex. The government in which he lived was wise enough to see that this was no question of civil jurisdiction, or we should all have been involved by authority in vortices. In fact the vortices have been exploded, and the Newtonian principles of gravitation is now more firmly established, on the basis of reason, than it would be were the government to step in and to make it an article of necessary faith. Reason and experiment have been indulged, and error has fled before them. It is error alone which needs the support of government. Truth can stand by itself. Subject opinion to coercion: whom will you make your inquisitors? Fallible men; men governed by bad passions, by private as well as public reasons. And why subject it to coercion? To produce uniformity. But is uniformity of opinion desireable? No more than of face and stature. Introduce the bed of Procrustes then, and as there is danger that the large men may beat the small, make us all of a size, by lopping the former and stretching the latter. Difference of opinion is advantageous in religion. The several sects perform the office of a Censor morum over each other. Is uniformity attainable? Millions of innocent men, women and children, since the introduction of Christianity, have been burnt, tortured, fined, imprisoned: yet we have not advanced one inch towards uniformity. What has been the effect of coercion? To make one half the world fools, and the other half hypocrites. To support roguery and error all over the earth. Let us reflect that it is inhabited by a thousand millions of people. That these profess probably a thousand different systems of religion. That ours is but one of that thousand. That if there be but one right, and ours that one, we should wish to see the 999 wandering sects gathered into the fold of truth. But against such a majority we cannot effect this by force. Reason and persuasion are the only practicable instruments. To make way for these, free inquiry must be indulged; and how can we wish others to indulge it while we refuse it ourselves. But every state, says an inquisitor, has established some religion. "No two, say I, have established the same." Is this a proof of the infallibility of establishments? Our sister states of Pennsylvania and New York, however, have long subsisted without any establishment at all. The experiment was new and doubtful when they made it. It has answered beyond conception. They flourish infinitely. Religion is well supported; of various kinds indeed, but all good enough; all sufficient to preserve peace and order: or if a sect arises whose tenets would subvert morals, good sense has fair play, and reasons and laughs it out of doors, without suffering the state to be troubled with it. They do not hang more male-factors than we do. They are not more disturbed with religious dissentions. On the contrary, their harmony is unparallelled, and can be ascribed to nothing but their unbounded tolerance, because there is no other circumstance in which they differ from every nation on earth. They have made the happy discovery, that the way to silence religious disputes, is to take no notice of them. Let us too give this experiment fair play, and get rid, while we may, of those tyrannical laws. It is true we are as yet secured against them by the spirit of the times. I doubt whether the people of this country would suffer an execution for heresy, or a three years imprisonment for not comprehending the mysteries of the trinity. But is the spirit of the people an infallible, a permanent reliance? Is it government? Is this the kind of protection we receive in return for the rights we give up? Besides, the spirit of the times may alter, will alter. Our rulers will become corrupt, our people careless. A single zealot may commence persecuter, and better men be his victims. It can never be too often repeated, that the time for fixing every essential right on a legal basis is while our rulers are honest, and ourselves united. From the conclusion of this war we shall be going down hill. It will not then be necessary to resort every moment to the people for support. They will be forgotten therefore, and their rights disregarded. They will forget themselves, but in the sole faculty of making money, and will never think of uniting to effect a due respect for their rights. The shackles, therefore, which shall not be knocked off at the conclusion of this war, will remain on us long, will be made heavier and heavier, till our rights shall revive or expire in a convulsion.

SOURCE: Andrew A. Lipscomb and Albert Ellery Bergh, ed., *The Works of Thomas Jefferson*, Memorial Edition, 20 vols., (Washington, DC: Thomas Jefferson Memorial Association, 1903), II: 179-191, 201-208, 217-225.

2. THOMAS JEFFERSON AND JOHN ADAMS ON THE NATURAL ARISTOCRACY

John Adams and Thomas Jefferson—the "North and South Poles of the American Revolution"—are two of America's greatest founding fathers. Both were revolutionaries, political philosophers, politicians, statesmen, diplomats, and both served as vice-president and president of the United States. They were also friends. The Adams-Jefferson friendship began in 1775 when they met at the Second Continental Congress in Philadelphia. They served together on the committee responsible for drafting the Declaration of Independence, and they became particularly close in the mid 1780s when they both served as American diplomats in France (Jefferson) and England (Adams). Their friendship began to fray in the late 1780s and early 1790s when the two men differed over their competing views on the French Revolution and American domestic politics, and then it ended abruptly in 1801 after Jefferson's victory over Adams in the presidential election of 1800. The two men did not correspond with each other for the next eleven years. Their friendship was restored through the relentless efforts of their mutual friend, Benjamin Rush, who worked behind the scenes for almost two years to bring these two men back into good will with each other. The result was one of the most extraordinary correspondences in American history. Now both out of political office, the two old men in the declining years of their lives used their correspondence to wander together through history, philosophy, theology, literature, and politics. In the two letters below, Adams and Jefferson discuss what they mean by "natural aristocracy," and the role that it should play in American life. Remarkably, Adams and Jefferson both died on July 4, 1826, exactly fifty years to the day after the Americans' declaration of independence.

JOHN ADAMS TO THOMAS JEFFERSON, SEPTEMBER 2, 1813

. . . Now, my Friend, who are the αριϛτοι ["aristocrats"]? Philosophers may answer, "The Wise and Good." But the world, mankind, have by their practice, always answered, "the rich the beautiful and well born." And Philosophers themselves in marrying their childen prefer the rich, the handsome, and the well descended to the wise and good.

What chance have talents and virtues in competition, with wealth and birth? and beauty?

Haud facile emergunt, quorum Virtutibus obstant
Res Angusta Domi.

One truth is clear, by all the world confessed
Slow rises worth, by poverty depresseed.

The five pillars of aristocracy are beauty wealth, birth, genius and virtues. Any one of the three first can, at any time, over bear any one or both of the two last.

Let me ask again, what a wave of publick opinion, in favour of birth has been spread over the globe by Abraham, by Hercules, by Mahomet, by Guelphs, Ghibellines, Bourbons, and a miserable Scottish chief Stuart, by Zingis by ____, by ____, by, a million others. And what a wave will be Spread by Napoleon and by Washington! Their remotest cousins will be sought, and will be proud, and will avail themselves of their descent. Call this principle, prejudice, folly, ignorance, baseness, slavery, stupidity, adulation, superstition, or what you will, I will not contradict you. But the fact, in natural, moral, political, and domestic history, I cannot deny, or dispute, or question.

And is this great fact in the natural history of man, this unalterable principle of morals, philosophy, policy, domestic felicity, and daily experience from the creation, to be overlooked, forgotten, neglected, or hypocritically waived out of sight, by a Legislator, by a professed writer upon civil government, and upon constitutions of civil government? . . .

You may laugh at the introduction of beauty among the pillars of aristocracy. But Madame du Barry says, "*la véritable royauté c'est la beauté*," and there is not a more certain truth. Beauty, grace, figure, attitude, movement, have, in innumerable instances prevailed over wealth, birth, talents virtues and every thing else, in men of the highest rank, greatest power, and, sometimes, the most exalted genius, greatest fame, and highest merit.

SOURCE: Selections of a letter from John Adams to Thomas Jefferson, September 2, 1813, in Charles Francis Adams, ed., *The Works of John Adams,* 10 vols., (Boston: Little, Brown and Company, 1856), 10:64-66.

THOMAS JEFFERSON TO JOHN ADAMS, OCTOBER 28, 1813

. . . I agree with you that there is a natural aristocracy among men. The grounds of this are virtue and talents. Formerly, bodily powers gave place among the aristoi. But since the invention of gunpowder has armed the weak as well as the strong with missile death, bodily strength, like beauty, good humor, politeness and other accomplishments, has become but an auxiliary ground of distinction. There is also an artificial aristocracy founded on wealth and birth, without either virtue or talents; for with these it would belong to the first class. The natural aristocracy I consider as the most precious gift of nature for the instruction, the trusts, and government of society. And indeed, it would have been inconsistent in creation to have formed man for the social state, and not to have provide virtue and wisdom enough to manage the concerns of the society. May we not even say, that that form of government is the best, which provides the most effectually for a pure selection of these natural aristoi into the offices of government? The artificial aristocracy is a mischievous ingredient in government, and provision should be made to prevent its ascendancy. On the question, what is the best provision, you and I differ; but we differ as rational friends, using the free exercise of our own reason, and mutually indulging its errors. You think it best to put the pseudo-aristoi into a separate chamber of legislation, where they may be hindered from doing mischief by their coordinate branches, and where, also, they may be a protection to wealth against the Agrarian and plundering enterprises of the majority of the people. I think that to give them power in order to prevent them from doing mischief, is arming them for it, and increasing instead of remedying the evil. For if the co-ordinate branches can arrest their action, so may they that of co-ordinates. Mischief may be done negatively as well as positively. Of this, a cabal in the Senate of the United States has furnished many proofs. Nor do I believe them necessary to protect the wealthy; because enough of these will find their way into every branch of the legislation, to protect themselves. From fifteen to twenty legislatures of our own, in action for thirty years past, have proved that no fears of an equalization of property are to be apprehended from them. I think the best remedy is exactly that provided by all our constitutions, to leave to the citizens the free election and separation of the aristoi from the pseudo-aristoi, of the wheat from the chaff. In general they will elect the real good and wise. In some instances, wealth may corrupt, and birth blind them; but not in sufficient degree to endanger the society.

It is probable that our difference of opinion may, in some measure, be produced by a difference of character in those among whom we live. From what I have seen of Massachusetts and Connecticut myself, and still more from what I have heard, and the character given of the former by yourself, . . . who know them so much better, there seems to be in those two states a traditionary reverence for certain families, which has rendered the offices of the government nearly hereditary in those families. I presume that from an early period of your history, members of these families happening to possess virtue and talents, have honestly exercised them for the good of the people, and by their services have endeared their names to them. In coupling Connecticut with you, I mean it politically only, not morally. For having made the Bible the common law of their land, they seem to have modeled their morality on the story of Jacob and Laban. But although this hereditary succession to office with you may in some degree be founded in real family merit, yet in a much higher , it has proceeded form your strict alliance of Church and State. These families are canonized in the eyes of the people on the common principle "you tickle me, and I will tickle you." In Virginia we have nothing of this. Our clergy, before the revolution, having been secured against rivalship by fixed salaries, did not give themselves the trouble of acquiring influence over the people. Of wealth, there were great accumulations in particular families, handed down from generation to generation under the English law of entails. But the only object of ambition for the wealthy was a seat in the King's Council. All their court then was paid to the crown and its creatures; and they Philipized in all collisions between the King and people. Hence they were unpopular; and that unpopularity continues attached to their names. A Randolph, a Carter, or a Burwell must have great personal superiority over a common competitor to be elected by the people, even at this day. At the first session of our legislature after the Declaration of Independence, we passed a law abolishing entails. And this was followed by one abolishing the privilege of primogeniture, and dividing the lands of intestates equally among all their children, or other representatives. These laws, drawn by myself, laid the axe to the rood of pseudo-aristocracy. And had another which I prepared been adopted by the legislature, our work would have been complete. It was a bill for the more general diffusion of learning. This proposed to divide every county into wards of five or six miles square, like your townships; to establish in each ward a free school for reading, writing and common arithmetic; to provide for the annual selection of the best subjects from these schools, who might receive at the pubic expense a higher degree of education at a district school; and from these district schools to select a certain number of the most promising subjects to be completed at an university, where all the useful sciences should be taught. Worth and genius would thus have been sought out form every condition of life, and completely prepared by education for defeating the competition of wealth and birth for public trusts. My proposition had, for a further object, to impart to these wards those portions of self-government for which they are best qualified, by confiding to them the care of their poor, their roads, police, elections, the nomination of jurors, administration of justice in small cases, elementary exercises of militia; in short, to have made them little republics, with a warden at the head of each, for all those concerns which, being under their eye, they would better manage than the larger republics of the country or State. A general call of ward-meetings by their wardens on the same day through the State would at any time produce the genuine sense of the people on any required point, and would enable the State to act in mass, as your people have so often done, and with so much effect, by their town meetings. The law for religious freedom, with made a part of this system, having put down the aristocracy of the clergy, and restored to the citizen the freedom of the mind, and those of entails and descents nurturing an equality of condition among them, this on education would have raised the mass of the people to the high ground of moral respectability necessary to their own safety, and to orderly government; and would have completed the great object of qualifying them to select the veritable aristoi, for the trusts of government, to the exclusion of the pseudalists; and the same Theognis who has furnished the epigraphs of your two letters, assures us that "ονδεμιαν πω Κυρν· άγαθοι πολιν ώλεσαν άνδ ρες." Although this law has not yet been acted on but in a small and inefficient degree, it is still considered as before the legislature, with other bills of the revised code, not yet taken up, and I have great hope that some patriotic spirit will, at a favorable moment, call it up, and make it the key-stone of the arch of our government

With respect to aristocracy, we should further consider, that before the establishment of the American States, nothing was known to History but the man of the old world, crowded within limits either small or overcharged, and steeped in the vices which that situation generates. A government adapted to such men would be one thing; but a very different one, that for the man of these States. Here everyone may have land to labor for himself, if he chooses; or, preferring the exercise of any other industry, may exact for it such compensation as not only to afford a comfortable subsistence, but wherewith to provide for a cessation form labor in old age. Everyone, by his property, or by his satisfactory situation, is interested in the support of law and order. And such men may safely and advantageously reserve to themselves a wholesome control over their public affairs, and a degree of freedom, which in the hands of the *canaille* of the cities of Europe, would be instantly perverted to the demolition and destruction of everything public and private. The history of the last twenty-five years of France, and of the last forty years in America, nay of its last two hundred years, proves the truth of both parts of this observation.

But even in Europe a change has sensibly taken place in the mind of man. Science has liberated the ideas of those who read and reflect, and the American example has kindled feelings of right in the people. An insurrection has consequently begun, of science, talents, and courage against rank and birth, which have fallen into contempt. It has failed in its first effort, because the mobs of the cities, the instrument used for its accomplishment, debased by ignorance, poverty and vice, could not be restrained to rational action. But the world will recover from the panic of this first catastrophe. Science is progressive, and talents and enterprise on the alert. Resort may be had to the people of the country, a more governable power from their principles and subordination; and rank, and birth, and tinsel-aristocracy will finally shrink into insignificance, even there. This, however, we have no right to meddle with. It suffices for us, if the moral and physical condition of our own citizens qualifies them to select the able and good for the direction of their government, with a recurrence of elections at such short periods as will enable them to displace an unfaithful servant, before the mischief he mediates may be irremediable.

I have thus stated my opinion on a point on which we differ, not with a view to controversy, for we are both too old to change opinions which are the result of a long life of inquiry and reflection; but on the suggestion of a former letter of yours, that we ought not to die before we have explained ourselves to each other. We acted in perfect harmony, through a long and perilous contest for our liberty and independence. A constitution has been acquired, which, though neither of us think perfect, yet both consider as competent to render our fellow-citizens the happiest and the securest on whom the sun has ever shone. If we do not think exactly alike as to its imperfections, it matters little to our country, which, after devoting to it long lives of disinterested labor, we have delivered over to our successors in life, who will be able to take care of it and of themselves. . . .

SOURCE: Selections of a letter from Thomas Jefferson to John Adams, October 28, 1813, in Andrew A. Lipscomb and Albert Ellery Bergh, ed., *The Works of Thomas Jefferson*, "Memorial Edition," 20 vols., (Washington, DC: Thomas Jefferson Memorial Association, 1903), 13: 394-404.

3. PATRICK HENRY
A BILL ESTABLISHING A PROVISION FOR TEACHERS OF THE CHRISTIAN RELIGION
JANUARY 1, 1784

Patrick Henry (1736-1799) was a Virginia planter, self-educated lawyer, revolutionary, patriot, politician, orator, constitution-maker, and founding father. He twice served as governor of Virginia (1776-1779 and 1784-1786). Henry was a proponent of the common eighteenth-century view that Christianity was principally responsible for maintaining a morally virtuous society. To that end, Henry proposed to the Virginia General Assembly in 1784 "A Bill Establishing a Provision for Teachers of the Christian Religion," the purpose of which was to support Christian teachings broadly conceived, believing that Christian morality could restrain men's vices, improve their morals, and preserve societal peace. The bill proposed implementing a general tax assessment that would fund Christian teachers and religious education in Virginia. Each taxpayer could choose which Christian denomination would receive their tax money. If no denominational preference were indicated, the taxpayer money would go to a general education fund. Henry's bill was viewed as a compromise between having an established Anglican Church (which Virginia did before the Revolution) and complete separation of church and state, which many people were now pushing for. The question raised by Henry's bill was: Is the proper role of government in a free society to inculcate religious virtue in its citizens by violating their rights. Henry's bill faced significant opposition, particularly from James Madison and Thomas Jefferson (see below), who were proponents of a separation of church and state. Henry's bill was ultimately defeated in a statewide movement for disestablishment and religious freedom.

Whereas the general diffusion of Christian knowledge hath a natural tendency to correct the morals of men, restrain their vices, and preserve the peace of society; which cannot be effected without a competent provision for learned teachers, who may be thereby enabled to devote their time and attention to the duty of instructing such citizens, as from their circumstances and want of education, cannot otherwise attain such knowledge; and it is judged that such provision may be made by the Legislature, without counteracting the liberal principle heretofore adopted and intended to be preserved by abolishing all distinctions of preeminence amongst the different societies or communities of Christians;

Be it therefore enacted by the General Assembly, That for the support of Christian teachers, per centum on the amount, or in the pound on the sum payable for tax on the property within this Commonwealth, is hereby assessed, and shall be paid by every person chargeable with the said tax at the time the same shall become due; and the Sheriffs of the several Counties shall have power to levy and collect the same in the same manner and under the like restrictions and limitations, as are or may be prescribed by the laws for raising the Revenues of this State.

And be it enacted, That for every sum so paid, the Sheriff or Collector shall give a receipt, expressing therein to what society of Christians the person from whom he may receive the same shall direct the money to be paid, keeping a distinct account thereof in his books. The Sheriff of every County, shall, on or before the___ day of___ in every year, return to the Court, upon oath, two alphabetical lists of the payments to him made, distinguishing in columns opposite to the names of the persons who shall have paid the same, the society to which the money so paid was by them appropriated; and one column for the names where no appropriation shall be made. One of which lists, after being recorded in a book to be kept for that purpose, shall be filed by the Clerk in his office; the other shall by the Sheriff be fixed up in the Court-house, there to remain for the inspection of all concerned. And the Sheriff, after deducting five per centum for the collection, shall forthwith pay to such person or persons as shall be appointed to receive the same by the Vestry, Elders, or Directors, however denominated of each such society, the sum so stated to be due to that society....

And be it further enacted, That the money to be raised by virtue of this Act, shall be by the Vestries, Elders, or Directors of each religious society, appropriated to a provision for a Minister or Teacher of the Gospel of their denomination, or the providing places of divine worship, and to none other use whatsoever; except in the denominations of Quakers and Menonists, who may receive what is collected from their members, and place it in their general fund, to be disposed of in a manner which they shall think best calculated to promote their particular mode of worship.

And be it enacted, That all sums which at the time of payment to the Sheriff or Collector may not be appropriated by the person paying the same, shall be accounted for with the Court in manner as by this Act is directed; and after deducting for his collection, the Sheriff shall pay the amount thereof (upon account certified by the Court to the Auditors of Public Accounts, and by them to the Treasurer) into the public Treasury, to be disposed of under the direction of the General Assembly, for the encouragement of seminaries of learning within the Counties whence such sums shall arise, and to no other use or purpose whatsoever.

THIS Act shall commence, and be in force, from and after the _____ day of _____ in the year _____

SOURCE: Patrick Henry, A Bill Establishing a Provision for Teachers of the Christian Religion, ContextUS: https://contextus.org/Patrick_Henry%2C_A_Bill_Establishing_a_Provision_for_Teachers_of_the_Christian_Religion.1?lang=en&with=About&lang2=en

4. JAMES MADISON
A MEMORIAL AND REMONSTRANCE AGAINST RELIGIOUS ASSESSMENTS
1785

James Madison wrote "A Memorial and Remonstrance Against Religious Assessments" in 1785 in response to Patrick Henry's "A Bill Establishing a Provision for Teachers of the Christian Religion." The historical background relative to both Henry's bill and Madison's response can be found in two events of the time: first, the disestablishment of Anglican Church in the wake of independence; and second, the rise of several Protestant denominations in Virginia, such as the Baptists, Presbyterians, and Methodists, all of which had been growing in numbers and influence in rural Virginia as a result of the Great Awakening. These dissenting, non-establishment churches opposed Henry's bill, arguing that it infringed upon their religious liberty. Madison's "Memorial and Remonstrance" was a tour-de-force in support of disestablishment, separation of church and state, and religious freedom. The "Memorial and Remonstrance" listed fifteen arguments against taxpayer support for religion, including most importantly: 1) that religion is a matter between individuals and their God, and must not be regulated government; 2) that civil government should have no jurisdiction over religious beliefs or practices; 3) that taxpayer support for religion via government redistribution would lead to religious and political corruption; 4) that true religious faith flourishes best when it is supported by voluntary contributions, not taxes. Madison's "Memorial and Remonstrance" was a key document in rallying opposition and ultimately defeating Henry's bill. In the place of Henry's bill, Virginia instead adopted Thomas Jefferson's "Virginia Statute for Religious Freedom" in 1786, which Madison helped to steer through the state legislature.

TO THE HONORABLE THE GENERAL ASSEMBLY OF THE COMMONWEALTH OF VIRGINIA A MEMORIAL AND REMONSTRANCE

We the subscribers, citizens of the said Commonwealth, having taken into serious consideration, a Bill printed by order of the last Session of General Assembly, entitled "A Bill establishing a provision for Teachers of the Christian Religion," and conceiving that the same if finally armed with the sanctions of a law, will be a dangerous abuse of power, are bound as faithful members of a free State to remonstrate against it, and to declare the reasons by which we are determined. We remonstrate against the said Bill,

1. Because we hold it for a fundamental and undeniable truth, "that Religion or the duty which we owe to our Creator and the manner of discharging it, can be directed only by reason and conviction, not by force or violence." The Religion then of every man must be left to the conviction and conscience of every man; and it is the right of every man to exercise it as these may dictate. This right is in its nature an unalienable right. It is unalienable, because the opinions of men, depending only on the evidence contemplated by their own minds cannot follow the dictates of other men: It is unalienable also, because what is here a right towards men, is a duty towards the Creator. It is the duty of every man to render to the Creator such homage and such only as he believes to be acceptable to him. This duty is precedent, both in order of time and in degree of obligation, to the claims of Civil Society. Before any man can be considered as a member of Civil Society, he must be considered as a subject of the Governour of the Universe: And if a member of Civil Society, who enters into any subordinate Association, must always do it with a reservation of his duty to the General Authority; much more must every man who becomes a member of any particular Civil Society, do it with a saving of his allegiance to the Universal Sovereign. We maintain therefore that in matters of Religion, no mans right is abridged by the institution of Civil Society and that Religion is wholly exempt from its cognizance. True it is, that no other rule exists, by which any question which may divide a Society, can be ultimately determined, but the will of the majority; but it is also true that the majority may trespass on the rights of the minority.

2. Because if Religion be exempt from the authority of the Society at large, still less can it be subject to that of the Legislative Body. The latter are but the creatures and vicegerents of the former. Their jurisdiction is both derivative and limited: it is limited with regard to the co-ordinate departments, more necessarily is it limited with regard to the constituents. The preservation of a free Government requires not merely, that the metes and bounds which separate each department of power be invariably maintained; but more especially that neither of them be suffered to overleap the great Barrier which defends the rights of the people. The Rulers who are guilty of such an encroachment, exceed the commission from which they derive their authority, and are Tyrants. The People who submit to it are governed by laws made neither by themselves nor by an authority derived from them, and are slaves.

3. Because it is proper to take alarm at the first experiment on our liberties. We hold this prudent jealousy to be the first duty of Citizens, and one of the noblest characteristics of the late Revolution. The free men of America did not wait till usurped power had strengthened itself by exercise, and entangled the question in precedents. They saw all the consequences in the principle, and they avoided the consequences by denying the principle. We revere this lesson too much soon to forget it. Who does not see that the same authority which can establish Christianity, in exclusion of all other Religions,

may establish with the same ease any particular sect of Christians, in exclusion of all other Sects? that the same authority which can force a citizen to contribute three pence only of his property for the support of any one establishment, may force him to conform to any other establishment in all cases whatsoever?

4. Because the Bill violates that equality which ought to be the basis of every law, and which is more indispensible, in proportion as the validity or expediency of any law is more liable to be impeached. If "all men are by nature equally free and independent," all men are to be considered as entering into Society on equal conditions; as relinquishing no more, and therefore retaining no less, one than another, of their natural rights. Above all are they to be considered as retaining an "*equal* title to the free exercise of Religion according to the dictates of Conscience." Whilst we assert for ourselves a freedom to embrace, to profess and to observe the Religion which we believe to be of divine origin, we cannot deny an equal freedom to those whose minds have not yet yielded to the evidence which has convinced us. If this freedom be abused, it is an offence against God, not against man: To God, therefore, not to man, must an account of it be rendered. As the Bill violates equality by subjecting some to peculiar burdens, so it violates the same principle, by granting to others peculiar exemptions. Are the Quakers and Menonists the only sects who think a compulsive support of their Religions unnecessary and unwarrantable? Can their piety alone be entrusted with the care of public worship? Ought their Religions to be endowed above all others with extraordinary privileges by which proselytes may be enticed from all others? We think too favorably of the justice and good sense of these denominations to believe that they either covet pre-eminences over their fellow citizens or that they will be seduced by them from the common opposition to the measure.

5. Because the Bill implies either that the Civil Magistrate is a competent Judge of Religious Truth; or that he may employ Religion as an engine of Civil policy. The first is an arrogant pretension falsified by the contradictory opinions of Rulers in all ages, and throughout the world: the second an unhallowed perversion of the means of salvation.

6. Because the establishment proposed by the Bill is not requisite for the support of the Christian Religion. To say that it is, is a contradiction to the Christian Religion itself, for every page of it disavows a dependence on the powers of this world: it is a contradiction to fact; for it is known that this Religion both existed and flourished, not only without the support of human laws, but in spite of every opposition from them, and not only during the period of miraculous aid, but long after it had been left to its own evidence and the ordinary care of Providence. Nay, it is a contradiction in terms; for a Religion not invented by human policy, must have pre-existed and been supported, before it was established by human policy. It is moreover to weaken in those who profess this Religion a pious confidence in its innate excellence

and the patronage of its Author; and to foster in those who still reject it, a suspicion that its friends are too conscious of its fallacies to trust it to its own merits.

7. Because experience witnesseth that ecclesiastical establishments, instead of maintaining the purity and efficacy of Religion, have had a contrary operation. During almost fifteen centuries has the legal establishment of Christianity been on trial. What have been its fruits? More or less in all places, pride and indolence in the Clergy, ignorance and servility in the laity, in both, superstition, bigotry and persecution. Enquire of the Teachers of Christianity for the ages in which it appeared in its greatest lustre; those of every sect, point to the ages prior to its incorporation with Civil policy. Propose a restoration of this primitive State in which its Teachers depended on the voluntary rewards of their flocks, many of them predict its downfall. On which Side ought their testimony to have greatest weight, when for or when against their interest?

8. Because the establishment in question is not necessary for the support of Civil Government. If it be urged as necessary for the support of Civil Government only as it is a means of supporting Religion, and it be not necessary for the latter purpose, it cannot be necessary for the former. If Religion be not within the cognizance of Civil Government how can its legal establishment be necessary to Civil Government? What influence in fact have ecclesiastical establishments had on Civil Society? In some instances they have been seen to erect a spiritual tyranny on the ruins of the Civil authority; in many instances they have been seen upholding the thrones of political tyranny: in no instance have they been seen the guardians of the liberties of the people. Rulers who wished to subvert the public liberty, may have found an established Clergy convenient auxiliaries. A just Government instituted to secure & perpetuate it needs them not. Such a Government will be best supported by protecting every Citizen in the enjoyment of his Religion with the same equal hand which protects his person and his property; by neither invading the equal rights of any Sect, nor suffering any Sect to invade those of another.

9. Because the proposed establishment is a departure from that generous policy, which, offering an Asylum to the persecuted and oppressed of every Nation and Religion, promised a lustre to our country, and an accession to the number of its citizens. What a melancholy mark is the Bill of sudden degeneracy? Instead of holding forth an Asylum to the persecuted, it is itself a signal of persecution. It degrades from the equal rank of Citizens all those whose opinions in Religion do not bend to those of the Legislative authority. Distant as it may be in its present form from the Inquisition, it differs from it only in degree. The one is the first step, the other the last in the career of intolerance. The magnanimous sufferer under this cruel scourge in foreign Regions, must view the Bill as a Beacon on our Coast, warning him to seek

some other haven, where liberty and philanthrophy in their due extent, may offer a more certain repose from his Troubles.

10. Because it will have a like tendency to banish our Citizens. The allurements presented by other situations are every day thinning their number. To superadd a fresh motive to emigration by revoking the liberty which they now enjoy, would be the same species of folly which has dishonoured and depopulated flourishing kingdoms.

11. Because it will destroy that moderation and harmony which the forbearance of our laws to intermeddle with Religion has produced among its several sects. Torrents of blood have been spilt in the old world, by vain attempts of the secular arm, to extinguish Religious discord, by proscribing all difference in Religious opinion. Time has at length revealed the true remedy. Every relaxation of narrow and rigorous policy, wherever it has been tried, has been found to assuage the disease. The American Theatre has exhibited proofs that equal and compleat liberty, if it does not wholly eradicate it, sufficiently destroys its malignant influence on the health and prosperity of the State. If with the salutary effects of this system under our own eyes, we begin to contract the bounds of Religious freedom, we know no name that will too severely reproach our folly. At least let warning be taken at the first fruits of the threatened innovation. The very appearance of the Bill has transformed "that Christian forbearance, love and charity," which of late mutually prevailed, into animosities and jealousies, which may not soon be appeased. What mischiefs may not be dreaded, should this enemy to the public quiet be armed with the force of a law?

12. Because the policy of the Bill is adverse to the diffusion of the light of Christianity. The first wish of those who enjoy this precious gift ought to be that it may be imparted to the whole race of mankind. Compare the number of those who have as yet received it with the number still remaining under the dominion of false Religions; and how small is the former! Does the policy of the Bill tend to lessen the disproportion? No; it at once discourages those who are strangers to the light of revelation from coming into the Region of it; and countenances by example the nations who continue in darkness, in shutting out those who might convey it to them. Instead of Levelling as far as possible, every obstacle to the victorious progress of Truth, the Bill with an ignoble and unchristian timidity would circumscribe it with a wall of defence against the encroachments of error.

13. Because attempts to enforce by legal sanctions, acts obnoxious to so great a proportion of Citizens, tend to enervate the laws in general, and to slacken the bands of Society. If it be difficult to execute any law which is not generally deemed necessary or salutary, what must be the case, where it is deemed invalid and dangerous? And what may be the effect of so striking an example of impotency in the Government, on its general authority?

14. Because a measure of such singular magnitude and delicacy ought not to be imposed, without the clearest evidence that it is called for by a

majority of citizens, and no satisfactory method is yet proposed by which the voice of the majority in this case may be determined, or its influence secured. "The people of the respective counties are indeed requested to signify their opinion respecting the adoption of the Bill to the next Session of Assembly." But the representation must be made equal, before the voice either of the Representatives or of the Counties will be that of the people. Our hope is that neither of the former will, after due consideration, espouse the dangerous principle of the Bill. Should the event disappoint us, it will still leave us in full confidence, that a fair appeal to the latter will reverse the sentence against our liberties.

15. Because finally, "the equal right of every citizen to the free exercise of his Religion according to the dictates of conscience" is held by the same tenure with all our other rights. If we recur to its origin, it is equally the gift of nature; if we weigh its importance, it cannot be less dear to us; if we consult the "Declaration of those rights which pertain to the good people of Virginia, as the basis and foundation of Government," it is enumerated with equal so-lemnity, or rather studied emphasis. Either then, we must say, that the Will of the Legislature is the only measure of their authority; and that in the plen-itude of this authority, they may sweep away all our fundamental rights; or, that they are bound to leave this particular right untouched and sacred: Ei-ther we must say, that they may controul the freedom of the press, may abol-ish the Trial by Jury, may swallow up the Executive and Judiciary Powers of the State; nay that they may despoil us of our very right of suffrage, and erect themselves into an independent and hereditary Assembly or, we must say, that they have no authority to enact into law the Bill under consideration. We the Subscribers say, that the General Assembly of this Commonwealth have no such authority: And that no effort may be omitted on our part against so dangerous an usurpation, we oppose to it, this remonstrance; ear-nestly praying, as we are in duty bound, that the Supreme Lawgiver of the Universe, by illuminating those to whom it is addressed, may on the one hand, turn their Councils from every act which would affront his holy pre-rogative, or violate the trust committed to them: and on the other, guide them into every measure which may be worthy of his [blessing, may redound to their own praise, and may establish more firmly the liberties, the prosper-ity and the happiness of the Commonwealth.

SOURCE: "Memorial and Remonstrance against Religious Assessments, [ca. 20 June] 1785," *Founders Online*, National Archives, https://founders.ar-chives.gov/documents/Madison/01-08-02-0163.

5. THOMAS JEFFERSON
A BILL FOR ESTABLISHING RELIGIOUS FREEDOM
1777/1785

Thomas Jefferson (1743-1826) drafted "A Bill for Establishing Religious Freedom" in 1777 while he was a member of the Virginia Committee of Revisors (a political body appointed to revise Virginia's antiquated, prerevolutionary laws). The bill was subsequently submitted to Virginia's General Assembly in 1779 while Jefferson was serving as Governor of the state. The bill was debated but not adopted. In October 1785, James Madison brought the bill forward again while Jefferson was in Paris serving as the United States Ambassador to France. The Virginia Statute for Religious Freedom was subsequently adopted on January 16, 1786. Readers should recall that the Anglican Church was the government-supported, established church in Virginia prior to the Revolution. This meant that Virginians were forced to pay taxes to support the Anglican Church, while other Christian denominations (particularly the Baptists, Presbyterians, and Methodist) faced various forms of discrimination and restriction. Jefferson was a strong proponent of religious freedom and the separation of church and state. His ideas crystallized into his bill for establishing religious freedom, which, he maintained was a natural right. Jefferson believed that thought and government compulsion were anathema to one another. Jefferson argued that "God hath created the mind free" and that the only path to God was through "reason alone." The core principles of Jefferson's bill included: 1) that individuals should never be compelled to think or worship a certain way through government coercion; 2) that men must be free to use their reason to profess and maintain their religious opinions; 3) that the inculcation of religious opinions is not a proper object or function of government in a free society; and 4) that the ascent to truth is only possible through reason and freedom.

Well aware that the opinions and belief of men depend not on their own will, but follow involuntarily the evidence proposed to their minds; that Almighty God hath created the mind free, *and manifested his supreme will that free it shall remain by making it altogether insusceptible of restraint*; that all attempts to influence it by temporal punishments, or burthens, or by civil incapacitations, tend only to beget habits of hypocrisy and meanness, and are a departure from the plan of the holy author of our religion, who being lord both of body and mind, yet chose not to propagate it by coercions on either, as was in his Almighty power to do, *but to extend it by its influence on reason alone*; that the impious presumption of legislators and rulers, civil as well as ecclesiastical, who, being themselves but fallible and uninspired men, have assumed dominion over the faith of others, setting up their own opinions and modes of thinking as the only true and infallible, and as such endeavoring to impose them on others, hath established and maintained false religions over the greatest part of the world and through all time: That to compel a man to furnish contributions of money for the propagation of opinions which he disbelieves *and abhors*, is sinful and tyrannical; that even the forcing him to support this or that teacher of his own religious persuasion, is depriving him of the comfortable liberty of giving his contributions to the particular pastor whose morals he would make his pattern, and whose powers he feels most persuasive to righteousness; and is withdrawing from the ministry those temporary rewards, which proceeding from an approbation of their personal conduct, are an additional incitement to earnest and unremitting labours for the instruction of mankind; that our civil rights have no dependance on our religious opinions, any more than our opinions in physics or geometry; that therefore the proscribing any citizen as unworthy the public confidence by laying upon him an incapacity of being called to offices of trust and emolument, unless he profess or renounce this or that religious opinion, is depriving him injuriously of those privileges and advantages to which, in common with his fellow citizens, he has a natural right; that it tends also to corrupt the principles of that *very* religion it is meant to encourage, by bribing, with a monopoly of worldly honours and emoluments, those who will externally profess and conform to it; that though indeed these are criminal who do not withstand such temptation, yet neither are those innocent who lay the bait in their way; *that the opinions of men are not the object of civil government, nor under its jurisdiction*; that to suffer the civil magistrate to intrude his powers into the field of opinion and to restrain the profession or propagation of principles on supposition of their ill tendency is a dangerous falacy, which at once destroys all religious liberty, because he being of course judge of that tendency will make his opinions the rule of judgment, and approve or condemn the sentiments of others only as they shall square with or differ from his own; that it is time enough for the rightful purposes of civil government for its officers to interfere when principles break out into overt acts against peace and good order; and finally, that truth is great and will prevail if left to herself; that she is the proper and sufficient antagonist to error, and has nothing to fear from the conflict unless by human interposition disarmed of her natural weapons, free argument and debate; errors ceasing to be dangerous when it is permitted freely to contradict them.

We the General Assembly of Virginia do enact that no man shall be compelled to frequent or support any religious worship, place, or ministry whatsoever, nor shall be enforced, restrained, molested, or burthened in his body or goods, nor shall otherwise suffer, on account of his religious opinions or belief; but that all men shall be free to profess, and by argument to maintain, their opinions in matters of religion, and that the same shall in no wise diminish, enlarge, or affect their civil capacities.

And though we well know that this Assembly, elected by the people for the ordinary purposes of legislation only, have no power to restrain the acts of succeeding Assemblies, constituted with powers equal to our own, and that therefore to declare this act irrevocable would be of no effect in law; yet we are free to declare, and do declare, that the rights hereby asserted are of the natural rights of mankind, and that if any act shall be hereafter passed to repeal the present or to narrow its operation, such act will be an infringement of natural right.

SOURCE: These excerpts are taken from "Considerations on the Nature and Extent of the Legislative Authority of the British Parliament" ([1768] 1774), *Collected Works of James Wilson,* edited by Kermit L. Hall and Mark David Hall, with an Introduction by Kermit L. Hall, and a Bibliographical Essay by Mark David Hall, collected by Maynard Garrison (Indianapolis: Liberty Fund, 2007). Vol. 1.

6. BENJAMIN RUSH
"THOUGHTS UPON THE MODE OF EDUCATION PROPER IN A REPUBLIC"
1786

Benjamin Rush (1746-1813) was a Philadelphia physician, politician, social reformer, politicians, revolutionary patriot, revolutionary, and founding father. He was also one of the first founding fathers to turn his attention to education and the cultural conditions necessary for republican government, and, more particularly, to the question: How shall America's children be educated for life in a free society? Rush was probably unique amongst the founding generation for the emphasis he placed on modeling American education in alignment with classical standards of moral virtue. He was a proponent of a form of education and a curriculum that emphasized moral, religious, and political instruction to create virtuous republican citizens. He implored his fellow Americans to break free from chains of the colonial and monarchical ways of thinking about education and adopt the model of classical republican education. Shockingly, Rush was a proponent of the moral and political principles contained Declaration of Independence at the same time that he argued in "Thoughts Upon the Mode of Education Proper in a Republic" for a form of education that would teach American children to believe that they do not belong to themselves but are instead "public property." For Rush, the primary virtue that young Americans should be taught was self-sacrifice. One wonders how Rush could reconcile the individual "pursuit of happiness" with the idea of converting American children into what he called "republican machines." He even goes so far as to promote the educational practices of ancient Spartans.

The business of education has acquired a new complexion by the independence of our country. The form of government we have assumed has created a new class of duties to every American. It becomes us, therefore, to examine our former habits upon this subject, and in laying the foundations for nurseries of wise and good men, to adapt our modes of teaching to the peculiar form of our government.

The first remark that I shall make upon this subject is that an education in our own is to be preferred to an education in a foreign country. The principle of patriotism stands in need of the reinforcement of prejudice, and it is well known that our strongest prejudices in favor of our country are formed in the first one and twenty years of our lives. The policy of the Lacedamonians is well worthy of our imitation. When Antipater demanded fifty of their children as hostages for the fulfillment of a distant engagement, those wise republicans refused to comply with his demand but readily offered him double the number of their adult citizens, whose habits and prejudices could not be shaken by residing in a foreign country. Passing by, in this place, the advantages to the community from the early attachment of youth to the laws and constitution of their country, I shall only remark that young men who have trodden the paths of science together, or have joined in the same sports, whether of swimming, skating, fishing, or hunting, generally feel, through life, such ties to each other as add greatly to the obligations of mutual benevolence.

I conceive the education of our youth in this country to be peculiarly necessary in Pennsylvania while our citizens are com posed of the natives of so many different kingdoms in Europe. Our schools of learning, by producing one general and uniform system of education, will render the mass of the people more homogeneous and thereby fit them more easily for uniform and peaceable government.

I proceed, in the next place, to inquire what mode of education we shall adopt so as to secure to the state all the advantages that are to be derived from the proper instruction of youth; and here I beg leave to remark that the only foundation for a useful education in a republic is to be laid in RELIGION. Without this, there can be no virtue, and without virtue there can be no liberty, and liberty is the object and life of all republican governments.

Such is my veneration for every religion that reveals the attributes of the Deity, or a future state of rewards and punishments, that I had rather see the opinions of Confucius or Mohammed inculcated upon our youth than see them grow up wholly devoid of a system of religious principles. But the religion I mean to recommend in this place is the religion of JESUS CHRIST.

It is foreign to my purpose to hint at the arguments which establish the truth of the Christian revelation. My only business is to declare that all its doctrines and precepts are calculated to promote the happiness of society and the safety and well-being of civil government. A Christian cannot fail of being a republican. The history of the creation of man and of the relation of our species to each other by birth, which is recorded in the Old Testament, is the best refutation that can be given to the divine right of kings and the strongest argument that can be used in favor of the original and natural equality of all mankind. A Christian, I say again, cannot fail of being a republican, for every precept of the Gospel inculcates those degrees of humility, self-denial, and brotherly kindness which are directly opposed to the pride of monarchy and the pageantry of a court. A Christian cannot fail of being useful to the republic, for his religion teacheth him that no man "liveth to himself." And lastly, a Christian cannot fail of being wholly in offensive, for his religion teacheth him in all things to do to others what he would wish, in like circumstances, they should do to him.

I am aware that I dissent from one of those paradoxical opinions with which modern times abound: that it is improper to fill the minds of youth with religious prejudices of any kind and that they should be left to choose their own principles after they have arrived at an age in which they are capable of judging for themselves. Could we preserve the mind in childhood and youth a perfect blank, this plan of education would have more to recommend it, but this we know to be impossible. The human mind runs as naturally into principles as it does after facts. It submits with difficulty to those restraints or partial discoveries which are imposed upon it in the infancy of reason. Hence the impatience of children to be informed upon all subjects that relate to the invisible world. But I beg leave to ask, Why should we pursue a different plan of education with respect to religion from that which we pursue in teaching the arts and sciences? Do we leave our youth to acquire systems of geography, philosophy, or politics till they have arrived at an age in which they are capable of judging for themselves? We do not. I claim no more, then, for religion than for the other sciences, and I add further that if our youth are disposed after they are of age to think for themselves, a knowledge of one system will be the best means of conducting them in a free inquiry into other systems of religion, just as an acquaintance with one system of philosophy is the best introduction to the study of all the other systems in the world.

I must beg leave upon this subject to go one step further. In order more effectually to secure to our youth the advantages of a religious education, it is necessary to impose upon them the doctrines and discipline of a particular church. Man is naturally an ungovernable animal, and observations on particular societies and countries will teach us that when we add the restraints of ecclesiastical to those of domestic and civil government, we produce in him the highest degrees of order and virtue. That fashionable liberality which refuses associate with any one sect of Christians is seldom useful to itself or to society and may fitly be compared to the unprofitable bravery of a soldier who wastes his valor in solitary enterprises without the aid or effect of military associations. Far be it from me to recommend the doctrines or modes of worship of any one denomination of Christians. I only recommend to the persons entrusted with the education of youth to inculcate upon them a strict conformity to that mode of worship which is most agreeable to their consciences or the inclinations of their parents.

Under this head, I must be excused in not agreeing with those modern writers who have opposed the use of the Bible as a schoolbook. The only objection I know to it is its division into chapters and verses and its improper punctuation which render it a more difficult book to read well than many others, but these defects may easily be corrected, and the disadvantages of them are not to be mentioned with the immense advantages of making children early and intimately acquainted with the means of acquiring happiness both here and hereafter. How great is the difference between making young people acquainted with the interesting and entertaining truths contained in the Bible, and the fables of Moore and Croxall, or the doubtful histories of antiquity! I maintain that there is no book of its size in the whole world that contains half so much useful knowledge for the government of states or the direction of the affairs of individuals as the Bible. To object to the practice of having it read in schools because it tends to destroy our veneration for it is an argument that applies with equal force against the frequency of public worship and all other religious exercises.

The first impressions upon the mind are the most durable. They survive the wreck of the memory and exist in old age after the ideas acquired in middle life have been obliterated. Of how much consequence then must it be to the human mind in the evening of life to be able to recall those ideas which are most essential to its happiness, and these are to be found chiefly in the Bible. The great delight which old people take in reading the Bible, I am persuaded, is derived chiefly from its histories and precepts being associated with the events of childhood and youth, the recollection of which forms a material part of their pleasures.

I do not mean to exclude books of history, poetry, or even fables from our schools. They may and should be read frequently by our young people, but if the Bible is made to give way to them altogether, I foresee that it will be read in a short time only in churches and in a few years will probably be found only in the offices of magistrates and in courts of justice.

Next to the duty which young men owe to their Creator, I wish to see a SUPREME REGARD TO THEIR COUNTRY inculcated upon them. When the Duke of Sully became prime minister to Henry the IVth of France, the first thing he did, he tells us, "Was to subdue and forget his own heart." The same duty is incumbent upon every citizen of a republic. Our country includes family, friends, and property, and should be preferred to them all. Let our pupil be taught that he does not belong to himself, but that he is public property. Let him be taught to love his family, but let him be taught at the same time that he must forsake and even forget them when the welfare of his country requires it.

He must watch for the state as if its liberties depended upon his vigilance alone, but he must do this in such a manner as not to defraud his creditors or neglect his family. He must love private life, but he must decline no station, however public or responsible it may be, when called to it by the suffrages of his fellow citizens. He must love popularity, but he must despise it when set in competition with the dictates of his judgment or the real interest of his country. He must love character and have a due sense of injuries, but he must be taught to appeal only to the laws of the state, to defend the one and punish the other. He must love family honor, but he must be taught that neither the rank nor antiquity of his ancestors can command respect without personal merit. He must avoid neutrality in all questions that divide the state, but he must shun the rage and acrimony of party spirit. He must be taught to love his fellow creatures in every part of the world, but he must cherish with a more intense and peculiar affection the citizens of Pennsylvania and of the United States.

I do not wish to see our youth educated with a single prejudice against any nation or country, but we impose a task upon human nature repugnant alike to reason, revelation, and the ordinary dimensions of the human heart when we require him to embrace with equal affection the whole family of mankind. He must be taught to amass wealth, but it must be only to increase his power of contributing to the wants and demands of the state. He must be indulged occasionally in amusements, but he must be taught that study and business should be his principal pursuits in life. Above all he must love life and endeavor to acquire as many of its conveniences as possible by industry and economy, but he must be taught that this life "is not his own" when the safety of his country requires it. These are practicable lessons, and the history of the commonwealths of Greece and Rome show that human nature, without the aids of Christianity, has attained these degrees of perfection.

While we inculcate these republican duties upon our pupil, we must not neglect at the same time to inspire him with republican principles. He must be taught that there can be no durable liberty but in a republic and that government, like all other sciences, is of a progressive nature. The chains which have bound this science in Europe are happily unloosed in America. Here it is open to investigation and improvement. While philosophy has protected us by its discoveries from a thousand natural evils, government has unhappily followed with an unequal pace. It would be to dishonor human genius only to name the many defects which still exist in the best systems of legislation. We daily see matter of a perishable nature rendered durable by certain chemical operations. In like manner, I conceive that it is possible to analyze and combine power in such a manner as not only to increase the happiness but to promote the duration of republican forms of government far beyond the terms limited for them by history or the common opinions of mankind.

To assist in rendering religious, moral, and political instruction more effectual upon the minds of our youth, it will be necessary to subject their bodies to physical discipline. To obviate the inconveniences of their studious and sedentary mode of life, they should live upon a temperate diet, consisting chiefly of broths, milk, and vegetables. The black broth of Sparta and the barley broth of Scotland have been alike celebrated for their beneficial effects upon the minds of young people. They should avoid tasting spirituous liquors. They should also be accustomed occasionally to work with their hands in the intervals of study and in the busy seasons of the year in the country. Moderate sleep, silence, occasional solitude, and cleanliness should be inculcated upon them, and the utmost advantage should be taken of a proper direction of those great principles in human conduct–sensibility, habit, imitation, and association.

The influence [of] these physical causes will be powerful upon the intellects as well as upon the principles and morals of young people.

To those who have studied human nature, it will not appear paradoxical to recommend in this essay a particular attention to vocal music. Its mechanical effects in civilizing the mind and thereby preparing it for the influence of religion and government have been so often felt and recorded that it will be unnecessary to mention facts in favor of its usefulness in order to excite a proper attention to it.

In the education of youth, let the authority of our masters be as absolute as possible. The government of schools like the government of private families should be arbitrary, that it may not be severe. By this mode of education, we prepare our youth for the subordination of laws and thereby qualify them for becoming good citizens of the republic. I am satisfied that the most useful citizens have been formed from those youth who have never known or felt their own wills till they were one and twenty years of age, and I have often thought that society owes a great deal of its order and happiness to the deficiencies of parental government being supplied by those habits of obedience and subordination which are contracted at schools.

I cannot help bearing a testimony, in this place, against the custom which prevails in some parts of America (but which is daily falling into disuse in Europe) of crowding boys together under one roof for the purpose of education. The practice is the gloomy remains of monkish ignorance and is as unfavorable to the improvements of the mind in useful learning as monasteries are to the spirit of religion. I grant this mode of secluding boys from the intercourse of private families has a tendency to make them scholars, but our business is to make them men, citizens, and Christians. The vices of young people are generally learned from each other. The vices of adults seldom infect them. By separating them from each other, therefore, in their hours of relaxation from study, we secure their morals from a principal source of corruption, while we improve their manners by subjecting them to those restraints which the difference of age and sex naturally produce in private families.

I have hitherto said nothing of the AMUSEMENTS that are proper for young people in a republic. Those which promote health and good humor will have a happy effect upon morals and government. To increase this influence, let the persons who direct these amusements be admitted into good company and subjected by that means to restraints in behavior and moral conduct. Taverns, which in most countries are exposed to riot and vice, in Connecticut are places of business and innocent pleasure because the tavern-keepers in that country are generally men of sober and respectable characters. . . .

From the observations that have been made it is plain that I consider it as possible to convert men into republican machines. This must be done if we expect them to perform their parts properly in the great machine of the government of the state. That republic is sophisticated with monarchy or aristocracy that does not revolve upon the wills of the people, and these must be fitted to each other by means of education before they can be made to produce regularity and unison in government.

Having pointed out those general principles which should be inculcated alike in all the schools of the state, I proceed now to make a few remarks upon the method of conducting what is commonly called a liberal or learned education in a republic.

I shall begin this part of my subject by bearing a testimony against the common practice of attempting to teach boys the learned languages and the arts and sciences too early in life. The first twelve years of life are barely sufficient to instruct a boy in reading, writing, and arithmetic. With these, he may be taught those modern languages which are necessary for him to speak. The state of the memory, in early life, is favorable to the acquisition of languages, especially when they are conveyed to the mind through the ear. It is, moreover, in early life only that the organs of speech yield in such a manner as to favor the just pronunciation of foreign languages.

I do not wish the LEARNED OR DEAD LANGUAGES, as they are commonly called, to be reduced below their present just rank in the universities of Europe, especially as I consider an acquaintance with them as the best foundation for a correct and extensive knowledge of the language of our country. Too much pains cannot be taken to teach our youth to read and write our American language with propriety and elegance. The study of the Greek language constituted a material part of the literature of the Athenians, hence the sublimity, purity, and immortality of so many of their writings. The advantages of a perfect knowledge of our language to young men intended for the professions of law, physic, or divinity are too obvious to be mentioned, but in a state which boasts of the first commercial city in America, I wish to see it cultivated by young men who are intended for the counting house, for many such, I hope, will be educated in our colleges. The time is past when an academical education was thought to be unnecessary to qualify a young man for merchandise. I conceive no profession is capable of receiving more embellishments from it.

Connected with the study of our own language is the study of ELOQUENCE. It is well known how great a part it constituted of the Roman education. It is the first accomplishment in a republic and often sets the whole machine of government in motion. Let our youth, therefore, be instructed in this art. We do not extol it too highly when we attribute as much to the power of eloquence as to the sword in bringing about the American Revolution.

With the usual arts and sciences that are taught in our American colleges, I wish to see a regular course of lectures given upon HISTORY and CHRONOLOGY. The science of government, whether it relates to constitutions or laws, can only be advanced by a careful selection of facts, and these are to be found chiefly in history. Above all, let our youth be instructed in the history of the ancient republics and the progress of liberty and tyranny in the different states of Europe.

I wish likewise to see the numerous facts that relate to the origin and present state of COMMERCE, together with the nature and principles of MONEY, reduced to such a system as to be intelligible and agreeable to a young man. If we consider the commerce of our metropolis only as the avenue of the wealth of the state, the study of it merits a place in a young man's education, but, I consider commerce in a much higher light when I recommend the study of it in republican seminaries. I view it as the best security against the influence of hereditary monopolies of land, and, therefore, the surest protection against aristocracy. I consider its effects as next to those of religion in humanizing mankind, and lastly, I view it as the means of uniting the different nations of the world together by the ties of mutual wants and obligations.

CHEMISTRY by unfolding to us the effects of heat and mixture, enlarges our acquaintance with the wonders of nature and the mysteries of art; hence it has become in most of the universities of Europe a necessary branch of a gentleman's education. In a young country, where improvements in agriculture and manufactures are so much to be desired, the cultivation of this science, which explains the principles of both of them, should be considered as an object of the utmost importance.

In a state where every citizen is liable to be a soldier and a legislator, it will be necessary to have some regular instruction given upon the ART OF WAR and upon PRACTICAL LEGISLATION. These branches of knowledge are of too much importance in a republic to be trusted to solitary study or to a fortuitous acquaintance with books. Let mathematical learning, therefore, be carefully applied in our colleges to gunnery and fortification, and let philosophy be applied to the history of those compositions which have been made use of for the terrible purposes of destroying human life. These branches of knowledge will be indispensably necessary in our republic, if unfortunately war should continue hereafter to be the unchristian mode of arbitrating disputes between Christian nations.

Again, let our youth be instructed in all the means of promoting national prosperity and independence, whether they relate to improvements in agriculture, manufactures, or inland navigation. Let him be instructed further in the general principles of legislation, whether they relate to revenue or to the preservation of life, liberty, or property. Let him be directed frequently to attend the courts of justice, where he will have the best opportunities of acquiring habits of arranging and comparing his ideas by observing the secretion of truth in the examination of witnesses and where he will hear the laws of the state explained, with all the advantages of that species of eloquence which belongs to the bar. Of so much importance do I conceive it to be to a young man to attend occasionally to the decisions of our courts of law that I wish to see our colleges and academies established only in county towns.

But further, considering the nature of our connection with the United States, it will be necessary to make our pupil acquainted with all the prerogatives of the federal government.

He must be instructed in the nature and variety of treaties. He must know the difference in the powers and duties of the several species of ambassadors. He must be taught wherein the obligations of individuals and of states are the same and wherein they differ. In short, he must acquire a general knowledge of all those laws and forms which unite the sovereigns of the earth or separate them from each other.

I have only to add that it will be to no purpose to adopt this or any other mode of education unless we make choice of suitable masters to carry our plans into execution. Let our teachers be distinguished for their abilities and knowledge. Let them be grave in their manners, gentle in their tempers, exemplary in their morals, and of sound principles in religion and government. Let us not leave their support to the precarious resources to be derived from their pupils, but let such funds be provided for our schools and colleges as will enable us to allow them liberal salaries.

By these means we shall render the chairs–the professorships and rectorships of our colleges and academies–objects of competition among learned men. By conferring upon our masters that independence which is the companion of competency, we shall, moreover, strengthen their authority over the youth committed to their care. Let us remember that a great part of the divines, lawyers, physicians, legislators, soldiers, generals, delegates, counselors, and governors of the state will probably hereafter pass through their hands. How great then should be the wisdom, how honorable the rank, and how generous the reward of those men who are to form these necessary and leading members of the republic!

I beg pardon for having delayed so long, to say anything of the separate and peculiar mode of education proper for WOMEN in a republic. I am sensible that they must concur in all our plans of education for young men, or no laws will ever render them effectual. To qualify our women for this purpose, they should not only be instructed in the usual branches of female education but they should be instructed in the principles of liberty and government, and the obligations of patriotism should be inculcated upon them. The opinions and conduct of men are often regulated by the women in the most arduous enterprises of life, and their approbation is frequently the principal reward of the hero's dangers and the patriot's toils. Be sides, the first impressions upon the minds of children are generally derived from the women. Of how much consequence, therefore, is it in a republic that they should think justly upon the great subjects of liberty and government!

The complaints that have been made against religion, liberty, and learning have been made against each of them in a separate state. Perhaps like certain liquors they should only be used in a state of mixture. They mutually assist in correcting the abuses and in improving the good effects of each other. From the combined and reciprocal influence of religion, liberty, and learning upon the morals, manners, and knowledge of individuals, of these upon government, and of government upon individuals, it is impossible to measure the degrees of happiness and perfection to which mankind may be raised. For my part, I can form no ideas of the golden age, so much celebrated by the poets, more delightful than the contemplation of that happiness which it is now in the power of the legislature of Pennsylvania to confer upon her citizens by establishing proper modes and places of education in every part of the state.

The present time is peculiarly favorable to the establishment of these benevolent and necessary institutions in Pennsylvania. The minds of our people have not as yet lost the yielding texture they acquired by the heat of the late Revolution. They will now receive more readily than five or even three years hence new impressions and habits of all kinds. The spirit of liberty now pervades every part of the state. The influence of error and deception are now of short duration. Seven years hence the affairs of our state may assume a new complexion. We may be riveted to a criminal indifference for the safety and happiness of ourselves and our posterity. An aristocratic or democratic junto may arise that shall find its despotic views connected with the prevalence of ignorance and vice in the state, or a few artful pedagogues who consider learning as useful only in proportion as it favors their pride or avarice may prevent all new literary establishments from taking place by raising a hue and cry against them, as the offspring of improper rivalship or the nurseries of party spirit.

But in vain shall we lavish pains and expense in establishing nurseries of virtue and knowledge in every part of the state, in vain shall we attempt to give the minds of our citizens a virtuous and uniform bias in early life, while the arms of our state are opened alike to receive into its bosom and to confer equal privileges upon the virtuous emigrant and the annual refuse of the jails of Britain, Ireland, and our sister states. Of the many criminals that have been executed within these seven years, four out of five of them have been foreigners who have arrived here during the war and since the peace. We are yet, perhaps, to see and deplore the tracks of the enormous vices and crimes these men have left behind them. Legislators of Pennsylvania!–Stewards of the justice and virtue of heaven!– Fathers of children who may be corrupted and disgraced by bad examples, say–can nothing be done to preserve our morals, manners, and government from the infection of European vices?

In a republic where all votes for public officers are given by ballot, should not a knowledge of reading and writing be considered as essential qualifications for an elector? And when a man who is of a doubtful character offers his Vote, would it not be more consistent with sound policy and wise government to oblige him to read a few verses in the Bible to prove his qualifications than simply to Compel him to kiss the outside of it?

SOURCE: From "A Plan for the Establishment of Public Schools and the Diffusion of Knowledge in Pennsylvania; to Which Are Added, Thoughts upon the Mode of Education Proper in a Republic. Addressed to the Legislature and Citizens of the State" (Philadelphia: Thomas Dobson, 1786).

Part Six:

Revolution and Slavery

1. THE FOUNDERS' PRIVATE THOUGHTS ON SLAVERY

Slavery is, along with marriage, the world's oldest social institution. It has existed on all five continents and through all time. Euro-African slavery was introduced into Britain's American colonies sometime—the precise date is unknown—in the seventeenth century. By the middle of the eighteenth century, chattel slavery existed in all thirteen of Great Britain's American colonies. Prior to the years of imperial crisis, there was virtually no intellectual, cultural, or political opposition to the "peculiar institution." The American movement for independence, as summed up in the principles of the Declaration of Independence, changed everything. The American Revolution unleashed the world's first anti-slavery movement. The Declaration's first two self-evident truths—that all men are created equal and that they are endowed by their Creator with certain unalienable rights, among which are the rights to life, liberty, and the pursuit of happiness—could not be reconciled with the practice of slavery. American patriots and revolutionaries were stung—and stung deeply—with the charge of hypocrisy when the English Tory Samuel Johnson asked them in 1775, "How is it that we hear the loudest yelps for liberty among the drivers of Negroes?" All of America's founding fathers judged chattel slavery to be a "necessary evil," which sums up their challenge. Morally, they all viewed slavery—including slaveholders—as morally evil, but many, particularly those in the South, viewed slavery as economically necessary, at least for the time being. The real differences amongst the revolutionaries and founders concerned how to deal with slavery in practice. If slavery were to end in the United States, the difficult questions were how and when. More specifically, the greatest challenge confronted by American revolutionaries on the slavery question was how to deal with what might be called the post-emancipation problem. In other words, if slavery were to be abolished, what would happen to the former slaves? With some justification, the revolutionaries feared social chaos, economic destruction, and racial war. Among the difficult questions confronted by post-1776 Americans on the slavery question were: 1) should slaveowners be compensated and by whom, 2) should freed slaves be integrated into white society, returned to Africa, or settled in the trans-Appalachian West? These questions had no easy or good answers. In the meantime, all of the northern states began the process of gradually dismantling slavery in the thirty years after independence. In the private correspondence below, readers can see the difficult and sometimes tortured views held by the revolutionary generation as they contemplated how to deal with slavery.

PATRICK HENRY TO ROBERT PLEASANTS, JANUARY 18, 1773

I take this oppo. to acknowledge the receipt of A Benezets Book against the Slave Trade. I thank you for it. It is not a little surprising that Christianity, whose chief excellence consists in softening the human heart, in cherishing & improving its finer Feelings, should encourage a Practice so totally repugnant to the first Impression of right & wrong. What adds to the wonder is that this Abominable Practice has been introduced in ye. most enlightened Ages, Times that seem to have pretentions to boast of high Improvements in the Arts, Sciences, & refined Morality, h[ave] brought into general use, & guarded by many Laws, a Species of Violence & Tyranny, which our more rude & barbarous, but more honest Ancestors detested. Is it not amazing, that at a time, when ye. Rights of Humanity are defined & understood with precision, in a Country above all others fond of Liberty, that in such an Age, & such a Country we find Men, professing a Religion ye. most humane, mild, meek, gentle & generous; adopting a Principle as repugnant to humanity as it is inconsistant with the Bible and destructive to Liberty.

Every thinking honest Man rejects it in Speculation, how few in Practice from conscienscious Motives? The World in general has denied ye. People a share of its honours, but the Wise will ascribe to ye. a just Tribute of virtuous Praise, for ye. Practice of a train of Virtues among which yr. disagreement to Slavery will be principally ranked.--I cannot but wish well to a people whose System imitates ye. Example of him whose Life was perfect.--And believe m[e], I shall honour the Quakers for their noble Effort to abolish Slavery. It is equally calculated to promote moral & political Good.

Would any one believe that I am Master of Slaves of my own purchase! I am drawn along by ye. general inconvenience of living without them, I will not, I cannot justify it. However culpable my Conduct, I will so far pay my devoir to Virtue, as to own the excellence & rectitude of her Precepts, & to lament my want of conforming to them.--

I believe a time will come when an oppo. will be offered to abolish this lamentable Evil.--Every thing we can do is to improve it, if it happens in our day, if not, let us transmit to our descendants together with our Slaves, a pity for their unhappy Lot, & an abhorrence for Slavery. If we cannot reduce this wished for Reformation to practice, let us treat the unhappy victims with lenity, it is ye. furthest advance we can make toward Justice [We owe to the] purity of our Religion to shew that it is at variance with that Law which warrants Slavery.--

Here is an instance that silent Meetings (ye. scoff of reverd. Doctrs.) have done yt. wch. learned & elaborate Preaching could not effect, so much preferable are the genuine dictates of Conscience & a steady attention to its feelings above ye. teachings of those Men who pretend to have found a better

Guide. I exhort you to persevere in so worthy a resolution, Some of your People disagree, or at least are lukewarm in the abolition of Slavery. Many treat ye. Resolution of your Meeting with redicule, & among those who throw Contempt on it, are Clergymen, whose surest Guard against both Redicule & Contempt is a certain Act of Assembly.--

I know not where to stop, I could say many things on this Subject; a serious review of which gives a gloomy perspective to future times.

SOURCE: Patrick Henry to Robert Pleasants, January 18, 1773. From Teaching American History: https://teachingamericanhistory.org/document/patrick-henry-to-robert-pleasants/ (accessed December 29, 2024).

ABIGAIL ADAMS TO JOHN ADAMS, SEPTEMBER 22, 1774

I have just returnd from a visit to my Brother, with my Father who carried me there the day before yesterday, and call'd here in my return to see this much injured Town. I view it with much the same sensations that I should the body of a departed Friend, only put of[f] its present Glory, for to rise finally to a more happy State. I will not despair, but will believe that our cause being good we shall finally prevail. The Maxim in time of peace prepare for war, (if this may be call'd a time of peace) resounds throughout the Country. Next tuesday they are warned at Braintree all above 15 and under 60 to attend with their arms, and to train once a fortnight from that time, is a Scheme which lays much at heart with many.

Scot has arrived, and brings news that he expected to find all peace and Quietness here as he left them at home. You will have more particulars than I am able to send you, from much better hands. There has been in Town a conspiracy of the Negroes. At present it is kept pretty private and was discovered by one who endeavourd to diswaid them from it—he being threatned with his life, applied to Justice Quincy for protection. They conducted in this way—got an Irishman to draw up a petition to the Govener telling him they would fight for him provided he would arm them and engage to liberate them if he conquerd, and it is said that he attended so much to it as to consult Pircy upon it, and one [Lieut.?] Small has been very buisy and active. There is but little said, and what Steps they will take in consequence of it I know not. I wish most sincerely there was not a Slave in the province. It allways appeard a most iniquitious Scheme to me—fight ourselfs for what we are daily robbing and plundering from those who have as good a right to freedom as we have. You know my mind upon this Subject. . .

SOURCE: Abigail Adams to John Adams, 22 September 1774," *Founders Online,* National Archives, https://founders.archives.gov/documents/Adams/04-01-02-0107.

ALEXANDER HAMILTON TO JOHN JAY, MARCH 14, 1779

Col Laurens who will have the honor of delivering you this letter, is on his way to South Carolina, on a project, which I think, in the present situation of affairs there, is a very good one and deserves every Kind of support and encouragement. This is to raise two three or four batalions of negroes; with the assistance of the government of that state, by contributions from the owners in proportion to the number they possess. If you should think proper to enter upon the subject with him, he will give you a detail of his plan. He wishes to have it recommended by Congress to the state; and, as an inducement, that they would engage to take those batalions into Continental pay.

It appears to me, that an expedient of this kind, in the present state of Southern affairs, is the most rational, that can be adopted, and promises very important advantages. Indeed, I hardly see how a sufficient force can be collected in that quarter without it; and the enemy's operations there are growing infinitely serious and formidable— I have not the least doubt that the negroes will make very excellent soldiers, with proper management; and I will venture to pronounce, that they cannot be put in better hands than those of Mr. Laurens. He has all the zeal, intelligence enterprise, and every other qualification requisite to succeed in such an undertaking. It is a maxim with some great military judges, that with sensible officers, soldiers can hardly be too stupid; and on this principle it is thought that the Russians would make the best troops in the world if they were under other officers than their own. The King of Prussia is among the number who maintain this doctrine, and has a very emphatical saying on the occasion, which I do not exactly recollect— I mention this, because I frequently hear it objected to the scheme of embodying negroes that they are too stupid to make soldiers. This is so far from appearing to me a valid objection that I think their cultivation (for their natural faculties are probably as good as ours) joined to that habit of subordination which they acquire from a life of servitude, will make them sooner become soldiers than our White inhabitants. Let officers be men of sense and sentiment, and the nearer the soldiers approach to machines perhaps the better.

I foresee that this project will have to combat much opposition from prejudices and self-interest. The contempt we have been taught to entertain for the blacks, makes us fancy many things that are founded neither in reason nor experience; and an unwillingness to part with property of so valuable a kind will furnish a thousand arguments to show the impracticability or pernicious tendency of a scheme which requires such a sacrifice. But it should be considered, that if we do not make use of them in this way, the enemy probably will; and that the best way to counteract the temptations they will hold out will be to offer them ourselves. An essential part of the plan is to give them their freedom with their muskets. This will secure their fidelity, animate their courage, and I believe will have a good influence upon those who remain, by opening a door to their emancipation. This circumstance, I confess, has no small weight in inducing me to wish the success of the project; for the dictates of humanity and true policy equally interest me in favour of this unfortunate class of men.

While I am on the subject of Southern affairs, you will excuse the liberty I take, in saying that I do not think measures sufficiently vigorous are pursuing for your defense in that quarter. Except the few regular troops of South Carolina we seem to be relying wholly on the militia in that and the two neighbouring states. These will soon grow impatient of service and leave our affairs in a very miserable situation. No considerable force can be uniformly kept up by militia—to say nothing of obvious and well known inconveniences, that attend this kind of troops— I would beg leave to suggest, Sir, that no time ought to be lost in making a draft of militia to serve a twelve month from the States of North and South Carolina and Virginia. But South Carolina being very weak in her population of whites may be excused from the draft on condition of furnishing the black batalions. The two others may furnish about 3,500 men in and be exempted on that account from sending any succours to this army. The states, to the Northward of Virginia will be fully able to give competent supplies to the army here; and it will require all the force and exertions of the three states I have mentioned to withstand the storm which has arisen and is increasing in the South.

The troops draft must be thrown into batalions and officered in the best manner we can. The supernumerary officers may be made use of as far as they will go.

If arms are wanted for these troops and no better way of supplying them is to be found—we should endeavour to levy a contribution of arms upon the militia at large— Extraordinary exigencies demand extraordinary means— I fear this Southern business will become a very *grave* one. . . .

SOURCE: Alexander Hamilton to John Jay, [14 March 1779]," *Founders Online,* National Archives, https://founders.archives.gov/documents/Hamilton/01-02-02-0051.

JOHN ADAMS TO ROBERT J. EVANS, JUNE 8, 1819

I respect the Sentiments and motives which have prompted you to engage in your present occupation so much that I feel an Esteem and affection for your person, as I do a veneration for your assumed signature of Benjamin Rush. The turpitude, the inhumanity, the cruelty, and the infamy of the African commerce in slaves, have been so impressively represented to the public by the highest powers of eloquence, that nothing that I can say would increase the just odium in which it is and ought to be held. Every measure of prudence, therefore, ought to be assumed for the eventual total extirpation of slavery from the United States. If, however, humanity dictates the duty of adopting the most prudent measures for accomplishing so excellent a purpose, the same humanity requires that we should not inflict severer calamities on the objects of our commiseration than those which they at present endure, by reducing them to despair, or the necessity of robbery, plunder, assassination, and massacre to preserve their lives, some provision for furnishing them employment, or some means of supplying them with the necessary comforts of life. The same humanity requires that we should not by any rash and violent measures expose the lives and property of those of our fellow-citizens, who are so unfortunate as to be surrounded with these fellow-creatures by hereditary descent, or by any other means without their own fault I have, through my whole life, held the practice of Slavery in such abhorrence, that I have never owned a negro or any other slave, though I have lived for many years in times, when the practice was not disgraceful, when the best men in my vicinity, thought it not inconsistent with their character, and when it has cost me thousands of dollars for the labor and subsistence of free men, which I might have saved by the purchase of negros at times when they were very cheap.

If any thing should occur to me, which I think may assist you, I will endeavor to communicate it to you. . . .

SOURCE: John Adams to Robert J. Evans, June 8, 1819, in *The Works of John Adams*, ed. Charles Francis Adams, 10 vols. (Boston, MA: Little, Brown and Company, 1856), 10: 379-380.

THOMAS JEFFERSON TO JOHN HOLMES, APRIL 22, 1820

I thank you, dear sir, for the copy you have been so kind as to send me of the letter to your constituents on the Missouri question. It is a perfect justification to them. I had for a long time ceased to read newspapers, or pay any attention to public affairs, confident they were in good hands, and content to be a passenger in our bark to the shore from which I am not distant. But this momentous question, like a fire bell in the night, awakened and filled me with terror. I considered it at once as the knell of the Union. It is hushed, indeed, for the moment. But this is a reprieve only, not a final sentence. A geographical line, coinciding with a marked principle, moral and political, once conceived and held up to the angry passions of men, will never be obliterated; and every new irritation will mark it deeper and deeper. I can say, with conscious truth, that there is not a man on earth who would sacrifice more than I would to relieve us from this heavy reproach, in any *practicable* way. The cession of that kind of property, for so it is misnamed, is a bagatelle which would not cost me a second thought, if, in that way, a general emancipation and *expatriation* could be effected; and, gradually, and with due sacrifices, I think it might be. But as it is, we have the wolf by the ears, and we can neither hold him, nor safely let him go. Justice is in one scale, and self-preservation in the other. Of one thing I am certain, that as the passage of slaves from one state to another, would not make a slave of a single human being who would not be so without it, so their diffusion over a greater surface would make them individually happier, and proportionally facilitate the accomplishment of their emancipation, by dividing the burthen on a greater number of coadjutors. An abstinence too, from this act of power, would remove the jealousy excited by the undertaking of Congress to regulate the condition of the different descriptions of men composing a state. This certainly is the exclusive right of every state, which nothing in the Constitution has taken from them and given to the general government. Could Congress, for example, say, that the non-freemen of Connecticut shall be freemen, or that they shall not emigrate into any other state?

I regret that I am now to die in the belief, that the useless sacrifice of themselves by the generation of 1776, to acquire self-government and happiness to their country, is to be thrown away by the unwise and unworthy passions of their sons, and that my only consolation is to be, that I live not to weep over it. If they would but dispassionately weigh the blessings they will throw away, against an abstract principle more likely to be effected by union than by scission, they would pause before they would perpetrate this act of suicide on themselves, and of treason against the hopes of the world. To yourself, as the faithful advocate of the Union, I tender the offering of my high esteem and respect.

SOURCE: Thomas Jefferson to John Holmes, April 22, 1820, in Andrew A. Lipscomb and Albert Ellery Bergh, ed., *The Works of Thomas Jefferson*, Memorial Edition, 20 vols., (Washington, DC: Thomas Jefferson Memorial Association, 1903), 15: 248-250.

2. RICHARD WELLS
"A FEW POLITICAL REFLECTIONS SUBMITTED TO THE CONSIDERATION OF THE BRITISH COLONIES"
1774

Richard Wells was born in Cutthorpe, Derbyshire, England (1734), and he died in Philadelphia, Pennsylvania (1801). Wells was a Quaker and a merchant in Philadelphia. The Quakers were amongst the first Americans to condemn slavery and call for its abolition. Wells's antislavery pamphlet is notable not only for its religious and humanitarian arguments against slavery, but, more importantly, for its claim that chattel slavery was inconsistent with the moral principles of the Revolution. The colonists could not, he argued, "reconcile the exercise of SLAVERY with our professions of freedom, founded on the law of God and nature, and the common rights of mankind." Wells understood that to not extend the right of freedom to the enslaved was inconsistent and hypocritical. He called for immediate steps to end the slave trade and the eventually emancipation of the slaves.

SO loud and important is the present cry for liberty, that it cannot but rouse every man who has the welfare of his country at heart; and it becomes every man's duty to exert himself on the occasion. We have, my Brethren, a dangerous slippery path to tread: Let us then carefully pick our way, and attentively inspect every road that is pointed to our view.—Let us patiently hear and consider every opinion that is offered with candor. Let us not reject, with contempt, whatever disagrees with our own private sentiments. In the multitude of counsel there is wisdom. . . .

NOW, my brethren, I will beg leave to come close to the point, and call for an examination of our own conduct—Let us try if it will square with our pretensions, whether we can reconcile the *exercise of* SLAVERY with our *professions of freedom*, founded on the law of God and nature, and the common rights of mankind—I beseech you, brethren, with dispassionate and disinterested minds to survey the subject—Can we suppose that the people of England will grant the force of our reasoning, when they are told, that *every colony* on the continent is deeply involved in the inconsistent practice of *keeping their fellow creatures* in *perpetual bondage*? So much has been wrote on this subject by abler pens, that it may be difficult to set it in so new and striking a point of light as to gain your attention; but whilst the evil remains, the same arguments will necessarily arise; nor will they ever lose their force. In vain shall we contend for *liberty*, as an *"essential in our constitution,"* till this barbarous inhuman practice is driven from our borders. Let him who claims an exemption from the controul of Parliamentary power, shew to the world, by what right, human or divine, he keeps in cruel slavery his *fellow man*. We declare with a joint voice, that ALL *the inhabitants of America* are entitled to the privileges of the inhabitants of Great-Britain; if so, by what right do we support slavery?—the instant a slave sets his foot in England he claims the protection of the laws, and puts his master at defiance; if British rights extend to America, *who* shall detain him in bondage? If his pretended owner can shew no personal contract with the unfortunate African, is there a court on the continent, that would unrighteously declare him a slave? You say you bought them of those who had a right to sell.—I dispute it—on behalf of the injured Blacks, I dispute it, and call on you to shew your title. When a servant is offered for sale in the colonies, are we contented with the Captain's asseverations?—no—we call for the indenture, the personal contract; if *that* is not to be produced, where is the man who will be hardy enough to sell him? If he is indebted for his passage, he is at liberty to make his own bargain with the purchaser, and enters into a voluntary temporary servitude; even if he be a *convict*, and has *forfeited his life* to the laws of his country, and is respited for transportation, I presume no Captain ever came over unprovided with authentic documents from the records of Newgate; though many contend, that servitude is no part of their sentence, as being inconsistent with the liberty of an Englishman, and I have been assured that some, on their landing in America, have demanded their liberty.—If this be the case—if the English constitution guards the liberties of men, who have been condemned to die for the breach of their own country's laws, how comes it that *we* undertake to inflict so barbarous a punishment upon the natives of Africa, for *their* transgressions in Guinea, which is the last wretched argument of refuge, which the advocates for slavery insist on; and that not content with *gloriously* taking up the cause of an Ethiopian savage government, and *nobly* becoming their *honourable executioners*, we visit the sins of the fathers to the latest generations; but if we admit the propriety of the argument, I request on behalf of the injured and distressed, that you produce the records of their courts, or the proofs of their crimes; if you do neither, what better testimony do you shew for your possession than the house-breaker or highway-man? —Wherever a man claims and supports his property, he shall undoubtedly recover it. Now every slave, by his personal appearance, makes *that* claim,— he forever carries about him the strongest proofs in nature of his *original right*—he is the first grand link, and unless his pretended owner shall deduce a regular chain of conveyance, I contend that, by the laws of the English constitution, and by our *own declarations*, the instant a Negro sets his foot in America, he is as free as if he had landed in England. If *force* and *power* are the only important links in the title, what arguments can we advance in *their* favour, which will not militate against ourselves, whilst England remains superior by land and by sea.

SHALL a climate, a colour, or a country, determine the miserable inhabitants as slaves and vassals to the rest of the world; or from what quarter shall we derive our reasonings, to prove and support our tyrannizing power?—Is there such a thing with Englishmen—high claiming Englishmen—as *partial* liberty? Has the Almighty decreed *us* their masters, and degrading the workmanship of his hands, stamped slave to eternity on their foreheads? By what law has he thus vested us with barbarous and cruel sway? Is it possible we can sit down in the cool of the day, and laying our hands on our bosoms, say we believe they were formed for our servants? On the other hand I would ask, Is there a single argument to be adduced in support of *our* right to their services, which would not equally hold in favour of *their* enslaving *us*, if we were trepanned into their country? But why need I argue on the point? I cannot consent to believe that there is a single slave holder on the continent, who is from principle a tyrant. Their interests are so nearly connected with the subject, that their judgments are misled. With such men it is hard to contend; their reason lies buried and concealed; when called forth it appears with reluctance, and urges its efforts with enervated force. Yet many there are in the several colonies, who are earnestly concerned in this important cause.— To *you*, my brethren—*you* genuine sons of liberty, they look for support. Let us set foot to foot and shoulder to shoulder, to expel this horrid demon from our land.—How oft is my heart sunk into sorrowing sympathy with these poor and unfortunate wretches. When I hear of the brutal cruelties exercised over them, by their inhuman owners, when I view these usurpers of human freedom, basking in the beams of success, and bowling through life with undaunted career, I look up with wondering eye to the great and Almighty Author of our being, and am lost in contemplating the dispensations of his Providence.

THE noble, spirited and virtuous Assembly of Virginia, not long ago petitioned his Majesty for leave to pass an act to prohibit the importation of slaves, as inconsistent with the principles of humanity; but the petition was rejected. Yet should the colonies, with their joint voice at the Congress, make a forcible remonstrance against the iniquity of the slave trade, it would breathe such an independant spirit of liberty, and so corroborate our own claims, that I should dare to hope for an intervening arm of Providence to be extended in our favour. Should the colonies gain permission to pass prohibitory acts against future importations, I should then, with expectant joy, look forward for the glorious dawning of a day of liberty.

UNIMPORTANT as this may seem to some, I hesitate not to pronounce, that the true interests and welfare of America are more intimately connected with it, than with the repeal of every act which now agitates the continent— *one* we might probably out grow in a series of years, but *the other* would "strengthen with our strength," and involve us in endless perplexities. If a stop could be put to the importation, the grand difficulty would be over. Means might soon be devised to discharge this unhappy race amongst us, and wear out the monstrous badge of unrighteousness. To the Congress I would earnestly urge this weighty point, and to the internal policy of every government I would press the necessity of removing every legal obstruction, which stands as a bar to their freedom. I am unacquainted with the general laws of emancipation in the southern and the eastern colonies, but those of Maryland, Pennsylvania and New- Jersey have fallen within my knowledge. In the first, any slave holder may set his slaves at liberty without charge or encumbrance, provided they are not aged or infirm, but in Pennsylvania the law requires a bond of indemnification of thirty pounds, to prevent the slave becoming a burthen to the township, and the law is so worded as to admit of a doubt, whether such bond totally discharges the master's estate; and in some cases the courts, before whom such emancipation is to be declared, have so far exerted their power, as to refuse admitting the security, though undoubtedly good, and the slaves intended for freedom healthy and young; by which means, they were kept in bondage against the inclinations of their owners. In New- Jersey, the law requires a security of two hundred pounds, but the assembly of that province, at their last session, took up the matter on virtuous principles, and made an essay towards "*an act for the more equitable manumission of slaves,*" by which any person declaring his Negro free, before proper authority, at the age of twenty one, may do it without charge or encumbrance, and for every year exceeding that age, the owner so intending to set him free, is to pay into the hands of the overseers of the poor, the sum of twenty shillings, which shall be a total discharge: This with a few discretionary restrictions is published in their votes, for the inspection of their constituents, and it is hoped by every lover of liberty, that it will pass into a law at the next sessions.

WERE the colonies as earnest for the preservation of liberty, upon its *true* and *genuine* principles, as they are to oppose the supremacy of an English parliament, they would enter into a virtuous and *perpetual* resolve neither to import, nor to purchase any slaves introduced among them after the meeting of the Congress. A resolve so replete with liberty, so truly noble, would indelibly convey to future ages a memorable record of disinterested virtue; whilst thousands, ten thousands yet unborn, might bless them in their native shades, carving on the smooth bark of every tree, NOBLE AMERICANS. With grateful hearts might they look up "*to the unknown God,*" and urge this ardent prayer— *Great and Almighty ruler of the Universe, shower down the choicest of thy blessings on yon western climes.*

SOURCE: "A few political reflections submitted to the consideration of the British colonies, by a citizen of Philadelphia." In the digital collection *Evans Early American Imprint*

Collection. https://name.umdl.umich.edu/N10868.0001.001. University of Michigan Library Digital Collections. Accessed December 26, 2024.

3. THOMAS PAINE
"AFRICAN SLAVERY IN AMERICA"
1775

Thomas Paine (1737-1809) was America's most radical thinker on all margins. He saw further than most Americans, and he was one of the first people in America to call for the abolition of slavery. In his 1775 pamphlet on "African Slavery in America," Paine condemned slavery as morally repugnant, and he called for the emancipation of all slaves in America. Slavery, he argued, "proved contrary to the light of nature, to every principle of Justice and Humanity, and even good policy." He referred to slave traders as "Man-Stealers," and he claimed that the slave is the "proper owner of his freedom, has a right to reclaim it." Freedom is, Paine claimed, a "natural, perfect right of all mankind." A few weeks after Paine's pamphlet was published, America's first anti-slavery society in America was formed in Philadelphia. Paine was a founding member of the organization.

TO AMERICANS:

That some desperate wretches should be willing to steal and enslave men by violence and murder for gain, is rather lamentable than strange. But that many civilized, nay, Christianized people should approve, and be concerned in the savage practice, is surprising; and still persist, though it has been so often proved contrary to the light of nature, to every principle of Justice and Humanity, and even good policy, by a succession of eminent men, and several late publications.

Our Traders in MEN (*an unnatural commodity!*) must know the wickedness of the SLAVE-TRADE, if they attend to reasoning, or the dictates of their own hearts: and such as shun and stiffle all these, wilfully sacrifice Conscience, and the character of integrity to that golden idol.

The Managers the Trade themselves, and others testify, that many of these African nations inhabit fertile countries, are industrious farmers, enjoy plenty, and lived quietly, averse to war, before the Europeans debauched them with liquors, and bribing them against one another; and that these inoffensive people are brought into slavery, by stealing them, tempting Kings to sell subjects, which they can have no right to do, and hiring one tribe to war against another, in order to catch prisoners. By such wicked and inhuman ways the English are said to enslave towards one hundred thousand yearly; of which thirty thousand are supposed to die by barbarous treatment in the first year; besides all that are slain in the unnatural ways excited to take them. So much innocent blood have the managers and supporters of this inhuman trade to answer for to the common Lord of all!

Many of these were not prisoners of war, and redeemed from savage conquerors, as some plead; and they who were such prisoners, the English, who promote the war for that very end, are the guilty authors of their being so; and if they were redeemed, as is alleged, they would owe nothing to the redeemer but what he paid for them.

They show as little reason as conscience who put the matter by with saying — "Men, in some cases, are lawfully made slaves, and why may not these?" So men, in some cases, are lawfully put to death, deprived of their goods, without their consent; may any man, therefore, be treated so, without any conviction of desert? Nor is this plea mended by adding — "They are set forth to us as slaves, and we buy them without farther inquiry, let the sellers see to it." Such man may as well join with a known band of robbers, buy their ill-got goods, and help on the trade; ignorance is no more pleadable in one case than the other; the sellers plainly own how they obtain them. But none can lawfully buy without evidence that they are not concurring with Men-Stealers; and as the true owner has a right to reclaim his goods that were stolen, and sold; so the slave, who is proper owner of his freedom, has a right to reclaim it, however often sold.

Most shocking of all is alledging the sacred scriptures to favour this wicked practice. One would have thought none but infidel cavillers would endeavour to make them appear contrary to the plain dictates of natural light, and the conscience, in a matter of common Justice and Humanity; which they cannot be. Such worthy men, as referred to before, judged otherways; Mr. Baxter declared, *the Slave-Traders should be called Devils, rather than Christians; and that it is a heinous crime to buy them.* But some say, "the practice was permitted to the Jews." To which may be replied,

1. The example of the Jews, in many things, may not be imitated by us; they had not only orders to cut off several nations altogether, but if they were obliged to war with others, and conquered them, to cut off every male; they were suffered to use polygamy and divorces, and other things utterly unlawful to us under clearer light.

2. The plea is, in a great measure, false; they had no permission to catch and enslave people who never injured them.

3. Such arguments ill become us, *since the time of reformation came*, under Gospel light. All distinctions of nations and privileges of one above others, are ceased; Christians are taught to *account all men their neighbours; and love their neighbours as themselves; and do to all men as they would be done by; to do good to all men; and Man-stealing is ranked with enormous crimes.* Is the barbarous enslaving our inoffensive neighbours, and treating them like wild beasts subdued by force, reconcilable with the *Divine precepts!* Is this doing to them as we would desire they should do to us? If they could carry off and enslave some thousands of us, would we think it just? — One would

almost wish they could for once; it might convince more than reason, or the Bible.

As much in vain, perhaps, will they search ancient history for examples of the modern Slave-Trade. Too many nations enslaved the prisoners they took in war. But to go to nations with whom there is no war, who have no way provoked, without farther design of conquest, purely to catch inoffensive people, like wild beasts, for slaves, is an height of outrage against humanity and justice, that seems left by heathen nations to be practised by pretended Christian. How shameful are all attempts to colour and excuse it!

As these people are not convicted of forfeiting freedom, they have still a natural, perfect right to it; and the governments whenever they come should, in justice set them free, and punish those who hold them in slavery.

So monstrous is the making and keeping them slaves at all, abstracted from the barbarous usage they suffer, and the many evils attending the practice; as selling husbands away from wives, children from parents, and from each other, in violation of sacred and natural ties; and opening the way for adulteries, incests, and many shocking consequences, for all of which the guilty Masters must answer to the final Judge.

If the slavery of the parents be unjust, much more is their children's; if the parents were justly slaves, yet the children are born free; this is the natural, perfect right of all mankind; they are nothing but a just recompense to those who bring them up: And as much less is commonly spent on them than others, they have a right, in justice, to be proportionably sooner free.

Certainly, one may, with as much reason and decency, plead for murder, robbery, lewdness and barbarity, as for this practice. They are not more contrary to the natural dictates of conscience, and feeling of humanity; nay, they are all comprehended in it.

But the chief design of this paper is not to disprove it, which many have sufficiently done; but to entreat Americans to consider.

1. With what consistency, or decency they complain so loudly of attempts to enslave them, while they hold so many hundred thousands in slavery; and annually enslave many thousands more, without any pretence of authority, or claim upon them?

2. How just, how suitable to our crime is the punishment with which Providence threatens us? We have enslaved multitudes, and shed much innocent blood in doing it; and now are threatened with the same. And while other evils are confessed, and bewailed, why not this especially, and publicity; than which no other vice, if all others, has brought so much guilt on the land?

3. Whether, then, all ought not immediately to discontinue and renounce it, with grief and abhorrence? Should not every society bear testimony against it, and account obstinate persisters in it bad men, enemies to their country, and exclude them from fellowship; as they often do for much lesser faults?

4. The great Question may be — What should be done with those who are enslaved already? To turn the old and infirm free, would be injustice and cruelty; they who enjoyed the labours of the their better days should keep, and treat them humanely. As to the rest, let prudent men, with the assistance of legislatures, determine what is practicable for masters, and and best for them. Perhaps some could give them lands upon reasonable rent, some, employing them in their labour still, might give them some reasonable allowances for it; so as all may have some property, and fruits of their labours at the own disposal, and be encouraged to industry; the family may live together, and enjoy the natural satisfaction of exercising relative affections and duties, with civil protection, and other advantages, like fellow men. Perhaps they might sometime form useful barrier settlements on the frontiers. Thus they may become interested in the public welfare, and assist in promoting it; instead of being dangerous, as now they are, should any enemy promise them a better condition.

5. The past treatment of Africans must naturally fill them with abhorrence of Christians; lead them to think our religion would make them more inhuman savages, if they embraced it; thus the gain of that trade has been pursued in oppositions of the redeemer's cause, and the happiness of men. Are we not, therefore, bound in duty to him and to them to repair these injuries, as far as possible, by taking some proper measure to instruct, not only the slaves here, but the Africans in their own countries? Primitive Christians, laboured always to spread the *divine religion*; and this is equally our duty while there is an heathen nation: But what singular obligations are we under to these injured people!

These are the sentiments of JUSTICE AND HUMANITY.

SOURCE: William M. Van der Weyde, ed. *The Life and Works of Thomas Paine*, Patriots Edition, 10 vols. (New Rochelle, NY: Thomas Paine National Historical Association, 1925), 2: 3-10.

4. THOMAS JEFFERSON
SELECTIONS FROM NOTES ON THE STATE OF VIRGINIA
1785

Thomas Jefferson's (1743-1826) relationship to slavery was complicated and conflicted. He was born on a slave plantation, and he grew up in a slave culture. He inherited his father's plantation and slaves at a relatively young age, and he married into a wealthy slave-owning family. He owned hundreds of slaves over the course of a lifetime. At the time of his death in 1826, he owned approximately 130 slaves, only a fraction of which he freed. From early in his life, he recognized that slavery was immoral, and he said so. In 1774, he wrote in his Summary View of the Rights of British-America *that "the rights of human nature" are "deeply wounded by this infamous practice." In 1779, he proposed to the Virginia legislature a bill for the gradual emancipation of slavery, but it did not pass. The bill did not pass because most slaveholders could not solve the post-emancipation problem, namely, what to do with the slaves after emancipation. Like most southerners, Jefferson thought that whites and a freed black population simply could not live together without the serious possibility of a race war. Jefferson considered creating a free black state in the trans-Appalachian West, but he recognized that such a solution was fraught with innumerable problems. The first selection below from* Notes on the State of Virginia *is painful to read for a twenty-first-century audience, but it is important to note that it represented a somewhat enlightened view as Jefferson attempted to scientifically identify the differences between whites and blacks. In the second selection from the* Notes, *Jefferson is blunt in his assessment of the moral effects of slavery on whites, which his describes as a form of "unremitting despotism." Jefferson trembled for his country when he reflected that "God is just," suggesting that slaveowners will pay for their sin.*

QUERY XIV: *The administration of justice and the description of the laws?*

. . . To emancipate all slaves born after passing the act. The bill reported by the revisers does not itself contain this proposition; but an amendment containing it was prepared, to be offered to the legislature whenever the bill should be taken up, and further directing, that they should continue with their parents to a certain age, then be brought up, at the public expense, to tillage, arts, or sciences, according to their geniuses, till the females should be eighteen, and the males twenty-one years of age, when they should be colonized to such place as the circumstances of the time should render most proper, sending them out with arms, implements of household and of the handicraft arts, seeds, pairs of the useful domestic animals, &c. to declare them a free and independent people, and extend to them our alliance and protection, till they shall have acquired strength; and to send vessels at the same time to other parts of the world for an equal number of white inhabitants; to induce whom to migrate hither, proper encouragements were to be proposed. It will probably be asked, Why not retain and incorporate the blacks into the state, and thus save the expense of supplying by importation of white settlers, the vacancies they will leave? Deep rooted prejudices entertained by the whites; ten thousand recollections, by the blacks, of the injuries they have sustained; new provocations; the real distinctions which nature has made; and many other circumstances will divide us into parties, and produce convulsions, which will probably never end but in the extermination of the one or the other race.—To these objections, which are political, may be added others, which are physical and moral. The first difference which strikes us is that of color. Whether the black of the negro resides in the reticular membrane between the skin and scarfskin, or in the scarfskin itself; whether it proceeds from the color of the blood, the color of the bile, or from that of some other secretion, the difference is fixed in nature, and is as real as if its seat and cause were better known to us. And is this difference of no importance? Is it not the foundation of a greater or less share of beauty in the two races? Are not the fine mixtures of red and white, the expressions of every passion by greater or less suffusions of colour in the one, preferable to that eternal monotony, which reigns in the countenances, that immovable veil of black which covers all the emotions of the other race? Add to these, flowing hair, a more elegant symmetry of form, their own judgment in favor of the whites, declared by their preference of them as uniformly as is the preference of the Oranootan for the black woman over those of his own species. The circumstance of superior beauty, is thought worthy attention in the propagation of our horses, dogs, and other domestic animals; why not in that of man? Besides those of color, figure, and hair, there are other physical distinctions proving a difference of race. They have less hair on the face and body. They secreteless by the kidnies, and more by the glands of the skin, which gives them a very strong and disagreeable odor. This greater degree of transpiration, renders them more tolerant of heat, and less so of cold than the whites. Perhaps too a difference of structure in the pulmonary apparatus, which a late ingenious[1] experimentalist has discovered to be the principal regulator of animal heat, may have disabled them from extricating, in the act of inspiration, so much of that fluid from the outer air, or obliged them in expiration, to part with more of it. They seem to require less sleep. A black after hard labor through the day, will be induced by the slightest amusements to sit up till midnight or later, though knowing he must be out with the first dawn of the morning. They are at least as brave, and more adventuresome. But this may perhaps proceed from a want of forethought, which prevents their seeing a danger till it be present. When present, they do not go through it with more coolness or steadiness than the whites. They are more ardent after their female; but love seems with them to be more an eager desire, than a tender delicate mixture of sentiment and sensation. Their griefs are transient. Those numberless afflictions, which render it doubtful whether heaven has given life to us in mercy or in wrath, are less felt, and sooner forgotten with them. In general, their existence appears to participate more of sensation than reflection. To this must be ascribed their disposition to sleep when abstracted from their diversions, and unemployed in labor. An animal whose body is at rest, and who does not reflect, must be disposed to sleep of course. Comparing them by their faculties of memory, reason, and imagination, it appears to me that in memory they are equal to the whites; in reason much inferior, as I think one could scarcely be found capable of tracing and comprehending the investigations of Euclid: and that in imagination they are dull, tasteless, and anomalous. It would be unfair to follow them to Africa for this investigation. We will consider them here, on the same stage with the whites, and where the facts are not apochryphal on which a judgment is to be formed. It will be right to make great allowances for the difference of condition, of education, of conversation, of the sphere in which they move. Many millions of them have been brought to, and born in America. Most of them, indeed, have been confined to tillage, to their own homes, and their own society: yet many have been so situated, that they might have availed themselves of the conversation of their masters; many have been brought up to the handicraft arts, and from that circumstance have always been associated with the whites. Some have been liberally educated, and all have lived in countries where the arts and sciences are cultivated to a considerable degree, and have had before their eyes samples of the best works from abroad. The Indians, with no advantages of this kind, will often carve figures on their pipes not destitute of design and merit. They will crayon out an animal, a plant, or a country, so as to prove the existence of a germ in their minds which only wants cultivation. They astonish you with strokes of the most sublime oratory; such as prove their reason and sentiment strong, their imagination glowing and elevated. But never yet could I find that a black had uttered a thought above the level of plain narration; never seen even an elementary trait of painting or sculpture. In music they are more generally gifted than the whites, with accurate ears for tune and time, and they have been found capable of imagining a small catch. Whether they will be equal to the composition of a more extensive run of melody, or of complicated harmony, is yet to be proved. Misery is often the parent of the most affecting touches in poetry.—Among the blacks is misery enough, God knows, but no poetry. Love is the peculiar cestrum of the poet. Their love is ardent, but it kindles the senses only, not the imagination. Religion, indeed, has produced a Phyllis

Whately; but it could not produce a poet. The compositions published under her name are below the dignity of criticism. The heroes of the Dunciad are to her, as Hercules to the author of that poem. Ignatius Sancho has approached nearer to merit in composition; yet his letters do more honor to the heart than the head. They breathe the purest effusions of friendship and general philanthropy, and show how great a degree of the latter may be compounded with strong religious zeal. He is often happy in the turn of his compliments, and his style is easy and familiar, except when he affects a Shandean fabrication of words. But his imagination is wild and extravagant, escapes incessantly from every restraint of reason and taste, and, in the course of its vagaries, leaves a tract of thought as incoherent and eccentric, as is the course of a meteor through the sky. His subjects should often have led him to a process of sober reasoning; yet we find him always substituting sentiment for demonstration. Upon the whole, though we admit him to the first place among those of his own color who have presented themselves to the public judgment, yet when we compare him with the writers of the race among whom he lived and particularly with the epistolary class in which he has taken his own stand, we are compelled to enrol him at the bottom of the column. This criticism supposes the letters published under his name to be genuine, and to have received amendment from no other hand; points which would not be of easy investigation. The improvement of the blacks in body and mind, in the first instance of their mixture with the whites, has been observed by every one, and proves that their inferiority is not the effect merely of their condition of life. We know that among the Romans, about the Augustan age especially, the condition of their slaves was much more deplorable than that of the blacks on the continent of America. The two sexes were confined in separate apartments, because to raise a child cost the master more than to buy one. Cato, for a very restricted indulgence to his slaves in this particular, took from them a certain price. But in this country the slaves multiply as fast as the free inhabitants. Their situation and manners place the commerce between the two sexes almost without restraint.—The same Cato, on a principle of economy, always sold his sick and superannuated slaves. He gives it as a standing precept to a master visiting his farm, to sell his old oxen, old waggons, old tools, old and diseased servants, and everything else become useless. . . . The American slaves cannot enumerate this among the injuries and insults they receive. It was the common practice to expose in the island Æsculapius, in the Tyber, diseased slaves whose cure was like to become tedious. The Emperor Claudius, by an edict, gave freedom to such of them as should recover, and first declared that if any person chose to kill rather than to expose them, it should be deemed homicide. The exposing them is a crime of which no instance has existed with us; and were it to be followed by death, it would be punished capitally. We are told of a certain Vedius Pollio, who, in the presence of Augustus, would have given a slave as food to his fish, for having broken a glass. With the Romans, the

regular method of taking the evidence of their slaves was under torture. Here it has been thought better never to resort to their evidence. When a master was murdered, all his slaves, in the same house, or within hearing, were condemned to death. Here punishment falls on the guilty only, and as precise proof is required against him as against a freeman. Yet notwithstanding these and other discouraging circumstances among the Romans, their slaves were often their rarest artists. They excelled too in science, insomuch as to be usually employed as tutors to their master's children. Epictetus, Terence, and Phædrus, were slaves. But they were of the race of whites. It is not their condition then, but nature, which has produced the distinction.—Whether further observation will or will not verify the conjecture, that nature has been less bountiful to them in the endowments of the head, I believe that in those of the heart she will be found to have done them justice. That disposition to theft with which they have been branded, must be ascribed to their situation, and not to any depravity of the moral sense. The man in whose favor no laws of property exist, probably feels himself less bound to respect those made in favor of others. When arguing for ourselves, we lay it down as a fundamental, that laws, to be just, must give a reciprocation of right: that, without this, they are mere arbitrary rules of conduct, founded in force, and not in conscience; and it is a problem which I give to the master to solve, whether the religious precepts against the violation of property were not framed for him as well as his slave? And whether the slave may not as justifiably take a little from one who has taken all from him, as he may slay one who would slay him? That a change in the relations in which a man is placed should change his ideas of moral right and wrong, is neither new, nor peculiar to the color of the blacks.
. . .

But the slaves of which Homer speaks were whites. Notwithstanding these considerations which must weaken their respect for the laws of property, we find among them numerous instances of the most rigid integrity, and as many as among their better instructed masters, of benevolence, gratitude, and unshaken fidelity. The opinion that they are inferior in the faculties of reason and imagination, must be hazarded with great diffidence. To justify a general conclusion, requires many observations, even where the subject may be submitted to the Anatomical knife, to Optical glasses, to analysis by fire or by solvents. How much more then where it is a faculty, not a substance, we are examining; where it eludes the research of all the senses; where the conditions of its existence are various and variously combined; where the effects of those which are present or absent bid defiance to calculation; let me add too, as a circumstance of great tenderness, where our conclusion would degrade a whole race of men from the rank in the scale of beings which their Creator may perhaps have given them. To our reproach it must be said, that though for a century and a half we have had under our eyes the races of black and of red men, they have never yet been viewed by us as subjects of natural history. I advance it, therefore, as a suspicion only, that the blacks, whether originally a distinct race, or made distinct by time and circumstances, are inferior to the whites in the endowments both of body and mind. It is not against experience to suppose that different species of the same genus, or varieties of the same species, may possess different qualifications. Will not a lover of natural history then, one who views the gradations in all the races of animals with the eye of philosophy, excuse an effort to keep those in the department of man as distinct as nature has formed them? This unfortunate difference of colour, and perhaps of faculty, is a powerful obstacle to the emancipation of these people. Many of their advocates, while they wish to vindicate the liberty of human nature, are anxious also to preserve its dignity and beauty. Some of these, embarrassed by the question, 'What further is to be done with them?' join themselves in opposition with those who are actuated by sordid avarice only. Among the Romans emancipation required but one effort. The slave, when made free, might mix with, without staining the blood of his master. But with us a second is necessary, unknown to history. When freed, he is to be removed beyond the reach of mixture. . . .

QUERY XVIII: *The particular customs and manners that may happen to be received in that State?*

It is difficult to determine on the standard by which the manners of a nation may be tried, whether *catholic* or *particular*. It is more difficult for a native to bring to that standard the manners of his own nation, familiarized to him by habit. There must doubtless be an unhappy influence on the manners of our people produced by the existence of slavery among us. The whole commerce between master and slave is a perpetual exercise of the most boisterous passions, the most unremitting despotism on the one part, and degrading submissions on the other. Our children see this, and learn to imitate it; for man is an imitative animal. This quality is the germ of all education in him. From his cradle to his grave he is learning to do what he sees others do. If a parent could find no motive either in his philanthropy or his self-love, for restraining the intemperance of passion towards his slave, it should always be a sufficient one that his child is present. But generally it is not sufficient. The parent storms, the child looks on, catches the lineaments of wrath, puts on the same airs in the circle of smaller slaves, gives a loose to the worst of passions, and thus nursed, educated, and daily exercised in tyranny, cannot but be stamped by it with odious peculiarities. The man must be a prodigy who can retain his manners and morals undepraved by such circumstances. And with what execrations should the statesman be loaded, who permitting one half the citizens thus to trample on the rights of the other, transforms those into despots, and these into enemies, destroys the morals of the one part, and the amor patriæ of the other. For if a slave can have a country in this world, it must be any other in preference to that in which he is born to live and labor for another: in which he must lock up the faculties of his nature, contribute as far as depends on his individual endeavors to the evanishment of the human race, or entail his own miserable condition on the endless generations proceeding from him. With the morals of the people, their industry also is destroyed. For in a warm climate, no man will labor for himself who can make another labor for him. This is so true, that of the proprietors of slaves a very small proportion indeed are ever seen to labor. And can the liberties of a nation be thought secure when we have removed their only firm basis, a conviction in the minds of the people that these liberties are of the gift of God? That they are not to be violated but with his wrath? Indeed I tremble for my country when I reflect that God is just: that his justice cannot sleep forever: that considering numbers, nature and natural means only, a revolution of the wheel of fortune, an exchange of situation, is among possible events: that it may become probable by supernatural interference! The Almighty has no attribute which can take side with us in such a contest.—But it is impossible to be temperate and to pursue this subject through the various considerations of policy, of morals, of history natural and civil. We must be contented to hope they will force their way into every one's mind. I think a change already perceptible, since the origin of the present revolution. The spirit of the master is abating, that of the slave rising from the dust, his condition mollifying, the way I hope preparing, under the auspices of heaven, for a total emancipation, and that this is disposed, in the order of events, to be with the consent of the masters, rather than by their extirpation.

SOURCE: Andrew A. Lipscomb and Albert Ellery Bergh, ed., *The Works of Thomas Jefferson*, Memorial Edition, 20 vols., (Washington, DC: Thomas Jefferson Memorial Association, 1903), 2: 191-199, 200-201, 225-228.

SUGGESTED READING

Adams, Randolph G. *Political Ideas of the American Revolution: Britannic American Contributions to the Problem of Imperial Organization, 1765 to 1775*. New York, NY: Barnes & Noble, Inc., 1932.

Adams, Willi Paul. *The First American Constitutions: Republican Ideology and the Making of the State Constitutions in the Revolutionary Era*. Lanham, MD: Rowman & Littlefield Publishers, 2001.

Bailyn, Bernard. *The Ideological Origins of the American Revolution*. Cambridge, MA: Harvard University Press, 1967.

Draper, Theodore. *A Struggle for Power: The American Revolution*. New York: Random House, 1996.

Handlin, Oscar and Handlin, Mary (eds). *The Popular Sources of Political Authority: Documents on the Massachusetts Constitution of 1780*. Cambridge, MA: Harvard University Press, 1966.

Kruman, Marc W. *Between Liberty and Authority: State Constitution Making in Revolutionary America*. Chapel Hill, NC: University of North Carolina Press, 1997.

Kurland, Philip B., and Ralph Lerner, eds. *The Founders' Constitution*. 5 vols., Chicago: University of Chicago Press, 1986.

McDonald, Forrest. *Novus Ordo Seclorum: The Intellectual Origins of the Constitution*. Lawrence, KS: University Press of Kansas, 1985.

_____. *Growth of the American Revolution: 1766-1755*. Indianapolis, IN: Liberty Fund, 1975.

Main, Jackson Turner. *The Sovereign States, 1775-1783*. New York, NY: Franklin Watts, Inc., 1973.

Mayer, David N. *The Constitutional Thought of Thomas Jefferson*. Charlottesville, VA: University Press of Virginia, 1994.

McIlwain, Charles Howard. *The American Revolution: A Constitutional Interpretation*. New York: Macmillan Company, 1924.

Middlekauff, Robert. *The Glorious Cause: The American Revolution, 1763-1789*. Oxford: Oxford University Press, 1982.

Nelson, William. *E Pluribus Unum: How the Common Law Helped Unify and Liberate Colonial America, 1607-1776*. Oxford: Oxford University Press, 2019.

Nevins, Allan. The American States: *During and After the Revolution, 1775-1789*. New York, NY: Augustus M. Kelley, Publishers, 1969.

Taylor, Robert J. (ed.) Massachusetts, *Colony to Commonwealth: Documents on the Formation of Its Constitution, 1775-1780*. New York, NY: W. W. Norton & Company, 1961.

Thompson, C. Bradley. *Political Thought of the American Revolution: A Reader*. Volume I: Imperial Crisis and Independence. Seneca, SC: Loco-Foco Press, 2024.

_____. *America's Revolutionary Mind: A Moral History of the American Revolution and the Declaration that Defined It*. New York: Encounter Books, 2019.

_____. *What America Is*. Seneca, SC: Loco-Foco Press, 2023.

_____. *John Adams and the Spirit of Liberty*. Lawrence, KS: University Press of Kansas, 1998.

Wood, Gordon S. *The Creation of the American Republic, 1776-1787*. New York: Norton, 1972.

_____. *The Radicalism of the American Revolution*. New York: Alfred A. Knopf, 1992.

About the Author

C. Bradley Thompson is a Professor of Political Science at Clemson University, where he teaches political philosophy. He is also the Executive Director of the Snow Institute for the Study Capitalism and the founder of the Lyceum Scholars Program.

During his academic career, he has also served as the Garwood Family Professor in the James Madison Program at Princeton University, a John Adams Fellow at the Institute of United States Studies (University of London), and a fellow of the Program in Constitutional Studies at Harvard University.

Thompson's research, writing, and teaching focus on the history of political philosophy, with a special emphasis on American political thought. His most recent book is *What America Is* (2023). In 2019, he published *America's Revolutionary Mind: A Moral History of the American Revolution and the Declaration that Defined It* (2019), which has been described as "may be the most important work of American history in generations" if not the "most important book of our time." His first book, *John Adams and the Spirit of Liberty* (1998), was awarded the "Best First Book in Political Theory" prize by the American Political Science Association. His second book, *Neoconservatism: An Obituary for an Idea* was published in 2010. Thompson has also edited two volumes of historical documents, *The Revolutionary Writings of John Adams* (2001) and *Antislavery Political Writings, 1833-1860: A Reader* (2003), and he was also a co-editor of *Freedom and School Choice in American Education* with Greg Forster (2011).

ABOUT LOCO-FOCO PRESS

Loco-Foco Press is an independent publishing company founded by C. Bradley Thompson in 2023. The name "Loco-Foco" refers to a radical political movement in New York City during the 1830s and 1840s, formed by working-class men and reformers who supported a free society defined by individual rights, constitutional government, laissez-faire capitalism, and abolitionism. The word "Loco-Foco" originated with "loco-foco" matches (self-igniting matches), which combines the Latin "loco," meaning "self-generated," with the Italian "fuoco," meaning "fire," symbolizing independent thought and initiative.

In the spirit of the Loco-Foco movement, Loco-Foco Press is dedicated to publishing the works of independent writers who value the principles and institutions of a free society. Loco-Foco Press will primarily publish books on history, philosophy, culture, politics, and economics, and it is particularly interested in publishing books that explore new and old ideas, and sometimes controversial ones. We encourage debate and disputation amongst our writers and readers in the pursuit of truth and wisdom. Loco-Foco Press will also republish "forgotten classics" in American moral, political, constitutional, and economic thought.

Made in the USA
Middletown, DE
07 April 2025

73896227R00257